BEYOND THE
LETTERED CITY

BEYOND THE LETTERED CITY

Indigenous Literacies in the Andes

JOANNE RAPPAPORT AND

TOM CUMMINS

Duke University Press   Durham and London   2012

Printed in the United States of
America on acid-free paper ∞

Designed by Heather Hensley

Typeset in Minion Pro by Tseng
Information Systems, Inc.

Library of Congress Cataloging-
in-Publication Data appear on the
last printed page of this book.

Duke University Press gratefully
acknowledges the support of
Georgetown University and
Harvard University, which
provided funds toward the
publication of this book.

FOR DAVID, KYLE, AND JIMMY

Contents

About the Series

Narrating Native Histories aims to foster a rethinking of the ethical, methodological, and conceptual frameworks within which we locate our work on Native histories and cultures. We seek to create a space for effective and ongoing conversations between North and South, Natives and non-Natives, academics and activists, throughout the Americas and the Pacific region. We are committed to complicating and transgressing the disciplinary and epistemological boundaries of established academic discourses on Native peoples.

This series encourages symmetrical, horizontal, collaborative, and auto-ethnographies; work that recognizes Native intellectuals, cultural interpreters, and alternative knowledge producers within broader academic and intellectual worlds; projects that decolonize the relationship between orality and textuality; narratives that productively work the tensions between the norms of Native cultures and the requirements for evidence in academic circles; and analyses that contribute to an understanding of Native peoples' relationships with nation-states, including histories of expropriation and exclusion as well as projects for autonomy and sovereignty.

By critically extending and reconceptualizing the concept of literacy as formulated in Angel Rama's *The Lettered City*, Rappaport and Cummins contribute in an absolutely central way to the goals of our series. A historical analysis of literacy as a social process that included interactions between oral and written texts and alphabetic and pictorial forms, their work pays attention to indigenous agency even as it highlights the inevitable embeddedness of literacy in a system of colonial domination. Focusing on the Northern

Andes, Rappaport and Cummins trace the emergence of a stratum of literate indigenous people and mestizos who, in effect, created an alternative indigenous lettered city. Composed of alphabetic and visual renditions, paintings, and legal documents and petitions, this indigenous lettered city forces us to rethink the notion of literacy as exclusively alphabetic, while also questioning it as simply a technology of production and reception of meanings. Instead, the authors demonstrate, literacy was a technology that, by framing the world ideologically from the perspective of the colonizer and encouraging the participation of literate and non-literate alike, ultimately helped consolidate and reproduce European hegemony in the Americas.

Illustrations

All photographs by the Authors unless otherwise indicated.

Acknowledgments

The research on which we base this study was funded by a Senior Collaborative Research Grant from the Getty Grant Program in 1995–96, permitting us to engage in interdisciplinary discussion and interpretation, and by a Fellowship for University Teachers awarded by the National Endowment for the Humanities to Joanne Rappaport in 2000–2001. Work on the book was completed under a National Endowment for the Humanities fellowship at the National Humanities Center, awarded to Joanne Rappaport in 2002–3. The archival documentation used in our analysis was collected by Joanne Rappaport under a Grant-in-Aid from the Wenner-Gren Foundation for Anthropological Research in 1989 and with Designated Research Initiative Funds from the University of Maryland Baltimore County in 1990, and by Tom Cummins during a sabbatical year from the University of Chicago in 2002. The Graduate School of Georgetown University, as well as Harvard University, provided the funding necessary to permit the reproduction of color images in this publication, for which we are grateful.

Thanks go to the directors of the archives we consulted, especially to Grecia Vasco de Escudero, director of the Archivo Nacional del Ecuador, and Jorge Isaac Cazorla, former director of the Archivo Histórico del Banco Central del Ecuador in Ibarra. Thanks also to Cristóbal Landázuri, director of MARKA—Instituto de Historia y Antropología Andina (Quito), and his students, for collaboration in the collection of archival materials and for the pleasure of a continuing dialogue over the past two decades. We are indebted to Mercedes López for her assistance in the collection of historical documentation on the Muisca in the Archivo General de la Nación and the Biblioteca Nacional de Colombia in Bogotá. We also appreciate the generosity of Rodolfo Vallín Magaña and Luis Gonzalo Uscátegui, for providing us with photos of the reconstructed murals of Sutatausa, and to Elías Sevilla Casas and Carlos Miguel Varona for the photo of the shaft tomb in Tierradentro. José Ramón Jouvé-Martín assisted us in converting microfilms from Ibarra into computer files, for which we are thankful.

The following individuals engaged us in fruitful conversation around the issues of colonial culture and indigenous literacy: Vincent Barletta, Kathryn Burns, Mélida Camayo, Carolina Castañeda, Quetzil Castañeda, Alicia Chocué, Joanne Moran Cruz, Carolyn Dean, Sarah Fentress, Michael Gerli, Bill Hanks, José Ramón Jouve-Martín, Walter Mignolo, Dana Leibsohn, Mercedes López, Frederick Luciani, Sabine MacCormack, Bruce Mannheim, Bruno Mazzoldi, Abelardo Ramos, Verónica Salles-Reese, Frank Salomon, Greg Spira, Gary Urton, and Marta Zambrano. We have benefited by the commentaries of the Georgetown University Standing Seminar in History and the students in "Alphabetic and Visual Literacy in Colonial Latin America" at Georgetown University in 1997 and 1999, the University of Chicago in 1999, and Harvard University in 2002, as well as from exchanges with the students of the Licenciatura en Pedagogía Comunitaria of the Consejo Regional Indígena del Cauca and anthropology students of the Universidad de Buenos Aires. Readings and critical commentary on selected chapters by Kalman Bland, Kathryn Burns, Gail Gibson, Paul Griffiths, Adam Jasienski, and Moshe Sluhovsky were helpful for uncovering the significance of our project beyond the Andes and Latin America. We are particularly grateful to Carolyn Dean and to the other reviewers for Duke University Press, who remain anonymous, for their suggestions.

Valerie Millholland of Duke University Press has helped to make this book a reality, providing along the way not only crucial assistance, but highly valued friendship. We also would like to thank Gisela Fosado for her help making sense of all the images and Sonya Manes for her patient and precise copyediting, as well as Adam Jasienski for preparing the index.

Portions of chapter 1 were included in a review essay for *Ethnohistory*, volume 49, number 3, pp. 687–701 (2002): "Imagining Colonial Culture." Chapter 5 was published in a slightly altered version in *Colonial Latin American Review*, volume 7, number 1, pp. 7–32 (1998) under the title, "Between Images and Writing: The Ritual of the King's *Quillca*." Chapter 6 was published in a different version in *Latin American Literary Review*, volume 26, number 52, pp. 174–200 (1998) as "The Reconfiguration of Civic and Sacred Space: Architecture, Image, and Writing in the Colonial Northern Andes."

Introduction

From 1574 until his death in Madrid in 1590, Don Diego de Torres, the hereditary chief or cacique of the Muisca town of Turmequé, near Bogotá, fought a legal battle to regain the rights to his chiefdom, taken from him by members of the Royal Court, or Audiencia, in Santafé de Bogotá in a move to block his efforts to denounce the multiple abuses that Spanish authorities had committed against the indigenous population there. Don Diego, son of a Spanish conquistador and the sister of the cacique of Turmequé, was a mestizo and an educated, highly literate, and cosmopolitan colonial actor who produced innumerable legal petitions in impeccable Castilian Spanish, all signed with a clear and precise hand.[1] He was fully aware of the genres through which he should formulate his various texts, and he was conversant enough in the laws of the Indies to address his needs and complaints properly.[2] Furthermore, he understood the need for graphic representation as part of his presentation, perhaps in response to the royal questionnaire known as the Relaciones Geográficas of 1571. In his petition presented to the king in 1586, he includes two European-style maps, made two years before (figures 1 and 2). They form an integral part of Don Diego's document—he addresses Philip II directly, in word and in image—that voices his hopes that the king would remedy the abuses committed in the areas represented by the maps. One of them represents the indigenous communities and the jurisdiction of the Province of Tunja, in which Turmequé was situated; the other configures the same for Santafé de Bogotá. These are the earliest carto-

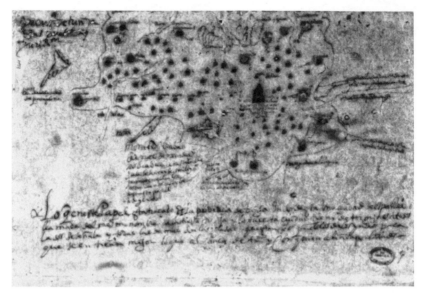

FIGURE 1 Map of the province of Tunja, its towns and jurisdiction, artist unknown, ca. 1586, AGI/S, MP Panama 7. Ink and paper. Courtesy of Archivo General de Indias, Seville.

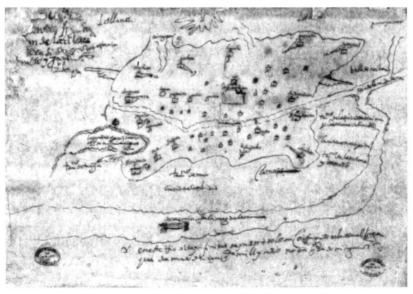

FIGURE 2 Map of the province of Santafé, its towns and borders, artist unknown, ca. 1586, AGI/S, MP Panama 8. Ink and paper. Courtesy of Archivo General de Indias, Seville.

graphic documents we know for Colombia and they were meant to demonstrate in the visual channel the place described in prose in the document, a place where one could still see similar mistreatment—"verlo ocularmente," as he states—such that "it would require a thick book" (Sería hacer un libro de gran volumen) to describe it all (AGI/S 1586b, 232r). Don Diego de Torres turned the pen to two different acts, writing and drawing, but toward a single purpose, the defense of his rights and those of his community.

To accomplish this, the cacique of Turmequé did not just send his letters to Spain. Rather, he traveled twice in his forty years to the Royal Court, where he was granted audiences on multiple occasions and where he socialized with the elite of Santafé and Madrid society. While in Spain he married a Spanish woman, to whom he left his estates in the New Kingdom of Granada (AGI/S 1633); he also served in Spain as executor of the will of Alonso de Atagualpa, grandson of Atahualpa, the last pre-Hispanic Inca ruler. Accused of leading a general native rebellion in the Bogotá region, Don Diego did not neglect his American subjects; he maintained close relations with most of the caciques of the Muisca area, as well as in other regions of Colombia to which he traveled.[3]

Indigenous Peoples and the Lettered City

This sophisticated and prolific man, who moved with ease between indigenous and Spanish society, was not altogether unusual in the colonial Spanish American world. Other members of the Andean and Mexican native nobility composed petitions and myriad other documents that are clear indications of the eloquence of the colonial indigenous voice. Among them are figures more well-known than Don Diego de Torres—such as Felipe Guaman Poma de Ayala (1980 [1616]), Diego Muñoz Camargo (1981 [1585]), and Inca Garcilaso de la Vega (1723 [1609])—whose writings are today considered to be part of the colonial literary canon. Nonetheless, notwithstanding the exceptional nature of Guaman Poma, Muñoz Camargo, and Garcilaso's contributions, they were, essentially, petitions to the Crown (Adorno 1986; González Echevarría 1990), a quotidian activity common among members of the colonial elite—both European and indigenous—throughout Latin America.[4] In fact, written documents, many of which had some form of legal status, constituted one of the primary channels of communication between native peoples and Europeans, as well as between Europeans themselves. Indeed, the Spanish American world was, as Ángel Rama (1996 [1984]) has aptly suggested, a "lettered city," a social constellation built on an ideology of the primacy of the written word; within this system, the urban landscape was constituted as a literate scenario for indigenous conversion and domination, structuring the exercise of power by native actors and Spaniards alike. Legal documents functioned as prime vehicles for transforming native perceptions of time, space, and the discourses of power (Abercrombie 1998a; Rappaport and Cummins 1994). Stored and circulated within the indigenous community, where these papers were transmitted across generations of hereditary chiefs, the written record became a source of legitimacy and authenticity, as well as a vehicle that significantly reconfigured the native memory, since only those historical referents that were legally acceptable in the Spanish worldview were transmitted in writing to future readers.

This process of reconfiguration began very early, especially within the native communities that almost immediately allied themselves with the Spanish conquerors, such as the Tlaxcalan lords in central Mexico or the Wanka ethnic lords from Jauja, in central Peru. For example, in 1567, several of the bilingual sons of the Wankas, including the principal cacique Felipe Guacar Paucar, traveled to Spain with their own notaries to petition the court for rewards for their loyalty to the Crown (AGI/s 1563). Some of them were able to meet with the king, who in written documents granted them not only certain rights and privileges, but also bestowed upon them the use of coats of arms, bringing them into the visual field of Spanish symbolic power (Murra 1998, 55–56). This interaction between political power on the one hand, and image and text on the other, was more fully realized later, when the Tlaxcalan lords of Mexico presented themselves before Philip II at the Royal Court in Madrid. There, the mestizo historian Muñoz Camargo, official interpreter of the 1583–85 Tlaxcalan embassy, personally presented the Codex Tlaxcala to the king (Acuña 1981, 9–12). The Codex consisted of the history of the Tlaxcalan community and its early service to the Crown, illustrated with 156 pen-and-ink drawings. Two years later, the cacique of Turmequé—another mestizo—presented his *relación* to the royal court. Perhaps, Don Diego de Torres met with Diego Muñoz Camargo or Inca Garcilaso de la Vega at court. It was a "new world" that, within less than a hundred years, had suddenly become very small. These lords, who sprang from such diverse social and cultural realities, shared very similar concerns in defense of their own standing and that of their communities. Passivity in the face of the symbolic techniques of colonial power was inconceivable for these gentlemen. Rather, they actively engaged with the written word and pictorial image at the highest levels of political and cultural power.[5]

Our task, then, is to present the traces of this sustained engagement with literacy, so as to understand the nature of the intellectual participation of indigenous peoples in the social formation of colonial Latin America. More precisely, it is through the examination of the nature of visual and alphabetic inscription among native peoples of the northern Andes (today, Colombia and Ecuador) that we can recognize not only such traces, but their implications. Literacy is not a univocal term for us. Rather, we understand it to comprise a complex constellation of channels of expression, both visual and alphabetic, which functioned in the colonial Andean world within an ideological system that saw the two as inextricably interconnected and as prime tools for reorganizing the worldviews and everyday lives of native South Americans. In this respect, our aim is not that of exploring literacy as a technology in the unilinear evolutionary manner of the early theorists of the topic (Goody 1977, 1987; Havelock 1986; Ong 1982; cf. Street 1984). Instead, we propose to engage in a specific historical analysis of how literacy operated as a social process in relation to orality and bodily experience by examining a series of historical cases, following in the footsteps of medieval and early modern historians, art historians, and literary scholars (Camille 1989; Clanchy 1993; Fox 2000; Johns 1998; Justice 1994; Smail 1999; Stock 1983, 1990) and ethnographers (Bowen 1991; Messick 1993) who have examined the introduction of Western alphabetic literacy into previously oral societies or into communities that did not use the Roman alphabet and have taken visuality as seriously as the command of the alphabet. Like our fellow Latin-americanists (Gruzinski 1993 [1988]; Hanks 2000; Mignolo 1995), we take the implications of alphabetic and visual literacy to be inextricably entangled with an analysis of Spanish colonial domination and how writing and pictorial expression functioned as both a measuring stick of cultural hierarchy in a colonial world and as a vehicle for incorporating native peoples into the colonial project.[6]

Contours of Literacy

The role of alphabetic writing within the colonial Latin American social formation is not an isolated phenomenon. It would be an error to imagine literacy as restricted to the production and reception of alphabetic writing; literacy also includes the visual, which must be understood in relation to the written word. Colonial cultural politics, as it sought to impose systems of Western European sociability, was enacted through an engagement with both image and text. Literacy, in this sense, can be understood as an inter-related strategy. It imparted a system of referentiality that, in the colonial context, fostered the expression of a divine and secular power that was embedded within a hierarchy of natural authority. Learning to look at pictorial images within the paradigms of European visual culture, as well as learning to conduct oneself within the architectural grid of the Spanish-style town, form as much a part of colonial literacy as learning to read the alphabetic text of a catechism. Both the alphabetic and the visual systems of representation are abstract, concerned with looking and decoding, and in the colonial era, both skills were intimately connected to the didactic, religious, and legal practices of Europeans in the New World as they were directed toward native peoples (Bryson 1988; Durston 2007; Gruzinski 1999, 2001 [1990]; Mannheim 1991; Mignolo 1995; Pagden 1982).

Our interpretive move connecting alphabet with visual image is not merely an analytical tool. Visual and alphabetic literacy were, in fact, perceived by colonial-era Spaniards and native Andeans as being intimately related. In a continuation of the medieval notion of the fundamental identity of pictures and writing, both of which were believed to produce images in the mind when read aloud and memorized (Carruthers 1990, 1998; Clanchy 1993; Huot 1987; Yates 1966), literacy was not understood by colonial Latin Americans as being entirely alphabetic in nature. The most extensive book on memory is the *Rhetorica christiana*, written in Latin by Diego Valadés (1579), probably a mestizo from Tlaxcala. Valadés discusses and illustrates two ways to know letters. One is by the sound: the letter *a* is to be recognized by the initial sound "a," as in "Antonio." Another is to recognize a letter by its form, in association with an object: an open compass or ladder represents the letter *a* (figures 3 and 4). Valadés follows the convention of European illustrations of a "visual alphabet" as used in the art of memory (Sherman 2000, 150–52); however, he also localizes it by including indigenous Mexican forms to facilitate learning. Valadés's "visual alphabet" is not directed toward reading or writing a text, but instead is meant as a tool for recalling from memory texts that can then be recited out loud.[7]

The alphabet and literacy were thus both something visual and very much a part of orality. This oral aspect is also captured in the 1611 dictionary of Sebastián de Covarrubias Orozco (1995 [1611], 706), which defines *leer*—"to read"—as, "To pronounce with words that which is written in letters" and "to teach a discipline publicly."[8] The two forms of literacy, visual and alphabetic, were thus mediated by orality, a practice common to Spaniards and natives

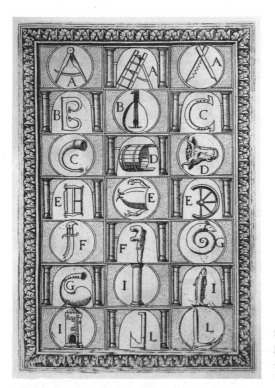

FIGURE 3 Alphabet with European figures, Diego Valadés, *Rhetorica christiana* (Perugia, 1579). Engraving.

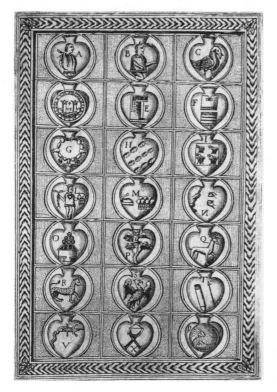

FIGURE 4 Alphabet with European figures, Diego Valadés, *Rhetorica christiana* (Perugia, 1579). Engraving.

alike. Alphabetically written teachings furnished the basis for oral presentations in which visual materials supplied crucial pedagogical tools. Sermons were among the most common texts read aloud to both Spanish and indigenous audiences while they observed religious paintings and sculptures, gathered in communal spaces of the church's interior or in the exterior plaza. However, in sermons prepared for a native audience, the spheres of administrative documents and religious images were drawn together through ontological analogy such that various forms of colonial culture and society overlapped in unexpected ways (Lima, Concilio de, 1990 [1585], 653). We will detail such juxtapositions in the following pages, probing the ideological substratum that underlay not only the introduction of the alphabet and the naturalistic pictorial image, but also inspired particular ways of promoting urban life among native peoples, infused public administration with a ritualization of the written word, and attuned the indigenous inner eye to particular visual templates which generated miraculous visions. That is, we see literacy as larger than writing and painting, encompassing a diverse range of experiences in the colonial world, something performative and embodied in specific ways by individuals of particular social groups.

By bringing together a variety of interrelated documentary and visual materials, we will analyze the means by which literacy contributed to the constitution and reconstitution of European institutions in native northern Andean society, primarily among the Muisca (Chibcha), Pasto, and Nasa (Páez) ethnic groups; the former two were the largest aboriginal populations north of the boundaries of Tawantinsuyu, the Inca empire. We have chosen to concentrate our analysis on the northern Andes, what is today Colombia and Ecuador, in an effort to focus on Andean culture in a non-Incaic setting. We intend in this way to expand what is more broadly meant by Andean. Along with examining excellent evidence for indigenous deployment of literacy in this area, both in the defense of communities before the Spanish administration and in their internal social and political life, by focusing on a region beyond the Inca sphere of influence, we gain new insights into the colonial process, precisely because this area was never part of the state-level constellation of Tawantinsuyu. Such a vantage point permits us to compare and contrast a multiplicity of adaptations to European literacy by various ethnic groups. Given that the Spaniards sought to impose Quechua and Incaic models upon northern Andean peoples, northern ethnic groups exhibit a distinctive overlay of native and imported elements of Andean culture that can be analyzed in the course of the study of the implications of literacy for the region. Nonetheless, we do not see the northern Andes as an isolated or discrete colonial culture in relation to the colonial formations in Peru. In contrast, Bogotá and Quito were politically and ecclesiastically linked to the metropolitan center of Lima and to Spain. Not only did the viceroy in Lima hold ultimate jurisdiction in this area, but important doctrinal publications, such as the 1585 catechism of the Third Council of Lima (Lima, Concilio de 1990 [1585]), held religious authority there, as well. So, at times we turn to examples from the central Andes, where we often find more ample documentation, as well as unique or telling acts that articulate the colonial intersection between visual and alphabetic literacy.

Literacy, in its broadest sense, is a critical component of what has come to be called colonial discourse, a heterogeneous set of communicative strategies and practices proper to the colonial situation. Colonial discourse was at once local and international; it was transcultural in nature, its expressive forms overlapping a diverse set of colonial actors—Europeans and American-born Europeans, Native Americans, African populations, and the *castas,* the numerous groups that arose out of their mixture (mestizos, mulattos, etc.). The study of colonial discourse has been tremendously useful for studying the process of cultural formation from the sixteenth century to the eighteenth, as it provides a window for examining the multiple and conflicting voices of colonial actors, as well as for viewing members of subordinated groups, such as indigenous peoples, as active agents in cultural creation (Seed 1991). Literacy, in our extended understanding, is fundamental to the study of colonial discourse. Writing provided one of the most important interfaces of the different groups inhabiting the colonial landscape, while images created a common focus for devotion, imagination, and fear, as well as for economic and political interests. And although these forms of literacy created the symbolic arena within which the various European colonizers, both secular and religious, could construct and implement a policy of colonization and conversion to Christianity, it is also through literacy that the indigenous colonized could textually describe and visually present themselves to their colonizers and press their demands in the colonial political arena.

Too often, however, the process of acquiring literacy is understood as the process of shifting from an oral to a written culture, such that a native person becomes learned in the European textual tradition. Participation in literacy implies more than learning to read alphabetically inscribed texts and produce Western forms of pictorial representation. Native literacies emerging out of the colonial context were richer than mere adaptations to European practices of reading and viewing; they also transformed them, spawning intertextual readings that interacted with indigenous forms of recording and representation, including knot records (khipus), textiles, and sacred geography. That is, literacy is not always—nor ever was—a passive process in which forms of authority and power are reproduced through mechanical everyday practice. When literacy is taken up and used by subaltern groups, it becomes what Steven Justice (1994, 24) calls "assertive literacy." The copying in the colonial period of documents and images, or the creation of new ones by subordinated social groups acting in relation to dominant ones, were acts that engaged with these media and their technology. Out of this engagement emerged the historical specificities of colonial culture and society. So too, the orthodox making and veneration of images became heterodox almost immediately, thereby transforming the shared space of the visual field into a multiple one in which all eyes may be focused on the same image, but what is being seen is not the same (Cummins 1998a). With these features in mind, it is possible to view literacy as a crucial arena within which colonial culture was contested and negotiated by native peoples and their Spanish overlords.

Manuscript Interculture

In the late eighteenth century, in a dispute over maize lands in the warm country of Puntal, the Pasto caciques of Tuza presented a series of packets of legal papers comprising a range of documents produced over the course of two and a half centuries, bound roughly together by thread (ANE/Q 1792b).[9] Carefully stored in home archives by generations of hereditary chiefs, this documentation legitimized their strategies of expansion into productive warm-country territory (Powers 1995, 124–27). In addition to the rich historical information contained in these pages, the Tuza document packets can also be approached in terms of their form and materiality: the ways in which such documents are written, compiled, conserved; how they are related to one another and to nonwritten referents in an intertextual series; the ritual uses to which they were put. They are an example of what could be called a "manuscript interculture," participated in by both native Andeans and members of the dominant Hispanic society. We intentionally employ the term *interculture* in place of *culture* here, borrowing from Thomas Abercrombie's work on colonial Bolivia (1998a, 114–15), to emphasize the fact that the written word provided a creative interface within which members of different cultural traditions expounded upon and adjusted to an unequal relationship born of colonialism (1998a, 215). This literary contact zone (Pratt 1992) developed over time, producing complementary and contradictory interpretations on the part of both native and European readers and writers, whose self-perceptions and views of the Other were imbued with colonial metaphors and cultural typologies in which the categories of "indigenous" and "Spanish" took on new meanings (Gruzinski 1999, 211–13).

Our focus on textual literacy goes beyond the obvious point that alphabetically written archival documents provide the major source of our information on the colonial period. We intend to focus on writing's critical role as an arena for the playing out of cultural differences and the appropriation of cultural forms, particularly in the struggles surrounding the production of legal discourse. In the colonial context, such struggles most frequently took place in the space of handwritten manuscripts. The manuscript constitutes a particular form of writing that reproduces features proper to orality:

> Each manuscript is unique (as is each oral performance). It is the work of one or more human individuals. Both processes respond to their environment, vary over time and according to circumstance (oral poetry can be rained out, a written line can detour around a hole in the parchment, a leaf or the writing on it can wear away). It is modified by its audience (as the oral performer tailors his performance to audience reaction, as members of the audience react to one another, as the manuscript text is mediated by generations of glosses). The handwritten text as product resembles the mechanically reproduced book; the process of its creation mimics the unique, occasional nature of oral tradition and oral performance. The rhetorical nature of orality, too, carries over into the realm of the manuscript text, always conditioned by and elaborated according to its circumstantiae. . . . The manuscript text is constituted by the individuals who created it: scribe, rubricator, corrector, illuminator. In the case of the scribe, these traces include individual hands (no matter how formalized), the variants caused by minor distractions whose causes are lost to us forever (a bird flying through a window), misreadings, misunderstandings, interference of dialects, poor eyesight, an aching back, and a host of other quirks that situate the product squarely in the process of its creation in a way that the printed book can never be. (Dagenais 1994, 17)

Handwritten, displaying the penmanship of the scribe, exhibiting corrections and revisions, idiosyncratic in its partial reproduction of generic models, with an abundance of marginalia only sometimes providing a direct gloss of the contents (Barletta 1999; Camille 1992), the manuscript, John Dagenais argues, is the antithesis of the printed book. The performance that engenders the manuscript is embodied within its very form, unlike the printed book, whose discourse, he contends, is standardized, reified, and removed from the conditions of its production. However, recent authors have insightfully suggested that print culture only developed modern standards of veracity and uniformity over time as a result of specific economic and political arrangements that fostered such appreciations of the possibilities of print (Johns 1998). Nonetheless, the dichotomy of manuscript versus print is hardly relevant to the case we are studying, because manuscripts were the only objects of alphabetic literacy that could be produced within the colonial indigenous community. Printing presses were few and very far between in the colonial Americas, and natives in general had little familiarity with the mechanical reproduction of the printed page. Of course, the printed page was ever present, but it was something that was to be read aloud, perhaps even to be copied, and this was done by hand. What Dagenais contributes to our understanding of colonial indigenous literacy is not so much the distinction between manuscript and print, as the fluid nature of the manuscript and the ways in which fluidity is embodied in its visual form.

The mechanics of writing by hand was a meaningful activity in itself, often a subject of pictorial representation in Mexican and Andean colonial manuscripts. Natives and Europeans are depicted seated at tables replete with the instruments of their profession. In Guaman Poma de Ayala's *Nueva corónica y buen gobierno* (henceforth, *Nueva corónica*) (1980 [1616], 828; figure 5), a native scribe, identified as a *quilcacamayo*—literally, "maker of writing"—is seated at a desk with a half-written document before him. The image is not meant to depict the literal act of writing; rather, it displays the scribe as a person looking downward and away, pen in hand and laid to paper, but not forming a letter. The page is, in fact, turned away from the scribe and placed parallel to the picture plane, so that the viewer can see it. On the desk are arranged the instruments of writing: an extra quill, ink blotter, ink and case for the quills. A similar image is found in the colonial Mixtec manuscript of Yanhuitlán, in which the Dominican friar Domingo de Santa María, the priest of the village of Tepozcolula, is depicted seated at a table, holding a quill pen and writing, while two Mixtecs, Seven Deer and Ten Monkeys, approach him (figure 6). Here, in a Mexican manuscript, the image of Western writing is subtly infused with Mixtec writing, conveying the names of the

FIGURE 5 Native scribe, Felipe Guaman Poma de Ayala, *El primer nueva corónica y buen gobierno*, p. 814 (824), 1616. Ink and paper. Courtesy of Royal Danish Library, Copenhagen.

FIGURE 6 Seven Deer and Ten Monkeys approach Dominican monk, Codex Yanhuitlán, f.29r, artist unknown, 1545–50, Archivo General de la Nación, Mexico City. Ink and paper.

two individuals through a place-glyph composed of a mountain and a copper axe (Jiménez Moreno and Matos Higuera 1940 [1545–50], 65).

These two images, one from Mexico and one from Peru, consciously register through iconography the complexity of the scribe's work. By work, we do not only mean the intellectual exercise of writing, but the physical task itself. For as Justice notes in relation to English medieval literacy, "the laboriousness of writing—the recalcitrance of pen and the resistance of paper, the variability of ink, and the job of sharpening—meant that the activity had to enter consciousness as something more than the extension of reading or thought" (1994, 24, n. 34). In taking up writing, indigenous authors came to understand themselves, along with mimicking the symbolic technology of writing, as inhabiting and working differently in space, working at a task to produce an object. It meant working with an alien surface—paper—that was produced far away and brought with great labor and expense to the farthest reaches of the empire.[10] Writing often meant being indoors and seated in a chair at a table; such furniture was listed in native wills with great frequency, as we will describe in the coming chapters.

The same elements and tasks of the native author were employed, albeit for different effect, in the act of drawing. Although the tasks of making an image and making a letter require different conceptual skills and abilities—the conversion of sound and the conversion of sight to a graphic system—they employ the same tools: pen, ink, paper, and the gesture of the hand. The graphic elements of the word and the image are distinguished only through cultural recognition of the communicative system through which the lines are inscribed on paper. Our own Western frames of reference lead us to see written text and drawing as discrete (Goodman 1976, 127–73). However, the act of making them is the same. In fact, these two culturally separate tasks are brought together in one of the most remarkable drawings by Guaman Poma (1980 [1616], 784) of a principal cacique seated behind a large table (figure 7). Unlike Guaman Poma's image of the scribe, who is depicted as a passive cipher, the cacique is shown as an active agent. He turns to listen to a member of his community, who gestures as he speaks. At the same time, the cacique steadies a piece of paper with his left hand and writes with the other. The pen touches the paper in the process of forming a word, the continuation of a clearly legible text that is turned upside down from the perspective of the viewer/reader. This is, then, the precise moment of transformation of the oral into the written. But what, precisely, are we seeing beyond that? The figure is speaking Quechua, which we learn from the heading. The cacique is listening

FIGURE 7 Cacique principal, Felipe Guaman Poma de Ayala, *Nueva coronica y buen gobierno*, p. 770 (784), 1616. Ink and paper. Courtesy of Royal Danish Library, Copenhagen.

to his Quechua utterance, but is simultaneously translating it into Spanish as he writes, something that is instantiated in almost all Andean documents when testimony is given in a "mother tongue," but inscribed in Spanish.[11]

But there is another instance of simultaneity when we ask about visual, rather than linguistic, decoding. Is the viewer to read the text or to see it as depicting writing? It is both, although we can only read what is written if we turn Guaman Poma's manuscript upside down and assume the position of the cacique. If we look at the drawing head on, we see that it is writing, but without necessarily being able to read it precisely. Here, then, the operations of drawing and writing become undifferentiated and equivalent in relation to the Quechua orality imagined to be shared by the two figures. The lack of differentiation between drawing and writing is most clearly realized at the precise moment that the next letter is about to be formed. Suddenly and effortlessly, Guaman Poma swaps modes of Spanish symbolic technology and begins to draw, the letter becoming the tip of the pen; his graphic gesture now flows up the curved line that articulates the contour line of the quill. Only at this instant is the distinction between writing and drawing completely effaced: when the tip of the pen represents simultaneously the instrument of writing and drawing, as well as a sign for these two activities. That is, Guaman Poma shifts from writing a word to making a drawing, so as to express the nature of both the communication between the speaking and listening figure, and the production of a document. We would argue that this is a natural act, rather than a calculated one on the part of Guaman Poma; that is, he feels perfectly at ease in the physical transition from one code of line making to another, as it is the same gesture and set of instruments.[12]

Moreover, the viewer must turn the manuscript upside down to read what is written/drawn, something that Guaman Poma presumably also had to do to create this part of the drawing. But when the reader/viewer rotates the page, he or she is placed behind the image of the cacique, looking over his shoulder, so to speak: it is as though the viewer were moved deep into the picture plane. Guaman Poma's own position as artist/viewer at this point does not simply mirror the cacique in the image; he becomes the cacique: his right hand is drawing the right hand that is writing, just as his left hand and the cacique's are holding the paper to steady it. In many ways, this image complicates the distinction between the graphic reproduction of sound and vision. Nelson Goodman argues in *Languages of Art* that realism is not a matter of "any constant or absolute relationship between picture and its object but a relationship between the system of representation employed in the picture and the standard system" (1976, 38). Here, Guaman Poma is careful both in word and drawing to appeal to the standard system, so that he might in fact produce something that gives a real and effective representation of the Andean experience, as well as a portrait of his own creative act.

Whereas Guaman Poma's drawing both depicts and performs a colonial orality congealed in picture and writing, the 1633 will of Don Andrés, the Muisca cacique of Machetá, displays the dynamic oral component of colonial manuscript culture (AGN/B 1633a). Don Andrés dictated his desires to the notary, who recorded the numerous possessions, landholdings, debt relationships, and pious bequests enumerated in this lengthy testament of a wealthy man. In the process, the cacique recurrently backtracked, remembering possessions and directives that he had forgotten to include in their proper position in the will. As a result, the document recapitulates his haphazard oral performance. A literate man, Don Andrés frequently referred to papers validating his possessions and the debts owed him, so that his will conjures up the image of man on his deathbed, shuffling through his files and composing his will according to what he finds. The feeling of eavesdropping on a meeting in progress that one derives from reading Don Andrés's will is apparent in more modest documents, as well. Juana Sanguino, an urban *india* from Bogotá who worked as a servant for a Spaniard named Bartolomé Sanguino, provides early on in her 1633 will for burial in the Church of Our Lady of Las Nieves, the parish of many of Santafé's indigenous inhabitants (AGN/B 1633d, 142v).[13] However, this provision is revoked at the end of the two-page testament in favor of interment in Santafé's Cathedral, in a tomb belonging to her employer. Presumably, Juana Sanguino was notified of the possibility of this burial site by the notary, Estacio Sanguino Rangel, a relative of her benefactor—in fact, she requests his permission to be interred there in the very text of the will (1633d, 143v). Thus, her testament provides a window onto a notarial process, in which a last-minute reminder by the notary causes her to backtrack and alter her last wishes.

In essence, then, if we take a manuscript as an object and appreciate the ways in which its contents unfold on the space of the page, we can get a sense of how it was composed. Kathryn Burns (2005) notes that the very process of drawing up notarial documents, which generally took place in stages, is reflected in colonial-era manuscripts. Clients frequently signed blank pages, allowing notaries and their assistants to compose entries after the fact in their official record books. This practice left visual traces of scribal procedure on the written page, such as the crowding of print into a space too small for its contents or extra-large writing where too much space had been reserved. But notwithstanding the manuscript's oral tone, in an era in which manuscripts were far more ubiquitous than the printed word, scribal writing emitted an aura of authority deriving from its perceived uniformity, its embellishments, and its relation to the holy scriptures (Ross 1994, 232–34). In colonial Latin America, the authority of the manuscript originated in its control by the state apparatus, the official notaries (Herzog 1996) whose scribblings were hardly uniform and were frequently illegible—as indigenous litigants sometimes complained—but were surrounded by a mystique of "respect, awe, and obedience" (Ross 1994, 234). Their aura was intensified by the rituals to which manuscripts were subjected (Seed 1995), a theme we will treat in detail in later chapters.[14]

Colonial-era manuscript production and reception were mediated by numerous gatekeepers and impinged upon by particular cultural contexts.

A number of factors are key to understanding these manuscripts. The language of transmission, which was not necessarily that of the petitioners or litigators, was mediated at the grassroots by scribes, artists, town criers, interpreters, missionaries, and catechumens, dissolving the notion that these documents had a single author. Many indigenous writers and readers were forced to work through interpreters—nonnative speakers of indigenous languages, whose level of proficiency is never remarked upon in the documentation—or to compose briefs and letters in Spanish, which was a second language for most of them, resulting in documentation that does not entirely capture the intent of its authors. In the Pasto case, there is a double overlay, since documents were frequently written in Spanish, based upon testimony collected in Quechua, among people whose native language was Pasto. Quechua was probably introduced among the Pasto under Spanish domination, given that only a small number of Pasto chiefdoms were brought under Incaic control, and then only for the space of a decade or so (Landázuri 1995).[15] In addition to the pitfalls inherent in translation, scribes and notaries frequently mediated the transcription of these documents with their own glosses of what was translated, producing an imperfect record of the already-defective account supplied by the interpreter.

The people who penned letters and petitions were influenced by the institutions and methods by which literacy was taught, the legal networks in which they were enmeshed, and their geographic location. Although there were schools established for caciques throughout the Andes (AGI/S 1577; AGI/S 1604,16r–v; AGN/B 1576; ANE/Q 1695, 67r; Cárdenas Ayaipoma 1975–76; Galdo Gutiérrez 1970; Hartmann and Oberem 1981; Jaramillo Uribe 1989; R. Wood 1986), the extent of indigenous literacy varied by region. In the northern Andes, considerably more Pastos than Muiscas could sign their names, if the presence of chiefly signatures on documents is any indication of the acquisition of literacy skills. In contrast, there is no evidence at all for Nasa literacy in this period. Many Pastos and Muiscas claimed proficiency in Castilian Spanish—the documents frequently designate bilingual witnesses and litigants as *ladinos*, or native people who spoke Spanish. In contrast, there is little evidence that the Nasa were bilingual in Spanish and Nasa Yuwe (the Nasa language) in the colonial era, except possibly for a handful of caciques. Differences in literacy across the region may be due to the relative isolation of the Pastos in comparison to the Muiscas. It is likely that the Pastos were forced to assume by themselves the most elementary documentary procedures, given the arduous journeys they had to undertake to reach a notarial office in the provincial capitals of Pasto or Ibarra. The Muisca, in contrast, were able to secure the services of notaries and lawyers in the nearby cities of Santafé and Tunja, obviating the need for native people to learn to write contracts, wills, or petitions; the huge indigenous presence in the capital of the Audiencia, including both servants and artisans, as well as caciques, only reinforced their dependence upon the official gatekeepers of the legal world.[16] In addition, the vicious struggle over the fate of the indigenous population between the Church of the New Kingdom of Granada and the Audiencia of Santafé—the latter allied with powerful Spanish settlers—meant that the Muisca enjoyed less direct access to the sort of literacy necessary for a relatively unmediated participation as legal actors (Ares Queija 1989; Gálvez Piñal 1974; Rojas 1965). The Pasto Province was, in comparison, a backwater of the Audiencia of Quito, and thus to some degree cushioned from such struggles.[17] In the case of the Nasa, geographic isolation operated conversely, hampering the acquisition of literacy within this small and rebellious group that was not as integrated into the colonial state's administrative apparatus as were the Muisca and Pasto. Hence, the Nasa had less need of literate expertise. Such differences in access to literacy are significant, given that the processes of production and reception of manuscripts were conditioned upon mastery of this skill. These variations lead us to interpret literacy as more than a technology: literacy is better understood as a set of practices deeply embedded within social, political, and economic realities. Social arrangements deeply impacted upon the ways that literacy was employed in the colonial era (Gee 1988; Graff 1987).

The legal framework of manuscript composition determined the extent to which genre boundaries could be transgressed and indigenous petitioners could be considered authors. The existence of mediators, particularly notaries and scribes, alerts us to the fact that colonial-era literacy was much more than simply the ability to read and write. It also involved a familiarity with legal precepts and formulas, the province of notaries, judges, and other specialists. Brinkley Messick, writing about legal literacy in Yemen, captures this point compellingly:

> In the legal document genre, entextualization rests on a double movement, a double relation. The first is a movement from Text to text, that is, from law on the books to the document; while the second is from the world (as event) to text, from a specific human undertaking, such as a sale, to the document. Behind a given document text is the law, in front

of it is the world. . . . The writer, the notary, through his document text, mediates both the reproduction of the Text and the incorporative 'translation' of the world. (1989, 35)

The manuscript, at least of the legal sort, is the product of a collaborative—or adversarial—vision of the world that was, in the case of the northern Andes, necessarily interethnic. The law and its gatekeepers were European, while the litigants belonged to a range of subordinated ethnic groups. Notaries mediated law and document, filtering translations of indigenous observations of the world into acceptable legal discourse. In this sense, we can only comprehend indigenous literate production as an intercultural phenomenon.

In a highly insightful interpretation of sixteenth- and seventeenth-century notarial manuals used in the New Kingdom of Granada—the sorts of manuals that someone like Don Diego de Torres, cacique of Turmequé, would have consulted—Juan Felipe Hoyos García (2002, chap. 6) argues that the role of the notary was to convert raw testimony into colonial legal truth, by guiding witnesses into providing him with testimonial material that he could insert into his own text. The notarial document, unlike testimony, obeyed a specific legal epistemology and was marked by a distinct set of linguistic usages. It rearranged witnesses' statements so that their contents fit within certain categories:

> [There is a] . . . correlation among types of knowledge that are specified through expressions of two types of knowledge: "ciencia cierta" [complete certainty], "público y notorio" [public and well known] and "pública voz y fama" [widely stated] all shared in the direct knowledge of acts, but the latter two distinguished between public occurrences and traditions; "creencia" [belief] and "común opinión" [common opinion] specified that the testimony was inferential based on inconclusive facts, while "común reputación" [commonly reputed] was also an inference, but of the causes, based upon the effects . . . that were perceived but inconclusive; "oídas" [things heard] and "tiempo inmemorial" [time immemorial] shared in indirect knowledge—through verbal description—of a fact, determining from whom or how it had been heard and its temporal distance from whoever had learned it directly. (2002, 121–22)[18]

The notary could never be certain that indigenous witnesses fully understood these legal categories; he could not trust them to classify the truth value of their statements according to a European epistemology. In fact, in many Andean languages epistemological concerns are marked by precise referential validators, frequently in the form of suffixes, whose classifications of types of knowledge differ considerably from those outlined by Hoyos (Hardman 1988; Howard-Malverde 1990; Rojas Curieux 1998); some linguists have suggested that these meanings carry over into nonstandard usages in popular Andean Spanish as well (Zavala 1996). The extent to which the epistemologies embedded in native languages conflicted with the epistemology that the notary was at pains to draw out of the testimony of indigenous witnesses, underscores the ambivalences inherent in these collaborative texts.[19]

Finally, manuscript production was accompanied by ritual acts, both sacred and secular, in which alphabetic, visual, and gestural symbols intermingled. Signatories to legal briefs vowed by the sign of the cross that their testimony was true, simultaneously making the sign of the cross on their bodies and placing their signatures on documents in which notaries had already drawn crosses next to the description of the ritual act. Recipients of royal decrees demonstrated their obedience to the Crown by kissing manuscripts that bore the royal seal, subsequently placing them on their heads. As a will was drawn up, testator, notary, and witnesses recited the prayers to which the testaments alluded. We must think of literacy as more than simply the ability to reproduce or decipher writing. It was part of a much more complex performative process marked by extraliterate ceremony, as well as by graphic notation. The significance of these performances was sometimes interpreted quite differently by native peoples and by Spaniards, both of whom assigned their own meanings to ceremonial acts. Moreover, while it might be appealing to ascribe these rituals to the native cultures to which colonial indigenous litigants belonged—which is what Andeanists have traditionally done—many of these ceremonies are of European origin, demonstrating that oral culture had a hold over Europeans, as well as native Andeans (Clanchy 1989; Fox 2000).

The Visuality of Literacy

The precise nature of the relationship between text and image has always been unstable in Western thought and practice, and the two have been articulated in various forms (Bedos-Rezak 1993; Derrida 1987; Goodman 1976; Marin 1988; Mitchell 1986). The simultaneous introduction in the Americas of both modes and their relationship as the preferred means of symbolic communication of legal, social, historical, and religious knowledge has never been fully addressed, particularly in the Andes, where literacy as both a cognitive and visual system supplemented and supplanted pre-Columbian systems that depended upon different chains of historical referents and visual cues from those articulated in written or visual European texts.[20] The pre-Columbian northern Andes knew no alphabetic or hieroglyphic literacy; nor did pictorial representation take a narrative form. Thus, in 1574 Don Francisco Guillén responded to a royal questionnaire, stating that the natives of Muzo, near Bogotá, had no writing nor painted boards to keep records of their past, and that what they knew was passed down to them, presumably in the oral channel, from their parents and grandparents (AGI/S 1574).

Northern Andeans had to come to terms with more than a new technology of inscription and a novel set of literary genres. Because theirs was a "nonliterate" society before the Spanish invasion, they had to learn to recognize the surface-ground relationship between paper and graphic mark as a concrete manifestation of language. The introduction of this new technology was embedded within European administrative and philosophical systems that redrew the contours of Andean social and topographic space, as well as native hearts and minds. The encounter of Andean and Spanish technologies and ideological systems under conditions of European domination produced a distinctly colonial culture of communication.

When we refer to visual literacy, we are not speaking exclusively of the ability of Andean natives to read the message contained in European art forms, although, as we will demonstrate, the Spaniards made analogies between the referentiality of paintings and that of legal documents. Alphabetic writing merged with other forms of representation in the colonial world. The most celebrated example of native Andean literacy, Felipe Guaman Poma de Ayala's *Nueva corónica* is itself an object of representation within the pictorial realm. One of his illustrations depicts the presentation of his book to the king by the author himself (figure 8; Guaman Poma 1980 [1616], 961). This imaginary scene suggests that among other things, writing is something to be seen, handled, and exchanged rather than being just a text to be read. At the same time, Guaman Poma's text supplements his black-and-white drawings by describing color, sound, and movement, thereby providing descriptively that to which neither written word nor pictorial line could directly refer. In the larger context of colonial cultural interaction, text and image are interwoven visually in religious images, such as the murals in the native Church of San Juan Bautista in Sutatausa, Cundinamarca (figure 9), where

FIGURE 8
The author's
presentation to
and discussion
with the king
of Spain, Felipe
Guaman Poma de
Ayala, *El primer
nueva corónica
y buen gobierno*,
p. 961 (975), 1616.
Ink and paper.
Courtesy of Royal
Danish Library,
Copenhagen.

FIGURE 9 Names and portraits of donors and caciques, mural in the nave of the Church of
San Juan Bautista, artist unknown, ca. 1620, Sutatausa, Cundinamarca.

written names and the painted faces of patrons interact with the biblical subject matter represented in the pictorial narrative, so as to establish a permanent record of the relationship established between specific individuals and a universal sacred iconography.

In order to trace the connections in the Andes between the introduction of new forms of literacy and the implantation of a colonial ideology based upon writing and vision, it is necessary to consider diverse forms of literacy within their broader ethnographic contexts and to comprehend what mediates their production. In the alphabetic sphere, we are concerned primarily with analyzing administrative documents, given that it was through legal writing that native northern Andean peoples communicated with the colonial state; the lengthy chronicles and relaciones written by native authors in colonial Peru and Mexico are almost nonexistent in this region. But beyond interpreting documents in terms of their written contents, we must examine them in their nonliterary aspect as objects and as visual images, turning our attention toward signatures and their deployment, to watermarks, to seals, to marks, to the layout of the page (Goody 1977; Messick 1993; Street 1984), all of which acquire contrasting and contradictory meanings within the dual cultural filters through which native peoples and Europeans interpreted arrangements in topographic space and on the written page (Adorno 1986). This approach provides a deeper understanding of how both native Andeans and Spaniards with varying degrees of literacy confronted, grasped, and transformed the meaning of these documents.[21] The same legal papers can also be apprehended as objects, as tangible things which can be stored, exhibited, forged, copied, kissed, associated with a variety of other things in a meaningful series (Clanchy 1989, 1993). By taking this direction, we are further able to enhance our comprehension of the ethnographic context in which literacy is produced and maintained. Furthermore, we also need to appreciate alphabetic documents as forms of orality, forms of inscription in which both native peoples (Goody et al. 1988; Hanks 2000) and Europeans (Bedos-Rezak 1993; Neuschel 1989, 130–31) embedded oral conventions.

At the same time, we need to comprehend visuality through alphabetic documentation. The visual world becomes the subject not only of experience and exegesis, but the object of textual description. That is, the use of figural language to "paint" an image through words is crucial for Christian religion, legal inheritance, land transactions, and history (Smail 1999). The process of ekphrasis can be examined through catechisms and sermons that explain how people should see and react to narrative biblical representations, devotional images, and miraculous icons as well as how they could come to understand Christian dogma through analogies drawn from visual representational practices.[22] With regard to the mundane world, the issue can be studied in the language of wills, loans, and sales contracts that describe objects and places. In other words, the visual and the alphabetic are intimately associated at multiple levels in the colonial Andean world.

We also need to look at the intertextuality and intervisuality of these different forms of documentation to comprehend how both Spaniards and Andeans understood visual and alphabetic literacy as working in fundamentally the same way in the formation and characterization of the world. This interaction can be seen at the level at which writing and pictorial images were didactic colonial strategies for conversion and acculturation. It is no accident that many catechisms begin with a syllabary, as they were used simultaneously to teach, along with reading, the doctrine as it was explained through sermons keyed to visual representations (Romero Rey 1988, 19).[23] A similar set of relationships between colonial image and text exists in the colonial legal structure, where the portrait of an individual, a historical scene of some colonial event, or a map denotes its subject just as the written document does, and could be presented by the litigant to the authorities. As already mentioned, the Muisca hereditary lord, Don Diego de Torres, submitted as accompanying evidence in his sixteenth century bid to retain his *cacicazgo*, two maps of the territories and indigenous towns of Santafé de Bogotá and Tunja. Guaman Poma de Ayala also presented portraits of his ancestors, as well as a map, in an attempt to legally regain lands near Guamanga (Guaman Poma de Ayala 1991 [1594–1646]; cf. Adorno 1993).[24] That all forms could be presented together as evidence in a court of law underscores the relationship between text (testimony/speech) and image (portrait/person, map/territory). They are equally traces of things not present, although they are incommensurate because ekphrasis cannot reproduce the plenitude of the pictorial image; nor can the pictorial image reproduce the temporal nature of the narrative. For this very reason, both forms are necessary.

The Organization of this Book

While our examples have been of exemplary individuals, in the chapters that follow we will explore how the literate world was penetrated by less well-known folk: Pasto and Muisca testators, local caciques in struggles over succession to the chiefship, Nasa communities seeking to protect or reclaim lands, Pasto notaries. All of them, whether noble or commoner, prominent or obscure, moved within a world in which their dealings with nonnative colonial actors were premised upon intercultural negotiation and dialogue using heterogeneous cultural codes. As we shall demonstrate, the literate arena provides a prime site for discovering the intricacies of colonial culture. What we mean by this will be the subject of the first chapter, where we will argue that it is impossible to comprehend the colonial northern Andes as a territory in which culturally discrete groups of Europeans and native peoples lived parallel lives. Instead, we must conceive of the colonial panorama as a space of transculturation (Ortiz 1995 [1947]), in which a new colonial culture was engendered, although it was experienced differently by members of distinct groups, by men and by women, by the powerful and the powerless.

Literacy, whether alphabetic or visual, is premised by a diversity of genres of expression. We begin our exploration with a look at the genres at work in the colonial northern Andes: which Spanish alphabetic and visual genres were most prevalent and how they were altered by indigenous authors, how they related in intertextual series with native genres of expression, how they interpenetrated one another. The first half of the book will explore how the native voice operated in a region in which the alterity of native culture was most commonly shown through its absence, an issue we will begin to probe in the next chapter. We will trace the ways in which indigenous readers and viewers appropriated the literate production of both Spaniards and other native peoples. Only after we make clear the foundations of alphabetic and visual literacy, will we turn to the interaction of the two literacies within the colonial ideological matrix, exploring how literate ideology was validated by ceremony and how it restructured the indigenous experience of space. That is, in the first half of the book—chapters 1 through 4—we hope to explode common notions of literacy as a technology that is exclusively alphabetic in character, by examining practice among indigenous literates (in the broadest sense) and the metagenres upon which they based their activities. The second half—chapters 5 through 6 and the conclusion—aims to demonstrate that literacy is much more than a technology, a command of crucial skills for production and reception. Instead, it furnishes an ideologically charged way of experiencing the world that in the Americas solidified European domination and was participated in by literates and illiterates alike.

Imagining Colonial Culture

Andean peoples appropriated European representational forms within a colonial context that was more than a mere backdrop to their actions: it came to be an integral component of their worldview. The transculturating nature of colonial indigenous life problematizes the neat distinctions we have traditionally made between native and European worlds in our historical treatments of Latin America. Here are colonial indigenous figures, such as Don Diego de Torres, who defy radically polarized interpretations. Don Diego exemplifies the mestizo of noble native rank, living in a world in which such appellations were not necessarily intrinsic to individuals, but were highly contingent, given that movement across ethnic categories was fluid in this period, mediated by class distinctions and by gender (Kuznesof 1995; Schwartz 1995). Don Diego's intimate participation in the "lettered city" and in the world of Christian notions of morality and history (Adorno 1986) were part of the privileges accorded to the nobility. However, the ethnic and political basis of his claim to noble status came from the fact that he served as cacique of Turmequé and traced his chiefly privilege through his maternal line. These ambiguities and contradictions belie the stereotype of a hermetically sealed and unchanging colonial indigenous sphere. How are we to make sense of such a multifaceted individual who moved within a social space in which cultural codes and practices were disputed and contested by native people and Europeans alike? How can we contextualize Don Diego's cultural discourse within a colonial system that was not characterized by primordial and discrete cultural categories, but where ethnic classifications were explicitly recognized as operating simultaneously as tools for domination, as modes of accommodation, and as vehicles of resistance? To what extent can we capture the ethos of a world in which, like our own, people lived radically multicultural realities that at the time were not noted as at all remarkable or "hybrid" (Dean and Leibsohn 2003)?

Studies of the colonial Andes have, until recently, tended to classify cultural groups into two isolated "republics," following the model of the administrative division of the Spanish colonial world into the two republics of the Spaniards and the *indios*, without paying attention to the intricate connections and interfaces bridged by celebrated individuals such as Don Diego de Torres, as well as less well-known folk such as the testators Juana Sanguino and Don Andrés, the cacique of Machetá.[1] It is only in the past decade that scholars have begun to publish texts which reject the analytical utility of this Spanish juridical arrangement, focusing instead on the emergence of a colonial culture in which the two republics were not so much closed worlds, as they were critical scenarios within which representations and, ultimately, power, were wielded by colonial administrators and indigenous agents alike. In this view, the two republics are not so much an analytical model, as a hinge for interpreting systems of inequality within which indigenous subjects strove to consolidate newly structured native communities.

A good example of this perspective is the work of the art historian Carolyn Dean (1999), who argues—in her study of a seventeenth-century series of paintings of Corpus Christi processions in Cuzco—that these depictions of colonial hereditary lords in Incaic regalia represent not so much a resurgence of Inca iconography providing ethnographic evidence on pre-Columbian lifeways, as they proclaim the triumph of Spanish Christianity and embody indigenous alterity through costume. Corpus thus served as a stage for the Christian profanation of Incaic cosmology and, on a secular level, functioned as an arena in which Andean symbols could be deployed to consolidate an indigenous power structure under the guidance of the Crown. For Dean, the seemingly Incaic components of colonial culture cannot be taken at face value, but must be reevaluated within the colonial administrative and religious system. Thus, Dean suggests, colonial culture is best comprehended as a complex process of "relexification," in which Andean syntax was used to frame European utterances (1999, 127, 168).

Colonial Culture and Mestizaje

Under such circumstances, it becomes difficult to separate the threads of colonial culture into discrete culturally marked bundles. The weave can be better appreciated as a series of "entangled objects" (Thomas 1991), in which the voices of numerous cultural actors from different historical periods are inextricably intertwined. Instead of visualizing the process of cultural contestation as the confrontation of two opposite poles, we hope, after Serge Gruzinski (1999, 213), to look at it as a "series of modulations" that unfold over time, as much among Europeans as among native Andeans, both of whom belonged to heterogeneous social constellations marked by a multitude of cultural, racial, occupational, and gender identities that could be altered by administrative petition.[2] As Laura Lewis (2003) so elegantly demonstrates in her study of the negotiation of caste in colonial Mexico, the interaction of Spaniards, indios, Africans, mulattos, and mestizos involved the cross-fertilization of discourses and practices, ranging from European law to indigenous witchcraft and African ritual.[3] Cultural forms moved in all directions, mediated by the colonial status hierarchy and the European legal framework that bolstered it. However, members of subordinated castes were not without recourse to their own sources of power over those hailing from the dominant categories; they countered colonial power with ritual practices that drew upon all of the cultural traditions, but focused on the potency of indigenous witchcraft.[4] Indeed, systems of power and of representation were entangled in the Spanish colonial world.

The end result is a complex colonial culture, which in current language might be called "hybrid." Hybridity has come to substitute for *mestizaje*—the process of becoming mestizo—in much contemporary writing. Commonly, it has not been seen as a process, but as a moment of confrontation and mixing (García Canclini 1989; Rosaldo 1995). This sort of approach produces a kind of "ethnographic present in the past," which has not been useful for studying the *longue durée* of cultural change that unfolded over the centuries of Spanish domination (personal communication, Claudio Lomnitz-Adler). In order to avoid this difficulty—and in an attempt to sidestep the biological metaphor embodied by the notion of hybridity, which implies sterility—we will choose to speak instead of "colonial culture."[5]

There is a concrete date from which we can begin to speak of colonial culture in the Americas—1492. However, the sedimentation and interpenetration of diverse cultures has much deeper roots that antedate the Spanish colonial empire. The political administration of cultural heterogeneity and the ways in which individuals assumed identities within the colonial social hierarchy were not only proper to the Spanish domination of America. Such institutions as the *encomienda* (a grant made to conquerors for control over the tribute of subject populations), the *doctrina* (the village-level structure of Christian indoctrination), and the *requerimiento* (the proclamation read to military rivals requiring them to submit to Christianity or die in war), were all appropriated from the Reconquista, or Reconquest, the centuries-long process whereby the Catholic kings of Castile seized control of the Iberian Peninsula from the Moors (Fletcher 1992; Garrido Aranda 1980; Seed 1995). In other words, the cultural entanglement at play in the Americas emerged on the back of previous and ongoing Iberian experiences, resulting in institutions whose meaning is considerably more complex than can be accounted for by the polarity of Spanish versus indigenous or by a notion of hybridity that privileges initial contact.

Individuals such as Diego de Torres, Inca Garcilaso de la Vega, and Diego Muñoz Camargo, all mestizos who politically and culturally identified themselves with their maternal aristocratic roots, personally experienced this tremendous heterogeneity upon landing in Seville, the port of disembarkation from the Americas. There, they wandered the mazelike pathways of the medieval city, unlike the accustomed grid of intersecting straight streets that characterized the spatial organization of the colonial urban communities in which they were raised. As they roamed through the city, they encountered Spanish Christian culture superimposed on Roman, Visigothic, and Islamic foundations. The mosques of Seville and Córdoba had long ago been converted to cathedrals, and the Alhambra of the Nasarid dynasty in Granada was recently transformed by its juxtaposition with the Renaissance geometry of Charles V's palace. How this phenomenology played out in the minds of these colonial figures, perhaps expanding their awareness of cultural, social, and political complexity, is not easy to gauge. But at the very least, they did not feel alone or unique. Rather, they felt connected to a larger enterprise in which at times, their world in America was a projection of desires or plans — architectural, political, and social — not realized in Spain. They might be said to have a double vision: they possessed the grounds for a comparison that constituted both the inverse of the terms employed by the Spaniards who migrated to the New World, and a conceptual vantage point molded by the asymmetrical political and social relations in which their daily lives transpired.

We do not assume, therefore, that colonial cultural mixing is a neutral or unilateral process. Instead, our view of colonial culture incorporates the notion that in ethnically stratified Spanish American society, the appropriation of cultural elements and the production of colonial identities must be approached through the close consideration of the workings of power, both of the colonizers and of the colonized (Bhabha 1994, 50). For Homi Bhabha (1994, 2), writing about British colonialism of the nineteenth and twentieth centuries, cultural hybridity—his terminology, not ours—arises from the fluidity of place and identity brought on by the tremendous movement of peoples throughout the world, which was initiated by European colonialism. In a sense, he is reimagining the imagined community of Benedict Anderson (1983), so as to allow for the differences that punctuate the creation of global communities. In each context, culture is rearticulated in relation to the political, economic, and social roles of the different actors. In Bhabha's view, the tradition of the colonized is not something that "survives" from the past; instead, it is continually "reinscribed" as it intersects with the transformative power of the culture of the colonizer. This means that for Bhabha, "cultural hybridity" is all about articulating difference through negotiation in concrete situations of social asymmetry, and not about the fusion of primordial traditions.[6]

This process of the reinscription of tradition within a dominant culture is something embedded in modernity and the rise of European global domination, whose beginnings are apparent in the Spanish colonial project (Mignolo 2000). It is something recognizable both in the Andes and in Mexico. The mid-seventeenth-century Inca nobility of Cuzco displayed their alterity in the paintings of Corpus Christi by wearing colonial Inca clothes and symbols.[7] Guaman Poma claimed legal right to the territories of Chupas by drawing the portraits of his ancestors, thereby forcing the viewer to acknowledge his legitimacy by appeal to profound cultural difference located temporally before the Spanish conquest. However, other native nobles, such as the northern Andean caciques with whom we are concerned, claimed their new "traditional" rights by emphasizing their cultural and political integration within Spanish norms. Such claims were already scripted as responses to questions in the formulaic presentations of *probanzas de meritos* (service reports), such as were presented by the Bolivian native functionary

Don Fernando Ayra de Arritu, principal cacique and governor of Copoatá in 1639. One of the questions related to the activities of Don Fernando Chinchi, his father:

> If they knew that Don Fernando Chinchi was a person that with his great diligence, industry and care, as being a very devote in the worship of God, had made and built in the pueblo de Copoata one of the most sumptuous and best churches that there is in the entire province . . . because he was a good, God-fearing Christian obeying the instructions of the magistrates, [and was] very intelligent and able and that he always conducted himself and his person with great luster and as such he always appeared in the dress of a Spaniard and carried offensive and defensive weapons with the permission and license of the lord of Monteclaros, who was Viceroy at that time. (AGI/S 1634, 8v)[8]

Rather than pointing out the cacique's alterity, this passage emphasizes his success at conforming to Spanish dictates and mores.

Like Don Fernando Ayra de Arritu, Don Diego de Torres's cultural identity is that of someone who seeks his traditional chiefly authority not by wielding signs of tradition, but by their apparent absence. His legal briefs and other documentation surrounding his struggle to retain his *cacicazgo* do not point to the ways in which his behavior varied from that of Spaniards (AGI/S 1576, 1590); to the contrary, they enhance his resemblance to Europeans. He states in his briefs that he had a European-born servant, Luis de Quero, whom he took with him when he returned to the New Kingdom of Granada in 1579 (AGI/S 1579, 215); in fact, he also had a European wife (Rojas 1965). Don Diego emphasizes and values his Spanish descent and his Christianity in his documents, while his adversaries accuse him of being an idolater (Hoyos García 2002, 101–2). The absence of a discourse of alterity on the part of Don Diego is true as much in the visual evidence he submits, as it is in his writings. His maps display no traces of his own juxtaposed identities, in contrast to indigenous maps from Mexico (Gruzinski 1999; Leibsohn 1994, 2000; Mundy 1996). The representation of place is not inscribed by local iconic forms, but in cartographic conventions that are completely within European terms. Don Diego submits his evidence in the form of geographic maps, in which the salient topographical features are not indicated by indigenous symbols, as occurs in Mexican and a few early Peruvian maps; nor are indigenous terms provided in written form. Instead, simple cursive lines outline mountains and major bodies of water. The area described by the map is outlined and areas lying outside the periphery are indicated by Spanish names, such as *llano*, a term used today to refer to the low plains that extend seemingly without end toward Amazonia and the east. Stylized hands point toward salient features, such as major towns or important waterways. Moreover, the two maps perform in relation to each other as ever-reducing areas of administrative geography. The first map demarcates the province of Santa Fé, centered by the provincial capital, Santafé de Bogotá. The second map focuses the viewer more closely upon the Spanish city of Tunja, just north of Santafé, and the towns under its regional jurisdiction, among which Turmequé belongs.

The maps and the *relación* in which they are bound are indicative of the northern Andean documentation, in which native peoples are not self-identified through an appeal to cultural alterity in language or form. This absence of signs of cultural difference becomes apparent when the northern Andes corpus is compared with the use of native languages and graphic systems in myriad legal and political documents in colonial Mexico and, to a lesser extent, in Peru. The difference owes, perhaps, to the fact that the pre-Columbian Inca and Aztec states came to represent the indigenous cultures against which the Spaniards positioned themselves, whereas northern Andean chiefdoms were often portrayed as unorganized societies (*behetrías*), which were not at a level of political and social development that merited the incorporation of their cultural forms into the colonial formation of the New Kingdom of Granada. As a result, the Andean referents that crop up in the northern Andean documentation are a product of a European-inspired classification of Andean societies, reflecting colonial values and mores. While colonial northern Andean indigenous actors certainly employed different cultural codes from those of Europeans in their dealings with the Spanish administration or among themselves, these were not played up in the documentation issuing from the pen of Don Diego de Torres or that of other caciques (AGI/S 1624, 1755).

The Doubling of Don Diego

Perhaps more appropriate to Don Diego's predicament is the notion of "double consciousness," coined at the turn of the twentieth century by W. E. B. Du Bois, an African American sociologist whose writings contain theoretical tools for making sense of identity beyond the confines of modern North America, although Latin Americanists have not made use of his profound insights:

> After the Egyptian and Indian, the Greek and Roman, the Teuton and Mongolian, the Negro is a sort of seventh son, born with a veil, and gifted with second-sight in this American world—a world which yields him no true self-consciousness, but only lets him see himself through the revelation of the other world. It is a peculiar sensation, this double-consciousness, this sense of always looking at one's self through the eyes of others, of measuring one's soul by the tape of a world that looks on in amused contempt and pity. One ever feels his twoness—an American, a Negro; two souls, two thoughts, two unreconciled strivings; two warring ideals in one dark body, whose dogged strength alone keeps it from being torn asunder. (Du Bois 1989 [1903], 2–3)

In Du Bois's view, North American Negroes were caught between and profoundly aware of possessing two identities, both of which defined them, but one of which (Negro) excluded them from being fully recognized as belonging to the other (American).

The Du Boisian scholar Nahum Chandler finds this perspective to be exceptionally fruitful for problematizing the question of identity in general. In Chandler's view, identity is for Du Bois a relationship, not a primordial given. In this sense, both African American and Euroamerican identities have been forged historically in a relational process (Chandler 2000, 273–74). As we shall discuss below, a clear understanding of Don Diego de Torres as a colonial actor requires that all of the identities at work in colonial Santafé and in Spain be problematized in a similar fashion. Chandler goes on (2000, 276–83) to analyze an eighteenth-century slave narrative in terms of how the early modern relationship between the self-conscious slave author and his owner provides the ground upon which both identities were negotiated. In this sense, Du Boisian double consciousness might prove to be eminently applicable to the parallel predicament of Don Diego de Torres, a mestizo claiming membership in the indigenous aristocracy in an era in which not only the problematic identities of such castes as mestizo and mulatto were being defined, but the nature of membership in the African, indigenous, and Spanish categories, as well. In our discussion below of the quandaries faced by a mestizo cacique, we will try to capture a sense of how indigenous identity was defined in the colonial New Kingdom of Granada. Before that, though, we must take a brief look at how other colonial identities were forged in relation to indigenous ones, because if we are to think through how the concept of double consciousness might be applicable to the analysis of identity formation in the Spanish colonial setting, we must reformulate it within the historical conditions of sixteenth- and seventeenth-century Spanish America.

Portraits of Mestizaje

Colonial Spaniards in the Americas saw themselves as belonging to "quasi-autonomous kingdoms" under the rule of the Spanish Crown. Unlike colonies,

> each part of this cluster was deemed to possess its own identity, its own native nobility, and its own government. All parts owed allegiance to the sovereign, but all were self-governing commonwealths with their own customs and culture, their own customary laws and fueros. Mexico and Peru were considered by their inhabitants to be no different from the Netherlands, Aragon, or Naples. (Pagden 1987, 63)

These settlers—the *criollos*—attempted, early on in the colonial period, to forge marital ties with the indigenous nobility as a means of attaining a social mobility denied them in Spain and constituting their right to occupy key administrative posts in America (1987, 68).[9] However, they simultaneously erected a social hierarchy with themselves at the top and native peoples and African slaves at the bottom. This hierarchy was expressed in eighteenth-century casta paintings, a genre particular to Mexico that depicted extensive classifications of racial intermixture. Such typologies reflected more the ideal than the real, given that the incredible profusion of categories and their careful positioning in a hierarchy were not applied on the ground; these paintings were meant for viewing by the colonial and Spanish elite (Katzew 1996).[10] In the wake of Reconquista repudiation of non-Catholic elements on the Iberian Peninsula—that is, Muslims and Jews—Spanish settlers in the Americas were obsessed with the notion of purity of blood, leading them to confront the paradox of defining themselves in relation to the array of identities generated on the ground:

> The existence of this racial pyramid, and of the Indian's position at the very base of it, had the effect of both reenforcing and unsettling the whites' view of themselves and of their relationship with the conquered

and enslaved races over whom they ruled. Within such a society, white-
ness was frequently considered to be sufficient for one to claim membership in the elite. . . . But it was also a society that tolerated a large degree
of racial mobility, and this made it difficult for the criollos to make any
unassailable claims to purity of blood (*limpieza de sangre*). . . . Such racial
fluidity seriously undermined the criollo sense of being a closed white
elite and consequently made the notion of interbreeding with Indians,
however noble, very unattractive. The Americans, as they came to call
themselves, were to have a culture that was "Mexican" or "Peruvian" —
Spanish in customs and rooted in an understanding of a mythical Indian
past. But it was to be white, español, by blood. (Pagden 1987, 69–70)

Spanish identity was, hence, considerably more contentious than the traditional polarized model of identity in the Americas would suggest. Arrayed in
confrontation were those classified by color — criollos, Africans, aboriginal
populations, *castas* (mixed populations) — as well as Spanish identities predicated upon religious difference or political affiliation — Catholics, Muslims,
Jews, *conversos* (converts to Christianity), Aragoneses, Castilians, Neapoli-
tans. Criollos were white in relation to other populations in the Americas,
but in practice they identified themselves as members of particular royal
courts, or Audiencias — Quito, the New Kingdom of Granada, Lima — in
relation to Spain. Where the two orders intersected — for example, in the
struggle between criollos and the Crown over the idea of separate republics
for Spaniards and native people, a framework which wrested control of aboriginal populations from the settlers — contradictions erupted (1987, 66).

The quandaries of this process of defining relational identities in a new
world can be captured as we look at a unique group portrait from the northern Andes (plate 1). Commissioned by Juan de Barrio y Sepúlveda, a judge,
or *oidor*, of the Royal Court of Quito, it was painted as a gift to be sent
to King Philip III for his viewing pleasure (AGI/s 1600, 21v). The portrait
commemorated the peace that Barrio y Sepúlveda had achieved with the
individuals represented, who were important to the Spanish defense of the
Pacific coast against pirates such as Sir Francis Drake. But what is important for us is the relation between the subjects of the portrait and its painter,
and how this is resolved in the painting. The author of the portrait is Andrés
Sánchez Gallque. We can imagine Sánchez Gallque at the end of his work
as he stands before the canvas upon which he has just painted his signature, today the oldest surviving signed portrait from South America. He has

painted a group of three sitters, Don Francisco de la Robe, age fifty-six, and his two sons, Don Pedro, twenty-two, and Don Domingo, eighteen. They are mulatto leaders from the Esmeraldas coast of Ecuador. Gallque has been asked to paint the group portrait in Quito to commemorate their 1597 "pacification" and conversion to Christianity by Barrio y Sepúlveda. This achievement was deemed worthy enough by the oidor to commission the portrait. It now resides in Madrid, in the Museo de América. The letter that accompanied this gift to the Crown explains:

> As it would seem Your Majesty would like to see those barbarians depicted (who up until now have been invincible) and being something very extraordinary, I send them (in this portrait) with its letter and this document to Your Majesty. . . . They are all painted very faithfully as they are and as they usually appear, except for the dress which, after they pledged peace and obedience to Your Majesty and possession taken and they were placed in your royal dominion, then [clothing] was given them just as you see in the portrait. Because they are not civilized people and in their land, which is hot, they wear no more than mantles and shirts like the rest of the indios. They are very intelligent and they are cunning and sly, they understand Spanish although they speak awkwardly. They have been great warriors against the indios of other pagan provinces. [The indios] greatly fear them because they kill many of them and those they capture are ruled as slaves and they are terrible, determined, and cruel in their punishment. They have never been subdued by Spaniards. (AGI/s 1600, 1v–2r)[11]

Andrés Sánchez Gallque, the artist, was a native Andean with a Christian name. We can imagine him standing before the three mulattos and painting them dressed in the clothing of *gente política*, "civilized people." In what clothes, one can wonder, was Sánchez Gallque himself dressed as he painted? Clothing functioned as a sign of degrees of class, ethnicity, and power in the colonial Andes, something that was understood by Spaniards, natives, Africans, and mestizos alike (Adorno 1982, 51–106). Whatever he may have been wearing, Sánchez Gallque stood before the mulattos from Esmeraldas as a representative—and a producer—of the European culture to which the mulattos had recently submitted. The portrait, the production of which physically joins all four men for a brief time in a kind of intimacy, is itself the indisputable sign that separates them socially and culturally. Up until now, as Barrio y Sepúlveda's letter states, the portraits of Don Francisco and his sons would have been impossible. But as their wildness had now been subdued, they were brought to Quito to be "painted very faithfully as they are and as they usually appear." However, they are depicted so as to appear before the king as his subjects, like any other. They hold their spears, now ready to defend the coast against the king's enemies, most especially Francis Drake. They doff their hats in the anticipated presence before the king.

What is important is that although they may appear "as they are" in terms of their physiognomy, costume, and body ornament, they do not appear to be anywhere in particular. That is, the three-quarter length composition of the portrait and its neutral background work visually to disembody Francisco de la Robe and his sons from any recognizable connection to a real, physical space: they are not necessarily imagined as standing on the same surface, or even in the same room, as the artist or the viewer. Now, although these are common enough conventions for portraiture, here they create a distance between the viewer and the subject, a colonial distance that Sánchez Gallque managed to factor into the portrait. No matter how the volume of their bodies presses close to the picture surface or how vivid and tactile the texture of their clothing appears, the viewer is arrested from engaging with them. There is something too startling in the black faces studded with gold that appear above the ruffled collars and in the black hands that emerge from ruffled cuffs, holding spears. The frame is no longer a window into a place the viewer may imaginatively penetrate; instead, it is a barrier behind which the three men stand. There is absolutely no recession into the picture; the three figures may appear in the immediate foreground, but the horizontal structure of the composition, the verticality of the spears held forward, and the rhythmic use of color create a sense of barrier and distance. Even gesture and its meaning are unsettled as a code for understanding between viewer and subject. The hats held in their hands address the viewer through courtly etiquette, but the gestures do not register as being meaningful to the subjects. These are not their normal clothes, so how can the tipping of the hat mean to them what it does to the king?

The act of painting is a cultural performance that indicates the social status of the artist, in this case, Sánchez Gallque, a colonial painter and a member of the confraternity of Nuestra Señora del Rosario in the Church of Santo Domingo in Quito. The physicality of that space was constituted, in part, by the Spanish city in which he lived and the architectural setting in which he painted. In this space, he has become the observer, not the observed, and he creates an image that disavows any pictorial reference that might suggest any kind of reciprocal relation between viewer and subject. Yet that cultural space is also defined by what it is not—the space inhabited by the vast majority of natives and mulattos, who are not painted. It is Sánchez Gallque's signature on the canvas over the illusionistic painted surface that indicates physically and visually his presence in the painting, while indicating he is not part of it. There is no similarity between artistic gesture and writing, as we found in Guaman Poma's drawing of the cacique writing. Sánchez Gallque's writing is a mark of individuation and separation, as both artist and Christian, a sense of self reified by such cultural acts as painting the Other. His signature, identifying him as the producer of the image, indicates physically and socially on which side of the canvas he stood when the portrait was painted. For Sánchez Gallque, the canvas is a cultural divider between his subjects and him. As a painter, he transcends the cultural and social space of his subjects, a space he theoretically shares with Don Francisco and his sons, given that he is an indio. But at the same time, as a colonial painter, he occupies the same cultural space as that of the viewer, which stands in contrast to the pictorial space of the subject.

The Double Identity of Don Diego de Torres

Like Sánchez Gallque, at once a painter and an indio, Don Diego de Torres claimed two identities. He was both a Muisca cacique and a mestizo, the first through his mother's family—as heir to the chiefdom of Turmequé, formerly occupied by his maternal uncle—the second through his conquistador father. This made him at once the hereditary lord of Turmequé and the son—and later, half-brother—of its *encomendero*, the Spaniard granted the right to collect royal tribute from its inhabitants. Don Diego's predicament arose from the fact that different groups interpreted his dual identity according to their own political requirements. The population of Turmequé and neighboring Muisca communities recognized him as cacique, in hopes that he would use his position to defend them against settler abuses. So did Crown officials in Spain, ever-preoccupied by the usurpation by Santafé officials of their royal prerogatives. But the local administrators in Santafé de Bogotá, attentive to the threats Don Diego posed to their extensive exploitation of the encomienda system, rejected his claim to the cacicazgo on the grounds that he was not an indio, but a mestizo. His two identities were at once mutually exclusive for the settlers of Santafé and overlapping for Don Diego and his allies in Spain.

The cacique of Turmequé was a member of the first generation of mestizos in a part of the Andes in which the mixed population was exceedingly low throughout the colonial period (Gutiérrez de Pineda and Pineda Giraldo 1999, vol. 1, 107).[12] He was, moreover, unusual in the sense that he was the mestizo product of a union between Spanish and Muisca nobility, bestowing upon him special rights not accorded to mestizo commoners, for example, the Crown's recognition of his chiefly identity (1999, 329). His is not simply the case of a mestizo, but of one who hoped to be accepted as indigenous nobility in a society characterized by ethnic stratification, an aspiration he shared with a small number of other mestizo chiefly pretenders (Gutiérrez de Pineda and Pineda Giraldo 1999). Thus, his self-identification in the legal briefs he produced is as a member of the native nobility: he signs his name as "cacique of Turmequé" and used the noble title of "Don."

Don Diego spoke both Muisca and Spanish, making him a kind of indio ladino, which significantly demarcates his own deployment of identity as a hereditary lord straddling the administrative boundary between the indigenous and Spanish worlds. In fact, ladino was an infinitely slippery classification, including both Spanish-speaking indios and mestizos, a diverse and heterogeneous range of individuals (Adorno 1991, 234), making for a highly relational sense of identity:

> Considering the single stereotypical label of indio ladino, in spite of the range of caste and class concealed thereby, the individuals so identified constantly had to adjust their positions as subjects. The search for and adjustment to various models of identity belie the multiple subject positions that the colonial subject seemed destined to take, not merely sequentially but most often simultaneously. (ibid., 258)

Don Diego acted as a ladino in his public performances. In a public meeting over idolatry in the native community of Sogamoso, for instance, he preferred to preach in Spanish, thus compelling his Muisca listeners to follow his interventions through an interpreter and making the words of his sermon and his ladino qualities immediately apprehensible to his Spanish observers (Restrepo 2001; Rojas 1965, 111). The officials of the Royal Court in Santafé, however, consistently attempted to deny him his bilingualism, in this way reinforcing his mestizo identity. For example, while he was in prison, the cacique was not permitted to speak Muisca (Rojas 1965, 207). In a contradictory combination of American and Iberian modes of identity production, he was falsely accused by the Audiencia of urging his subjects to reject Christianity by fomenting idolatry—identity based on religion (Gál-vez Piñal 1974, 39). That is, he was accused of surreptitiously indoctrinating the people of Turmequé when he addressed a native audience in their own language. This contradictory accusation classifies Don Diego as indio in order to ultimately expropriate his cacicazgo on the grounds of his mestizo identity, demonstrating how slippery ethnic classification could become in the New Kingdom of Granada and underlining the anxieties that Spanish settlers felt as they attempted to define Don Diego's particularity.

But Don Diego did not openly identify as ladino, a category charged in the colonial era with negative overtones (Adorno 1991), as the sixteenth-century writer Pedro de Quiroga expresses in a fictional dialogue between a Spaniard, Barchilón, and an indio ladino, Tito:

> Barchilon: I admit, Tito, that I am in certain admiration of your ability and tongue and how you speak my language as if it were your own, although according to what you have told of your life it is not so surprising, but what deception, you walk among us in the dress of an indio, who would think such of you if they were to see you among other indios! (Quiroga 1992 [1562], 65)[13]

Cognizant of the slippery nature of ladinos, Don Diego himself maligns them in one of his briefs to the king:

> And the worst evil is that the poor indios who are taken to rent out their services are paid in brass or alloys, or in less than a third of the wage they earned by they who come for them, using them as miserable and wanting beings. And when they collect the aforementioned rent, there is another greater maltreatment and it is that many *alguaciles* (minor officials) who are *indios ladinos* and some Spaniards, who do not carry staffs of office, who on the pretext of picking them up rob them and bribe them and commit a thousand other outrages deserving of severe punishment and appeal. (Rojas 1965, 57)[14]

Nevertheless, it is Don Diego's own chameleonlike ladino behavior that provokes the harsh response of the Santafé elite to his appeals.

Nahum Chandler (2000) warns his readers that it is not only necessary to explore how identity is produced among subaltern groups; it is crucial to analyze identity production among superordinate populations as well.[15] The term *ladino* provides a critical handle for making sense of the anxieties that fostered the production of colonial Spanish identities in the Americas, as well as for comprehending Don Diego de Torres's predicament. Sebastián de Covarrubias's seventeenth-century dictionary defines *ladinos* as those in Spain who spoke Latin elegantly (Covarrubias Orozco 1995 [1611], 697). However, he goes on to supply an additional definition: "The Morisco [Muslim converted to Christianity] or the foreigner who learned our language, with such care that we hardly distinguish him from ourselves, we also call ladino."[16] Thus, it is not just the bilingual Andean native who threatened the Spaniard because he resembled him; Moorish and Jewish converts to Christianity posed a threat similar to that of the indio ladino, both in terms of their ambiguous religious identity and the belief among Old Christians that they were able to speak secret and unintelligible languages (Silverblatt 2000, 534–35). The comparison is lexically based as well: remember that the language of Sephardic Jews is also called Ladino.[17] Similarly, the origin of the term *mestizo* lies in those medieval Spanish Christians who allied themselves with the Moors against King Rodrigo (Bernand 2001, in Gruzinski 1999, 37).

Both *ladino* and *mestizo* are terms bound up in the history of the Spanish state's assertion of its Christian identity, marked by the expulsion of Jews and Muslims. The 1492 Spanish invasion of America coincided with the triumph of the Reconquest of Spain from the Moors, compounding the anxieties inherent in the classification by Spaniards of both the American Other and the converso Other in relation to themselves (Pagden 1982). Thus, categories that should not have been at issue among native Andeans bled over from the Iberian arena into America, as the Spanish sought to erect boundaries around their own identity. For this reason, the eighteenth-century Nasa cacique Don Juan Tama y Calambás asserts that his descendants were *limpios de sangre*, pure of blood (ACC/P 1883 [1708], 2184r): that as members of the nobility there was no trace of Jewish or Moorish blood in their veins, despite the fact that there is little chance this would have been the case at such a late date and in such an isolated corner of the Andes.

As in medieval Spain, where Jewish conversos manipulated their alterity in order to achieve noble status in the Spanish court (Gerli 1996), some mestizos who shared Diego de Torres's predicament opted for the European side of the equation. Some even were ordained, such as Diego Valadés, who, like Muñoz Camargo, is believed to have been a mestizo, the offspring of a Spanish father and a Tlaxcalan mother. But unlike Muñoz Camargo or Don Diego de Torres, Valadés did not identify himself as Tlaxcalan. Rather, he became a Franciscan who would eventually travel to Spain, Trent, and finally, Rome, where he became associated with Pope Gregory.[18] In 1579 he published his

Rhetorica christiana in Perugia which, in a most singular way, manifests the transcultural roots of its author. In contrast, Don Diego de Torres opted for clearly political reasons in favor of identification with his Muisca mother's family.

To further complicate matters, however, Diego de Torres also distinguished himself from the native aspirants to the chiefly seat in Turmequé as a mestizo pretender. He writes in one of his legal briefs:

> You will understand that by virtue of being the son of a Spaniard and Christian the aforementioned President and Judges take my cacicazgo from me and that it would have benefited me more to be the son of an idolatrous Indian and not of a Christian, understanding that as son of a Spaniard and Christian, as I am, I should have a stronger case because I am of such good blood, flowing from Spaniards and Christians, which is why all the caciques of this kingdom love me. (AGN/B 1574, 409r)[19]

Here, Don Diego celebrates the superiority of his mestizo legacy by claiming that he inherited "good blood" from his European father, causing him to be a more reliable promoter of Christianity in Turmequé. While he distances himself from the abuses committed by Spaniards, he honors his European roots, thus distinguishing himself from the other pretenders to the cacicazgo and from his subjects. Thus, it is overly romantic to assume, from a twenty-first-century perspective, that Don Diego de Torres cleaved exclusively to his Muisca heritage; instead, as a mestizo he distinguished both indigenous and European identities according to their virtues and shortcomings.

The intricacies of identity construction for Don Diego de Torres force a reconsideration of the Du Boisian notion of double consciousness in the Latin American context. For Du Bois, there were two poles toward which African Americans were obliged to simultaneously align themselves: the dominant (white) American society and their identity as black Americans. In the sixteenth-century New Kingdom of Granada, in contrast, Don Diego could not negotiate two opposed identities. He was compelled to hew to the third, intermediate position of mestizo. As a mestizo, his identity was always relational, always in simultaneous affiliation with and opposition to the two poles. He could no more claim Spanish identity than he could fuse entirely with his mother's people, because he would be rejected by both sides. At the same time, he could not let go of his ties to both the indigenous and the European worlds, because it is precisely his positioning at the crossroads that facilitated his claim to chiefly status and propelled him to be an effective advocate for the community of Turmequé: a kind of double-double consciousness that articulates at once the twin poles of mestizo-European and mestizo-Muisca.

The Du Boisian notion of double consciousness was articulated in a particular historical context, in which a racial discourse was characterized by the polar opposites of "black" and "white." There was no space for intermediate categories, such as "mestizo" or "mulatto." The historical and geographical contexts of sixteenth-century Latin America were entirely different, with gradations between the poles in play. But the differences between double consciousness as explained by Du Bois and what we see in the New Kingdom of Granada go beyond the number of categories: we must also examine their nature. The categories of "indio," "mestizo," and "Spaniard" were not racial in nature; they were not based on the metaphor of population genetics, which only came into general usage in the nineteenth century. They overlapped, fused, and contradicted one another in complex ways that were quite distinct epistemologically from the twentieth-century racial system in Latin America and the United States (de la Cadena 2005; Rappaport 2009; Seth 2010). Moreover, the meanings of these categories were only becoming established during the first century of colonization, and would be transformed over time. For this reason, the concept of colonial culture as it emerged in sixteenth- to eighteenth-century Latin America provides a crucial venue for making sense of the play between literacy and ethnoracial classification.

A Middle Ground

The drama of colonial culture unfolded at the interface of these manifold and blurred identities. In contrast to Don Diego de Torres, many other native people were not as familiar with Spanish cultural codes, so that their interactions with the colonial world exhibit a kind of Bakhtinian "double voicing" (Bakhtin 1981 [1975], 324), in which their speech or actions expressed intentions that diverged from the readings made by their counterparts. Consequently, the incongruities that arose across the multiple cultural codes that colonial social actors employed resulted in confusion and misinterpretations (Cornejo-Polar 1996). Richard White (1991), a historian of early North America, illuminates the significance of these scenarios of double voicing through the concept of the "middle ground." This is the space in which a multiplicity of peoples continually adjusts their differences in relation to one another. The process engenders a series of "creative misunderstandings," through which values and practices are reinterpreted and reinvented. White's analysis depicts the middle ground of the Great Lakes region at the onset of colonialism, when Europeans and Native Americans were allies, trade partners, and neighbors, brought together at a moment of massive population movement. These contacts produced what could be construed as a *métis* (mestizo) culture, through which the members of the various groups communicated. The new cultural forms operated like a creole language, providing a meaningful context for intercultural contact. At the same time, they impacted upon the parallel cultural worlds internal to each of the groups, which continued to function, albeit with significant transformations. The notion of the middle ground provides a vehicle for comprehending how we can interpret the appearance of a colonial culture in Latin America, without losing sight of the continued resonance of local cultures, which were, similarly, in a constant state of flux.

White developed his notion of the middle ground through the study of an early contact situation characterized by symmetrical trading relationships between Native Americans and Europeans. This is quite distinct from that of three centuries of Spanish domination, in which the process of creative misinterpretation and the creation of new communicative contexts were shot through by the exercise of Spanish physical, economic, and spiritual power. Mary Louise Pratt's (1992) notion of the "contact zone"—which situates such interactions in contexts of coercion, inequality, conflict, and asymmetry of power—goes far in applying White's ideas to colonial Spanish America. Pratt's work is particularly relevant, since she suggests that within the contact zone, colonized subjects engaged the colonizers' forms of representation by merging them with autochthonous forms, producing what she calls "diglossic representations." She thus builds upon the concept that Fernando Ortiz, a midcentury Cuban anthropologist, termed "transculturation" (Ortiz 1995 [1947]: 97–103), which suggests that cultural transmutation operates in multiple directions and unfolds in a continuous fashion across time, creating new cultural representations. Ortiz develops his historical interpretation contrapuntally, "by illuminating the complex interaction between the subaltern and the dominant" (Coronil 1995, xl) in the course of the historical development of the Cuban agricultural economy, providing a scenario for exploring the emergence of Cuban culture. As a result of this approach, "Ortiz shows the extent to which . . . fixed and separate [cultural] boundaries are the artifice of unequal power relations" (ibid., xli).

A similar contrapuntal interpretive strategy is employed by Vicente Rafael

(1988) in an examination of Spanish colonial linguistic policy and its application in the process of the Christian conversion of the Tagalog of the Philippines. Rafael moves back and forth between Spanish and Tagalog readings of the conversion process, noting, on the one hand, how Europeans faced serious dilemmas in their attempts to translate Christian concepts into a non-Western language. The Tagalogs, on the other hand, responded by appropriating Castilian through a defensive strategy of fishing for appropriate lexical terminology with the intention of conveying an image of linguistic proficiency that they never achieved. Mark Thurner (1997) develops his own counterpoint for the postcolonial Andes, inquiring into the multivocality of key symbols, such as the parallel meanings of *republic*, and the univocality of other symbols, such as *indígena* for the native people of Huaráz and the Peruvian state. As Thurner explains, the nineteenth-century use of the term *indígena* to refer to native people was a republican conceptual and political move away from the colonial signifier *indio*, which denoted membership in one of the two colonial republics; the move to a less heavily loaded appellation denied the possibility of membership in a semiautonomous structure of authority, like the by-then-defunct República de Indios. Instead, the term *indígena* integrated native people into the broader base of the Peruvian citizenry. However, while creole republicans replaced *indio* with *indígena*, nineteenth-century indigenous authorities in Huaráz rejected the new appellation and called themselves *republicanos*. But not republicanos in the sense of the newly independent Peruvian republic. In contrast, they harked back to the indigenous republicanos who belonged to the colonial republic of the "indios," thus reasserting a prior notion of citizenship at odds with that of nonnative legislators.

The task set out by these scholars poses a dilemma. While our sights are set on an intercultural space that impacts the multiple cultural traditions that surround it, altering them inexorably, we must also keep in mind that the inhabitants of the colonial period were heterogeneous in their use of the new cultural codes. That is, colonial culture meant one thing to a Don Diego de Torres and quite another to an aged and monolingual Nasa woman living in isolated Tierradentro. Similarly, Don Juan del Valle, archbishop of Popayán, displayed a very different appreciation of the transculturating effects of his evangelization of the Nasa and the Guambiano from that of a mestizo shoemaker, living just a few blocks from Popayán's main plaza where the archbishop's palace was located. How can we grasp the complexities of this intercultural space without losing sight of the diversity of ways it was experienced? We turn to another northern Andean example to probe this issue, this time, from northern Ecuador.

A Misinterpreted Inca

In early 1667, Don Alonso Florencio Inca, a descendant of the Inca royal family in Cuzco, was named *corregidor*, or district administrator, for Ibarra, in the Audiencia of Quito (Espinosa 1995).[20] But a month after his arrival in Ibarra, Don Alonso Inca was already on trial, accused first of improper etiquette toward Spaniards and of deriving his authority from his relationship to the Inca and later, more menacingly, of idolatry, specifically, of promoting the worship of rulers (Espinosa 1995, 89–94). Don Alonso Inca's behavior had enraged local Spaniards because he insisted upon showing greater respect to native authorities than to Europeans (ibid., 89). The festivities surrounding his arrival in Ibarra had alarmed the authorities, since local native communities greeted him with pantomimes of the Inca and his queen, paying him obeisance as though he were the Inca. Moreover, he was said to have proclaimed himself "King of the indios" and to have displayed a genealogical painting depicting his descent from Huayna Capac, the last Inca monarch, as well as a fine Incaic textile he said belonged to the Inca (ibid., 88–89). By mid-1667 the Inca corregidor was bound for trial in Lima, cutting short his contentious political career (ibid., 102).

While earlier scholars have interpreted the documentation from Don Alonso Florencio Inca's trial as evidence of an indigenous messianic response to European rule (Klumpp 1974), Carlos Espinosa (1990, 1995) reads the testimony as a scenario in which the intricate intersections of interlocking cultural traditions are misinterpreted to devastating effect. In the case of Don Diego de Torres, who was literate, the hundreds of pages of petitions he wrote provide us with evidence for exploring the notion of double consciousness in a northern Andean setting. In early seventeenth-century Ibarra, colonial culture was also performed and disputed within a literate arena, but this time in the visual channel.

The frightened Spanish settlers of Ibarra took Don Alonso Inca's performance to advocate literally the return of the Inca monarch, a reading very much in accordance with their anxiety over the emergence of rebellions such as those of Peru, where descendants of the last Inca emperor constituted themselves as a rival monarchy (Burga 1988; Flores Galindo 1988; Moreno Yáñez 1976). However, a different reading might conceptualize the new corregidor's appeal to public spectacle: his staging of the ancient Incaic past and his display of textiles and genealogical paintings that link him to the Inca dynasty could be seen as obeying a strictly European framework for civic celebration. Don Florencio Inca's use of Incaic symbols was an acceptable performative strategy drawn upon by the Cuzqueño indigenous nobility to legitimize their political status in the Spanish administrative" arena, as the Corpus Christi paintings demonstrate (Dean 1999). It constituted, moreover, a practice indulged in by the Crown itself, which sometimes staged the encounter of the Inca with the Spanish viceroy, using public pageantry to solidify its dominion over conquered Americans (Espinosa 1995, 92–98). Unfortunately for Don Alonso Inca, however, both the indigenous and Spanish worlds were heterogeneous in their application of cultural codes. His performance was misread by key players who saw idolatry where he may have meant to convey political legitimacy through appeals to alterity.

On the one hand, at the heart of the European community itself, there raged a struggle between local colonists bent upon controlling the native population for their own benefit, in opposition to a Crown that sought to regulate the settlers' activities. Espinosa argues that the baroque spectacle of the Inca paying homage to the Spanish monarch, which had played to crowds at viceregal festivities in Lima, was a staging of "the crown's requirement that the Indians be consensual agents" to conquest (1995, 97).[21] But when wielded by an indigenous agent, however official his standing in the colonial administrative hierarchy, such a spectacle ran against the interests of the local colonists, who felt slighted by the new corregidor. Like the colonial administrators of Santafé de Bogotá who persecuted Don Diego de Torres against the orders of the Crown, the Ibarra colonists used their own interpretation of the actions of this errant member of the indigenous nobility to delegitimize him.

On the other hand, the indigenous followers of Don Alonso Inca clearly went too far in enacting his connection to Inca ruler Huayna Capac, overstepping his own performance, which, in a different context, would have been thoroughly acceptable in the colonial arena. According to Espinosa, Don Alonso's subordinates "pressed an allegory of colonial relations into a putatively real correlation of forces. Or, alternatively, they transformed a historical representation into an actual presence in the here and now. This transgression from fiction or past to present was not plausible" (1995, 100). The native leaders of Ibarra, too, acted against a colonial backdrop. They understood such spectacles to be part of the colonial order and read them according to colonial codes. But they committed the error of attempting to direct these new forms of representation toward overturning the colonial order. Such misreadings, grounded as much in the varied interests of colonial actors as in the transculturated performances that they commonly employed to bolster their claims, are typical of what we call colonial culture, a complex and heterogeneous social formation that was incomparably more messy than the usual stereotype of two hermetically sealed cultural worlds.

Alterity, Literacy, and Colonial Culture

The three examples we describe in this chapter—Andrés Sánchez Gallque's portrait of the three mulatto chieftains of Esmeraldas, Don Diego de Torres's legal struggle with the Royal Court in Santafé de Bogotá, and Don Alonso Florencio Inca's disastrous foray into colonial pageantry—all highlight, in different ways, how the expression of alterity (or lack thereof) was intimately connected with forms of literacy. The workings of pidgin and creole languages provide a useful metaphor for making sense of the array of engagements with colonial culture presented by our three case studies; such an approach has been used by anthropologists to make sense of indigenous organizations' appropriations of anthropological discourse to assert their alterity in the contemporary Latin American political scene (Jackson 1989).

Both pidgins and creoles are languages born of cultural contact, melding elements of the languages of their speakers with those of the languages of the colonizers, in an effort to permit communication in a multicultural colonial context. It was once thought that pidgins were "vehicular languages," that is, languages with simplified structures that filled a limited array of communicative needs; creoles, in contrast, were the full-blown languages with native speakers, which eventually evolved out of pidgins (Jourdan 1991, 191). However, linguists are no longer sure that creoles necessarily emerge out of pidgins, nor that pidgins cannot be full-blown languages in their own right. The opposition upon which linguistic arguments depend is no longer between a second language (pidgin) and a mother tongue (creole), but between a secondary language (or pidgin) and a main language (or creole) (ibid., 194). This distinction shifts the terms of discussion considerably, because it does not focus as much on structure as on usage.

We do not intend to indulge in the wholesale importation of a linguistic model into the interpretation of social life, a process fraught with peril. Nonetheless, the pidgin/creole discussion does assist in conceptualizing how colonial actors could appropriate foreign idioms and imbue them with different sorts of indigenous content, while continuing to identify in other contexts with their native cultural groups. It suggests that the colonial culture adopted by the individuals highlighted in our case studies was as complex and complete as were the aboriginal cultures, and that indigenous actors in the colonial period did not necessarily see one as supplanting the other, or as incommensurate. Therefore, we need to look at how and when each was deployed and by whom, not to assume that they contradicted one another. For some of the actors we will be presenting in the coming chapters, colonial culture is a kind of a secondary language, which individuals employ when they move beyond the home sphere. For others, it has become a main language, at least in the literate channels in which they are communicating. The ways in which alterity is highlighted or downplayed depends in part upon the kind of language that these actors use in particular contexts.

Employing a European visual idiom, the native Quiteño painter Sánchez Gallque played up the alterity of his mulatto subjects by emphasizing their clothing and adornments in ways that suggest the persistence of American and African cultural forms (the gold jewelry and the spears). Sánchez Gallque's othering of the three men in the portrait discussed earlier also conveys an incomplete and ambiguous adoption of European culture (the Spanish clothing and accompanying gestures). We know little of the intentions of the mulattos depicted in the portrait: Francisco de la Robe and his sons. For them, the transcultural appropriations that are depicted were probably part of a secondary language they did not entirely command. Perhaps the spears they normally carried and the gold adornments that local indigenous people wore were part of a generalized idiom that they understood, but the Spanish clothing almost certainly was not, according to the letter that accompanied the painting. While Sánchez Gallque highlighted the alterity of his subjects in the portrait, however, his own cultural difference was entirely muted. Although he was an Andean native, he communicated in a European style of painting that had become his main idiom in those contexts in which he assumed the ethnically unmarked position of an artist. In this sense, like his fellow painters who were of European or mestizo descent, his own alterity was not at issue in this painting and was, therefore, not expressed there. Instead, he distanced himself from his subjects, converting them into Others.

Don Diego de Torres, unlike Sánchez Gallque, was a mestizo, and one who labored to gain recognition of his native noble status. He achieved this primarily through writing, by producing a series of documents that do not

distance him culturally from his fellow mestizo residents of the New Kingdom of Granada. Instead, he was at pains to distinguish himself according to
very distinct criteria: he asserted a noble identity that at once identified him
as a native, though in the position of assuming all of the trappings of high-
status Europeans, including their clothing, their language, their liberty of
movement across the Atlantic, and their direct access to legal literacy and to
the ear of the king. In this sense, the assertion of cultural alterity is not Don
Diego's objective. Nor would the idiom of colonial culture—which is his
main language—be an appropriate vehicle for asserting alterity, when what
he is claiming is nobility. Clearly, the Crown recognized what Don Diego was
up to. The Royal Court legitimized his elite status. However, the settlers of
Santafé de Bogotá did not. As Sánchez Gallque othered his mulatto sitters,
the colonial officials did so to Don Diego. They emphasized his alterity by
condemning him as an idolater and by demonstrating their fears of his linguistic powers of persuasion. They also highlighted his difference by focusing on what they perceived as a contradiction between his stated Indianness
and what they held to be his essential character as a mestizo: how could he
be a member of the native nobility if he was not entirely native? They, too,
spoke in a colonial idiom, using it differently from Don Diego.

Finally, Don Alonso Florencio Inca, the presumed pretender to the de-
funct Inca throne, melded his basic language with his secondary language in
such a way that it was unclear which idiom was which to both his indigenous
followers and his settler opponents. Don Alonso Inca's debacle takes place
in a later period, when colonial culture was more consolidated, when several generations of ladinos, mestizos, and Inca descendants had learned to
defend themselves in the colonial world, to make it on the colonizer's terms.
For them, as for the members of the colonial Inca nobility whose portraits
Carolyn Dean and Dana Leibsohn (2003) write about, people who wore both
Chinese silks and Andean textiles, such a combination was not at all remarkable—just like it is no longer remarkable to see modern indigenous people
using burros, or even motorcycles. But Don Alonso Inca miscalculated the
extent to which his use of Incaic images would become grist for the mills of
the settlers of Ibarra, who "othered" him with the aim of deposing him. He
also misjudged the indigenous locals, who did not read these symbols as
colonial, but as rehabilitated pre-Columbian icons effective for overturning
the colonial order. His errors landed him in deep trouble. He assumed that
both his adversaries and his followers spoke the same colonial cultural language as he did.

The technologies of visual and alphabetic literacy supplied critical scenarios in which alterity and sameness could be claimed and disputed by all of these actors. Literacy provided sites for the expression of intersecting and divergent colonial discourses by Spaniards, natives, and mestizos alike. It is to the painted canvas and the written page that we turn now, to see how less exemplary indigenous actors negotiated the same cultural space, exploring, first of all, the genres of expression they employed and the extent to which they were able to imbue these genres with native content.

Genre/Gender/*Género*

"QUE NO ES UNO NI OTRO, NI ESTÁ CLARO"

GÉNERO:

In Spanish it is commonly understood as sex, as masculine or feminine gender, or as what is strictly called species, such as: there is a type of lamb that has six horns. It warrants a condition: There is a type of men who have a propensity towards evil. In mode (by that I mean a conditional): It is a type of intense mockery to play with hands. Term and mode of proceeding: A type of a well-reared child should respect his elders.

[Comunamente en castellano, se toma, o por sexo, como género masculino o feminino, o por lo que en rigor se llama especie, como: ay un género de carneros que tienen seys cuernos. Vale condición: Ay género de hombres que quieren ser llevados por mal. Por modo: Es un género de burla muy pesado jugar de manos. Termino y modo de proceder: En genéro de buena *criança* el moço deve respetar al anciano.]

SEBASTIÁN DE COVARRUBIAS OROZCO *TESORO DE LA LENGUA CASTELLANA O ESPAÑOLA* 1995 [1611]

*G*énero is, by its etymological nature, a multifaceted word. When employed, it works to define, to distinguish, and to categorize so as to bring into proper focus social and cultural specificities. This means that first and foremost género is about the boundaries of representation and recognition. It is a term that is critical to the articulation of Western art and artistic practices and with regard to the visual arts of which this chapter is concerned, this sense of discretion is its defining element. Francisco Pacheco, the father-in-law of Diego Velázquez, wrote in his *El arte de la pintura* that "painting is the art that teaches to imitate with lines and colors. This is the definition. In order to explain it, it is necessary to know that all definitions should consist of genre and difference. Genre, according to logicians, is a common reason that belongs to many different species; difference is all that by which a species is distinguishable from all others of the same genre" (Pacheco 1990 [1649], 75).[1] That is, for example, there are many different portraits, and all portraits belong to the genre of portraiture, or else they are not portraits. However, as we shall see, in practice it is more complicated than that.

Género for Pacheco, following Italian theorists such as Alberti but most especially Lomazzo, is used in its broadest discretionary sense for organizing the conditions of artistic practice and production.[2] But within painting, género acts to distinguish one type of painting from another. So, for example, in 1599, the court artist, Juan Pantoja de la Cruz uses the word *género* instrumentally in his description of the fifth room of the treasury in the Alcázar of Madrid to differentiate between the kinds of paintings hung there and their relation to each other. Here, the royal portraits of Charles V and Philip II by Titian were hung with other portraits that together created an extended allegory of imperial rule (Cummins 2005, 16). Concerning a painting that depicted Philip II defending the church against her enemies, Pantoja de la Cruz writes, "This painting is burdened by the genre of devotional painting and there it is valid and here it is not."[3] The phrase is enigmatic, as *allí* (there) and *aquí* (here) have no reference other than within the sense of genre as he employs the term. That is, for Juan Pantoja de la Cruz there exists some notion of a proper relationship among the heterogeneity of images, such that one of them, a devotional painting perhaps similar to Cabrera de Córdoba's frontispiece,[4] an allegorical image of Phillip II defending the church, seems out of place in the midst of imperial portraits of Charles V, Philip II, Inca kings, and the Conquest of Peru (ibid., 16–17).

Género is more multifaceted in translation to English as it becomes, simultaneously, "genre" and "gender." But género as genre/gender is still about clarity, propriety, and proper distinction. It is possessed of a quality or condition that can be recognized and agreed upon, be it human gender, animal species, or categories of representation. Hence Covarrubias and Pantoja de la Cruz, although talking about different forms of representation, are in agreement as to the clarity that the term *género* brings in making sense of the world. The problem of genre, then, is to keep those distinctions clear so as to form states of knowledge and being. The desire for order, however, is always conditioned by an alternative, which in the case of the binary gender/genre distinction is, at the very least, a third possibility. Covarrubias also clearly articulates this possibility, but not in his dictionary of 1611. It appears a year before in his book *Emblemas morales*. Emblem 64 depicts a full-length figure standing in the countryside wearing a dress and sporting a beard (figure 10). The text below reads:

> I am hic, & hac, & hoc I declare myself
> I am man, I am woman, I am a third
> Which is neither one, nor the other, nor is it clear
> Which of these things am I. I am a Third
> a horrendous and strange monster.
> They take me as a sinister and bad omen
> Warning each one that looks upon me
> That he is another me. If he lives effeminately.
>
> [Soy hic, & hac, & hoc Yo me declaro
> Soy Varon, soy mujer, soy un tercero
> Que no es uno ni otro, ni está claro
> Qual de estas cosas sea. Soy Tercero
> De los q como a mõstro horrédo y raro
> Me tienen por siniestro y mal aguero
> Aduierta cada qual q me ha mirado
> Que es otro yo. Si vive afeminado]
> (Covarrubias 1610, 164)

Spanish as a language fails here to be able to express alterity, and it is only within the structure of Latin—hic, hac, hoc: Masculine, Feminine, Neuter— that the ambiguity of androgyny can be expressed. Alterity is an embodied third state of being, one that is feared and loathed ("me tienen por siniestro y mal aguero," or "they take me as a sinister and bad omen"). Neither male, nor female by recognition, one must declaim/decline oneself ("Yo me declaro"), as it is not clear. The gender of género fails when the borders of recognition between male and female are blurred ("Que no es uno ni otro, ni está claro," or "Which is neither one, nor the other, nor is it clear"). It is as if Jacques Derrida read this passage of Covarrubias's when he wrote that "the genre has always in all genres been able to play the role of order's principle: resem-

FIGURE 10
Emblem 64,
Sebastián de
Covarrubias
Orozco,
*Emblemas
morales* (Madrid:
L. Sánchez, 1610).
Woodcut.

blance, analogy, identity and difference, taxonomic classification, organization, and genealogical tree, order of reason, order of reasons, sense of sense, truth of truth, natural light and sense of history" (Derrida 1981, 51–52).

In his emblem, Covarrubias puts into doubt this structuring binary of order in several ways, as we shall discuss. More importantly, if it is put into doubt in Spain at the level of the imaginary at a most fundamental level of order—gender—then, what of the colonial world? What of the mestizo, mulato, and indio ladino? They, too, blur multiple boundaries of race, ethnicity, class, and culture, and are produced by the sexual relations of male and female. The mestizo offspring stand between the two republics: that of the Spanish and of the indios—two worlds not meant to mix. Mestizos, mulattos, and ladinos are never to be truly trusted, but are ever present, as the Spaniard Pedro de Quiroga suggests in his *Coloquios de la verdad*, a dialogue written in Lima in 1562 (1992), and the Andean Guaman Poma writes and draws in his *Nueva corónica i buen gobierno* (1980 [1616]). One could believe, with slight alteration, that Covarrubias's "they take as sinister and bad omen," written to refer to the third sex, stands also for those who are neither Spanish nor indio nor African. Yet, as we have discussed in chapter 1, the colonial world becomes blurred to such an extent that some individuals can choose which language to speak, which category of being to be, Spanish or indio, or, conversely, to be neither. Such choices are really open to only a few elite individuals, most often mestizos, such as Garcilaso de la Vega, el Inca, Diego de Torres, cacique of Turmequé, Diego Muñoz Camargo, and others. Their claims to self-identification are often contested by vested interests of differing communities—Spaniards in the New Kingdom of Granada could claim that Diego de Torres was not the rightful heir to Muisca authority, or the Tlaxcalans could deny Diego Muñoz Camargo membership in their community—so that they could not lay claim to certain rights and privileges.

And so, just as Covarrubias points to a third gender, composed from the elements of the other two so as to be neither male or female and both, the colonial world is an amalgamation, one of constantly blurred boundaries. In fact one of the great mestizo authors of the Andean world addresses this new historical condition quite forcefully. In the last section of the first volume of the history of the Incas, Garcilaso de la Vega, el Inca, details the things that did not exist in the Americas before the arrival of the Spanish and that were, consequently, brought there. One chapter of this section goes beyond the natural history of animals and plants and is entitled "The New Names for Naming the Different Generations" (Nombres nuevos para nombrar diversas generaciones), in which he writes:

> We are forgetting the best that has come to the Indies which are the Spaniards and the Negroes, who have since been brought here as slaves in order to serve them [the Spaniards] because before then they were unknown in my land. From these two nations have been created others there [Peru], mixed in all sorts of manner, they are called by different names, in order to distinguish among them. . . . The children of a Spanish mother and father, born there [America], are called Criollo, or Criolla, which means that they are born in the Indies. This name was invented by the Negroes as its use shows. It means among them Negroes [those] who are born in the Indies, they invented it to distinguish those who come from here, born in Guinea, from those who are born there, as they hold those who are born in their country in greater esteem and higher rank [*cali-*

dad] than those who are born outside of it, and the parents take offense if they are called Criollos. Similarly the Spaniards have introduced this word into their language in order to name those who are born there [the Americas]. Thus both Spaniards and Africans born in the New World are called Criollos. For the Negro who comes from here is simply called Negro or Guineo. For the child of a Negro and Indian they say Mulato or Mulata. Their offspring are called Cholo, which is a word that comes from the Island of Barlovento, and means dog. . . . For the children of Spanish and Indian parents, we call ourselves Mestiços, which means, we are a mixture of both nations: [the term] was given by the first Spaniards who had children with Indian wives, and as it is a name given by our fathers, and because of what it signifies, I call myself [mestizo] publicly and with great honor. However in the Indies, if someone says thou art a Mestiço, or you are a Mestiço, it is taken as an insult. . . . Of the children of a Spaniard and a Mestizo, they are called a Quatrraluos which means that have one [a fourth] Indian and three parts Spaniard. For the children of Mestizos and Indians they are called Tresaluos meaning that they have three parts Indian and one part Spaniard. All these names and others that I have left out, have been invented in my land in order to name the generations that have been [created] since the Spaniards arrived and therefore we can say that they have brought them with the other things that did not exist before. (Garcilaso 1723 [1609], 339–40)[5]

There are many things contained in this passage concerning the new "generations" in the Americas and the origins (inventions) of the terms that name them, and we shall return to some of them. For our immediate purposes, it is important to note that Garcilaso changes voice from third person to first person when he comes to account for his own self. He writes of the mestizo that they are "los Hijos de Español, y de India ó de Indio y Española, nos llaman Mestiços, por decir, somos mezclados de ambas Naciones: fue impuesto por los primeros Españoles, que tuvieron hijos en Indias; y por ser nombre impuesto por nuestros Padres, y por su significacion, me lo llamo Yo á boca llena, y me honrro con él." The last phrase is remarkably close to the first part of Covarrubias's text in which the androgynous figure speaks in the first-person voice "Soy hic & hac, & hoc. Yo me declaro Soy Varon, soy mujer, soy tercero." That is, Garcilaso also both proclaims and declaims himself proudly a mestizo, and as something unknown before, a mestizo is both Spaniard and indio and a third. This naming by Garcilaso de la Vega, el

Inca, is a different naming of the new than that which Columbus undertook when he discovered the Americas: Columbus recognized only what already existed and, therefore, named it accordingly, i.e., the West Indies (Todorov 1984, 25–26). Garcilaso embodies proudly both the name and the self which is named.[6]

It is also important to point out that just as Garcilaso de la Vega el Inca, Diego de Torres, and many others embody literally, physically, and culturally, the interstitial space, the "allegorical" figure in Covarrubias's emblem constitutes a third image made from the combining of the two others. The banner framing the figure bears a text in Latin "Neutrumque et utrvmque" meaning "Neither and both," a quote that comes from Ovid's *Metamorphoses* and that refers to the Hermaphrodite as a double being who was at the same time both sex and neither sex. The textual reference harkens to the classical world's notion of the hermaphrodite and blurred gender. The pictorial image that Covarrubias cites is altogether different, however. It is not classical: his visual source is a contemporary one. The bearded figure that is dressed in modern female clothes and stands in a landscape dotted with Renaissance buildings is a known person: the following page in the explanatory text identifies her as "the bearded lady of Peñaranda."[7] That is, the gendered state of being "neither and both" is not just the mythical/classical Hermaphrodite of Ovid, but it is a real state of being, something lived, just as the mestizo state of being neither and both in the early modern world of Spain and the Americas is real for Muñoz Camargo, Diego Valadés, the cacique of Turmequé, and so many others.

But equally important in terms of representation, Covarrubias's image is more than an illustration about androgyny and a third gender. By depicting a well-known individual, he mixes pictorial genres in his emblem of the third gender. The highly allegorical image is also a portrait. In fact, Covarrubias not only identifies the figure in the text, but he has taken for his model a specific and well-known portrait. It is Juan Sánchez Cotán's 1590 portrait of Brígida del Río, also known as "La Barbuda de Peñaranda," or "The Bearded Lady of Peñaranda" (Konečný 1994) (figure 11).[8] Covarrubias's image is therefore more than the mere illustration of the concept of a third sex, a third gender.[9] His image itself is a third genre, being neither allegory nor portrait, but both. It does not declare itself as the text does ("me declaro"). Instead, it manifests itself by appearance. Here, the economy of the image allows for a multitude of simultaneous understandings that the text must develop in a much slower, linear, and sequential fashion: "Soy hic &

FIGURE 11 Portrait of Brígida del Río, Juan Sánchez Cotán, 1590. Oil on canvas. Courtesy of Museo del Prado, Madrid.

hac & hoc. Yo me Declaro." The image is immediate and is at once both and neither, succinctly manifesting gender and genre as a possibility of being both and neither. This image, then, is different from the usual emblem. It is not just another clever game involving the relationship between text and image. Combining the reality of portrait with the allegory of emblem, Covarrubias produces a third image or genre/gender, so to speak.[10] To create the gender of difference, the order of genre is transgressed. No other image in Covarrubias's book of emblems leaves the genre of allegory to become real, but then none is real as an allegory. Only this image is both. The emblem mythologizes reality and demythologizes the classical pantheon (Konečný 1994, 831). The image is allegorical by its context and indexical by being a portrait.[11] Furthermore, the citation of Ovid is a reference to the textual authority of a classical source, whereas the citation of the known person is an appeal to the authority of experiential knowledge. This idea of authority, as well as the temporal dimension are, in this instance, heterodox.

Covarrubias's image is, of course, intended for a small literate public, armed with erudite references and the means to understand his book of emblems. Yet, the issues of genre and gender, which appear here in an intellectual emblem, are not unlike the historical conditions of "Golden Age Spain" and its empire. Here, genre, gender, and race are inextricably intertwined both in the intellectual imagination and the reality of social life.

Genre and the Religious Image

Genres and their deployment are not, then, neutral categories of distinction as Covarrubias at first might seem to suggest in his dictionary. Rather, genres are charged with a very strong purposefulness. Within the colonization of the Americas genres take a formative role in producing difference, as we shall discuss below. In terms of the pictorial, there is a rather marked differentiation between secular and religious images. In the Americas, secular images are really confined to just a relatively few genres: portraits, historical scenes, and maps. The vast majority of colonial Latin American images are religious images. This is especially true for the images within indigenous communities. Religious imagery might then be considered a secondary metagenre within which there are specific genres and subgenres that are based on differing criteria. The basic elements by which genres were understood appear in Vicente Carducho's *Dialogos de la pintura: Su defensa, origen, essencia, definición, modos y diferencias*, published in 1633:

> Genre . . . has a moral nobility and it is assumed that its motive and goal are virtue and honesty; through painting, the Holy Mother Church has sought to convert the creature into an image of his creator by means of holy images and through other acts of devotion, as attested to by saints and as the Councils have commanded; art is used for this purpose and to gain the fullest satisfaction, and the words of the Holy Tridentine Council that can be used to ascertain this, say as follows: All sacred images bear fruit, not only because they remind the people of the profits, gifts and grace that were done unto them by Christ, but more so because the miracles of the Lord, done by means of the saints and their wholesome examples, make themselves apparent to the eyes of the Faithful so that through them they might give thanks to God, and so that they might

compose their lives and habits in an imitation of the saints and exercise themselves in the adoration of God and in the embracing of piety. (Carducho 1633, 33v–34r)[12]

Carducho inserts into this Spanish tract on painting what had been promulgated at the twenty-fifth session of the Council of Trent (December 1543):

> That images of Christ, the Virgin Mother of God, and other saints are to be placed and retained especially in the churches, that due honor and reverence is to be given them, not, however, that any divinity or virtue (power) is believed to be in them by reason of which they may be worshipped, or that something is to be asked of them, or that any trust is to be put in images, as was done of old by the Gentiles who placed their hope in their idols, but because the honor which is shown to them is referred to the prototypes which they represent, so that by means of the images which we kiss and before which we uncover the head and prostrate ourselves, we adore Christ and honor the saints whose likeness they bear." (Schroeder 1978 [1564], 215–16)

We shall return, in chapter 5, to this passage as it appears in the catechism of the Third Council of Lima, but here it is important simply to note that what is expressed in the Council of Trent as a sixteenth-century Roman Catholic position is simply based on a venerable Christian defense of images. Basically, the Council of Trent reaffirmed the principles concerning images as established in 787 by the Second Council of Nicaea in its seventh session, when the members distinguished between absolute and relative worship and the rôle of images in the church. By citing the Second Council of Nicaea, the Council of Trent parallels (almost in typological form) the great threat of the eighth-century crisis of iconoclasm with that of the sixteenth-century iconoclasm of Protestantism.

It is important to understand, therefore, what the Second Council of Nicaea decreed. First, absolute worship is paid to the holy personage for his or her own sake. Relative worship is paid to a sign or, in this case, an image, not at all for its own sake, but for the sake of the thing signified:

> We declare that, next to the sign of the precious and life-giving cross, venerable and holy icons—made of colors or pebbles or any other material that is fit, may be set in the holy churches of God, on holy utensils, and vestments, on walls and boards, in houses and in streets. These may be

icons of our Lord and God, the Savior Jesus Christ, or of our pure Lady, the holy Theotokos, or of honorable angels or of any saint or holy man. For the more these are kept in view through their iconographic representation, the more those who look at them are lifted up to remember and have an earnest desire for the prototypes. And also [we declare] that one may render to them veneration of honor (*aspasmon kai timetiken proskynesin*); not true worship of our faith (*alethinen latreian*) which is due only to the Divine Nature but the same kind of veneration that is offered to the form of the precious and life-giving cross, to the holy gospels, and to other holy dedicated items. Also [we declare] that one may honor these by bringing to them incense and light are to be given to these as to the figure of the sacred and life-giving Cross, as was the pious custom of early [Christians]; for the honor to the icon is conveyed to the prototype. Thus, he who venerates the icon venerates hypostasis of the person depicted on it.[13] In this way the teaching of our holy Fathers—that is, the traditions of the Catholic Church which has accepted the gospel from one end of the earth to the other—strengthened. (Sahas 1986, 179)[14]

In fact, the Council of Nicaea prefaced this declaration by affirming that the council had acted merely to preserve "all the traditions of the Church . . . decreed in written and unwritten form. . . . One of these traditions is the making of iconographic representations—being in accordance with the narrative of the proclamation of the gospel—for the purpose of ascertaining the incarnation of God the Word, which was real, not imaginary, and for being an equal benefit to us as the gospel narrative. For those which point mutually to each other undoubtedly signify each other" (ibid., 178–79). That is, the incarnation (the word became Man) was real (Christ became Flesh). So, as the word is to flesh, so the narrative of the Gospel is to iconographic representation: that is, word and image mutually refer to the Real, which is God become Man.

If we then return to what Carducho writes in his tract on painting, a text intended to assert the nobility of painting as a practice, we find that the traditions affirmed by the Council of Nicaea and reaffirmed by the Council of Trent are at the core of artistic practice and interpretation. In all the texts, religious images are understood as instrumental within a set of deferred relations, that is, they refer to something exterior to the image itself. Nonetheless, all types of religious images bear fruit, as Carducho says, but they do so differently. Clearly, in the sixteenth century there are individual images of saints, Mary and Christ, either painted or sculpted, that are devotional images, as mentioned by the Council of Trent and the Second Council of Nicaea. These can be placed either in churches or in homes. Then, there are doctrinal images that make manifest to the faithful the tenets and history of the church. These can be subdivided into rather straightforward narrative pictures, or they can be more allegorical images in which a rich symbolic pictorial language expresses the mysteries of the faith.[15] These differences are easily recognizable and distinguishable by composition and iconography.

The rationale for this latter genre of images was clearly defined by Gregory the Great in his 599 letter to Serenus, bishop of Marseilles, who had destroyed the images in his diocese:

> It has recently come to our attention that your Fraternity saw some people adoring images and you smashed those images and threw them out of the churches. And we certainly applauded you for having had the zeal not to allow anything made by human hands to be adored, but we judge that you ought not to have smashed those images. For a picture is provided in churches for the reason that those who are illiterate may at least read by looking at the walls what they cannot read in books. Therefore, your Fraternity should have preserved them and should have prohibited the people from their adoration, so that both the illiterate might have a way of acquiring a knowledge of history, and the people would not be sinning at all in their adoration of a picture. (Gregory the Great 2004, 674 [Letter 9.209])

Here, Saint Gregory indissolubly links the state of illiteracy and the state of being barbarian as a Christian logic for the licit desire for images. This relationship between text and image is different from, but related to, the relationship between text and image as expressed in the Second Council of Nicaea, in which word and image exist in a mutually signifying relationship of reference to the Divine.

Saint Gregory's letter is often quoted in support of the use of images in the conversion and indoctrination of the natives because of the thinking that they were all both illiterate and barbarian; thus, this means of instruction was already ordained. However, the didactic use of images is only one of the genres that constitutes the range of Catholic images. Some images, for example, are distinct not by what is represented in the image but by what the image is: its ontology. That is, a miraculous image is significantly different from one that is not, even though the miraculous image may represent the same thing as one that is not. Nonetheless, neither the miraculous image nor the nonmiraculous one is in and of itself what it represents. In this sense, they are the same. Some miraculous images were "not made with hands" (*eikones acheiropoietai*), such as Virgin of Guadalupe, or there was divine intervention, such as in the Virgin of Copacabana and the Virgin of Chiquinquirá (plate 2), through which the miraculous is manifested by the transformation of a deteriorated devotional image into a beautiful new one that radiates light. After the Council of Trent (twenty-fifth session), such miraculous images were subject to extreme scrutiny: "No new miracles are to be accepted and new relics recognized unless they have been investigated and approved by the same bishop."[16] Moreover, the bishop was directed in all these matters to obtain accurate information through witnesses and to take council with theologians and pious men, and in cases of doubt or exceptional difficulty, to submit the matter to metropolitan and other bishops of the provincial synod "so however that nothing new, or anything that has not hitherto been in use in the Church, shall be resolved on, without having first consulted the Holy See" (Schroeder 1978 [1564], 217). Within Spain and its territories, these inquires took the same form as a legal trial, in which witnesses were called and interrogated according to a written set of standard questions (Cummins 1999). That is, there is an intersection between the genres of legal inquiry and miraculous inquiry. Most important, both procedures establish the relationship of hierarchy and power that produces a decided outcome and even the terms *juicio* (trial) and *abogado* (lawyer) are used in both. The outcome of a legal trial is termed *juicio*, just as the Last Judgment is the Juicio Final, while the trial lawyers and the heavenly intercessors are both called abogados. The iconography of the Last Judgment on church portals was used since at least the medieval period as the backdrop for secular trials, and certain executions were held in front of the main church portal in Spain and the Americas, the portals themselves known as *la puerta del perdón*, or "the portal of pardon," making reference to this spatially manifested ideological relationship. This intersection between the representations of temporal and celestial hierarchy, which is deeply embedded in European thought—beginning in Antiquity and traceable through to the Renaissance—finds added value in the New World when the new forms of authority have to be made manifest. As we shall see below, it is an intersection that even extends to the baptism of newly arrived slaves in the New Kingdom of Granada.

Pictorial Genres in the Americas

Genre/Género as revealed by Covarrubias is a powerful and complex concept concerned with order in the early modern world.[17] The establishment of the Western Catholic order was the ultimate task in the colonization of the Americas just as it was in Counter-Reformation Europe. In this sense, the various genres of Western visual forms became something even more significant as a critical element of colonization because in the colonies, the distinctions established by the traditions of the church were immediately at risk. Clarity in terms of understanding what was being seen could not be assumed; rather, it had to be explicit. More importantly, the concepts outlined above formed the basis of indoctrination in the Americas. Natives had to come to understand what it was that they were seeing in relation to what it meant or referred to.

In the New World, one must also rethink the concept of género in the greater sense as a defining characteristic of colonial culture. In terms of representation (pictorial, sculptural, and architectural), it was never enough to simply introduce the concept of idolatry and the distinction between truthful and deceitful images (although idolatry was an overriding concern). Of course in the beginning throughout the Americas, there may have been only the simple substitution of one image for another, such as Cortés's spontaneous destruction of Mexican religious images and their replacement by Christian ones (Gruzinski 2001 [1990], 32; Todorov 1984, 59–61) or the sustained campaign of placing Christian crosses over pagan sites as called for in the First Council of Lima (Vargas Ugarte 1951–54), or, the recasting of pagan temples as Christian churches. These were cultural and religious acts in which images were involved, but they were not about the nature of the licit image or what and how it meant. Moreover, these were iconoclastic acts that were more for the Spanish themselves, visually marking the remaking of the pagan landscape as a Christian one in which there was a tacit commensurability between European and indigenous images, operating in relation to each other, based on the experiences and actions of the Reconquista (the militant Christian capture of Islamic Spain). In fact, the experiences of the Reconquista laid the foundations for much of how the conquest and settlement of the Americas developed. Santiago Matamoro (Saint James the Moor Killer) eventually became Santiago Mataindio (Saint James the Indian Killer) and many of the Spanish political and social institutions employed in the Americas, such as the *encomienda*, had first been developed during the Reconquest. However, the historical condition of America was understood to be radically different than that of sixteenth-century Iberia, even if the tactics of conquest and evangelization were the same. Spain and America might physically exist together, but not at the same spiritual time. America existed in a state of being that was prior to evangelization, and as such analogies were most often made between the Christian efforts of the Spanish in the New World and the Christian confrontations in the Mediterranean world of Antiquity.[18] Precedents were also drawn from the Old Testament, where the deceit of the devil was found operating in the New World as in ancient biblical times. For example, José de Acosta notes that it should not seem unusual to find idolatrous rites in the New World that outwardly appear to be similar to Christian ones, because one finds the same demonic deception described in the Book of Judges, where "Michas, who was the priest of a false idol, used the same implements that were used in the tabernacle of the True God, the ephod and the teraphim and the rest" (Acosta 1940 [1590], 276). The devil's deceit was ubiquitous both temporally and spatially.

Idolatry, therefore, was a condition of mistaken worship that could be properly refocused on the true God by the teaching of the Gospels. After all, this is what happened in Antiquity when the Apostles went out to spread the Word to the pagan world. America was understood to be undergoing a similar conversion, and the evangelization of the Americas was paralleled with early Christian experiences in Europe and the subsequent triumph over their own pagan roots. However, this comparison was being made just as Renaissance Europe was rediscovering and valuing its own pagan past, and it should be noted that there was a social and cultural difference between ancient Rome and the Americas of the sixteenth and seventeenth centuries. As Acosta writes, "the Christian religion was founded by God with miracles because human agency was completely lacking in effect because the early Christians did not have the sufficient strength" (1984 [1588], 312). However, the pagans of Acosta's day—the Mexicans, Andeans, and the others—were quite different.

> The situation of our era is very distinct. Those to whom the priests announce the faith are inferior in everything: in reason, in culture, and in power, and those who announce the Gospel are superior in terms of the great age of Christianity by the number of its faithful, their wisdom and erudition and all other means of persuasion. (1984 [1588], 312)

The Mexicans, Andeans, and other Indians, according to Acosta's logic, lacked both the wisdom and intelligence of the Ancients.[19] This dichotomy between strong and weak cultures also defined an artistic difference between Renaissance Europe and Renaissance America. Juan Meléndez, a Dominican from Peru, writes about this distinction, directly stating:

> In many parts of Christendom especially in Rome there is so little risk of idolatry that they preserve the ancient statues of their idols, celebrating in them only the delicacy of their artistry and the antiquity of their marble, because as the Christian faith, by the grace of God, is so deeply rooted in the hearts of the faithful there that now does not run the risk anyone believes that there is divinity in the stones and so the palaces, gardens and galleries are filled with them.
>
> But in the Indies, as the original natives of those countries are still recently converted to the Faith, and it has only recently taken possession of the hearts of those descendents of the ancient pagan religion, that while there are many good Christians among them, there are still many weak ones, and all of them being generally of such easy nature that they can be moved by evil or weakness, as is more often the case, to return to their ancient idols, rituals and ceremonies and so it is that it is not permitted that their idols be either kept or preserved as they perpetuate their memory and demonstrate their antiquity. (Meléndez 1681, II, 61–63)[20]

The evangelical efforts in the Americas therefore focused on two fields: the external signs (images and rituals) and instruction. This meant that for the first time in the Americas there were now both true images and false images. Idolatry was a first cause in the distinction between Indians and Spaniards, and as a proposition idolatry would, of course, maintain a defining position in the Spaniards' relation to the Indian. Campaigns against idolatry and trials of idolaters would continue throughout the colonial period, even though at first these acts had no real impact on indigenous communities about the nature of their images.

Later, after the languages separating the two communities (Spanish and native) were both learned and taught, doctrinal instruction couched the nature of imagery within a binary of proper and improper veneration. But once past this divisional binary, the symbolic technology of Christian communication, be it textual or visual, was instrumentalized through genres and subgenres. The creation of these genres had a real impact on the creation of colonial order as well as on how it might be disordered.

For example, when it came time for the Third Council of Lima in 1571 to create the standardized sermons that would be preached in Quechua throughout the Andes for the next 200 years, the texts were composed following a clear standard in terms of style as well as dialectal and terminological levels (Durston 2007, 94). That is, a type of order through genre was called forth. One can understand the need to systematize language in terms of style and words: however, this systematization was deployed within a subgenre of sermons that were infantilizing in intent. The prologue of the *Tercero Catecismo y Exposición de la Doctrina Cristiana por Sermones* (Lima, Concilio de 1585: 4r-v) explains that the correct way of preaching to the Indians was to use a "plain, simple, clear, and brief style" ("modo . . . llano, senzillo, claro, y breve") mixed in with a few simple similes or analogies and frequent exhortations and exclamations which would appeal to their emotional natures (Indians were supposed to be more easily convinced by *afectos* than by *razones*, that is, emotions, rather than reason). The prologue criticizes contemporary preachers, who were going over the heads of their audiences by preaching to the Indians as if they were educated Spaniards: "They preach exquisite things or in a high style to the Indians, as if they were preaching in some court or university, and instead of doing good, they do great harm, because they obfuscate and confuse the limited and tender intellects of the Indians" (Lima, Concilio de 1990 [1585], 3).[21]

The demand for plain style is to be associated with the restricted range of genres produced in general by the Third Council, and especially with the minor role given to liturgical texts in the corpus.[22] What this means is that the native was never to be given the opportunity to achieve a higher state of intellect. Genre, here in relation to rhetoric, is deployed so as to separate and distinguish at multiple interrelated levels between plain and complex thought and between native and European (see, for example, sermon 29 of the *Tercero Catecismo*). In the context of the colonization of the Americas, genre takes a formative role in producing difference and if we move from the genre of textual sermons to pictorial ones, we find that there is also a hierarchy, one very different from the hierarchies of genre developed in the academies of the eighteenth century. For example, the colonial images presented within native churches in the Andes are less complicated, more direct, and produced in conjunction with the sermons. The extended allegories in colonial paintings are most often to be found in European churches and homes, whereas in the small churches of native villages we primarily see the more literal narratives of the most important passages in the Gospels, used

FIGURE 12
Franciscan
preaching to Aztecs,
Diego Valadés,
Rhetorica christiana
(Perugia, 1579).
Engraving.

as illustrations in the way that Gregory meant images to be used: as bibles for the illiterates.[23] We can see this in the engraving by Diego Valadés in his *Rhetorica christiana*, published in 1579. The engraving was intended for a very literate European audience and it illustrated how images were used in New Spain by friars for the indoctrination of native congregations. It depicts in a straightforward manner a Franciscan preacher delivering a sermon from a pulpit to a classicized native/pagan congregation (figure 12). The large figure of the friar stands in the foreground, above his flock, pointing to one of a series of images hanging from the nave's wall. These are images that pull down from a casing, making them easily transportable, a system that was used well into the nineteenth century in Colombia and elsewhere. The images illustrate the narrative of the Passion of Christ, a cycle that was soon painted as murals on the naves of native churches throughout the Americas.

Equally important, the sermons, written in native languages in an *estilo llano* (plain style) made reference directly to the standard set of images in these churches, so that priest and congregation could look together at the image of damnation or salvation as the translated words were spoken.[24]

As we have already discussed in the introduction to this chapter, genres are not as fixed as they attempt to be. Rather, pictorial genres can be reconfigured, mixed, and confused so as to express the change in various categories of being. If we are to think of artistic production in the Americas as innovative, transformative, and informative, then the category of genre must be as multiple and complex as Covarrubias understands it to be.

Of course, new genres or subgenres come to define different characteristics and preoccupations in each of the viceroyalties, especially in the late seventeenth century and the eighteenth. They recombine discrete images to produce new visions. For example, in Peru, "los ángeles" are called upon to protect and to fight against the ancient Andean gods, as written in the seventeenth-century poem by Fray Fernando Valverde about the Virgin of Copacabana (figure 13). In the frontispiece of *Santuario de N. Señora de Copacabana en el Perú*, one sees in the center the Virgin of Copacabana above a globe turned ninety degrees on its axis showing the Viceroyalty of Peru. Personifications of Faith and Grace stand on clouds on either side of the globe. Below the clouds and globe is this new world, composed of the reed shoreline of Lake Titicaca, the place of her sanctuary, and an Inca is seated in a darkened and rocky landscape. He looks up toward the Personifications while the cause of his darkened world, the devil, appears before him. In the poem, the archangel Baraquiel is described as a "luminous and eminent warrior" (luminoso y eminente guerrero) who defeats the telluric gods of the Inca, "the lightning, thunder, and wind" (el rayo, el relámpago y el viento). However, it is not just in the poems and the Quechua sermons, but also in the Andean vision that the angel takes on a new warriorlike guise (figure 14). In the late seventeenth century a new subgenre of angel paintings arose that responds to these Andean concerns. These militant angels appear within a series of twelve paintings known as *ángeles arcabuceros* (angels with muskets). They quickly become favored in the Andes, where we know that, for example, the Aymara caciques of Jesús de Machaca in the altiplano of present-day Bolivia had paintings of "twelve militant angels" (doce ángeles de marcha) in their residence. But they even appear in Lima—which we know from an engraving by the French engineer and spy Amédée Frezier—where we see them displayed in the interior of a Lima residence (figure 15).[25]

FIGURE 13 Our Lady of
Copacabana, Francisco
de Bejarano, frontispiece
of Fernando de Valverde,
*Santuario de N. Señora de
Copacabana en el Perú*, 1641.
Engraving.

FIGURE 14 *Ángel arca-
bucero*, artist unknown,
ca. 1720, Anonymous private
collection. Oil on canvas.

FIGURE 15 Lima interior with two ángeles arcabuceros paintings depicted as hanging on the wall, Amédée Frezier, *Relation du voyage de la Mer du Sud, aux côtes du Chili, et du Pérou, fait pendant les années, 1712, 1713, et 1714* (Paris: Chez Jean-Geoffroy Nyon, Etienne Ganneau et Jacques Quillau, 1716). Engraving.

Series of angels were painted in various guises throughout South America, including in the New Kingdom of Granada. For example, a series of twelve was painted in the second half of the seventeenth century and came to be placed in the Church of Sopó, Cundinamarca, north of Bogotá. Sopó was a Muisca town and it continued to render a cult to its ancient gods late into the sixteenth century, when it was mentioned in the extirpation campaign initiated by the archbishop of Santafé, Luis Zapata de Cárdenas. The town was for various reasons moved three times and remained rather obscure and poor, a place where the practice of idolatry continued until the eighteenth century. In 1753, the laundress of the church found an image of Christ at the column, known as El Señor de Sopó, on a rock drawn from a well. Quickly thereafter Sopó became the sanctuary of this miraculous image (Gamboa

Hinestrosa 1996, 27). We know from a 1758 map that the single-aisle church faced the plaza with an atrium cross and four small chapels at the corners, a configuration used throughout this area of the New Kingdom of Granada for native villages. The appearance of the miraculous image brought attention to the village and, with it, new wealth; it seems that the series of ángeles arcabuceros was placed in the church along the nave some time thereafter.[26]

How can this series of angels, those sexless beings that even Covarrubias's emblem on gender could not encompass, be portrayed both as manly defenders of Christianity and androgynous members of the celestial court? There are, of course, theological explanations, as Ramón Mujica Pinilla (1996) and others have outlined (Gamboa Hinestrosa 1996; Mesa and Gisbert 1983; Sebastián López 1986), but what is important for our discussion is that this new genre of genderless beings is de facto regendered through the blending of two genres. The sixteenth-century European interest in the images of the archangels was itself stimulated by the 1516 discovery of a fresco painting of the seven archangels with an inscription of their names and attributes in the Church of Sant' Angelo in Palermo, Sicily (Gamboa Hinestrosa 1996:47; Sebastián López 1986, 15). Almost immediately, in 1523, Charles V had a new chapel dedicated to the archangels built in Palermo. Their cult was taken to Rome by the Sicilian priest Angelo de Duca, where it was embraced by Pope Pius IV and further disseminated through the engravings of Hieronymus Wierix, Pieter de Jode, and Philippe Galle, and in printed books. These prints served as the first instance for many paintings of the angels both in Spain and the Americas. What is significant in the Americas is that a new genre appeared based upon a melding of two disparate sources. Here, the printed and painted images of angels were combined with a wholly different set of engravings, that is, the images that appear in Jacob de Gheyn's *Wapenhandelinghe* (*The Exercise of Armes*), first published in 1607 and translated into English and French the following year (figure 16) (Herzberg 1986; Merino 1958; Mesa and Gisbert 1983). The images illustrate the proper use of the military dress parade and the use of arms. This synthesis of two distinct genres creates something new, visually clarifying a new militant type of angel. This new category of painting is restricted, concerned with local ideas and concerns, in this case theological. Such a concern with the local, not the metropole, is basically the way in which new genres operated in the New World.

Different concerns give rise to an entirely different genre in Mexico. This genre, too, is about making clear that which is not; however it is physical, not metaphysical. Mexican artists during the eighteenth century give rise to

FIGURE 16 Military use of arms musketeer, Jacob de Gheyn, *Maniement d'armes, d'arqvebuses, movsqvetz, et piqves. En conformite de l'ordre de monseigneur le prince Maurice, prince d'Orange . . . representé par figures, par Jaques de Gheijn. Ensemble les enseignemeš par escrit a l'utilite de tous amateurs des armes, et ausi pour tous capitaines & commandeurs, pour par cecy pouvoir plus facillement enseigner a leurs soldatz inexperimentez l'entier et parfait maniement dicelles armes.* Amsterdam: Imprimé a Amsterdam chez R. de Baudous; on les vend ausi a Amsterdam chez Henrij Laurens. 1608. Engraving.

the now famous *casta* paintings (figures 17 and 18). We are not so concerned with the social history of race and its relation to the paintings as illustrations of it. What concerns us is the fact that these paintings are a local genre, restricted almost entirely to the Viceroyalty of New Spain. Like the ángeles arcabuceros, they are large and painted in series, and much like the ángeles arcabuceros, they are intended to make visible distinctions and relations. They are a new register, intended to put order through genre onto something that in reality could not be ordered. That is, the casta paintings as a series of

FIGURE 17 *Diseño de indio chichimeca*, Manuel de Arellano, 1711. Oil on canvas. Courtesy of Museo de América, Madrid.

FIGURE 18 *Diseño de india chichimeca*, Manuel de Arellano, 1711. Oil on canvas. Courtesy of Museo de América, Madrid.

conditions of being are no more mere illustrations than are the ángeles arcabuceros. They are sets of multiples, with each individual painting an iteration of a type, such that they change only slightly as one scans by eye or physically moves along the wall of a nave or a reception room. There is insistence about type and distinction through seriation.

The Andean angel paintings and Mexican casta paintings are rare in that they represent entirely new pictorial genres developed in and solely restricted to the different regions in the Americas. They demonstrate the artistic originality that was possible there. Nonetheless, these new genres are understandable within the general range of possibilities of colonial painting. A critical element is about making distinctions among things in a series, producing a viewing of multiples, and seeing the commonalities and differences between them. These two genres can therefore be understood to be linked through the effect to other series of paintings, such as the official portraits of viceroys and bishops. Such portraits occur within a series that is open ended, with the last in the series anticipating the next one. There is, thus, a temporal quality to these portraits that creates a nexus between the finite life of the individual and the enduring quality of the official position. Our point here is that these different genres can be seen as both distinct and related, and that they call upon a learned discrimination by the viewer. In general, the introduction and teaching of Western arts—be it music, sculpture, or painting—was not about the awakening of individual or collective creativity; it was, instead, a critical element in the subject formation of the native. How to see, how to interpret, and how to physically act in relation to images was a definitive part of the process of evangelization and colonization; within that process, the concept of genre is a defining characteristic of colonial visual literacy.

The New Kingdom of Granada: Northern Andean
Sacred Spaces and Ritual Practices

To address Western pictorial genres within a discussion of visual literacy as a colonial instrument, it is important to lay out some of the specific visual and ritual practices of the central parts of the New Kingdom of Granada, especially among the Muisca, who came under the scrutiny of extirpation by Spanish missionaries and priests. The textual descriptions of their iconoclasm are important insofar as they define how false images were characterized specifically in relation to native beliefs. Equally important are the descriptions of the architectural forms and spaces and the practices that took place in them. That is, one of the immediate objectives of visual literacy throughout the Americas was to impress upon native viewers the notion that some images (Catholic ones) were true images while other images (native ones) were false, and in turn, that some spaces were holy spaces while others were demonic. However, each native community had different practices and types of images, obliging friars and priests to accommodate themselves to local specificities. They had to learn almost as much as they had to teach, and it is from their descriptions that we can begin to understand some of the native precepts concerning images and the spaces in which they were seen and manipulated. We are not, therefore, attempting to reconstruct original meanings; rather, we are attempting to make use of Spanish accounts to explain how these images and objects were understood to be seen and used. As Carlo Ginzburg has demonstrated in his book *The Night Battles* (1983; see also Cummins 1998a), in the process of discursive entanglement, representational practices understood by the community to be licit and beneficial become something illicit and demonic. That is, one comes to recognize traditional practices within the terms by which they are opposed.

A description of the first mission to the New Kingdom of Granada begins like almost all others, stating that the friars had tried to plant the true faith and teach the natives the errors of their ways by which the devil had deceived them. One such mistaken belief was that the soul died with the body:

> From this they passed on to take the idols away from the natives and to burn them in their presence in order to confirm what they preached, that the figures were not nor could they be gods since they allowed themselves to be consumed and destroyed and that they were statues of metal, gold and copper, wood, string, cotton, merely instruments of the devil by which they were deceived. (Remesal 1620, 549, cited by Meléndez 1681, I, 416)[27]

The rooting out of pagan faith and the destruction of idols were nothing new. They had been going on since the discovery of Hispaniola and the Taíno. However, the mention of string (*hilo*) and cotton (*algodón*) as figures that were false gods and instruments of the devil is very unusual and specific to the highland region of the New Kingdom of Granada. It seems that in that area, images were made of bundled cotton. For example, the parish priest of Lenguazaque, in present-day Cundinamarca, Padre Fray Tomás de Acuña, burned idols made of sticks and cotton, which he found in a cave.

He also burned the wall hangings that adorned the cave walls (Meléndez 1681, I, 420). Another parish priest, Alonso Ronquillo, who burned nearly 300 cotton-and-stick idols in Bogotá, explains why these wall hangings needed to be destroyed. He first writes that the natives had so many different gods because they administered to almost every conceivable human need, including a deity of the night who received sacrifices from those who suffered from nightmares. We shall return to the issue of nightmares in the next section. It is important to note here his description of how, after a particular community was "reducida"—brought to a higher level of understanding, as we will discuss in chapter 6—as a result of his preaching, a powerful and old priest named Siqasiosa took him to a cave:

> The cave . . . was entered by going down a very dangerous and steep set of stairs cut into it and which measured some twelve feet long by six feet wide and it was covered with many mantas [cloths] painted with figures of incredibly horrendous demons of different types based on the evil spirit that appeared to the priests and the Friar removed them all up as well as all the idols that twenty *indios* could carry among which was a statue of an indio that the Friar made the native priest [Siqasiosa] carry himself.[28]

In fact, idols and caves are interdependent in the minds of the friars. Caves were seen as the places where important oracle images and the remains of ancestors were kept. For example,

> Not only were the Friars, with danger to their own lives, able to get rid of the idols, but they [extirpated] any other rites and ceremonies, such as did Friar Pedro Mártir de Cárdenas, the priest of the parish in Suesca [seventy-five kilometers north of Bogotá in the department of Cundina-marca] who was made aware of a cave where the indios practiced their idolatries and buried the bodies of *uchos* [mummies] who died as gentiles, [and] he went there with a mulatto named Martín Caballero. They removed the mud from the cave's entrance, and entering within they found more than a hundred and fifty bodies seated in a circle according to the tradition of their ancestors, and in the middle was seated their lord, or Cazique, who was differentiated from the rest by in his adornment of beads around his arms and neck and a headdress or turban on his head and next to him were small textiles that the Indios offered [to him]. He made them remove him as well as all the other bodies and carried them

by poles to the village's plaza where he set them on fire much to the consternation of the entire town. (Meléndez 1681, I, 422)[29]

Other priests speak of caves in which were kept both the bodies of the ancestors, and images of men and women made of cloth and sticks. Other objects, such as parrots and balls of wool, were also placed in them to be worshipped and consulted in some form or other. The images of birds were animated by ventriloquism, as will be discussed below. In fact, these images became a site of verbal disputation between the Franciscan priests and the native priests. What is important to recognize here is that the majority of the accounts point to three-dimensional objects as the idols that need to be destroyed, while painted images have no place in these discussions. Architecture, however, is critical, and it is an architecture of volume rather than mass that is described; that is, religious practices took place within interior spaces, rather than around solid pyramidal forms. Caves, either natural or manmade, seem to have been spaces the community entered, not only to visit its ancestors but also to perform religious acts and rituals. If we think about the subterranean funeral chamber caves of Tierradentro, which were artificially built by carving into the volcanic layer, then we can gain an idea of how these Muisca caves might have been understood to operate as spaces. The hollowed-out interiors found in Tierradentro took an architectural form that was probably not unlike above-ground residential structures, which, until very recently, were still being built by the Nasa in the southwestern highlands of Colombia (figure 19). The walls of the caves mimic an interior view in which one sees carved into the living rock a post and lintel system that supports a central beam and slanting rafters of a thatched roof. The interiors of these carved tombs were also painted to make the stone appear to extend even farther the illusion of the interior of a built structure above ground. Like the Muisca sanctuaries described above, the Tierradentro structures were visited and looted by Spaniards well into the eighteenth century.[30] Furthermore, although the Muisca sanctuaries were most often found within natural caves rather than manmade ones, we might imagine that these cave interiors, as described by sixteenth-century priests, were transformed into a pseudorealistic interior space complete with quasi-architectural features painted and covered with textiles.

Equally important, intense disputation about idolatry and proper veneration first took place around these Muisca spaces. For example, the Dominican Fray Diego Mancera, the parish priest of the Pueblo del Quiqui in the

FIGURE 19 Tomb, Tierradentro, ca. 800. Courtesy of Elías Sevilla Casas and Carlos Miguel Varona.

jurisdiction of Tunja, became aware that the *indios* of that town, as well as those of the surrounding area, had a common sanctuary where at certain times they all gathered to make offerings of emeralds, gold, and other items in idolatrous ceremonies:

> This sanctuary was in [the side of a] cliff into which they had dug and ex-cavated a cavernous space in the form of a very large room, into which one entered by a very wide door. This was closed on the outside by very tightly packed earth, such that one could not distinguish it [the entrance] from the side of the cliff itself. Within the room they had a great bird made of wood and covered with feathers, much larger than life size. The devil used this [image] as an instrument in order to speak with them, and to make speeches against the Holy Doctrine of the Gospels, which the friars preached to them, [and] to foretell things that would happen to

them, such that they turned their backs on the truth and believed these great lies. But all simple-minded people pay attention to such things, and they hold [the bird] in such great esteem, as it had been there for more than four hundred years in that place in which they venerated and obeyed it, sacrificing [to the image], among other many other offerings, innocent children, [and it] was attended in the room at night by many young maidens who were dedicated to its cult [and] who were changed from time to time. An old and very devout Christian Indian women told Friar Diego about this sanctuary, and of the great foolishness and abominations that were always committed in that place every time they gathered there, which were a great offense to God our Lord. (Meléndez 1681, I, 417)[31]

There are two points raised in this passage that need to be emphasized before we continue. First, this sanctuary is described as being an artificially made subterranean room, and therefore similar in nature to the known structures in Tierradentro. Second, this space was used to convene the community in ritual activity that focused on a cult statue of a large bird, which served as a kind of oracle.[32] Implicit in the friar's description is the belief that the sculpture of the talking bird was based both upon reality and the supernatural: in other words, some birds really did talk in the New Kingdom of Granada, and a talking bird could be a sign of demonic possession. For example, late into the eighteenth century, Fray Juan de Santa Gertrudis writes that "there was in the town of Santa Rosa [near the present-day town of Honda] a parrot the likes of which he had never seen because it talked so much and imitated all that it heard with such grace that another priest, after hearing the bird imitate all that they had said, hated the bird and said that that the parrot was possessed by the devil" (1970, I, chap. 6).[33] In the eighteenth century, a live talking bird was both uncanny and possessed, but in the sixteenth century, a larger-than-life sculpture of a bird was, for a Spanish priest, the very presence of the devil speaking.

It becomes clear, as one reads this passage, that the structuring component of this whole representational complex is mimicry. Mimicry appears in many guises. For example, the subterranean walls of the living rock are carved in order to mimic built structures; the statue of the bird mimics an actual bird that mimics the voice of man, and finally, ventriloquists in the cave mimic the mimicry of the birds by giving voice to the statue. Mimicry is, of course, by definition recursive, but here there seems to be a hierarchy that begins with the natural world's mimicking of the cultural world. At a first order, a bird mimics the voice of man, something real and observable, and then proceeds to operate at a second tier of copying, in which the cultural world of architecture built of organic material above ground, is recreated in the excavated walls of the subterranean chambers. This mimicry is not the mimesis of Western tradition in the sixteenth century; rather, it is an effective set of relations between the mundane and the supernatural and between the natural and the cultural worlds. Friar Diego Mancera's intent was to destroy this set of relations, which he understood to be demonic, but to do so he entered into it both physically and metaphorically. He disguised himself, dressing as (mimicking) an Indian, in order to enter the great hall at night. He was accompanied by the old *india*, so that the simulation was complete, and he was recognized as one of the community. But as he entered, his presence was detected by the supernatural and "the Lord allowed the demon to talk and the bird spoke in a loud voice: 'Get out, get the priest out of here.' The people rose up in commotion, shouting amongst themselves they began to ask where the priest was so they could kill him." The friar, sensing that he was recognized by the devil, fled the cave, unrecognized because of his disguise (Santa Gertrudis, 1970, 418).[34] He returned to the monastery and the very next day he revisited the sanctuary with his brothers, secular priests, and some soldiers. They entered the cave, where they "seiz[ed] the bird, as well as all the other idols of thread and the wooden figures of men and women that were placed around the bird, and . . . [took] them to plaza of the village where they are burned. A large number of the indios gathered to see the fire, most likely because on the one hand they wanted to see something so ancient that had been so wise and so hidden to the Spanish, and on the other hand, they were indignant to see something they so venerated be destroyed" (Meléndez 1681, I, 418).[35] At that point, those who were gathered there watching the bird idol burn rose up to kill the priest, at which point Father Mancera began to preach to them and in so doing, averted their intention of killing him, instead encouraging them to begin to understand the Gospels.

What needs to be noted here is that the Spanish priest enters into the mimicry through disguise in order to effect the disenchantment of the image. However, for Mancera, mimicry is a means to an end. Mimicry is instrumental, not transcendental: this is rooted in his Christian philosophical distinction between a thing and the representation of a thing, as we discussed above. Mancera's mimicry is intended to enable him to create a distance between the pre-Colombian object or image and the native colonial subject such that the affective hold that the object or image has over the native subject is broken. The object is to be seen and understood as being no more than an instrument of the devil, something deceitful both in appearance and substance. It is an act of disenchantment. It is an act of forceful physicality; it is also intended, though, to reorient how the native is now to see and understand an image or object. Disenchantment and destruction are the first acts in creating colonial visual literacy. We can see this disenchantment through the Christian engagement with the pre-Columbian object or image in a second battle by the same priest with a different demon:

> And in order that the indios recognize deceit of the demon the Padre made the demon manifest itself in the form in which it usually took when it talked to the yndios and at that point the demon took the form of a Guacamayo [parrot], whose appearance was the same that that priest had seen eating a chicken. And in the presence of the Spaniards who were gathered there, as well as the people in the house and the many yndios who were there, he spoke to the Guacamayo, and the father banished it to hell, something that the demon felt deeply, and with a thousand offerings of gold and silver, pearls and jewels and other earthly goods, he asked him to command him to go somewhere else. But as the priest did not accept these gifts, he again commanded him to hell; and making great threats to the priest, the demon which had taken the form of the bird disappeared. (Meléndez 1681, I, 419)[36]

There are many other similar passages in which the friars found themselves in underground chambers, face to face with sculptures activated through ventriloquism. In fact, it seems that these sacred spaces were almost everywhere and many of the new towns built for the Muisca, called either *resguardos* or *reducciones*, were situated near these ancient caves. This is true of such places as Chiquinquirá, Sutatausa, and Turmequé, towns that will be discussed in the following section. The point here is that the Muisca had a tradition of religious imagery and architecture that not only seems to have had considerable depth in time, but was distinct in its particular forms and practices from other areas of the Andes. As we have seen, the Spanish friars gave vivid descriptions of what they saw and how they had to act in specific ways to extirpate Muisca idolatry. In general, what is important in acts of extirpation is the battle with the offending images such that the new, Catholic images can assume their rightful place in the process of evangelization, taking the place of the discredited image. By rightful place, we mean that images begin to be categorized both by medium and by genre.

Colonial Images in the New Kingdom of Granada

There were multiple dimensions to the status of painting and sculpture within colonial culture. Early acts of substitution of one image for another were not about the distinctions framed by Pacheco's definition that "painting was an art that taught to imitate by color and line" (1990 [1649], 75). America was a world to be remade through the inculcation of such distinctions and definitions. At the center of that remaking were social, cultural, and political concerns. A remaking also meant the spatial organization of indigenous communities into newly built towns centered on the church, the place where images were produced and exhibited and discussed in catechism. The New Kingdom of Granada was no different from any other place in the Americas in this destruction and rebuilding. Between 1570 and 1580, for instance, the plan originally drawn up by the first president of the Real Audiencia, Andrés Díaz Venero de Leiva, led to the establishment of some 400 churches in native communities for their indoctrination into the Catholic faith. Laid out on a grid as was by then customary, the plaza was the center, its space demarcated at the corners by four *posas*, or small chapels. The church, the most important building, faced onto the plaza with a balcony over the portal that opened onto the single aisle of the nave. In many instances the conversion of the natives was directly manifested in the conversion of their idols into objects and images used to celebrate the Christian cult. Note, for example, the parish priest Fray Juan Martínez of the reducción/resguardo of Chipazaque:

> From the gold that he got from the idols he made a sculpted image of the Apostle Saint James, and a crown for Our Lady and it was made by the very same artistry of the Indians who had made the idols. The same was done by the Friar Pedro de Quiñones, parish priest of Guacheta, who being given golden idols by the indios as a result of his sermons, and who brought to the church on a feast day so that he could do as he liked; the Friar melted down the gold, which . . . after paying the King's fifth, there remained one hundred and forty pesos that was used to buy an image of Christ. (Meléndez 1681, I, 421)[37]

We can see such a conversion in a processional silver cross, made in the form of a Maltese cross, which comes from the parish of Pasca in Cundinamarca (figure 20). A small figure at the base represents the Virgin of the Immaculate Conception (figure 21). Around the belted circumference of the globe is inscribed a Spanish text that indicates that the cacique Don Alonso had the cross made in 1550 ("Este Estandarte iso el Casique Don Alonso 550"; figure 22).[38] Whether or not the processional cross was made from metal melted down from pre-Columbian images we do not know, but the area was a center of intense native metallurgy and one of the golden rafts that seems to represent the Muisca ritual in which their leader, "Zipa," covered his body in gold and, from his raft, he offered treasures to the Guatavita goddess in the middle of the sacred lake was found there.

As already mentioned, many of the resguardos, such as that of Pasca, were built near the ancient caves where the idols, ancestors, and oracle figures were kept. It is noteworthy in relation to the church spaces and their decorations that they were not so dissimilar to the interiors of the cave spaces, which as we have seen were quite ample and decorated with both wall hangings and paintings. The relationship between image and interior space however, was different. Narrative images were often painted on the lateral walls of the church's nave, such as at Turmequé during the period after Diego de Torres was cacique. Most of the surviving mural cycles in native churches were painted toward the end of the sixteenth century and at the beginning of the seventeenth, and they tend to follow a common pattern used throughout the Americas, depicting the most important narrative events of the Gospels, often meant to be viewed in direct relation to the spoken word of the priest.

If we return to the engraving by Diego Valadés depicting a Franciscan preaching to natives, we can acquire an idea of how these images were used. Here, we see the priest as he points to one of a series of paintings that depict the crucial narrative events of the Passion of Christ (plate 2). Such a narrative cycle was commonly depicted in native churches, such as in Sutatausa in Colombia, a Muisca resguardo (also known as reducción) whose church was erected in the sixteenth century (figure 23). It is like any other built in the native communities: a simple single-aisled structure with a narrative cycle depicting the Passion of Christ filling the interior lateral walls. The scenes depicted on the walls were taken from identifiable prints (Lara 1995, 259; Vallín 1998, 85), but in Sutatausa the print image is blown up into colored figures of superhuman size that are contained within an arched recess defined by painted fluted columns, such as can be noted in the scene of Ecce Homo (figure 24).

The illusion of the painted architecture amplifies the physical narrow-

FIGURE 22 Detail of processional cross, "Este Estandarte iso el Casique Don Alonso 550," ca. 1550–53, Pasca Cundinamarca. Silver. Courtesy of Jorge Mario Munera.

ness of the nave and at the same time it integrates the Gospel narrative into the actual space of the practicants. The viewer understands, at some level, that the overlapping of figures, the reduction in size of figures as they appear higher in the picture plane, the convergence of orthogonal lines and the foreshortening of anatomical elements all work together to create an illusionistic space in which the critical mythic events of the Gospels occur. Pictorial conventions become transparent so that these events detach themselves from the supernatural and appear in a knowable place. "God become man" turns into an experiential reality for the catechumen when the Word is seen (in murals) and spoken (in sermons). That is, many sermons written in native languages were meant to reinforce catechetical teachings (Durston 2007), and images made the story and its lesson visible. Valadés's engraving emphasizes this performative relationship. The straightforward descriptive scene unfolds within a church as a Franciscan friar stands above the congregation in a pulpit, simultaneously speaking and pointing toward the narrative scene of Christ carrying the cross. We are given to understand that this visual demonstration is taking place within the context of a sermon rather than a moment of catechetical instruction. Catechetical instruction through

FIGURE 23 Nave, looking toward the altar of the Church of San Juan Bautista, artist unknown, ca. 1620, Sutatausa, Cundinamarca.

FIGURE 24 Ecce Homo, right nave mural of the Church of San Juan Bautista, artist unknown, ca. 1620, Sutatausa, Cundinamarca.

FIGURE 25
Allegorical image
of monastic com-
pound in the New
World, Diego
Valadés, *Rhetorica
christiana* (Perugia,
1579). Engraving.

images is depicted in a different type of engraving created by Valadés (figure 25). Here, he anticipates by thirty years Covarrubias's emblematic image discussed at the beginning of this chapter. Valadés combines the genre of allegory and portrait to portray the Franciscan evangelical mission in New Spain. One sees an imagined enclosed space, a kind of walled garden in the center of which are represented the Holy Scriptures in the form of a great Renaissance cathedral being born on a litter by Martín de Valencia and the original twelve Franciscans who came to New Spain to spread the Gospels. These sixteenth-century monks are led by Saint Francis himself, who bears both poles of the front end of the litter while holding aloft a cross in his left hand. God the Father sits above the cupola, the author of the World. The twelve men bear the weight of Universal History on their shoulders as they bring it to the heathens of America. In the upper left, a Franciscan stands, pointing, before a painting of the Creation, as a group of natives sits before him. This is not an allegorical scene but a descriptive one, because it depicts the actual practice of instruction with different types of images. The Franciscan is identified by name, Pedro de Gante—or Peter of Ghent—instrumental in teaching the native elite how to paint and who created a rebuslike set of figures for use in the instruction of natives in Church prayers and doctrine. On the right side, another unidentified Franciscan points to a painting of the creation of the World. The four corners of the atrium are each marked by a domed structure in which instruction is given to men and women. They also recall the four chapels, or posas, that were built for native churches throughout the Americas, including in Sutatausa.

What is significant about the Sutatausa mural in this regard, is that the last part of the narrative cycle, Christ's crucifixion, has been covered over by a different mural that depicts the second coming of Christ and the portraits of caciques, presumably the patrons of the new mural. Christ appears seated on a rainbow, ready to judge, as the trumpet sounds, while the elect and damned divide into the right and left of him. The gaping maw of hell opens to receive the sinners, among whom is a native holding a painted *totuma*, or gourd vessel, used to drink corn beer, or *chicha* (see figure 30 on p. 138 and plate 7).[39] This Last Judgment image links the narrative events leading to Christ's crucifixion and His tortured death with the promise of either eternal salvation or the frightening possibilities of perpetual torment.[40] This promise and threat are immediately made local and linked to secular traditional authority because in addition to the insertion of the Last Judgment into the narrative cycle of the Christ's Passion, there are the names of Sutatausa's cacique, Don Domingo, and his captains, Don Lázaro, Don Juan Neaetariguia, Don Juan Corula, and Don Andrés (see figure 9 on p. 23).[41] At least one bust portrait of one of the men is still visible below the painted mural text, and there were probably others.

Donor portraits of native elites in conjunction with devotional images were relatively common in the sixteenth and seventeenth centuries in the New Kingdom of Granada. For example, the cacique of Turmequé, Diego de Torres and his wife are reported to be both depicted as donors wearing indigenous dress in the context of the image of the Virgin of the Rosary (Fajardo de Rueda 1999, 80). Donor portraits were not only commissioned by native political elite; they were also patronized by those natives who moved aggressively into the urban society of the New Kingdom of Granada. For example, in 1633 Luis Ximénez, "yndio ladino y criollo" of Bogotá, drew up his will, a document that reveals him to have been a very wealthy individual. He commended his soul to God and asked that his body be buried in his parish church of Our Lady of the Snows (Nuestra Señora de las Nieves, one of the predominantly native quarters of the city). He owned a number of different religious paintings and prints, as well as two small sculptures, one of San Antonio and the other of Santa Bárbara. Most of his belongings were to be sold to pay for his funeral, to pay debts, and to leave to his niece and his sister. One painting was to accompany him in death, however. This was "a canvas painting of Our Lady of the Rosary in which is painted the portrait of myself and my wife" (AGN/B 1633g, 67r–v).[42] He desired that on account of his devotion to the Virgin of the Rosary, the painting be placed in his parish church on the altar of Santa Bárbara, before which he was to be buried alongside his mother. Like the donor portraits in the murals of Sutatausa that were inserted into the already established iconographic program of the Stations of Cross, the devotional image of the Virgin of the Rosary with the donor portraits of Luis Ximénez and his wife, Felipa de Costilla yndia criolla, was inserted into the program of the altar. However, in this case, we find a very important transformational process in which a painting with donor portraits, created for their private piety, moved from the interior space of individual devotion to the public space of corporate worship, and this transformation occurs within the transition from life to death of the patrons.

In other paintings, the patrons are already inserted into the narrative content of the composition in anticipation of their death. For example, in 1656 the Confraternity of All Souls in the town of Cómbita in the province of Tunja commissioned the artist Gaspar de Figueroa to create a painting for their chapel (plate 3).[43] An inventory entry by Luis Cortés de Mesa describes the commission as "a painting of the souls of San Nicolás de Tolentino and the miracle of his descent into purgatory to act on behalf of his friend Fray Peregrino; prayers of devotion to San Nicolás are received during the mass for the week of All Souls, the painting by the hand of Gaspar de Figueroa, cost eight pesos."[44] The devotion of this confraternity to San Nicolás de Tolentino is logical, in that San Nicolás is an Italian thirteenth-century saint whose visions included seeing the souls in purgatory and he is considered their patron saint. He was petitioned on behalf of the recently dead and of those in purgatory, and a Latin text implores him to pray for the confraternity: ("ORAPRONIBISSANENICOLA"). The painting is, in fact, much more complex than Cortés de Mesa describes, and is composed of three distinct but related elements. In the middle ground on the right side of the canvas, one sees the members of the native Confraternity of All Souls in procession along with their cacique, Don Pedro Tabaco, and his wife. They surround San Nicolás, identifiable by his black Augustinian habit, who holds a silver paten and chalice, while a sacristan holds a censor and waves it over the paten. Two clerics, perhaps Augustinians, hold large candles, and a female figure wearing a native manta stares out at the viewer. It is her figure that draws attention both to the presence of the donors and the fact that they are of the native elite. Moreover, this part of the composition relates the local ritual activities of the confraternity with the subject of their devotion.

The foreground and background images bring the specificity of the patronage into the more universal elements of Christian doctrine: transubstantiation and the harrowing of souls in purgatory, essential parts of the catechetical teaching. In the background, one sees souls in purgatory who look upward to where God the Father appears with outstretched arms while Mary prays on their behalf. Ropes extend from the hands of two angels as they give a "life line" to the souls that move out of purgatory and into the celestial presence of God. In the foreground, a very different theme appears: the Mass of Saint Gregory. This is a rather common pictorial theme in the Americas, often directed toward indigenous communities, as it visually demonstrates the mystery of transubstantiation through Christ's appearance on the Altar as the critical words of the mass are said.[45] The conflation of this theme with that of the rescue of souls from purgatory is a post-Tridentine phenomenon. Saint Gregory is said to have taught that prayer hastens the release of the soul from purgatory. Jacobus de Voragine's *The Golden Legend* tells of how the saint prayed for the release of Trajan's soul. The souls being released from purgatory that are depicted in the mural therefore demonstrate the effectiveness of prayer; however, prayer is not sufficient in and of itself. The Christian must accept the mysteries of the church, the most important of which is on display in Gregory's celebration of the mass and the transubstantiation.[46]

This painting combines two distinct iconographic themes that are of importance to the native confraternity: the first is the Mass of Saint Gregory and his deliverance of souls from purgatory through prayer, while the second is the Devotion of San Nicolás. The intent and meaning of the conflation of the two themes are made clear by the presence of the devotees/patrons. The point is that varying genres and subgenres could be combined in paintings for native communities that fulfilled their own sociopolitical needs in specific ways. Here, for example, the iconography of Saint Gregory is used to promulgate the indigenous devotion of San Nicolás and to create a focus for the image of the community and its political hierarchy. The emphasis on the mass and the release of souls from purgatory also responds directly to the economy of the church itself, as inscribed in written wills and the purchase of indulgences (Cummins 2011, 221–23). Almost all indigenous testaments ask that some of the possessions be sold or debts collected and the proceeds be used for a mass said and prayers offered on behalf of the deceased. Paintings and altars, such as the one at Cómbita, anticipate the proscribed acts and rituals found in these wills and allow for the author to imagine and articulate the acts that will take place after his or her death. For example, Juan de Quintanilla, yndio ladino from the town of Ramiriquí in the province of Tunja, states in his will of 1617 that he takes as his advocate (*abogada*) "the most serene Queen of the Heavens of the Angels, Mother of God and Our Lady" (la serenisima reina de cielo de los angeles madre de dios y señora nuestra). He then implores that his executors insure his burial in the Church of Our Lady of the Snows, of which he is a parishioner. He requests that the funeral be accompanied by a priest and a sacristan with a tall cross and that mass be sung over the body and that another mass be said by the parish priest for the souls in purgatory all of which is to be paid for by the sale of his possessions (AGN/B 1617a, 42r–v).[47] What is significant about this document is that through the vehicle of the context of an individual's anticipated death, it narrates many of elements present in the painting of Cómbita: Mary as intercessor, mass, priest and sacristan, and finally purgatory.

If we return to the murals at Sutatausa, we find a similar conflation of differing genres. As the congregation sat facing toward the altar and the celebration of the mass, they would see two other native portraits painted on the lowest register of the columns of the *arco toral* (figures 23 above and 26 below). The figures are painted kneeling and facing inward, presumably toward the altar, with their hands clasped in prayer. They are dressed in Spanish blue full-length cloaks, but are identifiable as native elite by their haircut. Above them are two female saints, Santa Catalina on the left and Santa Úrsula on the right, for whom there was presumably a particular devotion in Sutatausa.

Another much more unusual portrait appears on the left side of the nave wall and is juxtaposed with the portrait of the cacique. It is a portrait of a female member of the native elite dressed in a beautifully detailed manta (shawl), holding a rosary between her clasped hands (plate 4). It would seem that these portraits were added at the same time that it was decided to add the Last Judgment scene with the donor portraits and inscriptions. The por-

FIGURE 26
Mural with the
portrait of a
cacique in prayer
at the right base
of the arco toral
of the Church of
San Juan Bautista,
artist unknown,
ca. 1620, Sutatausa,
Cundinamarca.
Courtesy of
Rodolfo Vallín.

trait of the *cacica* clearly shows that it was added after the Passion cycle was created, as she is painted over the bottom half of the painted framing column. These mural portraits of indigenous members in contemporary dress create a distinction between the universal history of Christ's suffering and the temporal political authority of the Muisca community that is, nonetheless, related in a hierarchical system. This is achieved by combining three genres within a comprehensible field of pictorial representation: that of the didactic Passion cycle, the apocalyptic scene of the Last Judgment, and the portrait. Of course, donor portraits are a common feature in Western religious painting, both in Europe and in the rest of the world. Here, however, one sees distinctions and differences marked through the bodies as they are displayed on the walls of this church. What is most characteristic is the attention given to the *manta* worn by the cacica (plate 5). The painted pattern of the native garment is clearly copied from observed reality.[48] It is also the only native object worn by any of the three figures.

Mantas begin to appear in indigenous wills as valued objects around the same time as this painting was executed. For example, the 1567 will of Juana, "india ladina cristiana," lists several mantas, including one from Portugal and still another one described as "una manta pintada de pincel" (a brush-painted manta; AGN/B 1567, 202r). The black linear abstract design of the cacica's manta in the portrait seems to correspond to this description. The 1630 testament of Beatriz, india of Chipaque (AGN/B 1630a, 47v), asks that her goods be sold to say prayers for her soul. The first object listed is "a painted manta," followed by the listing of a second one. As we have seen, Muisca textiles held more than a utilitarian place in that culture, a topic we will return to in more detail in chapter 6. Here, the presence of the cacica wearing a manta that is so highly detailed in its painted geometric design inserts the presence of Muisca representational value into the overall scheme of the murals. We are not arguing that there is any kind of subversive quality to this insertion of local value. Just the opposite: the high representational attention to the manta and its woven pattern in the portrait integrates local values of representation within the greater scheme of Christian representation. Here, whatever meanings the design on the manta might have within the context of an actual shawl that was woven and worn in the community are recontextualized within a naturalistic portrayal of an elite native woman performing the rosary. The viewer therefore can easily miss the fact that the design on the manta does not participate in the system of representation that depicts it.

The series of narrative mural and canvas paintings that depict the Passion in Sutatausa, Turmequé, and other Muisca towns are didactic, as they naturalize the native's participation within the system of Christian representation and belief. Their narrative function and pictorial conventions are intended to produce a clear and unambiguous representation of biblical truth. What the figures represented was based on the concept of likeness. The devotional images, such as the one commissioned by the confraternity in Cómbita, with donor portraits of the native elite, participate in the same structure of realistic imagery where imagination is not consciously called upon by the image to interpret what is visually presented.

The underlying concept of this type of pictorial representation is different from the murals painted in the Spanish colonial center of Tunja. In the murals painted during the late sixteenth century and early seventeenth in the houses of Juan de Castellanos and Juan de Vargas, one sees a complex set of allegorical images that combine classical motives, such as representations of Hercules and other classical deities with Christian symbols such as the paschal lamb and holy names, all derived from prints. The relationship among the various pictorial elements is not based on a narrative composition, but on a set of interlocking framing designs based on grotesque patterns (Sebastián López 1985 1992, 1995; Vallín 1998, 93–116). That is, very different genres of mural images were being created simultaneously within an interconnected area (the resguardos of Turmequé and Cómbita were subject to Tunja). This suggests that the intended audience was what dictated the kind of genre presented.

We know that churches such as the one in Sutatausa were used as places for indoctrination, liturgy, and corporeal punishment. Diego de Córdova Salinas (1957 [1651], 1060–61) recounts how one of his Franciscan brothers taught catechism to the natives in the area of Bogotá. He tells how the children were brought to the church every day, where they repeated out loud the principles of church doctrine. Moreover, on Sundays and feast days the entire community, whether they were Christians or not, were made to enter the church and do the same as the children. Then, those who were not yet Christian were required to leave, and mass was said for the faithful. After mass, the entire community was called together and the priests would take roll and review part of the Gospels and explain the need for the sacraments. Finally, the native community would repeat the Christian doctrine that had been taught to them. If anyone was absent without a legitimate reason, the priest whipped them on the back and fined them to pay to the adornment of the church.[49] In the end, doctrine came to be backed by the punishment of inflicted pain. There are many drawings in Guaman Poma de Ayala's manuscript in which Andeans are whipped by priests as well as by secular authorities. One drawing in particular depicts a priest whipping a six-year-old child attending indoctrination.[50]

The disciplinary aspect of the mural paintings in Sutatausa, Turmequé, and other Muisca towns may not seem so immediate, but its potential can perhaps be better understood through a description of similar paintings used in the conversion of slaves in coastal Colombia. The images surely had a different set of meanings in relation to their audience despite the same doctrinal aims. The description appears in the seventeenth-century biography of Pedro Claver written on the occasion of his canonization. Claver was a Jesuit who, in the latter part of his life, signed his name in Latin as "Petrus Claver, aethiopum semper servus" (Pedro Claver, eternal servant to the Ethiopian race), and was eventually canonized, becoming the "patron saint of slaves." Born in Spain, he entered the Jesuit order as a novitiate in 1602. He came to the New Kingdom of Granada in 1610, going on to study in Tunja and Fontibón. In Fontibón, he would have participated in the religious fervor of the community where

> coming to the church eight children of the community, dressed in very beautiful costume climbed upon a large platform and began to dance and sing to an organ to the appreciation of all, causing the entire city to shout the praises of the Jesuit Fathers not only for the great care they had shown teaching the Indians the Gospels and the law of God, but also teaching them vocal and instrumental music." (AGCG/R 1611–12, 73r)[51]

This description of a highly organized Christian ritual celebration demonstrates the Jesuit use of the arts (here, music and theater) in relation to the teaching of the communities' children as a means to conversion. More important, Claver came to understand the values of these procedures. He also would have visited the other Muisca settlements around Bogotá and Tunja; in resguardos such as Sutatausa, Quiqui, and Suesca he would have seen the doctrinal paintings and murals, and understood the role they had in catechetical instruction.

Claver did not stay in the cool highlands of Cundinamarca, but returned to Cartagena de Indias, where he had first landed. This was a great port for all kinds of traffic, where the emeralds, gold, and silver of the New Kingdom of Granada were loaded onto ships bound for Seville. Before this new world wealth could be loaded, the cargoes of the newly arrived merchants were taken off the ships and sold, the most consistent and valuable being the slaves from Africa. It was here in Cartagena that Claver found his mission, tending to the men, women, and children who were to be submitted to a life of perpetual misery in the Americas. With Christian charity, the slaves were first quickly placed before the image of Christ's suffering and presented with the threat of their own eternal damnation in addition to their worldly one. Their thoughts upon first seeing the tortured body of a man who looked like the Spanish masters themselves can only be imagined. What kind of living hell could this be? Although there is no record of these first impressions, we do have a most vivid description of the intended use of such paintings. It is found in the 1666 hagiography of Claver himself. The author, José Fernández, describes how the Jesuit set up a temporary altar on a patio for the newly arrived slaves. On it he placed a painting of the crucified Christ, which depicted most graphically all of his bloody wounds, and proceeded to baptize slaves before it.[52] Portraits of popes, cardinals, and kings were placed around the altar and thereby both authorized the procedure and joined in acknowledging and worshipping the mercy of the crucified Christ, whose blood was shed for all mankind. In other words, the paintings created an entire world of celestial and worldly hierarchy into which the newly baptized slaves entered. Just in case the necessity of this theater was misunderstood, however, part of the painting of the crucified Christ showed a neatly dressed African, a figure that represented those who had received baptism and God's blessing. Other, fiercer figures also appeared, representing those Africans who had refused God's mercy. In addition to their rough appearance, they were shown among monstrous beings with horrible open maws in which they were ensnared. According to the author of this description, these paintings, once seen by the Africans, were worth much more than any words of persuasion, as they created in slaves the fear of eternal damnation, the desire to flee from it and to accept the divine blood of the Sacrament (Fernández 1666, 140–41).[53]

In the frontispiece of this hagiography, we see the figure of Claver looming before two African slaves, swarms of tropical bugs around him (figure 27). Scale here clearly conjures up the moral and spiritual authority of Claver, just as the portraits of the kings, cardinals, and popes conveyed the hierarchy of terrestrial authority before the newly arrived slaves. The tonsured three-quarter figure of Claver is nearly twice the size of the two mature African slaves who look up and toward Claver just as they would toward the portraits, while Claver is turned toward the viewer/reader. He is depicted with individualized features that are clearly intended to be read as a lifelike portrait of the saint. The features of the two Africans are more generic and are to be read not as individual portraits of specific individuals, but as representatives of all Africans to whom Claver ministered.

The frontispiece lays out very economically how the protagonists will appear in the following several-hundred pages. No slave is ever given a name in the narrative of Claver's hagiography; rather, it is their bodies that are all important. This is because after their forced baptism, the slaves were sold at auction and often beaten and worked unmercifully, and it was here that Claver found the opportunity to perform his acts of charity and saintliness. We quote just two of a number of passages: "The pigsties in which the Negroes lived were for Our Father Claver gardens, their wounds flowers, their streaming sores were his fountains of sweetness, the odiferous vapors of wounds were sweet smells of delicate perfume [to him]" (Fernández 1666,

FIGURE 27
Portrait of
Pedro Claver,
Marcus Orozco,
frontispiece of
José Fernández,
*Apostólica, y
penitente vida
de el V.P. Pedro
Claver, de la
Compañía de
Jesús. Sacada
principalmente
de informaciones
jurídicas hechas
ante el Ordinario
de la Ciudad de
Cartagena de las
Indias . . .* (Zara-
goza: Diego
Dormer, 1666).
Engraving.

200–201).⁵⁴ These are not just metaphors for how Claver attended the slaves.
Claver's sanctity required the bodies of the slaves in the conditions in which
he found them, to demonstrate his true feelings. As such, he is described as
placing his mouth on the wounds of the unfortunate sick slaves and with his
tongue cleaning their wounds, most often of those who had leprosy. While
others, such as Saint Catherine of Siena and Saint Francis Xavier, occasionally performed similar pious acts, the number of times that Claver executed
these acts of humility with such effect on the lowly beings was something
to be greatly admired, according to his hagiographer. The details of Claver's
self-mortification in the wounds and sores of slaves are so excessive in this
narrative that we need not repeat the details. However, they find a counterpart in the description of the paintings and prints that Claver continually
placed before the slaves to preach of God's violence at the Last Judgment.

What is most telling of all is that the body of the slave is completely objectified, the slave bears no name in the narrative, and is never described as being more than "a Negro of so-and-so." That is, the slave's body is the site of desire that begets a portrait, here, the portrait of Claver.

Native communities are, of course, different from slave communities, but the underlying intent of the doctrinal images is the same: the bending of one's will to the authority of both the state and the church. For the natives, this use of images to create compliance came to be acknowledged through individual devotion and participation in the commissioning and maintenance of images both privately and within churches. Here, the distinction among religious genres is not necessarily clear, in that images can elicit prayers of petition and veneration, and can enter into the unconscious and reappear in visions and dreams, many of which place the dreamer in the presence of the divine in a wondrous sensation. The dreamers often recount their visions within the pictorial terms of local traditions. In some cases, the distinctions outlined above dissolve into nightmares.

There is a great deal of evidence that natives quickly entered into the purchase and commission of images for their own private devotions in their homes. For example, Francisco Texar writes in his 1633 will that when he married his wife, Inés Cosillo, they were quite poor, but that he eventually acquired a tile-making workshop. He proceeds to list a number of expensive items, including a painting of Saint Francis, as well as two large framed prints (AGN/B 1633e, 83r).[55] The cacique of Machetá states in his 1633 will that he owned a canvas painting of San Juan and a sculpture of Saint Lucy, for which he paid fifty pesos, which he gives to the church. He also states that he had two other canvas paintings, one of Christ and the other of Mary (AGN/B 1633a). In the same year, Ana de Coro, india ladina criolla, declared that she had commissioned Gaspar de Figueroa to paint the image of Our Lady of Mercy, for which she paid forty *patacones*. The painting was placed in the Church of Santa Bárbara in the parish of Santa Lucía de Jesús Nazareno in Santafé, where she was a sister in the confraternity of the Christ Child. It was hung on the altar, flush with the arco toral on the right, or Gospel side, of the church. Ana intended the image to increase the cult of the Virgin, for which she had a personal devotion. She therefore commissioned a work that was one of the earliest by a painter who would come to be one of the most prominent artists of Santafé, and who twenty-three years later, painted the devotional painting in Cómbita. She wished to be buried before the altar and painting, and she added the stipulation that the painting be kept in the church and on the altar forever, because she had given it so that mass for that devotion could be said (AGN/B 1630b, 79r).[56] Devotional paintings were not only placed in churches by individuals. Many individuals also kept paintings in their homes. Moreover, these private devotional paintings often referred to local miraculous images, such as the miraculous painting of Chiquinquirá.[57]

Miraculous images, such as the Virgin of Chiquinquirá, and their copies provided a genre of images that consoled by providing a physical site and visual manifestation for the living, whose immortal souls were otherwise threatened by other genres of religious images.[58] The latter images demonstrate in the most vivid terms the everlasting consequences of evil and sin (the Last Judgment, the Torment of Souls, the Devil). The fear of demonic struggle entered the unconscious as well as conscious life of native peoples throughout the Americas. Dreams and nightmares were imagined through the images that were seen in churches and the homes of the faithful (Cummins 1998a). In many cases, demonic visions were combated by the creation of other, either imagined or real images. For example, in 1600, a member of the town of Suesca had become exhausted by the continuous horrific and frightful visions that the devil beset upon him as a consequence of having accepted the tenets of the Christian faith. He prayed the rosary each day, a ritual object and act that freed him from these terrible apparitions. To ensure the safety of his house against these apparitions, he painted dozens of different colored crosses on the walls. In the nearby town of Chipazaque, a very agitated and pale member of the community came to confess and tell the priest, Fray Ángelo Serafino, of his nocturnal battles with the devil. The devil appeared to him at midnight as he sat chewing coca leaves. It appeared in the form of a ram, with long curved and disproportionate horns, and a body of wool ("cuerpo de lana"). This horrific vision seems to combine both traditional Christian images of the devil (ram and horns) with the idolatrous forms of Muisca images found in caves by the Spanish (cuerpo de lana). When Serafino called out the name of Jesus, the devil disappeared, only to return later to carry out his threats. The frightened man made a cross of the first sticks he could find and put them at the entrance of his house. The devil reappeared, first appealing to their friendship to open the door. The man replied that he did not want to be friends, and so the devil began to rant and rave, telling him to remove the accursed cross. Finally, after making great threats, he disappeared in a great clap of thunderous noise (Meléndez 1681, 1,

425–26).[59] The crosses used here are not like the processional crosses of liturgical ritual, such as the one commissioned by cacique Alonso of Pasca (figure 22). These painted crosses are very different: they perform a defense against the terrifying images conjured up in the imaginations of the faithful. They function in a real and direct way, just as miraculous images can, but here they are apotropaic, by what they represent, defending against the demonic visions created by the didactic paintings and sermons discussed above.

Genre and Native Media

Although the transmission of European visual literacy meant introducing image theory based upon Christian doctrine, it meant as well the European techniques of sculpting and painting. As we have mentioned, workshops based in different monastic communities, such as that of San Francisco in Quito, were established to train native artists to perform the tasks of visual production, just as they learned music making and instrument making. These monastic schools were most productive in the sixteenth century; however, by the seventeenth century, natives, like all other residents who sought a career in the arts, apprenticed themselves to established masters who had their own workshops. As at Sutatausa, the models of both canvas and mural paintings were prints that were imported from Flanders.[60] At the same time native artistic techniques were turned to producing new images for colonial needs. The featherwork of Mexico is perhaps the best known. New forms and iconography were adapted to this spectacular technique, and these objects immediately became appreciated both in Mexico and in Europe. Hernán Cortés, for example, writes to Charles V of his early encounter with Moctezuma: He "gave many of the these things (Aztec gold silver and featherworks) to your Majesty, and also other things that he had made from drawings I gave him, such as holy images and crucifixes" (Cortés 1986 [1520], 101–10). The desire for these new objects was almost immediate. Felipe de Guevara writes in his *Comentarios de la pintura* that the Mexicans had added something new and rare to the art of painting: painting with bird feathers (1788 [1560], 235). Guevara's remarks must be understood in the context of his assessment of European painting; they represented the high esteem that feather painting immediately garnered. In fact, liturgical objects and devotional images made of Mexican featherwork were spread all over the world as part of Spanish and Portuguese expansion. For example, already in 1548,

Mencía de Mendoza, one of the wealthiest women in Spain and cousin of Antonio de Mendoza, viceroy of New Spain, listed in the inventory of the goods she possessed, a Mexican feather painting of Saint Jerome and another of Mary Magdalene, along with paintings by Hieronymus Bosch and works of other notable northern and southern artists. Also listed in Mencía's inventory are two miters, both of which depicted in feathers the image of God the Father on one side and the Crucifixion and the instruments of the Passion on the other. One of them was decorated with the coat of arms of the Mendozas (AP/B 1548, 11r–v). As we shall see in this chapter and in chapter 4, one of the pictorial elements that is consistently integrated into the repertoire of native artists is the coat of arms, both those of Spaniards and of the native elite. It is a shared symbolic language that marks the hierarchy of class and authority.

The emergence of native media combined with new forms and objects (i.e., Christian images executed in featherwork) created things of wonder and brilliance that could manifest at the intersection of various native and European aesthetic and ideological positions (Russo 2002, 227–28). Such new objects could then be redeployed for an expanding Christian world. Hence, we find a feather painting of Ecce Homo that had come from New Spain in an inventory of the things that Philip II gave to the Jesuits to take to Africa for their evangelical mission to Monomotapa (Mozambique).[61]

Native artists could deploy various European genres differently, as the miters owned by Mencía de Mendoza suggest. In fact, a series of other miters that can be found in church treasuries and museum collections in Italy and other European countries were produced only slightly later and presumably in Michoacán. Indeed, the area of Michoacán became a locus of continuing native production of featherwork objects that had a broad appeal in Mexico, the Americas, and Europe.[62] This becomes very clear if we read the mid-seventeenth-century correspondence between Alexandro Favián in Mexico and Athanasius Kircher in Rome, in which they discuss a series of feather paintings to be sent to Rome, including one made for Pope Alexander VII and another, with the image of the Virgin of the Immaculate Conception, for his nephew, Cardinal Chisi. These religious feather paintings, commissioned and sent by Favián, are simply a continuation of a long-standing tradition first established by Cortés. However, the most unusual feather painting is the portrait *Emperor Leopoldo Ignacio* (1640–1705), made in Michoacán at tremendous cost.[63] The image was taken from a print, in which the portrait of Leopold was placed within the breast of the imperial Hapsburg eagle. The coat of arms of the seven electors were placed around the central motif.

The letter accompanying the portrait, and addressed to the emperor himself, states:

> My Letter for his Royal Imperial Majesty, it is left open for you, Reverend Father, so that you may read it before sending it along [to His Majesty, which details] with great marvel and astonishment the human artistry that had never before been created in this land, [and along with this letter] the portrait in feathers of which I have written various times before; a thing of great astonishment, surprise, and appreciation. There is no language in which to say, or to sing, or to exaggerate, the perfection and beauty with which those barbarians created a work of such comeliness and such piety, thanks to the infinite knowledge of God, who desired to give them His grace, which cannot simply exist in all other nations of the world . . . to create such an admirable wonder, that I do not believe another could have been made without the influence of the Majesty of God.
>
> The beauty and quality with which this painting was made, is confirmed by everyone in Michoacán, and they say that they have never before seen an object that would be so admirable and so premiere. . . . In the house of Pedroza y Zuniga, priest of the city of Pátzcuaro, in whose presence this object was made, ten master painters were brought to the task and spent over three months working on it. . . . (Remembrance of all that I am sending to Rome . . .) (Osorio Romero 1993, 84–85)[64]

One normally thinks of the genre of royal portrait as being created in and sent from Europe to the colonies in order to establish the presence of imperial authority (see Cañeque 2004 and chapter 5 of this book). Alexandro Favián's gift expresses something else, for as he says, this royal portrait in feathers demonstrates how native artists, even though they might be barbarian, can through the grace of God produce so prodigious a work as the one he sends. Its beauty and workmanship are beyond the capacity of any language to describe or even to sing, and so, it is something that can only be admired and marveled at by the direct experience of sight. Kircher understands Favián's longings and desires, in part because he reads them in the letter accompanying the portrait, addressed to the Holy Roman emperor, but which Favián had left open for him to see. And so, Kircher writes to Favián in return, that the portrait is indeed "a precious gift of feathers that here in Rome is admired by all" (Osorio Romero 1993, 93).[65] It is, in the end, the object seen that creates the marvel because its beauty is almost divine.

In the Andes, feathers were also used in pre-Columbian images; however, woven textiles are most often recorded in indigenous wills as some of the most prized native possessions. In chapters 3 and 6 we will discuss the prominence given to representing the Muisca manta in the portrait of the cacica in the Church of Sutatausa (plate 5), as well as their presence in native wills, along with paintings, prints, and small cult statues. The importance of maintaining traditions through textiles is attested to in the seventeenth-century southern Andes, where Inca *unkus* (tunics) were brought to weavers to be copied. At the same time, master Andean weavers created newly designed large-scale tapestries with Old Testament themes (Phipps, Hecht, and Esteras Martín 2004, 282–86) or armorial designs.[66] In addition, Andean-style unkus were woven to dress cult statues of Christ. In the northern Andes, in addition to textiles, a different type of material found new importance for embellishing all kinds of colonial objects. It is a substance called variously *mopa mopa* or *barniz de Pasto*. Like the featherwork of Mexico, mopa mopa was a pre-Columbian native medium, and the artists who worked it in the colonial period were natives. Both materials came from the lowland jungle areas, but the artists were concentrated in the highlands, where there was a much higher demand for the products. Moreover, both feathers and mopa mopa were used on objects that ranged from purely indigenous forms to purely European ones. Most importantly, however, mopa mopa, like featherwork, was used in such a way that it appears to imitate painting while still exhibiting the particularity of its unusual or exotic material. In the case of featherwork, it is the resplendence of the feathers that is manifest; in the case of mopa mopa, it is its brilliant colors, seemingly held suspended in the surface.[67]

This native material immediately came to the attention of the conquistadores in the northern Andes. The use of this "resin" is mentioned in relation to the history of Hernán Pérez de Quesada's 1541 campaign in the area of San Juan de Pasto, as retold by Lucas Fernández de Piedrahita in 1688. Fernández de Piedrahita interrupts his historical narrative of the conquest to write that his men were clearing a road through the valley called by the natives Mocoa

> and it is the same [place] from where later came the first paintings called Mocoa, that come from the Indies on tobacco boxes, small trunks, and a variety of vessels, [all of which are made in] wood, well esteemed in Europe for the skill with which they are worked now in the town of Pasto, where the creation of this type [of painted object] has passed [and which] is very much fancied by men of good taste. (1973 [1688], 505)[68]

Fernández de Piedrahita's text is similar to Cortés's passage about Mexican featherwork cited earlier, in that the conquistador/chronicler interrupts the drama of the events to express wonder and appreciation for a new artistic medium. Just as the correspondence between Kircher and Favián indicates the continued and widespread appreciation of and desire for Mexican featherwork in Europe, Fernández de Piedrahita makes it clear that objects covered in barniz de Pasto were desired not only in the New Kingdom of Granada, but in Europe as well. The center of mopa mopa production was, and still is today, the city of Pasto. This is similar to Michoacán, which became the center of featherwork production in the sixteenth century and continued that distinction into the nineteenth century. Just as the seventeenth century was a period of expanded featherwork in Mexico, the earliest, finest, and most diverse set of objects covered with barniz de Pasto come from the seventeenth century, but it is clear that the use of this material continued well into the eighteenth and nineteenth centuries (see Codding 2006).

The friar Juan de Serra Santa Gertrudis traveled throughout New Granada between 1756 and 1776. In a chapter entitled "Which Contains the Rare and Marvelous Things That Exist from Almaguer to the Putumayo River" (Contiene las cosas raras y maravillas que hay desde Almaguer hasta el río del Putumayo), he describes his confusion and then, wonderment, when he first encounters objects covered with mopa mopa:

I also saw in the priest's house a cupboard that held a silver plate and also what seemed to me to be the finest chinaware. And admiring that there were in that place such precious plates, I said to him: "Father, the chinaware you have is more valuable than the silver, the transport of a thing so fragile must have been very costly." He began to laugh and then told me: "You are not the first to be deceived, my dear Father. That is not porcelain from China, it is wood and it is varnished with a varnish that gives it this luster. The Indians get it from where you all are headed my dear Fathers, which the seed of a fruit that there is in these hills, and the Indians of Pasto prepare it and with it they varnish the surface of the wood with such artifice that imitates almost exactly the surface of china." I opened the cupboard and until I had it in my hands, I remained convinced that it was china. But taking it and realizing how light it was, I understood that it was varnished wood, because they even cover gourds, wooden cups and spoons in the same way. And [what is incredible] about these varnished things is that as much as you use them and as much as you clean them they never appear old nor lose their shine. The *encharoldos* that are produced in Spain are something akin to this, but this is much more lustrous.[69] (Santa Gertrudis 1956 [ca. 1775], I, 139–40)

Santa Gertrudis, in fact, goes on to visit and describe the places where mopa mopa was harvested.[70] He then continues on to Pasto, where the seeds were taken to be prepared into the "varnish," giving a very detailed account of the technique, which is still used there today to decorate many of the same items that Santa Gertrudis mentions. He writes:

While I was in Pasto, some Indians from Sibundoy came [to the city] and I met them in the plaza. They recognized me and came over to talk. I asked them why they had come and they responded that they had brought the juice and varnish of Condagua. I told them that I would like to see the varnish and they told me that they had already sold it. With this [news], I went with them to the house of the Indians who work the surface of wood with it [mopa mopa]. . . . The nut of the fruit that comes from trees that there are on the hillsides of the river called Condagua. It is a seed, really, that is no larger than an almond. It has a natural color that is somewhere between a yellow and a light green. These seeds are viscous and to make use of them, they chew them as if one were chewing soft wax. They combine all the chewed pieces into medium-sized balls to which they add the color that they desire.

Then, these men commission carpenters to make various pieces from cedar [such as] plates, platters, pitchers, cups, spoons, small pots, common cups, etc. They take the piece and draw a design with a small chisel and where they want the silver and gold to appear, they lay it in. Now prepared, they take a little ball of this varnish, flattening it they form it into a shape with four corners and above the heat of the fire, they pull the sheet of varnish, making it ever thinner until they get it to a thickness of a sheet of paper. They then heat the [wooden] piece and they cover it with the varnish and it immediately adheres to the surface. They immediately draw out the design that they have, next they place the varnish of color that they desire and they also uncover the golden silvered areas. But they [do it quickly] so that it does not get cold, because if it gets chilled, the varnish sticks and there is no way to get it off, and for this reason they always have a candle ready to heat the piece from time to time, and it becomes as lustrous as the ceramics of China. . . . I commissioned several pieces for my own use. (1956 [ca. 1775]: II, 76–77)[71]

What becomes clear in this passage is that by the eighteenth century there continued to be a widespread appreciation for, and trade in, objects decorated with mopa mopa.

Santa Gertrudis's description of how this material was worked is remarkable in its detail and accuracy. In 1995, we witnessed the same process in a small workshop in Pasto. Many of the same kinds of objects were covered using both a gloss- and matte-style mopa mopa. The description by Santa Gertrudis also makes clear that the artisans working with mopa mopa were extremely skilled and precise. Their abilities are clearly seen on extant objects decorated with mopa mopa in collections throughout the world. The designs are complex, combing figural (human, animal, and floral) with geometric patterning. The description of the quick working process implies an assured artistic handling, as the material hardened rapidly, the designs became fast, and they rarely faded.

Santa Gertrudis's description also reveals the continuing wonder that mopa mopa could evoke, something similar to the continuous wonder held by Europeans for Mexican featherwork. What is just as important is that this material transcended the boundaries between Andean and European artistic expression and desire. That is, mopa mopa also began to be used to enhance the surface of Andean wooden ritual vessels, known as *queros*. There are no known Inca queros from any archaeological context that have mopa mopa images, but the use of mopa mopa on queros quickly spread in the colonial period. By the seventeenth century, queros were fully covered with figural images that depict Inca rituals and myths (Cummins 2002a). These Andean objects come from the central Andes but are found as north as Pasto and in the wills of *curacas* (southern Andean hereditary lords). They often depict Inca rituals and myths. However, some of these vessels are covered with floral designs and coats of arms that were either conveyed upon Andean royalty by Spanish authority or were fabricated by the Andean nobility themselves (figures 31 and 32, p. 138).

As Santa Gertrudis notes, the objects decorated with mopa mopa that interested Europeans were primarily utilitarian—such as spoons, cups, and plates—and in this they fall into the same category of things as the Andean quero. One type of object was different: the wooden small writing desks and locked boxes. These objects were often emblazoned with the coats of arms of their owners. One of them has been identified as the desk of Cristóbal Bernardo de Quirós, who was the Bishop of Popayán from 1672 to 1684 (López Pérez 2006). His coat of arms is placed in the center of the interior side of the

FIGURE 28
Portable writing
desk decorated
with *mopa mopa /
barniz de Pasto*
coat of arms, late
1600s, Museo de
Arte Colonial,
Quito.

lid. The escutcheon, outlined in a gold line, contains the two upturned keys and the text "After God the House of Quiros." The coat of arms is set within a field of birds and flowers upon a background of gold and arranged facing toward the center in bilateral symmetry. A similar writing desk is now in the collection of the Museo de la Casa de la Cultura (figure 28 and plate 6). Like the desk of Cristóbal Bernardo de Quirós, a coat of arms (unidentified) appears in the inner side of the lid.

Mopa mopa was also used to decorate the frames of twenty-three oil-on-copper paintings depicting the life of the Virgin. The paintings were created in Flanders and likely in the workshop of Peter Paul Rubens, sometime between 1633 and 1650. Before 1657, they entered the Church of Our Lady of the Flight into Egypt (Nuestra Señora de Egipto) located to the east of the center of Santafé, most probably a donation by the cleric and patron Jerónimo de Guevara y Troya. The paintings were, of course, desired as a focus for the cult of the Virgin. Owing to the locus of their production (Flanders and Ruben's workshop), and the material they were made of (copper), they constituted a costly and prestigious donation (Aguilar 1990). Framing them was understood to be a valuable addition. In fact, frames are often valued more highly than paintings in church and private inventories; hence, the framing of this important series with caved wooden frames. Cut in low relief, a continuous series of flowers are seen from above, so that the four petals open to the viewer. Mopa mopa covers the carved surface with the colors of the Virgin. The golden leaves and red flowers are set on a golden ground. When new, the frames would have been brilliantly colored. The open-petal red flowers probably represented a rose, a symbol of the Virgin herself, just as the blue refers to her cloak.

Mopa mopa was also used to enhance church objects, such as a chest now in the Museo de San Francisco. It bears the inscription "facto en Quito en 1709" and combines flora and fauna designs similar to the images in the two writing desks made some twenty years earlier. But instead of a Spanish coat of arms in the center of the composition, there is a black-and-white disk. Unlike the figures of the animals and vegetation that are formed by solid areas of colors onto which were placed smaller pieces of mopa mopa to create detail, the disk has a linear quality that is more similar to the design of the cacica's mantle in the Sutatausa mural. The outer band is composed of three parallel black lines in a zigzag pattern. This part of the design gives a very kinetic, but controlled geometric quality to this part of the disk. This band encircles the center where a completely different equally abstract design is placed.[72] Here, the line becomes extremely fluid, as if two liquids, black and white, are in the process of being mixed. Together, one sees an extremely dynamic image contained within the disk that seems to derive clearly from an Andean iconography and style. It may represent the solar disk, which could be interpreted as Christian, but the mode and material of expression are New World.

The use of mopa mopa in a variety of forms and iconographies demonstrates phenomena that occurred throughout the Americas. One of the signs of the success of the conversion and civilizing of the natives was the retraining (as well as training) of them to produce Christian images. Be it in feathers, mopa mopa, or something else, objects and images were created by artists whose traditions were rooted in the deep past of their ancestors.

Conclusion

Artistic genres and their expression are an important element that defines some of the difficulties of creating an orthodox visual literacy in the New Kingdom of Granada, as well as throughout the Americas. For example, how one was to distinguish between genres was never really clear. This is something that Covarrubias manifests in his emblem, as we discussed at the beginning of this chapter. However Covarrubias's image was directed to a small, erudite public of common sensibilities and understandings. In the Americas, where there was a need to create a common visual imagination, the distinction between genres was created in part physically, that is, by place and context. For example, miraculous images and visions were kept under the control of the Spanish and creole churches, whereas the devotional images were permitted to occupy native spaces, be it in the church or in indigenous homes.[73] Public processions were one of the spaces where these domains intersected.

In relation to these spatial distinctions, genres operated differently. In general, however, looking at and understanding European images required learning to recognize in the painted image both the illusion of space and the creation of narrative. The act of recognizing and interpreting these visual properties was coupled with doctrinal instruction, so one would not be deceived into believing that the image was divine. There was within the new Christian images both *engaño* (enchantment) and *desengaño* (disenchantment), two positions that had to be held separately but simultaneously. In this sense, genres as they were taught and implemented were a disciplinary act that, as we shall argue, is fundamentally linked to the introduction of alphabetic literacy and creation of a lettered and painted world.

The Spanish colonial social formation, writes Ángel Rama using a stunningly apposite metonym, can be best comprehended as a "lettered city," a baroque edifice dedicated to the civilizing mission, within which architectural, administrative, political, and social practices were consolidated and ordered in relation to an ideology grounded in the primacy of the written word and the power of pens wielded in the service of empire (1996 [1984], 17). The preeminence of letters as a basis for empire filled a number of crucial functions. The administration of a world-wide empire, stretching from the Philippines to South America, could only be accomplished through the creation of far-flung networks of literate communication connecting Madrid to its colonies (ibid., 19; Elliott 1970). The lettered city was also central to the evangelizing project of the church—a textual community created around the holy scriptures—as well as to the intellectual formation of a creole elite (Rama 1996 [1984], 19–20), establishing as it did the absolute ascendancy of the Spanish language and of alphabetic communication over Native American tongues and systems of inscription and legitimizing Spanish for ensuring the spiritual welfare of humanity (Mignolo 1995; Pagden 1982).

Within this system, documents were worth more than simply their contents. They became objects subject to ritual manipulation, operating as symbolic representations of the colonizing project. Patricia Seed (1995) argues that the symbolic primacy of the written word in Spanish

America was unique among the European colonial powers of the time. Unfortunately, Seed makes the mistake of focusing exclusively on the ceremony surrounding the reading of the *requerimiento*, the statement read in Castilian to indigenous populations at the moment of conquest, whose purpose was to absolve Spain of responsibility for the consequences of invasion by reframing conquest as a just war in the service of the introduction of Christianity. Given that the requerimiento represents only a fleeting moment of initial contact and that we have no documentation of its use in the highlands of the New Kingdom of Granada, it is perhaps not the best example of the Spanish fetishization of the written word. However, the requerimiento is but one of a series of ritual acts connected to literacy that were aimed at consolidating the hegemony of the lettered city in the centuries after conquest. The drawing of maps prior to the founding of cities, the ritualized reading of written documents in the course of ceremonies granting possession of plots to individuals, and the ritual manipulation of royal decrees by colonial functionaries are better illustrations of how the continuous performance of literacy begat power in the Spanish colonies.

With literacy operating simultaneously as symbol and as the crystallization of an ideology of domination, the exercise of power was determined by the control of writing by *letrados*—the religious pedagogues and secular jurists entrenched in the upper reaches of the colonial bureaucracy. But even more so, the lettered city was maintained by notaries and their minions, who penned the numerous legal documents that oiled the Spanish bureaucratic machine. The latter were instrumental in the perpetuation of empire, functioning as the "documentary umbilical cord" between the metropolitan center and its colonial possessions (Rama 1996 [1984], 22, 33–34). These midlevel officials were ubiquitous in daily life. They were present at all trials. They certified the authenticity of a broad range of documentation that was written by nonspecialists. They were familiar with the legal formulas necessary for producing acceptable petitions, wills, and contracts. Thus, notaries not only created a bridge between the Crown and its colonial possessions, but also between the colonial administration and its subjects, whether they be aristocratic Spaniards, African slaves, or indigenous caciques.

Native Peoples and the Lettered City

The Spanish empire was characterized by a particular hierarchical character based on language and ancestry—we are loathe to refer to *race* in a colonial context that preceded the advent of "scientific" racial classification in the nineteenth century (Lewis 2003; Poole 1997). Rama (1996 [1984], 31) blames the lettered city for creating a form of colonial diglossia in which two kinds of languages coexisted parallel to one another: an elite, lettered, and rigidly codified discourse on the one hand, and a popular, quotidian, and fluid idiom on the other. Social hierarchy was replicated in a cultural stratification founded in notions of ancestry that divided the colonial administration into two republics, the República de Indios, whose bureaucracy engaged in all administrative and legal procedures relating to the indigenous population, and the República de Españoles, responsible for administering Spaniards, American-born populations of European descent (criollos), Africans, and the various racial admixtures (mestizos, mulattos, etc.) that labored in the service of the Europeans. Written language bound together each of these republics and connected one republic to the other.

In those Spanish American regions that had supported state-level societies before the Spanish invasion, the division between the two republics was explicitly expressed through writing. Intellectuals in the Catholic religious orders charged with converting Native Americans fashioned, in concert with native elites, what would come to be known as classical variants of Quechua and Nahuatl—the languages of the Incas and Aztecs, respectively—discriminating against other native tongues and ensuring the spread of these imperial languages beyond their pre-Columbian boundaries.[1] In their standardized written versions, Quechua and Nahuatl contrasted with the variety of vernaculars spoken at the local level which, in Mesoamerica at least, were employed by local notaries to produce such everyday legal documents as contracts and wills.[2] The creation of a classical written language, based upon the ritual speech of the pre-Columbian state, at once bolstered the power of the colonial indigenous elite and operated as a mechanism for controlling the native nobility within the colonial power structure (Klor de Alva 1989, 146–49): "Classical Nahuatl was clearly a device aimed at facilitating the movement of ideas from one set of discursive formations (Christianity, pre-contact ethics) to another (ethnic subordination, political order)" (ibid., 149).

Indeed, notwithstanding the elegance and significance of Rama's interpretation of Spanish America as a lettered city, we must move beyond his exclusive focus on the República de Españoles and on letrados, to consider the parallel lettered city that developed within the República de Indios and among the scribes and notaries that served them. Alphabetic literacy swiftly became one of the bulwarks of the indigenous elite—the hereditary chiefs (caciques and *cacicas*) and descendants of pre-Columbian nobility—who routinely engaged in the drafting of wills, of petitions, and of contracts with the aid of notaries and scribes. This chapter will inquire into the interplay of Spanish genres of alphabetic expression with native northern Andean genres of oral and spatial expression, focusing on how the Muisca, Nasa, and Pasto colonial nobility adapted Castilian legal writing to their own ends in the construction of a lettered city writ small, of which they formed the apex.[3] In the following pages, we will examine the various Spanish legal genres in which they wrote, the creation of new literate genres by indigenous authors, and in particular, the problems of identifying the native voice in a body of Spanish-language documentation that was not self-consciously transcultural, nor identified as such by its Spanish readers. On the surface, the writings we will be examining do not appear to be culturally heterogeneous in comparison to indigenous literate production in Mesoamerica and Peru, an indication of the northern Andean tendency to downplay alterity that we mentioned in chapter 1. First, however, let us briefly consider how indigenous literacy functioned in Mesoamerica and Peru.

Indigenous Literacy in Mesoamerica and Peru

Much has been written about indigenous vernacular literacy in colonial Mexico, where scribes at the local level drew up thousands of pages of documentation in Maya, Mixtec, Nahuatl, and Zapotec, among other languages, producing a transcultural corpus of documentation that incorporated native forms of address and formal speech, and which in the early colonial period juxtaposed alphabetic and hieroglyphic communication.[4] In the Andes, where pre-Columbian peoples were not alphabetically or hieroglyphically literate, but recorded statistics and narrative in khipu knot records that survived as a parallel literate system well into the postcolonial era (Salomon 2004), the alphabetic literacy introduced by the Spaniards did not encroach upon alternative vernacular recording systems. Hence, alphabetic literacy was almost entirely in the Spanish language, with the few exceptions of a handful of Quechua notarial documents and letters (Durston 2007; Mannheim 1991, 143–44), and mythic narratives written for use in the process of extirpation of native religion (Salomon and Urioste 1991). This holds as much for administrative documents, as for the well-known histories authored by native Andeans such as Inca Garcilaso de la Vega (1723 [1609]), Felipe Guaman Poma de Ayala (1980 [1616]), and Joan de Santacruz Pachacuti Yamqui (1993 [1613]), all of whom wrote in Castilian; in fact, Guaman Poma depicts a native scribe writing a document in Spanish—a will, to be precise, as we described in the previous chapter (Guaman Poma 1980 [1616], 814).[5]

The indigenous alphabetic literacy of Mesoamerica and Peru is transcultural in nature, merging native oral genres of formal speech and historical narration with Spanish literary genres to produce uniquely colonial literate discourses that are highly heterogeneous in nature. William Hanks (2000, 134–35) has called them "boundary works," suggesting that they operate simultaneously according to several sets of conventions originating in Europe and in native America:

> Official Maya is a "threshold" genre. . . . Works within this category were created to be doubly interpretable. On the one hand, the texts fit nicely into contemporary Spanish categories such as *carta* (letter), *información de derecho* (statement of rights), and *concierto* (agreement). Such a fit was necessary in order that the works be "regular," translatable, and intelligible to their Spanish addresses. But native conventions also laid claim over official Maya in at least some of its features, and lead to another reading. For instance, the texts are written in Maya, showing indigenous forms of address, along with prose and verse styles common to other kinds of native discourse. It is also typical of official Maya works that they arise as part of an intertextual series of two or more versions of what seems to be a single template. (2000, 159)

These Maya texts are susceptible to a close linguistic analysis that is virtually impossible in the Andean documentation, where Spanish predominates. In contrast to Mesoamerica, where native oral and literate forms mingled with the Roman alphabet on the written page to create new genres of alphabetic expression, native Peruvians compartmentalized their discourse into discrete documents. Colonial indigenous bureaucrats kept statistical data on khipus and also recorded them in Spanish-language documents, by order of their European overlords (Espinoza Soriano 1960, 223–24); southern Andean caciques' inventories of possessions were simultaneously cataloged on paper and in khipus (del Río 1990, 107). Orality in Andean languages was confined to the nonalphabetic channel, while indigenous testimony in alphabetic documents was either provided in Castilian or translated by an interpreter. Spanish discourse genres were isolated from Andean ones to a much greater extent than in Mexico.[6] In the two regions, indigenous expression achieved autonomy relative to the Spanish colonial administration via radically distinct channels.

The Native Voice in the Northern Andes

In the northern Andean documentation, compared to Mesoamerica and the southern Andes, we have exceedingly more limited access to the indigenous discursive contexts in which inscription occurred. While there are references to khipu use in modern indigenous Colombia, such artifacts were not preserved as they are for the southern Andes and their use has disappeared in the past fifty years, denying us access to parallel channels of inscription that might have existed in the colonial period.[7] Muisca and Pasto disappeared as living languages in the nineteenth century and in the case of Pasto, the colonial-era grammars and dictionaries ordered by church authorities (Burgos Guevara 1995, 473) have not been located in the documentary record, although they have been for the Muisca language (Anonymous 1987 [c.1607–20]). Thus, we have no entry into the oral genres that undoubtedly nourished native authors of the Spanish-language Muisca and Pasto documents that will form the core of archival material used here. Even if we wanted to excavate the multiple intertextual layers in the northern Andean documentation, we would be denied that privilege.

Most of the Spanish-language documents authored by native peoples were collaborative ventures in which Spanish notaries recorded native dictation or testimony, frequently passing through the additional filter of a mestizo interpreter. The palimpsestic nature of these documents, which routinely incorporate supporting documentation into the record, was seasoned by the practice of copying older briefs into legal records a century or more after they were written, thus passing into posterity numerous misreadings of the documentary record. Furthermore, *protectores de naturales*, Crown-appointed functionaries who served as defense attorneys for indigenous litigants and as intermediaries between the court and native communities, had a hand in the production of legal papers (Bonnett 1992). There is no single author, nor a single cultural or temporal identity of these writings, to which we might appeal in an effort to disentwine a colonial discursive product (Thurner 1997, 14). Instead, what we have to work with is a series of "entangled objects" (Thomas 1991), in which the voices of numerous cultural actors and of different historical periods are inextricably intertwined.

It would be a mistake to assume that the scribes of the Spanish colonial administration, who participated in the preparation of these documents, perceived literacy in the same functional way as we do today. This important fact muddies the waters, blurring what is "indigenous" and what is "European" in these papers. Until the end of the sixteenth century, the relationship between orality, literacy, and object was different from what we perceive today. Colonial-era Spanish writing—as was the case throughout Europe at the time—was fundamentally oral in nature, replicating in space the temporal dimension of oral communication through a refusal to appropriate the economy of expression that characterizes written communication. In other words, colonial literacy can be understood in part as oral communication set down in writing or as ritual acts described in detail, over and over again.[8]

The clearest examples of the orality of colonial Spanish writing are the numerous documents that record the process by which aboriginal communities were divested of their lands (ANE/Q 1685, 1693). These procedures were especially ubiquitous for the towns around the administrative center of Pasto, where the native Quillacinga population fell precipitously during the first half-century of conquest (Padilla, López Arellano, and González 1977, 40–41), leaving the Spanish with an opening for reassigning ownership of what they took to be underutilized lands. In order that these plots be freed for public auction, public announcement by a town crier was necessary. Frequently, the *pregonero*, as he was called in Spanish, was obliged to repeat his message some thirty times; his words—or a translation into Spanish of them—are reproduced, verbatim, as thirty identical sentences in the documentary record.[9]

Just as orality is reproduced in writing in colonial documents, ritual practice is relived through its inclusion in the legal record. Once again, Spanish scribes neglected the economy of expression that writing could afford. Instead of brief mentions of certain rituals that took place at designated sites with designated participants, the rituals are described in painstaking detail, over and over again. The nature of such ceremony was dictated in legal manuals. In a mid-sixteenth-century manual, for example, Gabriel de Monterroso y Alvarado (1609 [1563], 145r) specifies the language that legalized the efficacy of ritual, once it was inscribed on paper:

> By virtue of the aforementioned order, so-and-so [*fulano*] constable placed so-and-so in possession, or the judge in his person, taking him by the hand he placed him in the inheritance, or the house, and took him around it, and closed the doors (in the case of a house) and threw out of

it those who were inside, and took the keys of the house, and placed them in the hands of so-and-so as its tenant, all of which was done as a sign of possession.[10]

The northern Andean documentary record contains numerous examples of such strictures, affording not only a window into the relationship between ritual and writing, but also the creative ways in which such guiding principles were adapted to diverse situations:

> On the ninth day of the month of October of sixteen hundred and forty seven, having read the ruling of General Don Antonio de Santillana y Oyos at the request of Don Marcos Taques, governor of the indios of the town of Tulcán, I, Estéban Berdugo, resident in said town, granted possession to the aforementioned Don Marcos Taques. By virtue of the ruling entrusted to me I took Don Marcos Taques by the hand [and] gave him possession to the lands called Chunes and the hill of Chucanbut, as far as the bridge that descends to the river, following the high road until it reaches the town on the left-hand side reaching the hill of Tugteta and the hill of Tainguaput which divides the jurisdiction from [that of] Guaca. Uprooting some small plants and grass, Don Marcos Taques took possession of the aforementioned lands without any contradiction and I gave it to him by law in the name of Your Majesty in the presence of the Reverend Father Fr. Joseph de Rribera, who is the priest and vicar of the town and in the presence of Sergeant Bernardo Carballo and of Alonso Baes and Don Melchor G. Tulcanaza, *alcalde ordinario* of the town. In [affirmation of its] truth I sign my name. (ANE/Q 1647, 7v)[11]

Such statements were repeated, over and over, each time a possession to a plot was ceded from one disputant to another, eventually becoming part of the oral tradition of twentieth-century Pasto communities (Rappaport 1994, 102).

Written documents interacted with native forms of memory in an intertextual relationship. The territorial referents inscribed in the documentation of Don Marcos Taques's possession ceremony were also inscribed directly onto the territory. In some cases, houses and chapels were erected specifically to lay claim to a plot (ANE/Q 1656, 13v–14r; 1669, 17v–18r) and crosses were placed as boundary markers (ANE/Q 1767, 11r).[12] Notwithstanding these European forms of acknowledging boundaries, native forms of marking territory, such as the digging of *zanjas*, or boundary ditches, were engaged in by native and Spaniard alike (Caillavet 2000, 127–28; ANE/Q 1656, 10r–v, 19r). Pastos frequently called these ditches "ancient" or pertaining to *infieles*—"infidels" of pre-Columbian origin—and provided toponyms in the vernacular (AHBC/I 1674; ANE/Q 1689, 12v; ANE/Q 1709, 5v; ANE/Q 1733, 36v; ANE/Q 1759). Spaniards appear to have borrowed this technique from the aboriginal population for their own purposes of marking territories defined by European criteria (Caillavet 2000, 127). This indicates that the use of zanjas held intersecting but culturally different meanings for Europeans and Native Americans.[13] Other usages, such as that of redefining pre-Columbian terraces (*gradas*) as boundaries suggests the creation of colonial indigenous territorial conventions that reinscribed lands and their distinguishing features within a colonial reality (ANE/Q n.d.b, 5r–6v).

Key cultural information could also be crystallized in a characteristically native form in the written enumeration of the boundaries of lands, such as can be noted in the mid-eighteenth-century title to the Pasto community of Cumbal (NP/P 1908 [1758]), which includes a number of named boundary markers, or *mojones*, as well as natural features of supernatural importance, such as rivers and lakes. The colonial cacicazgo of Cumbal was organized into a hierarchy of sections, arrayed from north to south in parallel bands of territory (Rappaport 1994, chap. 2). Participation in political activities was structured according to the territorial hierarchy, with authorities from different sections assuming key administrative positions in a fixed rotational order that corresponds to the path of the sun between the summer and winter solstices. The enumeration of Cumbal's boundaries in its colonial title follows precisely that hierarchical order, which structures ritual and political life in the community today. Nevertheless, in the title, the symbolism of the section hierarchy is condensed into a list of mojones, limited to the administrative domain.

Possession to territory was thus inscribed on paper, on the land itself, and on the bodies of landholders, who rolled on the ground, tearing up bits of turf to symbolize the act of claiming possession. This ritual could take on special characteristics, depending upon the nature of the participants, such as in the case of a mid-eighteenth-century priest, whose possession ceremony also included the planting of a small wooden cross (ANE/Q 1735b, 100r).[14] Such signs could, however, also be erased from the landscape by way of similar ritual performances. In 1634, a series of plots in El Ángel was returned to the caciques of Tuza, after having fallen into the hands of Spanish landowners.

The restitution of the territory was accompanied by a possession ceremony identical to those we have already described, this time enacted "to symbolize this restitution" (ANE/Q 1634a, 8v). Animals belonging to the usurpers were to be ritually driven off the land and any buildings found there were ordered to be ceremonially destroyed, thus erasing from the very landscape any inscription of illegitimate claims to the territory. However, the cacique of El Ángel, Don Sebastián Guamanmira, thought better of destroying the houses and asked that they be preserved, so another possession ceremony followed close on the heels of the first one:

> And in conformity and noting the utility of leaving the cacique in possession of the houses and corrals, the judge ordered they desist from tearing them down. Taking Don Sebastian Guaman by the hands, he led him into the three houses and said that he gave him possession of them by virtue of their being built on his lands, so that he would possess them. (1634a, 10r)[15]

Thus, we cannot speak of alphabetic inscription as the sole means by which indigenous or Spanish litigators assumed control of territory. A combination of European and Pasto modes of marking the landscape contributed to the foundations of the indigenous lettered city, as did the symbiosis of native and Spanish ways of classifying these markers and the ceremonies that impressed possession upon the bodies of indigenous and European landholders. The lettered city transcends the strictly European, erudite, and alphabetic bounds placed on it by Rama.

Indigenous People and Notarial Writing

In order to comprehend the nature of the indigenous lettered city, the first step is to determine the nature of the genres of alphabetic expression that native peoples of the northern Andes used and transformed. Wills, contracts, and titles are Spanish legal genres, but in the colonial Andes, they were produced under particular local circumstances that subtly transformed their nature. The key word here is *subtle*, because these documents do not broadcast alterity. Instead, they champion conformity within a Spanish system, not the least because they were written in concert with colonial officials. The notarial papers of Ibarra—where many Pasto contracts, wills, and dispute records were registered—were drawn up by Spanish notaries, men whose offices were granted by the king of Spain. Ibarra's notaries undertook annual trips to the Pasto area, where they spent two weeks to a month recording the numerous legal matters of concern to native and Spanish local elites. The authenticity of these documents is predicated upon the presence of various individuals fulfilling a range of functions—including witnesses, interpreters, and other experts, such as land measurers. Only a limited number of (privileged) men—both Spaniards (or *criollos*) and indigenous nobility—could fill such roles, and for this reason, the same characters appear repeatedly in document after document, written in close succession.[16] Thus, notarial practice created a type of intertextuality based upon the demands of local legal procedure that determined the relationships between different genres of legal expression, as well as providing a transcultural interface in which Spanish officials, European landowners, and Pasto caciques created written artifacts of colonial culture.[17]

The notarial archives of Ibarra afford us a window onto how, when, and why the Pasto caciques of the Ibarra district sought official assistance for their legal needs. If we tabulate the 328 legal proceedings between 1593 and 1799 that have survived in this archive and to which Pastos were parties, we find that they fall into a number of categories. Most significant—188 entries, or almost 60 percent of the total documentation—were those simplest of papers, contracts written during land sales, including the sale of rural lands, of urban plots in Ibarra, and the creation of *capellanías* (private endowments producing revenue for pious bequests). The vast majority of these were written between 1640 and 1739. They include not only sales between Pastos and Spaniards, but also transactions among Pastos themselves and between Pastos and other indigenous people of the region; the two latter categories comprise roughly a third of the transactions. Clearly, protection of land rights and the increasing need for documentation of claims, on the one hand, and the need to sell lands, on the other, drove caciques to the notary. If we examine the contracts by decade, focusing on the sale of rural lands, it becomes evident that the number of sales grew from the end of the sixteenth century to the last two decades of the seventeenth, and then dropped off throughout the eighteenth. As caciques found themselves with lengthy tribute rolls inconsistent with the ever-more-reduced populations of their communities, beginning in the last two decades of the seventeenth century they had to sell off lands to meet their tribute obligations (Powers 1995); this is stated in some contracts. However, there is also a bell curve in the number of land sales between Pastos themselves that parallels the general trend, suggesting that contracts approved by notaries were necessary to protect land rights internally, as well as between Pastos and Europeans. Also during the seventeenth century, there appeared Pasto owners of urban lots in the provincial capital of Ibarra, a trend that all but vanished with the increasing impoverishment of caciques in the eighteenth century. As urban-based caciques became increasingly cosmopolitan, they began to endow capellanías, a trend that also disappeared in the eighteenth century.

The next-largest categories of notarial transactions are the registry of testaments, of which there are 25, with 20 of them by chiefly testators, and the recording of debt agreements, also 25 entries. Note that many of these wills were registered in Ibarra only after they were written in the home community, something we will come back to later in this chapter.[18] These categories are followed closely by the registry of papers regarding disputes over land (20); by the notarial validation of powers of attorney (18) that Pasto caciques gave to Spaniards, other Pastos, and even Inca nobility; and by the documentation of other disputes (16).[19]

As in Mexico (Lockhart 1992; Restall 1997), native Andeans served as notaries at the local level (Murra 1998; Spalding 1984, 217), although in contrast to Nahua and Maya scribes, who wrote in their vernaculars, Andean notaries wrote in Spanish with only very limited exceptions (Mannheim 1991, 143–44). In the Pasto area, we have two documents with indigenous scribal signatures, one a 1653 will from Carlosama prepared by Don Juan Guamialamag (ANE/Q 1653) and the other, a 1634 document from Tuza signed by Don Pedro Matías Huanamag (ANE/Q 1634a, 125v), who bears the title of *escribano del pueblo* (town notary).[20] The latter document is embedded within a lengthy dispute between the caciques of Tuza and several Spaniards who were occupying indigenous lands. It is a mere slip of paper written in a clear hand, bearing two brief paragraphs acknowledging delivery of a decree from Quito to a Spaniard accused of burning the church in Tuza, requiring he turn over a number of mules and horses to Don Diego Paspuel, governor of Tuza, followed by a statement of the actions the authorities had taken to confiscate the animals, legal procedures conducted before three native witnesses (figure 29).

In other circumstances, indigenous scribes with only temporary notarial titles and working in isolation from the Spanish authorities applied European literate conventions and legal procedures to local disputes, in an effort to ensure the legitimacy of their decisions for posterity. Thus, in 1654, when Don Marcos Taques, native governor of Tulcán, could find no European judge available to arbitrate a dispute over a will, he took upon himself that role.[21] Since there were no Spanish notaries in the area, he ordered that all

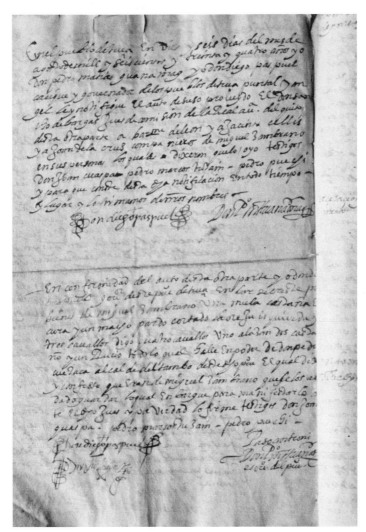

FIGURE 29 Dispute between the caciques of Tuza and several Spaniards, signed by Don Pedro Matías Huanamag, *escribano del pueblo*, 1634, ANE/Q, Indígenas, caja 3, 125v.

those who knew how to read and write present themselves to him, resulting in the temporary appointment of Tulcán native Juan Francisco Guapastal as notary (AHBC/I 1654). Guapastal penned a grammatically correct and legally accurate account of the proceedings. It accompanies the original will in the Ibarra notary archive where the documentation was subsequently deposited as protection against future claims. While Don Marcos and Juan Francisco Guapastal resolved the dispute without outside intervention, they framed their decision within the rubric of the broader colonial administration, "in the name of Your Majesty" (1654, 3v).

The Play of Genres

Colonial literate legal practice—it is almost redundant to juxtapose *literate* and *legal*, given that in the Spanish legal system, virtually all communications in the course of a dispute were made in writing—was based upon a series of genres that were transformed in the course of intercultural contact and conflict. The ideological supports of the literate system were supplied by those genres produced by friars. Their grammars and lexicons situated native languages within a Latin matrix and evaluated the capacity of these languages to reflect adequately upon spiritual matters (Harrison 1995), while their sermons and catechisms indoctrinated the indigenous faithful through reference to the written word and the narrative pictorial image.[22] A range of documents was produced within the República de Indios, the indigenous jurisdiction of the Spanish administration—including petitions and letters, documentation of land boundaries, contracts, wills, land and chiefly titles, and investigations into the activities of officials—some of these penned by native scribes and others by European notaries and lawyers working with ethnic lords. Documents produced within the República de Indios were guided by metageneric texts, such as notarial manuals and handbooks for priests, which classify types of documents and stipulate their contents and organization, lay out how many witnesses had to be present for the authentication of a legal paper, and describe how such documents could be falsified.[23]

As we shall describe, Andean local lords became embroiled in all sorts of disputes by employing specific legal genres, be they civil and criminal suits, wills, or contracts. To be able to use legal writing properly, these native leaders became aware of the published metagenres that controlled and gave order to the production of these specific kinds of religious, legal, and social documents. The knowledge of and possession by indios of such metatexts, especially legal ones, could be considered dangerous by Spaniards because native literacy empowered Andeans to use these texts in unintended and adversarial ways. For example, Bartolomé Álvarez writes in a bitter and sarcastic tone about the problems caused by *indios ladinos* in Peru toward the end of the sixteenth century. He cites two specific examples:

Among the virtues that Ladinos study is, one, to know how to compose a lawsuit and to make a petition in order to advance an accusation; for which end an indio ladino from a town called Andamarca in the province of Las Carangas bought a copy of Monterroso [y Alvarado, *Pratica civil, y criminal y instrvcion de escrivanos* 1609 (1563)] and in another pueblo called Coquemarca another ladino bought a copy of Las Partidas by King Alonso that cost 40 pesos. To comprehend their ignoble intent one need not look further than to the indio, who wishes to be lettered in order to create lawsuits without having studied what he ~~pretends~~ tries [to do]. And so, if we were to examine him, [we would find that] he would not know the law of God; and if [we ask] if he knows his catechism and prayers he is not able to understand it nor repeat it. And if we ask him who is your parish priest and [if] the parish priest examines him, it will be discovered that he doesn't know a word of the Christian doctrine nor believes if God exists; and [so] tries to raise a ladino child who does not know how to read or write and he will turn upside down Monterroso and the laws of Las Partidas only in order to cause problems. (Álvarez, 1998 [1588]: 269)[24]

The two books mentioned by Bartolomé Álvarez are fundamental texts for the establishment of a civil community in the New World.[25] The first text concerns teaching notaries how to create civil and criminal law cases. The second text, the *Siete partidas*, is even more important. It represents one of the various editions of the printed version of the foundational legal text of Spain. First compiled in the thirteenth century under the direction of Alfonso X, the *Siete partidas* became a much-copied manuscript that served as the guiding legal text of Spain both in terms of philosophy and practice (Alfonso X 1992 [1555]). The first printed edition appeared in 1491 and it was quickly reprinted more than a dozen times during the sixteenth century. Which of these editions was purchased by the ladino from Coquemarca is unclear and not important. What is clear, by what Álvarez says, is that the market gave native leaders access to some of most important books for learning how to legally defend themselves. They gained unmediated access to both the philosophical and technical underpinnings of the legal process. The acquisition of reading and writing by native people therefore did not just enhance their knowledge of church doctrine, as was hoped. It was also used to read these metatexts in order to produce their own documents. To someone like Álvarez, Andean literacy in general and these metagenres in particular would bring nothing but trouble.

Metagenres did not, however, completely control the character of documentary genres, nor the divisions between them. Once the contents of manuals entered into fields of activity and exchange, they took on different interpretive values, as Bartolomé Álvarez feared. For instance, Felipe Guaman Poma de Ayala's *Nueva corónica*—a lengthy report meant to be presented to the king of Spain as a letter documenting abuses against native people—took the genre of the sermon and transformed it into a type of historical writing, called the chronicle (Adorno 1986). González Echevarría (1990, 71–92) has argued that Garcilaso's *Comentarios reales*, a history of the Incas and of the conquest of Peru, might be better understood as a letter of appeal to the Crown, a genre known as a *relación*, thereby suggesting that the boundaries between historical writing and notarial rhetoric were blurred in the colonial period. In the northern Andean documentation, this kind of blurring of genres is not as obvious, probably because the collective nature of document writing and the participation of Spanish notaries, attorneys, and judges precluded the kind of generic experimentation enjoyed by Garcilaso and Guaman Poma, on the one hand, and by the more autonomous local scribes writing in the vernacular in Mexico, on the other. However, an examination of the genres of Pasto and Nasa documentary records indicates that indigenous authors and litigants did merge Spanish notarial genres with native forms of inscription in creative ways.

Contracts

Contracts are the form of documentation least susceptible to generic manipulation, given their brevity and their highly formulaic character. Typically, a contract legitimizing a land sale will stipulate little more than the following information: the names of buyers and sellers; the amount exchanged in the transaction and the terms of payment; the size and boundaries of the plot and the legal nature of its tenancy; and the conditions under which the contract was written, including the place and date of its signing, as well as the various participants in the notarial act (sellers, buyers, notaries, witnesses, etc.). Here is a brief example of a contract, entered into on 16 December 1692, between Doña Magdalena Guachán, cacica of the Pasto community of Guaca, and Sebastián Galíndez, a Spaniard or perhaps a criollo; it was offered as evidence by the caciques of Tuza in a dispute over lands in Puntal a century after its signing:

In the *villa* of San Miguel de Ibarra on the sixteenth day of the month of December of sixteen hundred and ninety two, before me, the public notary of the city council, and witnesses, Doña Magdalena Guachan, cacica of the town of Guaca, resident in this town, whom I swear I know: executed in her own [name] and in the name of her heirs and successors, the sale and placement in royal transaction by right of inheritance, now and forever, to Sebastián Galíndez, present [in his name] and for his heirs and successors, a piece of land that she owns and possesses, within the limits of the town of Puntal, in the place called Mumiar, comprised of approximately eight *cuadras* of land which she received and inherited from Doña Juana Guachan, her deceased mother. [It is] bounded from above and from below by the lands of Don Francisco Paspuel, cacique of the town of Tuza, to one side by the lands of Doña Maria Guachan, and to the other by those of Doña Francisca Guachan, [both] first cousins of the executor, with all its access routes [entradas y salidas], uses, customs, rights, and services, and whereby and in the form she has possessed them and her mother and others possessed them, free of pledges, obligations, and mortgages, in the price and quantity of seventy-two *patacones* which the buyer placed on the table in [denominations] of *reales de a dos* and change, which after being counted was taken and passed into the power of the executor in my presence and that of the witnesses, to which I, the present scribe, attest. . . . [signatures follow]. (ANE/Q 1792b, cuaderno 2, no pagination)[26]

While this particular contract was drawn up by an Ibarra notary, contracts were also written in indigenous communities without notarial intervention, but with all of the other formalities of the genre (ANE/Q 1727b; 1792b, cuaderno 4, no pagination).

Detailed toponyms whose meanings called attention to topographic features of importance to native peoples were included in contracts, thus imbuing notarial rhetoric with a native significance that could only be apprehended by Pasto speakers. The suffixes attached to place-names differentiate between various native forms of delimiting land (Caillavet 1982b), as the will of Don Sebastián Calisto, a cacique of the section of Yaputá, Carlosama, illustrates. Calisto distinguished between plots he called by the toponym Tirir. He referred to Tirir in conjunction to a *grada* (pre-Columbian agricultural terrace) called Yalguel, to the *tabla*, or band of land, named Tirir Yalcam, and to three tablas called Yalguesam Tirir (ANE/Q n.d.b, 6r–v; see also ANE/Q 1634b,

1681b). Note how the plot called Yalguel is transformed from an agricultural terrace into a boundary marker in this document and how suffixes—whose meanings are lost to us—were added to what appears to have been the root, "yal." Pre-Columbian topographic features were thus recast and inscribed into documents and as their function shifted in the colonial period, they were reinscribed in colonial form on the land. This is an eloquent illustration of the fact that colonial culture does not imply the juxtaposition of pre-Columbian survivals with Spanish cultural forms, but instead, the infusion of colonial indigenous and Spanish American symbolic systems. Inscription of Pasto toponyms into the Castilian literate record implied, moreover, the task of translation and interpretation, given that these place-names could only be imperfectly transcribed from an unwritten Andean language into the Roman alphabet, passing through the filter of Castilian phonology. That such toponyms were sometimes greeted with confusion by Spanish readers is evident in a 1680 sale of lands in Puntal, where the toponyms Guamal, Pilpuris Chalqualan, Pialtales, Quinamues, Usmaes, Quinangues, and Pialanpues are termed "esquisitos"—"exquisite" or perhaps, exotic—by witnesses (ANE/Q 1680, 7v and 9v).

Testaments

In theory, all good Christians in the colonial period were required to draw up wills before they died, although many native Andeans did not have the resources—nor, in some cases, the inclination—to do so. A quasi-sacramental act, the will allowed the faithful to balance salvation against wealth, by redirecting worldly possessions toward pious ends:

> The will was the religious and quasi-sacramental means of obtaining the aeterna without altogether losing the temporalia, a way of combining wealth with the work of salvation. It was an insurance policy contracted between the mortal individual and God, through the intermediary of the Church, a policy that had a dual purpose. In the first place, it was, as Jacques Le Goff puts it, a "passport to heaven." As such it guaranteed eternal wealth, but the premiums were paid in temporal currency, the pious bequests. The will was also a "laissez-passer," or permit, for use on earth. As such it legitimized and authorized the enjoyment–otherwise suspect—of property acquired during a lifetime, the temporalia. The premiums for this second guarantee were paid in spiritual currency,

the spiritual counterpart of the pious bequests, masses, and charitable endowments. So, on the one hand, the will provided an option on the aeterna; on the other, it rehabilitated the temporalia. (Ariès 1991, 191)

In the Spanish world, wills were considered, like confession, to be penitential acts (Eire 1995, 22), and their preparation unfolded within an intensely pious performance in which the testator, priest, notary, and witnesses engaged in prayer to resist the temptations of the devil, accompanied by processions of religious confraternities, and the act of alms giving by the dying to the poor (1995, 29–33).

The will functioned, therefore, on two planes. First, it reiterated the faith of the testator through formulaic invocations, meditations, and professions of faith, as well as through what are called pious bequests (*obras pías*) — provisions for masses to be said for the soul of the deceased and his or her family, as well as charitable contributions to institutions or directly to the poor. Second, it provided for the distribution of property to heirs, thus spiritually legitimizing wealth by detaching it from its owner before death (Eire 1995, 37–38). Carlos Eire has analyzed over 500 wills from sixteenth-century Madrid, demonstrating how they changed over the century in reaction to the 1563 Council of Trent. He notes in particular the surge in pious bequests and funerary ritual as Spain became increasingly more orthodox in the face of the rise of Protestantism in other parts of Europe. The value of Eire's work resides in its focus on systems of popular belief in Counter-Reformation Spain: how individuals, fearing their fates in the afterlife, participated in and transformed official structures of belief.

These structures were carried over to the Americas, where wills were also oriented toward spiritual ends, as admonishes an 1810 Mexican notarial manual that contains templates for testaments:

> The testament is a highly religious act and of very Catholic spirit because he who makes it looks toward depriving himself of worldly things, directing his objectives toward salvation, and as it is part (and not small) of easing the conscience by fulfilling one's obligations, paying one's debts and reinstating what belongs to others, pious bequests and other things that are incurred in testaments, it is necessary to solicit such an important means with extreme care, given that it is a medicinal memorial or remembrance for [ensuring] eternal health and is presumed as such in law. (Lara Valdés and Vidaurri Aréchiga 1998 [1810], 206)[27]

Indigenous Christians of Mesoamerica and the Andes prepared wills, in native vernaculars in Mesoamerica (Cline and León-Portilla 1984; Hill 1989; Kellogg and Restall 1998; Restall 1995) and in Spanish in the Andes (Abercrombie 1998b; Powers 1998; Salomon 1987–88), following formulas similar to those used in Europe. Unlike in Spain, where a quarter to half of the early modern population wrote testaments (Eire 1995, 20–21), the wills of indigenous Andeans that have been published are almost exclusively the last wishes of ethnic lords and members of the native nobility; some of these colonial Andean testators were members of powerful regional chiefly families (Caillavet 1982a, 1983; del Río 1990; Oberem 1993), while others were descendants of Atahualpa, the last Inca monarch (Estupiñán Freile 1988; Uzcátegui 1989).[28] This, in spite of the fact that religious authorities, such as the Synod of Bogotá in 1556, ordered parish priests to encourage their congregations on major feast days to consider preparing testaments (Romero 1960, 546).

Most scholars who have worked on colonial indigenous wills have mined them as evidence of pre-Columbian practices, as well as for information on colonial-era political intrigue and native material culture.[29] Nevertheless, these documents are also significant for the ways in which their authors project themselves onto the spiritual plane. Thomas B. Abercrombie (1998b) has analyzed a series of wills from colonial Bolivia, written by both caciques and *encomenderos*,[30] showing how these powerful political and social actors used their wills as a means to assuage their consciences and seek entry into heaven in spite of the offenses they had committed during their lives. The Spaniards stipulated sums left to indigenous communities in restitution for abuses perpetrated against them, while the hereditary chiefs generously contributed to the church to make up for having enriched themselves through the colonial system of domination.

Among the colonial Pasto, caciques also avidly sought to lessen their time in purgatory through pious bequests, although they were by no means as wealthy as were the Bolivian and Ecuadorian hereditary chiefs whose wills have been published, or the caciques of the Sabana de Bogotá who were rich in land and animals.[31] Of the thirty-nine Pasto wills we have studied, two-thirds are from the Pasto towns of the district of Ibarra (Guaca, Tulcán, and Tuza) and a third from the communities of the Pasto Province, to the north (Carlosama, Cumbal, Guachavéz, Sapuyes, and Túquerres). Two-thirds are by men and a third by women. The majority are from the seventeenth and eighteenth centuries—twenty-seven wills, with four from the sixteenth century and the remainder undated. The Pasto wills were all written in the communities, on the testators' deathbeds or in advanced old age, most by literate members of the community, although two were written by notaries, one an *escribano nombrado* (temporary notary) with a Spanish surname (ANE/Q 1585) and the other with a Pasto surname (ANE/Q 1653).

As in Spain, Andean wills were collective projects, in which actors as diverse as the testator, the parish priest, local literates, and indigenous authorities constructed the documents, probably using earlier wills and manuals as templates. Almost half of the Pasto wills exhibit deviations from the standard formula, including no signatures or missing sections, attributable to the lack of notarial participation in their writing.[32] Alonso de la Peña Montenegro's 1995 [1668] *Itinerario para parochos de indios*, a manual for priests working in indigenous communities, encourages readers to recognize these nonstandard wills:

> It is common among poor indios, who make testaments of the poverty [in which] they live, that their memorias are made by the hand of anyone who knows how to read, and as they have so little, rarely or never are there occasions for dispute, nor discord, nor do they arise in suits; but in some places there are rich indios, and among them live Spaniards, who have wealth, and in the distant towns it is not always possible to make a testament with all the formalities of Law, for lack of Notaries, and in these cases there is a clear doubt, and before resolving it I presuppose that although the testament might be void for external law, it is very probable that internally it is valid. (1995 [1668], 346–47)[33]

Peña Montenegro (1995 [1668], 345) specifies that for a will to be valid, the signatures of three witnesses are necessary if the will is made before a notary. The signatures of five *vecinos* (Spanish or criollo townspeople) suffice when there is no notarial at hand. Seven signatures are needed if the witnesses are not vecinos. In the Pasto wills, we found only five testaments that met these criteria, the majority written in the presence of fewer than seven indigenous witnesses, frequently an array of local officeholders. The notarial gatekeepers who commonly supervised the correct division of property between heirs and pious bequests were missing in most of these testaments.

In contrast, the Muisca wills we consulted were almost all vetted by notaries in Santafé de Bogotá, leading to more uniform documents with the proper number of witnesses, generally Spanish vecinos, paying closer attention to the various required formulas contained in proper testaments. Of eighty-eight Muisca wills consulted, only four were prepared by individuals without notarial status, although all were written by Spaniards, whether parish priests or local colonial officials (AGN/B 1665a, 1688c, 1758–59; Rodríguez Jiménez 2002, 159–62).[34] However, while some Pasto wills were clearly the product of indigenous hands and witnessed by indigenous observers, Muisca testators were all illiterate, with only one exception, Don Francisco Bojaca, the governor of Tabio; paradoxically, he had the final version of his will and codicils read to him through a royal interpreter (AGN/B 1665a). Less than a third of these wills are by individuals living outside of Santafé, the vast majority being authored by migrants to the city. Even those living in indigenous towns near Bogotá and Tunja owned house lots in the city, most of them testators of noble birth; unlike the Pasto wills, however, only eleven of the Muisca testaments were written by indigenous nobility—caciques, *capitanes*, and *gobernadores*. Fourteen of the Bogotá wills are from the sixteenth century, seventy-three from the seventeenth century, and one from the eighteenth century. Roughly a third (29) are by male testators and two-thirds (59) by female authors; many of the latter are urban widows.[35] Only one of the wills, by a rural cacique (AGN/B 1668c) has the collective quality so common to the Pasto wills, which were witnessed by the local authority structure: uprooted from their communities, Muisca migrants and caciques who traveled to Santafé to write their wills did not generally dictate testaments in the presence of indigenous authorities.

Clearly, the general contours of the Muisca wills differ from those of the Pasto area, suggesting that we cannot speak of a unitary form of indigenous literacy in the northern Andes. The Muisca, whose territory was considerably less isolated from the Spanish administration than were the Pasto and who made up a large proportion of the population of Santafé, seat of the Royal Court (Zambrano Escovar 2008), were, correspondingly, in closer contact with the literate world in general and with notaries in particular. Muisca caciques' testaments exhibit considerably more wealth than the wills of their Pasto colleagues, particularly in their ownership of hundreds—and sometimes thousands—of animals, as well as the presence of African and mulatto slaves listed as property (AGN/B 1609–10, 1633a; Rodríguez Jiménez 2002, 79–81). This suggests that their anxiety over properly composed documents led them to seek the services of notaries. However, the overwhelming presence in the notarial record of the testaments of Muisca commoners suggests that this was a colonial culture in which notaries played a ubiquitous role, while detours were made around such gatekeepers in Pasto.[36]

Only six of the Pasto wills studied include extensive pious bequests of the sort that Eire reports for post-Trent Madrid, three of them leaving all or most of the estate to the church to pay for masses to be said for the soul of the deceased (AHBC/I 1592, AHBC/I 1606; ANE/Q 1709). The vast majority of Pasto testators left only minimal bequests to the church; nine of the thirty-nine wills included no pious bequests at all.[37] The mass was thought to be the most effective means of ensuring salvation because in it "the sacrificial redemptive work of Christ was offered anew and could be selectively applied toward the suffering any Christian soul still owed in purgatory" (Eire 1995, 174). Interestingly, all but one of the six wills that contain extensive pious bequests were written in the three Pasto towns of the district of Ibarra, where caciques were considerably more wealthy than in the Pasto Province and where the indigenous nobility frequently maintained town houses, thus ensuring their more active participation in religious functions. These heredi-tary chiefs were similar to the regional caciques that Udo Oberem (1993, 15–17) has described for highland Ecuador, men who ruled over vast terri-tories and amassed considerable wealth. Among Muisca testators, a small number had no heirs and left their estates to the church and only four, all of them indigenous nobility, left extensive pious bequests, while five demanded elaborate funerals, some with 6 to 12 priests officiating (AGN/B 1629c, 1633a, 1665a). Nevertheless, even the most impoverished indigenous testators in Santafé, people with virtually no property at all, prepared wills (AGN/B 1567, 1617b, 1619a, 1630a, 1633d, 1633f, 1655a, 1655b; Rodríguez Jiménez 2002), sug-gesting that the spiritual benefits of the testament were of considerable con-sequence to them.[38] To give some idea of the range of pious bequests found in these testaments, let us look at two examples from the Pasto area, one in which only minimal property is dedicated to the testator's soul, and another in which the entire estate is left to the church.

Don Diego Guachocal Aza, cacique of Guachucal in the Pasto Province, wrote his will in August of 1589, in the presence of three Spaniards, Pedro de la Cadena, Alonso Daza, and Alonso Zambrando (ANE/Q 1589). Don Diego specified who was to receive his animals, his clothing, various ob-jects—including a songbook, a box, two masks, and drums—his land, and the various houses he owned. He laid down his last wishes as to the future of the cacicazgo, ordering the indigenous nobility who served under him to buy candles for his funeral, naming as his successor Don Alonso, his son-in-law, and requesting that two apparently defiant men, Don Pedro Guenza and Don Francisco Ypialput, submit to Don Alonso's authority. Don Diego, who apparently had many possessions, asked only for a funeral mass, to be said by Fr. Antonio Rodríguez, his parish priest, and asked for two additional masses to be said in his memory; in addition, he requested that the obligatory bequests be made to the *mandas forzosas*, the various charities associated with missions in the Holy Land.

In contrast, Doña Catalina Tuza (AHBC/I 1606), the daughter of the principal cacique of Tuza, a large community in the district of Ibarra, left almost her entire estate to the church, as she had no heirs. She requested that she be buried in a chapel next to the main altar of the church in Tuza, where her ancestors lay. Proceeds from her extensive landholdings would be spent on masses for her soul, to be held a year after her death, as well as for masses for her husband's soul, to be said on the days of Saint Catherine and Saint Andrew. She left 5 horses to various religious confraternities, as well as 3 cows and 110 sheep. In addition, numerous pieces of jewelry, including a gold chain, two silver bracelets, a red coral bracelet, a necklace of beads and silver, two gold rings, three pairs of silver and gold *tupus* (pins for fastening mantles), a silver spoon, a pewter plate, and four *llicllas*—a Quechua term used in Pasto (and Muisca) documents to refer to a woman's mantle, in this case, one of blue wool, another in the Huancavelica style, a spotted mantle, and a blue and yellow one made of *qompi* (fine) cloth—were all destined to pay for a battery of masses to be said for her soul. Additionally, she left two boxes for Tuza's church, one to hold frontals and the other for candles. Finally, two plates made in Quito were bequested for further masses. All of these masses were to be said for her soul to the Virgin Mary, Saint Peter, Saint Catherine, Saint Andrew, Saint John the Evangelist, Saint John the Baptist, the Archangel Saint Michael, and Saint Ann. Three masses were ordered for the soul of her husband. She remembered the souls in purgatory, requesting four masses be said for them. And she ordered two more masses for anyone else whom she had forgotten. All of these masses were to be said at her altar in Tuza, as well as at the church in Puntal, a warm country community in which the caciques of Tuza had lands, and where she wrote that "I am in the habit of going to mass there when I go to [work] my plots" (1606, 3r).[39] In order to ensure that her subjects be proper Christians, she asked that four masses be said in their name, "so that God brings them into true reason" (1606, 3r).[40] Having no direct heirs, she passed her chiefly authority to Don Pedro Cellin, so that he would govern the forty-four tributaries subject to her rule and so that he would give "council and exemplify God's teachings, receiving tribute and taking tribute to the house of the cacique" (1606, 4r).[41] The piety of Doña Catalina, while similar to that of the Madrileños described by Eire, is indeed, unusual among the Pastos.[42] However, it presents an extreme case of what is evident in the corpus of wills we consulted: that these are pious documents in which indigenous Christians strive to gain proximity to the divine, much as did their coreligionists throughout Spain's colonial holdings.

Notwithstanding the profoundly Christian tenor of Pasto testaments, these documents, like land contracts, were highly intertextual, in the sense that they also allude to indigenous forms of inscription embodied in material culture. The significance of visual genres that bore specific meanings in the northern Andean indigenous world—such as colonial-style lacquered beakers (*limbiquiros*), silver drinking vessels (*aquillas*), and the finely woven cloth (qompi) mentioned by Doña Catalina Tuza—were rearticulated in Spanish-language wills, as were the snail shells (*caracoles*) listed by Don Cristóbal Cuatín in 1592 (AHBC/I 1592; cf. ANE/Q 1589, 1624). Muisca testators, similarly, referred to the painted cotton mantles that were of great cosmological importance to them, as we will discuss in chapter 6 (AGN/B 1576, 202r–v; 1609–10, 373v; 1630n, 47v; 1633a, 97r; Rodríguez Jiménez 2002), as well as to gourds (*totumas*) from Arma and Urabá (AGN/B 1633a, 1629b, 1633e, 1633g, 1665a) and silver totumas (AGN/B 1665a,1633e, 1668c), both of which were presumably drinking-vessels.[43]

The importance of *queros* and other drinking vessels is underlined in the early colonial Muisca murals of Sutatausa, Cundinamarca, as discussed in chapter 2, where a depiction of the Last Judgment shows condemned souls en route to hell carrying a decorated gourd drinking vessel (called a *totuma* or *mate* in the documents) that was used throughout the Andes in native religious ceremonies (plate 7 and figure 30). Lacquered queros were also present in the inventory of objects (figures 31 and 32), many of them of ritual significance, found in an early eighteenth-century messianic movement in the Nasa area, where God was said to come down twice a week, dressed as a Franciscan friar, entreating followers to maintain themselves separate from Europeans, who would soon be destroyed by fire (AHT/B 1729; Rappaport 1980–81). In the Pasto area, vessels for drinking *chicha* (corn beer)—so despised by missionaries that an entire sermon of the 1585 catechism of Lima was dedicated to admonishing native Andeans for drinking (Lima 1990 [1585], 702–7)—are described in the wills as connected within a trade network that bolstered the political power of the caciques. Don Cristóbal Cuatín (AHBC/I 1592, 2r) owned a pair of mates like the one depicted in the Mouth of Hell scene in the Sutatausa mural, which had been sold to him by Juan Quaya, a member of the Tuza nobility. Quaya is undoubtedly the same

FIGURE 30 Detail of the Last Judgment, Mouth of Hell with figure holding a *totuma* (gourd), Church of San Juan Bautista, artist unknown, ca. 1620, Sutatausa, Cundinamarca. Courtesy of Rodolfo Vallín.

FIGURE 31 Colonial *quero* inlaid with *mopa mopa / barniz de Pasto*, ca. 1650, private collection.

FIGURE 32 Colonial quero inlaid with *mopa mopa / barniz de Pasto*, ca. 1700, Kamsá, Sibundoy valley, Colombia, Museo Rosero, Pasto.

mindalá, or status trader, cited by Grijalva (1937, 81–84) as having used his special access to prestige trade goods controlled by the pre-Colombian and colonial nobility as leverage for usurping political control from a cacique (Salomon 1986, 208–10).

Many of the objects inscribed into Pasto wills were Incaic in origin. Qompi cloth, for instance, was given by the Inca to the ethnic lords they conquered (Murra 1975, 145–70). The generic listing of such elements of Andean material culture in the written channel validated the authority of their owners by recourse to European interpretations of the meanings of Incaic power objects; this appropriation occurred in regions such as Tuza that had only briefly fallen under Inca control (Landázuri 1995). In other words, just as the Spaniards made the Incas the model against which to measure all native Andean peoples, the Pastos appropriated Incaic symbols to assert their colonial legitimacy, testimony to the transculturating influence of European perceptions of the Other in a colonial world in which many Others interacted.[44]

But such historically charged Andean objects cannot be isolated from their European counterparts, which intermingled with qompi, painted mantles, queros, and totumas in the pages of these wills. European clothing and textiles from Europe and Asia functioned as markers of chiefly status in an indigenous society in which only caciques dressed in Spanish-style garments. Beginning in the sixteenth century, Pasto hereditary chiefs listed numerous textiles of European origin which they valued enough to include in their wills and whose attributes were significant enough to incorporate in detail: a man's shirt woven of fine scarlet cloth with braided borders ("camiseta de grana con su pasamanos," in ANE/Q 1589, 48v), an unbraided woman's mantle made of Chinese damask ("vna liglla de damasco de la china sin pasamanos," in ANE/Q 1624, 87v), a lace-edged petticoat of fine red cloth ("una saya de escarlatilla con su encaje," in ANE/Q 1709, 9v), a Brittany cloth frontal edged in lace ("una palia de bretaña con sus encajes," in ANE/Q n.d.b, 7r), a damask cushion ("un cojin de damasco," in n.d.b, 7r), a black striped altar cloth with white silk fringes (n.d.b, 7v).[45] The testaments of female commoners from Bogotá similarly juxtapose Muisca painted mantles made of cotton with textiles acquired as trade-goods from Quito and Peru, mantles of European confection, silk from Asia, and a profusion of Spanish-style sewn garments made of European cloth, suggesting that even in poorer households women's wealth was not confined to the local Andean cultural domain.[46] The equal importance bestowed upon Andean and European objects indicates that for these testators, the juxtaposition of distinct cultural forms was not at all unique, but a thoroughly unremarkable occurrence (Dean and Leibsohn 2003).

These Andean and Spanish objects—some rearticulated simultaneously within a clandestine Andean ritual complex and a colonial system of power—cohabited the pages of testaments with other types of intertextuality. Various testators make reference to Christian images, both statues (*bultos*) and paintings (*lienzos*), which they passed on to their heirs (AGN/B 1629c, 1630b, 1633a, 1633c, 1633e, 1633g, 1665a, 1668c, 1758–59; AHBC/I 1674, 1713, 1739; ANE/Q 1624, 1689, 1709; Rodríguez Jiménez 2002, 60–68, 82–84). These are generally not described, beyond reference to their size or to the saints they represented, including such far-flung images as Our Lady of Copacabana (AHBC/I 1674) and such regional ones as Our Lady of Chiquinquirá (AGN/B 1665a, 1668c). In one instance, however, a poor urban woman described an image of the Virgin Mary which she planned to leave to her parish church in Bogotá in terms of its cost: 40 patacones for the painting, which was done by Gaspar de Figueroa; 13 patacones for its framing; and 66 patacones for gilding it, bringing to mind the medieval notion that was beginning to undergo transformations in early modern Europe, in which the value of a painting resided in its materials and labor, not in the artist's skill (Baxandall 1988, 8–27). Religious images provided an intertextual series in indigenous wills, relating alphabetic documents to religious texts, sermons, and devotional objects. The Spaniards likened such images to writing, emphasizing that they did not embody the saints themselves, but represented them: "And if they have crucifixes, images of Our Lady or of the saints, lead them to understand that those images are a form of writing which represents and leads to the understanding of those whom it represents." (Burgos Guevara 1995, 471).[47]

The intertextuality of wills extended to other alphabetic documents as well. We have already pointed to the relationship between the written word and topographic space in our discussion of the use of toponyms in contracts for land sales. The legalization of land claims via written documents stored by caciques in portable desks, or *escritorios* (AHBC/I 1674; ANE/Q n.d.b), which were sometimes decorated with the same mopa-mopa lacquerwork as were the queros called limbiquiros, created a series of entangled texts that testators engaged in their wills. Notarial documents were precious objects in the colonial period, frequently providing the only proof of the validity of statements and evidence, since even if testimony was oral, it was only certified as true when it was written into a document signed by a notary (Herzog 1996, 15, 19). For this reason, seventeenth-century Pasto chiefly testators and even poor Muisca urbanites routinely appealed to written documents in their possession to validate the belongings listed in their wills (AGN/B 1629a, 1633b, 1633f, 1633g, 1655c; Rodríguez Jiménez 2002, 52–55, 79–81, 136–39) and, simultaneously, used notarial testaments as a means for dividing up or managing even the most minuscule urban property (1630b, 1630c, 1633b, 1668a; Rodríguez Jiménez 2002, 182–84).

Don Francisco Paspuel Guachán de Mendoza, cacique of Tuza, wrote his testament in 1689 (ANE/Q 1689), including twenty-seven different plots of land, carefully delineated by boundaries, which he left to his children. Don Francisco's will provides a clear example of the growing confidence in which indigenous testators held the written word, motivated by the expansion of Europeans into their territory (Calero 1997). Don Francisco's will reveals attempts to access the past through oral tradition. He justifies possession of lands in Pialarquer by arguing that he learned of its boundaries from his ancestors, mojones marked by the ruins of his great-grandfather's house (ANE/Q 1689, 14v) But in the majority of his land bequests, Don Francisco refers to royal decrees, testaments, and other "legal papers inherited from my ancestors" (1689, 16r).[48] Sometimes, such references to documents are extremely detailed, as in the case of "bonds of protection from the Alcalde Ordinario of the city of San Francisco de Quito, the aforementioned Alcalde Ordinario who was named Torivio de Cortiguera, and another brief from Don Christoval Tusa to Don Francisco Tuspas, lord of said town of Tusa, for four more cuadras of lands" (ibid., 16v).[49]

The importance that Don Francisco Paspuel Guachán de Mendoza attributed to legal writing reveals much more than his need to transcend the primacy of the spoken word. It also underlines his quest for legimation by an alien authority whose legal system he saw as superior to his own or, in any case, as more binding. The titles he refers to, written in a language foreign to most Pastos of the period and accessible to only a small minority, did not provide unequivocal title to the land because they document the process of land loss, as is evident in continuous appeals in the wills to land grants (*composiciones*), which bestowed title to communities only after the lion's share of their lands were sold off to nonnative bidders (Calero 1997, 118–26). Yet Don Francisco and his colleagues had little choice in the matter, for if they lost such papers, or if notaries refused to provide them with copies, they forfeited their rights to the property that those papers validated (Herzog 1996, 20). Hence, indigenous wills refer not only to existing documentation, but to documentation that has fallen into the hands of others (AGN/B 1629a, 1633a,

1633e; ANE/Q 1677, 1711, 1792a) or that has yet to be notarized (AGN/B 1633e, 1665a; ANE/Q 1729).

The voices in these wills are, indeed, native. They project the continuing, although transformed, significance of the oral memory and of material culture—textiles, drinking vessels, musical instruments—in the maintenance of status hierarchies that emerged in their communities over the course of the colonial period. As in the Corpus Christi paintings that Carolyn Dean (1999) interpreted for colonial Cuzco, these seemingly "aboriginal" cultural representations have acquired new, colonial meanings. Even the plots of land they document are altered, producing European crops to pay tribute to the Crown, scattered over a landscape whose limits are traced according to Spanish conventions and are recorded in land titles. The testators do not dwell exclusively on items that might be seen as "indigenous." They also juxtapose them with objects that confer power in the Spanish world: religious images, legal documents, European and Asian textiles. The "indigenous voice" of these wills is clearly colonial in nature and, for this reason, appears less exotic, more thoroughly integrated into the Spanish legal landscape. And the objectives of their authors are colonial: to ensure that their burials are properly Christian and that their souls are saved and to guarantee that their heirs will have a place to live and work in the colonial world.

Titles

Along with providing native Andeans with a space in which they could express their own needs and aspirations, the genre of wills also imposed literary conventions that limited indigenous self-expression to a fairly narrow array of subjects, a restricted language, and a tightly defined set of objectives. In this sense, the testament as a genre had more or less the same structure and purpose across the northern Andes. However, the meaning of other legal documents was not as constant across cultural groups. A third, and very significant, genre of documentary expression (the first being testaments and the second contracts) was the multilayered documentation of disputes over land and chiefly succession, which, when the court ruled in their favor, provided caciques with crucial title to their territory and a legitimization of their authority. Such documentation is palimpsestic in nature: it layers copies of multiple legal briefs, ranging from complaints of disputants and testimony of witnesses, to the enumeration of boundaries of landholdings, peppering them with royal decrees that gave the parties involved the right to engage in legal action (Díaz Rementería 1977). In most cases, the native voice is muffled in these packets of papers. Complaints and petitions, for example, were generally composed by *protectores de naturales*, Crown officials who were charged with representing indigenous communities in court and who worked in consultation with their indigenous clients. The words of witnesses pass through a triple filter in this documentation: the interpretive screen of the translator who cast Pasto, Nasa, Muisca, or Quechua testimony in Spanish, the straightjacket of the list of questions—the *interrogatorio*—from whose text testimony rarely departs, and the pen of the scribe who committed the proceedings to paper. As we shall see in later chapters, the sentiments of indigenous disputants were most clearly apparent in their creation of an intertextual series out of the numerous pieces of written evidence they submitted to the courts.

Let us take a look at one such title, a very brief document dating from 1700, through which Don Juan Tama, a Nasa cacique from the district of Popayán, which lies to the north of the Pasto Province, acquired royal recognition of the boundaries of the community of Pitayó (ACC/P 1881 [1700]). Through this title, Pitayó became a *resguardo*, a circumscribed tract of land that could not be bought or sold, within which a tribute-paying indigenous community was governed by a cacique.[50] The title to Pitayó begins with a document dated 8 March 1700, a petition by Don Juan Tama requesting that he be recognized as cacique by virtue of his inheritance of the post from its previous incumbent, Don Jacinto de Moscay (ibid., 1133r–34r). Don Juan Tama's petition is granted in a royal decree issued in Quito, which follows the petition. The decree contains a listing of the boundaries of Pitayó (ibid., 1134r–35v), a statement of the mode of chiefly succession to be followed in the event of the cacique's death (ibid., 1135v–36r), and a description of the duties of the cacique with regard to the maintenance of the integrity of both the territory and the documents that legitimize its boundaries (ibid., 1136v–40r); it is signed by Don Felix Caro y Obregón and Don Marco Antonio Burgos y Arellano, judges, or *oidores*, of the Royal Court—the Audiencia—of Quito.

The decree granting rule to Don Juan Tama is followed by an earlier document, dated 11 February 1696, a petition by Don Jacinto de Moscay, then-cacique of Pitayó, who had traveled to Quito to acquire title to his holdings (ACC/P, 1881 [1700], 1140r–43v). Don Jacinto's petition, like the request made four years later by his successor, states the need to acquire title to the land and identifies Don Cruz Yucumal as his predecessor. Yucumal was a cacique who ruled without benefit of royal recognition—it took at least a century for the Spaniards to quell Nasa resistance and bring them under colonial rule, so he was probably the first cacique to fall under the Spanish administration. In his petition, Don Jacinto also names as his successor Don Juan Tama, whom he identifies as his nephew. Don Jacinto states that he will return to Pitayó—a month's journey from Quito—to await the Audiencia's decision, which did not arrive until 31 December of the same year. By that time Don Jacinto de Moscay had died (ACC/P, 1881 [1700], 1144r). The title ends with another petition by Don Juan Tama, dated 6 April 1698, requesting he be given the papers that his deceased uncle had been awaiting. This petition makes special mention of the need to include the rights to certain salt springs within the title (ibid., 1144r–45r). The petition was granted by the Audiencia (ibid., 1145r–v).

Don Juan Tama's title to Pitayó is a legalistic document, vetted by the Audiencia in Quito and rigorously following the conventions required of a petitioner to the Crown. As we shall see below, caciques frequently sought out legal assistance, acquiring expert representation of their interests before the Audiencia. Thus, Tama's and Moscay's petitions were the product of a collaboration between the caciques and more knowledgeable individuals who were familiar with the workings of the Audiencia. However, sometimes we find unexpected voices in resguardo titles. While Don Juan Tama asserted his political legitimacy for the Spaniards through the accepted legal channel of the title to Pitayó, he was also a key player in a very different sort of document, the title to Vitoncó (ACC/P 1883 [1708]), another of his subject communities. This title, at three folios, is even briefer than the title to Pitayó, and in it Tama inserts multiple appeals to native forms of legitimization. For instance, he cites his supposed supernatural origins as the "son of the stars of the aforementioned Tama Stream" (ibid., 2163v; figure 33).[51] He also claimed to have won the chiefdom thanks to his military triumph over Calambás, a neighboring ethnic lord, thus assuming what might be a native form of legitimacy (ibid., 2183v–84r). However, there is no documentation of Tama's conquest of a neighboring ethnic lord in the chronicle literature or in the archives, which suggests that he was reinterpreting an older oral tradition for use within a colonial power struggle (Rappaport 1998, 69–82). As in the title to Pitayó, the Vitoncó charter includes resguardo boundaries, but in this case they do not surround what in any period might be construed as the relatively constricted territory of Vitoncó. Instead, they erupt from Tierradentro, the isolated and mountainous district in which Vitoncó is located, to encroach upon the very limits of the city of Popayán, a day's travel on foot to the west (ACC/P 1883 [1708], 2163r–63v), where Tama claims his dominion extends

PLATE 1 Group portrait of Don Francisco de Arobe and his two sons, Don Pedro and Don Domingo, three mulatto gentlemen from Esmeraldas, Andrés Sánchez Gallque, 1599, Museo de América, Madrid. Oil on canvas. Courtesy of Museo de América, Madrid.

PLATE 2 Our Lady of Chiquinquirá, Alonso de Narváez, 1563, Basílica de Chiquinquirá, Colombia. Oil on cloth.

PLATE 3 San Nicolás de Tolentino and the souls in purgatory, Gaspar de Figueroa, 1656, Cómbita, Boyacá. Oil on canvas. Courtesy of Rodolfo Vallín.

PLATE 4 Mural with the portrait of a cacica and cacique in prayer at the left base of the arco toral of the Church of San Juan Bautista, artist unknown, ca. 1620, Sutatausa, Cundinamarca.

PLATE 5 Detail of mural portrait of a cacica in prayer at the left base of the arco toral of the Church of San Juan Bautista, artist unknown, ca. 1620, Sutatausa, Cundinamarca. Courtesy of Rodolfo Vallín.

PLATE 6 Detail, portable writing desk decorated with *mopa mopa / barniz de Pasto* coat of arms, late 1600s, Museo de Arte Colonial, Quito.

PLATE 7 Last Judgment, Mouth of Hell with figure holding a *totuma* (gourd), artist unknown, ca. 1620, Church of San Juan Bautista, Sutatausa, Cundinamarca.

PLATE 8 Patent of arms given by Charles V to Hernando Cortés, 7 March 1525, Harkness Collection, manuscript 1: f. 1r, Library of Congress, Washington, D.C. Paint, ink and gold leaf on vellum.

PLATE 9 Last Supper, artist unknown, ca. 1620, Church of San Juan Bautista, Sutatausa, Cundinamarca.

FIGURE 33 Modern Nasa depiction of the birth of Juan Tama, resguardo de Juan Tama, Santa Leticia, Cauca.

over the village of Paniquitá by dint of the fact that Vitoncó tributaries were resettled there to work in the haciendas of their encomendero. While the title to Vitoncó attempts to articulate an acceptable Spanish legal discourse in its references to the Nasa as tributaries of the Crown and their embracing of the Christianity brought by Vitoncó's parish priest, Don Matías de Viarroel, and its encomendero, Don Cristóbal de Mosquera y Figueroa, the document infuses a European genre of expression with a very distinct Nasa notion of where chiefly authority originates and operates. Moreover, unlike any other resguardo titles that we have seen, this is not a palimpsestic document, but a single, monolithic statement of Tama's regional hegemony.[52]

Documents such as Don Juan Tama's title to Vitoncó follow Spanish legal conventions to some extent, particularly in terms of the discourse they employ, and they are written in the Castilian language. Nevertheless, they fall completely outside of the legal system after which they are modeled. This genre has been called the "primordial title" by historians. Found for the most part in central Mexico, primordial titles attempt to authenticate community land rights by mimicking Spanish literary and legal conventions. They are usually written in native languages and sometimes carefully follow legal criteria and visual forms that were the rule a century or more before they were written. In this sense, they might be seen as "forgeries":

The Titulos primordiales are said to be fakes, in that their composition is as a rule much later than the events that they claim to establish and especially later than the dates that they bear. They are fakes in the way they report historically incorrect events—some even made up out of whole cloth—fakes entrusted with replacing authentic Titles that might never have existed or could have disappeared, whether destroyed, mislaid, sold or neglected by communities and pueblos that had become unable to decipher documents originally written in Spanish in the course of the sixteenth century. But quite obviously, the incomparable value of the Titles resides in the "forgery" itself, since they show in a relatively autonomous indigenous context a considerable creative effort combined with a perceptible mastery of writing. Thus one should from the outset avoid confusing our view with that of the Spanish, emphasizing that what is fake according to the criteria of historiography and colonial law can express a different apprehension of the past, a singular grasp of the event and of history. (Gruzinski 1993 [1988], 99)

James Lockhart, who sees these documents as one of the most "indigenous" of the broad corpus of written genres in the colonial period, emphasizes their heightened transcultural nature. While primordial titles are, indeed, transcultural products, it would be a misnomer to call them more "indigenous" than other documents. All of the documentation we have been considering is indigenous, but in a colonial sense, manifesting a range of strategies for survival in the colonial context. Mexican primordial titles of the sort referred to by Lockhart exhibit distinctive features, including handwriting and specific lexical and syntactic characteristics that date from a relatively late period after 1650, although they are cast as though they were written in the early colonial period. While they demonstrate a familiarity with Spanish literary conventions, they incorporate oral history and native modes of narration, lending a "mythic" flavor and providing a very particular indigenous view of how land rights were to be constituted (Lockhart 1992, 410–18; Wood 1998, 201–31).

Serge Gruzinski, in contrast to Lockhart, refuses to ground the orality of primordial titles exclusively in their pre-Columbian features, reminding us that Christian preaching and colonial administrative proceedings were also composed in the oral channel and served as models or sources for the contents of the titles (Gruzinski 1993 [1988], 112). Thus, he would have primordial titles be understood as innovations marked by transposition and adaptation, "a new type of tale, which marked a decisive moment in the appropriation of Christian discourse" (ibid., 113). In particular, the titles cast the pre-Columbian period as a backdrop separated from the colonial period, "a kind of general rehearsal in relation to the Christian foundation" (ibid., 123) of these communities. Gruzinski very rightly suggests that in them we learn that it was not the Spanish military invasion, so much as the arrival of Catholicism, which marks the historical vision of the titles, making them profoundly Christian documents (ibid., 123–24). They embody what Gruzinski calls "fossilized memories" that contributed to the construction of colonial identities (ibid., 126).

While true primordial titles have not been found in the Andes, there exist documents, such as the title to Vitoncó, which appear to play a similar role in the constitution of colonial Andean identity. Resguardo titles generally take the form of a compendium of royal decrees, acquired from the Crown by colonial actors through lengthy correspondence and multiple legal rulings channeled through the Audiencia in one of Spain's colonial jurisdictions in the Americas, as we saw in the title to Pitayó and as is the case in other titles (NP/P 1908 [1758]; Rappaport 1994, 106–9). Don Juan Tama mimics the genre with which he associates his document, but only imperfectly. Given that they emanated from Spain, resguardo titles were written in Castilian Spanish, as was Juan Tama's title. However, the title to Vitoncó was not validated by the Audiencia de Quito, the royal court that held jurisdiction over Tama's territory, as were the other resguardo titles we know for the region, including that of Pitayó. Instead, the title to Vitoncó states that Tama enlisted his encomendero in registering the title in a notarial office in the provincial capital of Popayán, an unlikely route for generating a title. This ambiguity is only compounded by the fact that the encomendero was a legal minor at the time of the title's authentication, suggesting that he could not legally have served as Tama's broker. There is, moreover, no royal seal on the title, a prerequisite for such a document, given that the seal stood in for the king in the ceremonies that accompanied its acceptance at the local level. The title to Vitoncó is probably an entirely local product, whose authenticity as a Spanish document was only validated with its inscription into the notarial record in the nineteenth century, when indigenous communities employed resguardo titles as an arm for defending their land rights in the face of privatization by the Colombian national state.[53]

The conditions of production of the title to Vitoncó help to explain its unusual contents. Unlike its sister title to Pitayó, also generated by Don Juan

Tama, which documents the legal procedure by which title was granted the cacique by the Audiencia de Quito, the title to Vitoncó is almost mythic in nature, narrating Tama's supernatural birth and his military rise to rule after vanquishing the cacique Calambás of a neighboring community. In this sense, the Vitoncó title mirrors its Mexican counterparts, which also inscribe oral histories and myth into a written genre in which they do not comfortably fit. Written in Spanish, as befits a document emanating from the Crown, the title was produced in a community which, in the eighteenth century, exhibited an exceedingly low index of Spanish-language proficiency and alphabetic literacy. The document is not even signed by Don Juan Tama, nor is it witnessed by other literates, as would have been the case were he incapable of producing a signature himself. In places, its syntax appears to depart from that of Spanish, suggesting it was written locally.[54]

We can only guess how this document was produced and then shielded from the dominant colonial society until a century and a half after its creation. Ethnographic comparison provides our only cue. All legal procedures undertaken by the Nasa today—or what is remembered by oral narrators—are accompanied by shamans, who determine when and where a judicial proceeding can take place and who can participate in it (Piñacué 1997, 31–52). It is likely that shamans also advised Don Juan Tama, just as a prominent shaman advises the resguardo council of Vitoncó today. As to how the document might have been used by the cacique and his associates, we are on firmer ground, having access to other colonial documents that hint at the reception of such papers. Don Juan Tama ruled at a time of massive population movement and the creation of new communities. He undoubtedly needed legal validation to cement his authority as a cacique and his dominion over the territory of Vitoncó. The title to Pitayó, which was approved in the Audiencia, served this purpose in the eyes of the Spaniards. Among his own people, however, it was not necessarily the legality of a title in the Spanish sense that legitimized Don Juan Tama's rule. Instead, his sovereignty may have been ensured for his indigenous followers by the material object that was the title. In regions adjacent to Vitoncó, colonial documents were prized as supernatural communications, as an inventory of belongings confiscated from an early eighteenth-century Nasa ceremonial center indicates. At the Alto de la Quebrada de las Cuevas, where God was said to appear in the guise of a Franciscan, commanding the Nasa to withdraw from colonial society, the watermark on writing paper was interpreted by the Nasa leader of this movement as divine approval of his mission (AHT/B 1729; Rappaport 1980–81). Thus, the alphabetic document—or the surface upon which it was written—was transformed from literate technology into cosmological object.

In this sense, literacy cannot be understood as the disembodied construction of receptacles carrying a standard corpus of information, with no regard to the context of reception. Instead, it must be appreciated in its performative dimension, whose meaning is reconfigured by its recipients. This was as true for pre-Columbian modes of inscription, such as the khipu knot-record and the lacquered beakers called queros that encoded historical referents, as it was for colonial-era Spanish-language literacy. Both khipus and queros formed part of performances in which multiple genres of expression were juxtaposed to enact history (Cummins 2002a; Urton 2003; Urton and Quilter 2002). The performativity of Spanish literacy, while distinct from its Andean counterpart, was also essential to its meaning in the colonial period. We have only to think of the ceremonial reception of royal decrees in the Spanish colonial world, a ritual in which the colonial official kissed the royal seal of the king and then placed the document on his head, an act recorded in all royal decrees—a ritual we will interpret later in this book.

Within colonial culture, the performative efficacy of the multiple literacies that crosscut indigenous and European genres of inscription and narration was played out in administrative and ritual space. For example, royal decrees read at the investiture of northern Andean caciques shared ritual space with native weavings, which were conferred upon new caciques in a culture in which textiles were a prime vehicle for inscription of memory and power. In the twentieth-century Pasto community of Cumbal, the ritual bestowal of land rights upon resguardo members can only occur once the indigenous council's staffs of office—themselves colonial Spanish objects that have become the almost exclusive province of indigenous authorities, serving as mnemonic devices for remembering past governors—are planted vertically in the ground according to what was once a widely practiced Iberian ceremony, followed by the reading of Spanish-language land documents (Rappaport 1994). We are not certain how, specifically, inscribed paper was ritualized by Don Juan Tama, but we do know that he lived in a world in which rituality was integral to both indigenous and Spanish literate forms.

Let us return for a moment to the 1654 document written by Pasto notary, Juan Francisco Guapastal, described above. Although the legal proceeding out of which Guapastal's record emerged was undertaken beyond the reach of the colonial administration and was most probably conducted in the now-extinct Pasto language, the indigenous notary drew up his report in Spanish. Ultimately, the written results of the trial were deposited in the notarial offices of the provincial center of Ibarra, becoming part of the colonial documentary record, thus explaining why they were composed in the colonial language. Don Juan Tama's title, however, only reached European eyes a century and a half after it was drafted. Why, then, was it composed in Spanish?

Given that the title to Vitoncó records the Spanish Crown's conferral of authority upon Don Juan Tama, a man who had already acquired legal title to other lands via the Audiencia in Quito, it is no accident that this document, despite its possibly "primordial" character, would be composed in Spanish. Notwithstanding its lack of official authentication, the efficacy of the document sprang from its linguistic, ritual, and visual connection to the República de Indios, within which Tama's authority was lodged. Whether or not the majority of the people of Vitoncó could read it, the graphic structure of the title and the Nasa and Spanish ritual practices within which it was undoubtedly ensconced, provided local validation of its significance. The title remained in the keeping of the Vitoncó authorities for three centuries after its creation, forming part of a lively oral tradition in which its most cosmological contents are still remembered.

In the end, Don Juan Tama consciously juxtaposed European literate conventions and Nasa narrative forms to produce a distinctly colonial product. While it is impossible to assert that northern Andean alphabetic documents departed significantly from the European genres upon which they are modeled, northern Andeans clearly infused their legal writing with an intertextuality of their own, one that emphasized nonliterate modes of demarcating territory and recounted lived and mythic experience according to local narrative conventions. In order to trespass upon the indigenous voice in these documents, however, we must appreciate them in their colonial context, as reinterpretations of what it meant to be Pasto, Nasa, or Muisca within a system of European domination. From this perspective, the assertions of Don Juan Tama regarding his military victory over Calambás, the emphasis on vernacular toponymy in Pasto contracts, the highlighting of Incaic representational forms such as queros and aquillas in Pasto wills, and Muisca donations of aboriginal textiles to fund Catholic masses, must all be understood as reinscriptions, both on paper and on the land and bodies of native peoples, which merge European and Andean forms of expression in unexpected and barely discernible ways. They employ a Spanish legal discourse and European legal conventions, while deploying Andean political intentions and symbols. They are imbued with a Christian intentionality, redirecting Andean referents toward Catholic spiritual ends. There is little in these documents that is "pre-Columbian," and much that is colonial. They stand as a testament to the versatility of native writers who, in the face of domination, forged new identities for themselves on the written page.

Up to this point we have only touched upon the conditions surrounding the production of legal documents. However, it is in the conditions of their transmission, reception, and subsequent use that we can further decipher the mechanisms by which an indigenous colonial culture emerged in the northern Andes. In particular, this can be achieved through the study of the types of written, visual, and oral evidence upon which indigenous litigants drew to bolster their legal cases. Here, we see native northern Andeans as readers and as interpreters, using texts in ways that engage European modes of analyzing and presenting oral, visual, and written evidence, at the same time that they serve their own interests by legitimizing themselves both before their own communities and colonial society. To accomplish this, we must look beyond written texts to various other cultural literacies, such as painting, sculpture, architecture, and music, to see how they intersect in this new system of legitimization.

Particularly useful in this exercise are Michel-Rolph Trouillot's ruminations upon how histories are constructed. Trouillot focuses on key moments in the production of history. For Trouillot, these are not discrete phases, but are, instead, entry points into a constant and simultaneous unfolding of history-making practices, which overlap upon one another. He begins with the creation of sources, such as the genres discussed in the previous chapter, which issue out of a process he calls "fact creation." This is followed by the creation of archives out of these sources, or "fact assembly." Facts must then be retrieved in a process of "narrative creation" and, finally, they must be attributed with retrospective significance, which he calls "the making of history" (Trouillot 1995, 26).[1] In this chapter, we will focus first on the latter three moments: the creation of archives, of narratives, and of retrospective significance.

We will not try to explicitly identify particular moments in our interpretation of native historical materials; rather, we will explore the sociocultural contexts in which we see them unfolding. Power is wielded during the process of history making, since those involved in attributing retrospective significance to narratives take advantage of the structural positions they occupy in order to authorize their histories. The category of *indio*, with all the cultural and legal baggage it carries, is a significant structural position that indigenous litigants move into and out of, as we have seen with Don Diego de Torres (see chapter 1), the mestizo cacique of Turmequé. Equally important is the position of the Pasto actors we will be looking at in this chapter, who operate within specific historical contexts that give rise to particular administrative arrangements impinging on their history making; for example, whether they are subject to the jurisdiction of the district of Ibarra or the Pasto Province, which, as we have already explained, makes a great deal of difference in terms of their adherence to Christianity, their command of literacy, and their projection of alterity. Finally, indigenous litigants are "voices aware of their vocality" (1995, 23) and of the different types of archives or memories upon which they can draw in their disputes.

Trouillot's suggestions can be considered more specifically within the field of literate production, to appropriate Pierre Bourdieu's notion. Bourdieu (1993) envisions social process as unfolding within nested and intersecting fields of power in which social actors articulate economic, political, or symbolic capital, with the former as the most encompassing of the fields. Within the colonial Latin American context, we could speak of a literate or lettered field of production, whose symbolic capital was controlled by erudite *letrados* and less aristocratic notaries and artists, as well as by priests. This field was accessed by other players in the lettered city, such as the indigenous litigants with whom we are concerned. Within the literate field, indigenous agents operating as subjects conscious of the power of the lettered city began to manipulate its very premises by consciously deploying orality and literacy according to multiple cultural criteria. As the medievalist Brian Stock describes with reference to the introduction of literacy in the European Middle Ages:

The coming of literacy heralds a new style of reflection. Individuals are aware of what is taking place, and this awareness influences the way they think about communication before reading and writing. An oral past that never existed may be brought to life and traditions given a legendary prehistory when they are only a couple of generations old. Alternately, a scriptural tradition that is the by-product of recent menaces to the preservation of verbal texts may be posited as eternal. In areas like this, the spoken and the written do not operate only in the external world. They also provoke subjective reactions. They provide us with insights into a system of mental representations in which "orality" and "literacy" play the roles of categories that classify a wide variety of social conventions having little or nothing to do with whether they are spoken or written. (1990, 7)

This sort of consciousness was present in the colonial Andes, embodied in the notion of "time immemorial," a legal term that pushed oral referents back to ancient times. When Pasto litigants juxtaposed an oral tradition from what they called time immemorial to an alphabetic document, playing one off against the other, they perceived "orality" and "literacy" as categories whose distinctive historical, legal, and cultural specificities could be used to different ends. On the one hand, they played oral history off documentation to display their alterity, in those cases in which they sought to preserve native lands using unrecorded evidence. On the other hand, when written documentation was available, it trumped orality, placing indigenous litigants firmly in a multiethnic and hierarchical world in which they fought their adversaries using the master's tools.

Also critical for our arguments are the insights of William Hanks (2000, 110–15), who argues in his analysis of sixteenth-century Maya-language documents from Yucatán, that legal briefs were arranged in intertextual series of almost identical writings with different signatories and dates. He suggests that the ways in which native literates assembled documentation into coherent collections followed criteria that diverged from those of Europeans. This is what Pasto disputants did when they attached oral histories from "time immemorial" to royal documents: they connected historical referents in what must have been for the Spanish judges, unexpected ways. But we will employ the notion of intertextuality more broadly than Hanks, taking into account how native disputants saw different types of texts, both alphabetic and nonwritten, as components of contextually specific assemblages. In the course of such an analysis it is important, however, to remember that the criteria used by indigenous litigants to arrange their evidence did not always demonstrate alterity. Frequently their criteria asserted the litigants' intimate insertion into the lettered city and colonial culture in general. Both positionings were simultaneously at play, whether the intertextual series was visual, alphabetic, or oral.

Hanks's application of the notion of an intertextual series to colonial-era documents is significant insofar as it leads us beyond the exploration of the conditions of their production, to a consideration of the trajectories of their readership: the various administrative levels through which documents passed, both within and beyond indigenous society, the ways in which legal papers were appropriated in the centuries after they were produced (2000, 280). Time and place are thus fundamental features of the construction and the reception of intertextual series. The intertextual series we will interpret juxtapose documentation from various time periods and places to create their narratives.

Finally, Gary Tomlinson's highly perceptive exposition of the problems inherent in the analysis of native-authored colonial documentation (Tomlinson 1996) reminds us that any interpretation of the northern Andean documentary record must not only remain cognizant of what Michel de Certeau (1988, 46) called "a dialogue with the dead"—between colonial authors and twentieth-century historians—it must also recognize that a similar dialogue took place between indigenous readers and writers themselves, who across the centuries read, cited, and manipulated the documentation of their ancestors in a circuit of readers, leaving a distinct mark upon what we know of these distant colonial actors.

In this sense, a modern reading of the Pasto documentation cannot only dwell on the evidence for its historical reconstruction of indigenous social structure, symbolism, or political intentions; it must consider, as well, native litigants as active framers of history, as agents who assembled archives and selected facts from them in their construction of legal and historical arguments. Moreover, their interpretations, recontextualizations, and modifications of earlier documents took place in dialogue with a living oral tradition, a space in which written evidence was transformed into oral narrative. That is, we must consider the particular way in which literacy operates in a "paraliterate" society in which "reading" was more than a mastery of the technology of literacy, but also involved the reception in heterogeneous social circles of the products of the lettered city, thereby expanding the purview of writing to a nonliterate milieu. Orality was itself recast within the documentation that Pasto readers—and twenty-first-century historians—studied. Such multiple readings played out against a backdrop of European and American colonial notions of proper evidence, of the nature of historical time, and of what it meant to be indigenous. Thomas Abercrombie (1998a), in his study of Bolivian Aymara historical memory, aptly terms these historical trajectories as "pathways of memory and power," writ on paper, in oral discourse, and upon the land itself, suggesting that these infinitely nested conversations and borrowings are a key component of colonial indigenous culture throughout the Andes, a culture that cannot, therefore, be Othered by painting it as exclusively oral.[2]

The following pages will begin by considering the nature of the trajectories of such assemblages among the Pasto. At the risk of appearing ahistorical, we will begin with a late eighteenth-century assemblage of documentary evidence by the caciques of Tuza, a kind of a "kitchen archive" (Behar 1986) stored in chiefly homes, which was destined for use in a centuries old dispute over lands. This case will help us to comprehend the specific circumstances under which the moment of "archive creation" took place, as well as the beginnings of the establishment of a narrative. From there, we will turn back to the seventeenth century and the town of Guachucal, where litigants in a long dispute over chiefly succession deployed oral and written evidence in their construction of a history of their ethnic lords, thus lending "retrospective significance" to their narratives. All of these cases focus exclusively on alphabetic literacy. The second half of the chapter will turn to the visual dimension of how literate genres of expression are brought into play in practice, focusing on maps and heraldry from colonial Ecuador and Peru.

Assembling Archives and Building Narratives:
Document Bundles in Tuza

In the late eighteenth century, the caciques of Tuza, in what is today northern Ecuador, presented a series of "notebooks"—or *cuadernos*, as they are called in the eighteenth-century labels affixed to the bundles—comprising a range of documents produced over the course of two and a half centuries, bound roughly together by thread. They were submitted as evidence in a dispute over maize lands in the vicinity of Puntal, which the nobility of Tuza had been cultivating since the sixteenth century (ANE/Q 1792b).[3] This documentation legitimized strategies of expansion by Pasto rulers into productive warm-country territory (Powers 1995, 124–27) and was the sort of evidence advanced in previous suits over territory that the high-altitude Tuzas coveted and the native lords of Puntal hoped to reclaim (AHBC/I 1634b, 1783). The Tuzas made their case by proving that they had legally purchased lands in Puntal, particularly in the vicinity of two hamlets called Cuesaca and Mumiar, by producing originals or copies of contracts, wills, and other transactions. They drove this point home in a 1791 document:

> So, what the indios of Tusa have done is to acquire those pieces of land by just and legitimate title, which is that of sale, and maintain themselves on them for a long time, even [time] immemorial. So that even if they did not hold a sales contract by which they acquired real control, it is necessary to confess that in the past more than one hundred years of possession, with their good faith and just title that they have shown, they would be the owners, if only by dint of prescription. (ANE/Q 1791, 38v)[4]

The genre of contracts that we described in the previous chapter must, therefore, not only be studied as internally produced documents, but also as legal papers that were read and employed in the centuries after they were drawn up. This documentation was organized into a series of "notebooks" whose contours were determined by the exigencies of legal proceedings dating to the late colonial period. When the Tuzas did not retain the necessary documentation, they turned to the ways in which they had inscribed themselves onto the land—through cultivation, boundary markers, and the erection of buildings—as proof of their possession, along with oral testimony. But as will become evident, the Tuzas were experts at deploying written documentation to back their oral claims.

The numerous "notebooks" of Tuza's caciques are carefully labeled with records of their contents and their owners. For example, the first packet reads:

> This notebook contains the very ancient documents [dating] from the year [one thousand] five hundred eighty and [one thousand] six hundred twenty nine, with a Royal Decree and other orders of protection for the lands of Mumiar in favor of Don Diego and Don Francisco Paspueles, Principal Caciques of all three towns of Tusa, Puntal and El Angel. It is in possession of Don Agustin Don Manuel Tussa = eleven folios. (ANE/Q 1792b, cuaderno 1, no pagination)[5]

This particular packet contains documentation dating from 1581, 1629, and 1692, emanating from both the Audiencia of Quito and local notarial registries.

Other packets, also containing the papers of several centuries, are more specific in their labels. Packet two, owned by a woman, serves as a case in point:

This notebook contains the deed of sale released by Doña Magdalena Guachan, cacica of the town of Guaca, in favor of Sebastian Galindes Cuerta, [for] a piece of land [measuring] eight cuadras that she inherited from her mother, Doña Juana Guachan, within the limits of the town of Puntal, in the site called Mumiar, and in the price of seventy two patacones = Item, contains the litigation over the same eight cuadras of land by Doña Maria Tuquer, descendent of Don Dionicio Paspuel Tusa and Doña Paula Cogollo against Doña Petrona Mainbas, wife of Don Matheo Garcia Paspueltusa, for which Doña Maria Tuquer received a favorable ruling, [lands] which the Puntal indios Don Santiago and Don Jasinto Guachagmiras and Don Cas. Paspuel, in the name of the community of the aforementioned indios, aspire to take from the descendents of said Doña Paula Cogollo: They are documents from the year of [one thousand] six hundred ninety two = In possession of Doña Maria Tuquer fourteen folios. (1792b, cuaderno 2, no pagination)[6]

Although the packet also contains petitions made over the course of the eighteenth century, these are not listed in the label. Documents not present in the collection, such as the 1740 will of Doña Paula Cogollo, are woven into a running narrative that surfaces at different points over the century of documentation, fashioned by different speakers, some Pasto and some Spanish; sometimes the narrative is embellished by details, such as the quantity of maize and barley harvested from the plot at any given point in time.

These packets contain crucial genealogical information, providing the caciques of Tuza with the names of numerous generations of ancestors and their exploits, facts that are integrated into complaints and petitions. Such missives generally begin with a lengthy genealogical description of the ancestors of the signatory, sometimes organized into lines that consist of five generations, a trope that constitutes a particularly colonial Andean— although not exclusively indigenous—form of narrative creation. In addition to the materials contained in this kitchen archive, the packets also point to the silences out of which history—as both practice and as narrative—is made (Trouillot 1995). For example, the eighth notebook, whose owner is not specified and which details the sale of the lands of Tustud in the hamlet of Mumiar, includes a 1700 petition by Doña Madalena Paspuel, who complains that the documentation of her claim to the land was stolen, thus hindering her from claiming her inheritance:

> I state that this india has informed me that at the death of the Don Carlos Paspuel, her father, there was left undivided among her brothers, Don Fernando Paspuel and Don Nicolas Paspuel, who are deceased, a piece of farmland in Mumiar. Since the documentation of the lands and the testament of Don Carlos, the father of my client, was left in the power of Don Fernando Paspuel, as the eldest brother, with his death, Don Carlos Paspuel, son of Don Fernando, her brother, appropriated said papers and lands and will not consent to my client or the sons of Don Nicolas occupying nor benefiting from them. So that justice be done and so that each party can make use of the rights which are theirs to their portion [of the lands], given that my client has sons who are tributaries and are paying tribute, it is in her interest that the piece of land be divided. (ANE/Q 1792b, cuaderno 8, no pagination)[7]

Doña Madalena's attorney demanded that "that said Don Carlos . . . not leave [Ibarra] . . . until he has shown Your Honor the will of said Don Carlos Paspuel, father of my client" (1792b).[8] Here is a silence or an absence which, like the documents preserved in the packet, serves as a point of departure for a narrative of family feud and intrigue that the Tuza-Puntal dispute fed upon and nourished over the years. It provides us with an example of how the idea of the power of the document, and not just its contents, contributed to the definition of the archive.

Embedded between mid-seventeenth-century documentation of land disputes by Doña Madalena's ancestors and the 1735 sale of these lands by Doña Madalena's sons, her petition makes reference to a series of other documents, including the 1661 testament of Doña Esperansa Gauilan (ANE/Q 1661), a previous owner of the plot, as well as sixteenth-century papers regarding its ownership. This is a nested set of several intertextual series, not just a single arrangement. The antiquity of these intertextual series, as well as those assembled in the other packets, is underlined in the label given to notebook eight:

> This notebook contains documentation of the legal sale made by Don Vicente Garcia Paspuel Tusa and Don Dionicio Paspuel, caciques of the town of Tusa, to Josef Vsuay, indio of the aforementioned town, [of] three cuadras of land which they held in Mumiar, jurisdiction of Puntal, which

they held and possessed by virtue of inheritance and division, as was the case for many other lands, as much in the aforementioned jurisdiction of Puntal, as in the Valley [of Apaqui], as is obvious and evident in the documentation of writs of protection and possession issued by the courts, which are inserted in this Notebook, whose age is such that some are more than two hundred years old and others one hundred and fifty, as can be noted. (ANE/Q 1792b, cuaderno 8, no pagination)[9]

Clearly, both the extent of the antiquity of these writs and the need to sample documents from different periods are significant criteria for the assemblers of the series, originating in the exigencies of colonial Spanish legal procedure.

Given the insertion into legal briefs of written evidence from earlier periods, most documentation of colonial litigation has this nested quality, ensuring that in any given packet of evidence there will be a series of papers that themselves contain reference to, copies of, or sometimes originals of earlier legal briefs; in other words, there are packets within packets. Each of them documents the ownership of specific plots by particular individuals and was assembled by their heirs. Thus, topography (plot location), genealogy (patterns of inheritance), and land tenure (the legal foundations of migratory and predatory trends) are crucial criteria for determining the organization of these discrete bundles of evidence. The entire aggregate of fourteen notebooks constitutes a polyphonic intertextual series in which long-dead Pasto caciques engage in dialogues with their ancestors, with the adversaries of their forerunners, with the colonial administrators and lawyers who represented them and who sometimes spoke for their forebears and—in the context of this extensive bundle of discrete documents—participate in an exchange with one another and with the caciques of Puntal, each from his or her own particular vantage points marked by territory, kinship, and trajectories of transmission of legal papers. Such are the "kitchen archives" of the Pastos, opening a window into the intertwined moments of historical creation that Trouillot calls "fact assembly" and "narrative creation." Unfortunately, these document bundles are preserved in the Quito archives, unattached to the record of the late eighteenth-century dispute for which they had been assembled, so we cannot tell how they were used to make history. Let us now step back a century to 1695 Guachucal, to see how such archives nourished narratives that had effects in the real world, as caciques were made and deposed in the course of disputes. Here, retrospective significance was given to the narratives.

The Attribution of Retrospective Significance:
The Chiefly Succession of Guachucal

The archives are full of disputes over cacicazgos, lengthy procedures that amass a century or two of documentation. Some of these disputes are underscored by contradictory claims founded upon contrasting legal systems, such as matrilineal succession in Pasto customary law and primogeniture in the Spanish system. Others are complicated by the massive population movements and the depopulation of the colonial period, which brought outsiders to communities as pretenders to chiefdoms (Powers 1995). In each of these confrontations, the legal record is constituted by numerous petitions by the various parties to the dispute and the royal decrees responding to each of these petitions, as well as by records of oral testimony and documentary evidence—such as wills, pedigrees, titles, and census documents—supporting the divergent claims. In this sense, the creation of sources and of archives is a product of the intersection of the practices of the colonial administration with indigenous agents who, as we have already seen, were not passive recipients of colonial justice, but actively engaged in the production of colonial legality, sometimes beyond the reach of Crown authorities. While the native voice is apparent in each of these individual documents—at a microlevel in Pasto toponyms, in references to parallel Andean forms of memory and inscription, and in particular brands of indigenous Christianity—it is also manifest in the conscious creation of an intertextual series by the litigants working in concert with their lawyers, in opposition to their adversaries, and before the court that decided the case. In such disputes, documents stored by caciques in their homes or retrieved from official archives were brought to light, their veracity debated, the rigor with which they followed notarial regulations contested, and their fidelity to customary law argued. The production, transmission, and reception of supporting documentary evidence were all in dispute. These are confrontations over correct literate and legal practice in which the timely juxtaposition of centuries of writing determined the outcome of the case. Furthermore, the indigenous litigants bolstered their documentary proof with oral testimony, itself only valid in written form and hence, an intercultural product of the interaction of indigenous witness, native or European translators, and Spanish scribes.

Such is the case of an extended litigation between Don Juan Bautista Ypialpud, hereditary cacique of the Pasto community of Guachucal in the

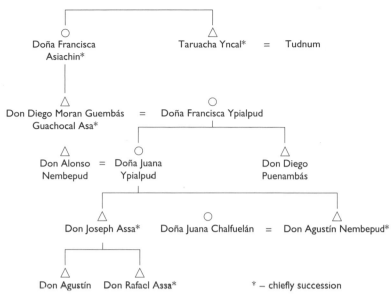

FIGURE 34 Reconstruction of the genealogy of the caciques of Guachucal: Don Rafael Assa's descent line, 1739.

late seventeenth century, and Don Rafael Assa, who disputed Don Juan Bautista's possession of the cacicazgo (ANE/Q 1695; AHBC/Q 1739). In 1695 Don Juan Bautista assembled as evidence of his right to the chiefdom an intertextual series of documents that hark back to a 1589 dispute over the succession. The royal decree in which this earlier dispute is registered contains a number of petitions from the early seventeenth century that cite chiefly wills and other important papers; it also records elements of chiefly history derived from oral tradition dating back to the time of the Spanish invasion in the 1530s. In an early seventeenth-century addition to this palimpsestic record, Don Alonso Nembepud (figure 34), one of the original sixteenth-century disputants and an ancestor of Don Rafael Assa, the litigant in 1695, argues that the legitimate cacique of the community was Don Diego Moran Guembás,

> who by another name is called Don Diego Guachocal Assa, who governed the indios of Guachocal as cacique and true lord more than fifty years, having inherited and succeeded to the chiefdom upon the death of Doña Francisca Asiachin his legitimate mother [and] true cacica and lady, who was from said town. [She] inherited her dominion from Taruacha Yncal cacique and lord, who was from said town since time immemo-

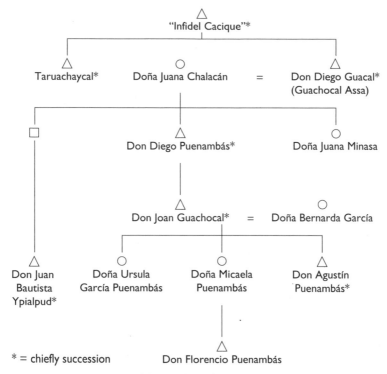

FIGURE 35 Reconstruction of the genealogy of the caciques of Guachucal: Don Juan Bautista Ypialpud's argument, 1739.

rial, having died without heirs at the hands of the first Spaniards who conquered these lands. She having been, as she was, his legitimate sister according to their law, and thus the chiefdom was justly inherited from her by Don Diego Moran Guambas. (ANE/Q 1695, 8v–9r)[10]

The depth of this oral memory, which includes recourse to complex anthroponyms, can be culled from the countertestimony of Don Diego Puenambás (figure 35), correcting the previous account:

Because Don Diego Guacal, my father, was the true cacique and natural lord of the town of Guachocal and true to the office and dignity as hereditary chief, he was commonly named Don Diego Guachocal Aça, which is the name of the town itself, as it is the use and custom in the entire Pasto Province for caciques to take the names of towns. To say that Don Diego Mueranbanpaz [Moran Guembás] is the same as Don Diego Guachocal Aça, [meant] he could only usurp the name because he was governor of the town. However, they were distinct and different people and it was Don Diego Guachocal Aça or Don Diego Guacal (who is the same), my father, and Don Diego Mueranbuenpaz, who was a commoner and since he was a ladino, he was named as governor, as is stated in the suit. Tarua-chaycal Guascal Aza, who was the principal cacique of the town when the Spaniards entered these lands, was the older brother of Don Diego Guachal, my father, who, having died without children, was succeeded by his brother. And she who is called Doña Francisca, a pretender to the succession, was a common indio in his service. . . . It falls upon me as son of the brother of Taraochayncal and the chiefdom and lordship, should succeed through the male line that existed and since all were his ancestors. (ANE/Q 1695, 10r–v)[11]

The various permutations of the name of the holder of the chiefly title at the time of the Spanish invasion—Taruacha Yncal, Taruachaycal Guascal Aza, even Taraochayncal—illustrate the slippery quality of the rendering of unwritten Pasto into literate Spanish, probably by a monolingual Spanish-speaking scribe.

Later in the record, a second royal decree was presented, which includes the following testimony, again from Nembepud, highlighting specifically his own (oral) memory of customary law:

Don Diego [Guacal] was not married to nor tended by Joana Chalacan, as is alleged in the petition. To the contrary, she was his concubine with many others he had. Nor was he a baptized Christian since he was born before there was a mission or baptism among the indios and the name of Don Diego was given him later by his employer, Esquibel, from which it can be inferred that he was not qualified for the cacicazgo nor had he any right to it. Another thing was that by inviolable custom and ancient law among our ancestors the sons did not succeed their fathers in the caci-cazgos. Instead, in the case of there being brothers and in the absence of nephews, sons of sisters, or cousins and other relatives of the possessor, as was verified with Don Diego Moran Guanpas my father-in-law and predecessor, who according to that law, succeeded in the cacicazgo after Don Diego, father of my adversary, since he was his cousin. . . . Now we have Josephe, who is the right and legitimate successor to the chiefdom and according to the Christian law in which we live now. (ANE/Q 1695, 51v–52r)[12]

Let us pause for a moment to unpack this complex group of quotations. Both disputants recall the time of the Spanish invasion when, in an un-recorded event, the cacique of Guachucal perished at the hands of European soldiers. The original hereditary chief is named, alternately, as Tarua-cha Yncal and as Taruachaycal Guascal Aza, the complex anthroponym we flagged above. Although we do not have access to the Pasto language, a close comparison with neighboring Pasto chiefdoms suggests that "Aza" distin-guished its bearer as a member of the chiefly lineage—it is alternately spelled "Aza," "Assa," and "Aça," since there is no orthographic consistency in the documents. Guascal most certainly is a chiefly surname, borne by one of the pretenders to the cacicazgo, as well as by the conquest-era cacique; the combination of "Guascal" and "Aza" later permutated into "Guachocal Aza," which, as Don Diego Puenambás states in his testimony, mirrors the name of the community. "Taruachaycal" remains, however, inaccessible due to the disappearance of the Pasto language. The oral memory of the custom of tracing cacicazgos matrilineally is tied to the narrative of the death of the conquest-era hereditary chief, since it is at this moment that primogeniture versus matrilineal descent becomes an issue. The nature of chiefly descent at the time of the Spanish invasion is argued at length in the pages and pages of testimony issuing from this dispute, pointing not only to the centrality of customary law in such documents, but also to the complex and intercultural ways in which legality was disputed in the colonial era, a problem we will re-turn to in the following sections.

However, the memory of Don Diego Moran Guembás—identified by one of the disputants as the same person who was also called Taruachaycal Guascal Aza—is also lodged in the written record, in particular, in a writ submitted as evidence to the court, in which he was named governor by the Crown, given his facility in the Spanish language (his identity as a *ladino*). There is much to disentangle here, for by identifying the former governor and pretender to the chiefdom as a ladino, the witness acknowledged him as someone who had facility in two languages and cultures, Spanish and indige-nous. *Ladino* is not a neutral category. Rather, it indicates an individual of slippery character. Ladinos were primarily caciques or sons of caciques but, as Bartolomé Álvarez (1998 [1588], 267) says, they were also spies used by the native elite against the Spaniards. There is, thus, an inherent untrustworthi-ness in someone who learns and uses Spanish, a stereotyping of indigenous speakers of Spanish that pervaded the colonial era. While the label func-tioned as a separator between indigenous and European, its use here betrays the participation of both categories, "indio" and "español," in a common colonial social formation (Adorno 1991).[13] Don Diego Puenambás, who presented this Spanish-language document as evidence, also framed it in Pasto oral tradition by alluding to the rules and prerogatives of chiefly succession: "Another thing was that by inviolable custom and ancient law among our ancestors the sons did not succeed their fathers in the cacicazgos." In addition, he effectively separated the pagan past from the Christian present by alluding to the critical function of Christianity as the pivot of the transition from customary to Christian law (Gruzinski 1993 [1988], 123–24, 126): "Now we have Josephe, who is the right and legitimate successor to the chiefdom and according to the Christian law in which we live now." The assembly of an archive, itself the product of the juxtaposition and reinterpretation of various sources produced by earlier indigenous litigants, unfolds here in a nuanced historical narrative very specific to its narrator, his noble position in both Spanish and Pasto society, and the time period in which he was speaking.

Interlude: "Time Immemorial"

Time is essential to these quotations, in which assertions are validated by appeal to the veracity of memory. Notwithstanding the deployment of native conventions of appropriate evidence and Pasto expressive forms contained in the document, the native voice is conditioned by Spanish legal convention, which is expressed as though it were a native form of memory. "Time immemorial" was an epistemological category for Spanish notaries and judges, one of an array of terms used to gauge how the knowledge provided in a testimony was acquired by the witness (Hoyos García 2002, 121). An early seventeenth century notarial manual used in the Bogotá area conveys the precision with which such a term would have been employed:

> For this it must be known that time is a brief movement, or a long one of movable things, and immemorial, when there is no memory to the contrary. . . . And in this case, the principle is understood of beginning to place things in their being, as to begin to own a thing; and because according to that, the discourse of time is needed, which no one can reach, the law provides that five things be decided. The first [being] the witnesses speak of forty years of knowledge. The other, that they heard it from others before them, who had seen it themselves, which is called firsthand (*primeras oidas*). The other, when they tell what they have heard

from others before them, which is called secondhand (*segundas oidas*). (González de Torneo 1614, 102v–3 in Hoyos García 2002, 121)[14]

Of course, as we move through the usages of this term over time and space, its meaning appears to vary significantly, diverging from the legal definition to one extent or another.

Customs and administrative arrangements are sometimes described in the Pasto documents as being in effect "from time immemorial" (*desde tiempo inmemorial*), "from the time of gentility" (*desde tiempos de la gentilidad*), and sometimes even "from the time of the Inca" (*desde el tiempo del ynga*); this, in a region that never fell under Incaic control.[15] Framed in terms of oral tradition and customary law, appeals to time immemorial were sometimes meant to refer specifically to pre-Columbian times (Caillavet 1983), thus conceptually isolating the colonial indigenous speakers from their non-Christian past (Espinosa 1995, 93–94). This occurs in Nembepud's testimony, when Don Reymundo Guaycal, chiefly pretender in 1735, provides in his petition a genealogy of his noble ancestors, stretching back to his *rebisabuelos*, or great-great grandparents, who lived in the late sixteenth century; this provides an approximation of the critical moment when the "time of gentility" ended (ANE/Q 1735a). Such a positing of a time depth of five generations is, itself, highly formulaic, appearing in other disputes over chiefly successions (ANE/Q 1771, 1r), as well as in Zapata de Cárdenas's commentary on the structural distance necessary to avoid marriage with close relatives (1988 [1576], 80–81), and in both indigenous and European models of kinship in Peru (Zuidema 1977). This use of European formulas for genealogical calculation suggests that "time immemorial" and related phrases were meant to signal the two opposed blocks of time, lying before and after the Spanish invasion.

But more frequently, the use of this formulaic expression referred to any point in the past, deriving from a Spanish legal convention that defined "time immemorial" as at least twenty years (Leal Curiel 1990, 12–13, cited in Spira 1998). O'Phelan Godoy (1993) argues that the notion was employed in the eighteenth-century Bourbon era as a way of criticizing far-ranging transformations in the colonial administration and its ritual by appealing to tradition or to custom. In Pasto documents from a range of periods, it is sometimes possible to calculate the time depth of time immemorial, as O'Phelan has done for Bourbon-era documentation. For example, a mid-seventeenth-century *cacica*, Doña Lucía Nem, widow of Don Joan Miscay, a lesser noble of Túquerres, alleges that the lands she inherited from him date back to "time immemorial": "My husband was in possession for many years [up] to today in continuation of that which his parents and ancestors held since time immemorial" (ANE/Q 1735b, 85r).[16] A 1660 petition by her husband dates his possession of the land back forty-five years and that of his ancestors, more than fifty years (1735b, 90r), providing a calculation for time immemorial of roughly a century. In another example, the authorities of Muellamués state that their community members had worked local haciendas "since time immemorial" (ANE/Q 1757, 1r, 4v); later on in the document, it appears this service began approximately a century before the complaint (1757, 28r, 52v). These are not cases of litigators lying to achieve their ends, but attempts to advance claims by transcending an imperfect paper trail through expanding the scope of written evidence by means of an appeal to oral tradition. As evidence was read and reread by successive generations, "time immemorial" thus became a colonial indigenous vehicle for asserting what was meant to appear as a more ancient authenticity, legitimizing rights by appeal to customary law and to the oral memory (Mills 1997, 62–63).

Similarly, oral and symbolic traditions inserted in the documentary record became elements of the scripted past, following European legal conventions through which orality and literacy became intertwined. In the 1690s, at the tail end of the lengthy dispute in Guachucal, various witnesses were called to attest to the genealogy of Don Juan Bautista Ypialpud, who was then cacique, and whose dispute with Don Raphael Assa resulted in this palimpsestic record.[17] The witnesses, some of whom spoke in Spanish and some of whom used interpreters, were confronted by the court with a written list of complex and precise questions, to which they replied, reproducing almost verbatim the words of their interrogator, as was the accepted legal practice (ANE/Q 1695, 82r–84r and 85r–95r). What appears as orality in the document is thus but a trace element, filtered through the questions of the interrogator, the voice of the interpreter, and the pen of the scribe. In an analysis of the nature of the legal transcript of the trial of the Red Brigades in the early 1980s, the Italian historian Alessandro Portelli (1991) highlights the fact that what we see in the legal record is a rendering by the trial judge, who erases the voice of oral witnesses as he writes legal briefs. The oral shape of the indigenous voice in these colonial Latin American documents is, similarly, elusive.

Finally, once the written record was internalized by Pasto witnesses, it was not all that easy for them to separate those narratives that they had acquired through oral tradition from the evidence that was read to them or commented upon by other readers. In effect, we are speaking of a "para-literate" system, where literacy involves much more than command of the technologies of reading and writing. Such was the case with the sermons of the Third Council of Lima, which were meant to be read or explained by the priest to the indigenous faithful in the vernacular (Lima, Concilio de 1990 [1585], 629–30), to the indigenous doctrinal assistants he had trained, or to the officeholders of the community (Peña Montenegro 1995 [1668], 319).[18] The ceremony that accompanied the arrival of a royal decree in an indigenous community also included its public reading, called its "publication."[19] When such a ritual act also included the translation of the decree into indigenous vernaculars, the written document entered into oral channels of communication:

> Being in the plaza of this town of Tussa, having come out of mass, being the spot destined for doctrinal teaching and the people of this town having congregated, including Don Tomatias [Tomas Matias?] Quatinpas, governor, and the other caciques and principals, with the participation of Miguel Rodrigues Moran, protector, appointed for this inspection by order of Your Honor the Lieutenant Corregidor General, who was present, by voice of Diego de Santa Maria, who assumed the role of town crier, I published the Royal Decree of Proclamation, in and according to its contents, I, the notary, explaining it in the General Language of the Ynga. (ANE/Q 1771, 11v)[20]

As a result, witnesses frequently alluded to papers that they had heard of from their elders, but which are described in such detail that it is clear that either their titles had entered into oral discourse, or the speaker was referring to a written list of documents during his testimony (ANE/Q 1656, 2v).

Reading the Archive in the Pasto Province

Thus, it is difficult to extricate orality from alphabetic literacy in dispute documents because by the seventeenth century, the Pastos were inextricably bonded with a colonial culture whose very nature was defined in part by legal discourse. The indigenous respondents, moreover, understood the value of writing and the legal conventions that underlay its use. The original royal decree which Don Juan Bautista Ypialpud brought to court in the 1690s includes reference to written documentation, in particular, the will of Don

Diego Guachocal Aza, whose chiefly pedigree was in question (ANE/Q 1695). Don Diego Puenambás, one of the sixteenth-century disputants, argues in his testimony that the testament is fraudulent:

> The other party grounded his argument in the fact that my party was named as son. It says in its date that [the will] was made on 18 August, fifteen hundred and eighty nine, and the decree handed down by this Royal Court in order to ascertain how my party was the legitimate son of Don Diego Guachocal Asa was the year fifteen hundred and eighty six, in which the royal decree makes mention of his father having died a long time before. Since my party was a child of small age, Don Diego Mueran-banpaz had entered into the governance of the chiefdom. . . . This being so as is evident in the rulings, my adversary, is notoriously false, as is the above-referenced so-called testament. (1695, 12r–v)[21]

So Don Diego Puenambás compared the various pieces of evidence to indicate that their dates were not consistent with the narrative of his adversary. But he went further, arguing that Nembepud's argument was not admissible, because it was not signed by a letrado, a high Crown functionary whose very name bespeaks the place of literacy in the architecture of the Spanish colonial administration (1695, 13v), what Ángel Rama has called the "lettered city."

The notions of truth and falsehood deployed here were dependent upon the exigencies of the lettered city, its administrative apparatus, and the legal principles upon which it was founded. Truth was lodged in the office of the notary, whose testimony was considered more valid than that of other actors and whose production of and access to correctly formulated papers prevailed over the oral memory (Herzog 1996, 20). Nevertheless, many of the papers upon which Pasto litigants were dependent were but imperfect likenesses of proper notarial rhetoric, lacking, for example, the requisite number of signatures, thus leaving indigenous disputants at a real disadvantage in the courts, as the following example from neighboring Carlosama illustrates:

> Before me, Captain Don Josep de Simon y Belasco, lieutenant governor, high justice, and corregidor of the aforementioned city and its provinces, Don Andres Garcia Yaputa exhibited the testament of Don Sebastian Yaputa, his deceased father, governor and principal cacique of the section of Yaputa, whose testament appears to be written in four folios of un-official paper [paper without a seal] without the authority of notary nor

judge and it appears to be signed by only four witnesses and that of the deceased. (ANE/Q 1736, 6r)[22]

The proper procedure for executing legal conventions and setting them on paper was also a matter of dispute, not just between Pastos and Spaniards, but within communities, whose members routinely argued among themselves over the order of steps in a proceeding (ANE/Q 1771, 30r–v). The construction of a hierarchical ranking of the validity of different genres of evidence was also in dispute in some cases. A 1783 confrontation over lands in Puntal hinged on whether or not testaments presented valid enough testimony to legitimize property rights, in comparison to notarized sale contracts (ANE/Q 1792b, cuaderno 12, n.p.).

Even when there was a modicum of consensus over legal procedure and the value of particular genres as evidence, disagreements erupted over the veracity of a document. Sometimes lawyers, judges, and litigants found it difficult to read the notarial handwriting of earlier centuries, as occurred in a mid-eighteenth-century dispute in Pastás:

> Don Luis took the commissioner judge and the indios to show them the boundaries of the hacienda of El Salado, as he claimed were contained in the titles he brought and showed the judge of land claims, [the latter], having looked at them, said that he could not find the boundaries of the upper part and that he did not understand the handwriting, because it was very old and that the titles should be copied in order to understand them. (ANE/Q 1753, 39v).[23]

However, copyists frequently had equal difficulty in deciphering notarial scrawlings, leading to further disputes over the veracity of documents. This was compounded by the fact that evidence was frequently presented in copied form, thus concealing the conditions of creation of documents and leaving litigants open to allegations of fraud.

It is thus not surprising that at times, fraudulent documents made their way into litigation. In a 1748 dispute over the chiefly succession of Pastás, three wills advanced as evidence did not fill the criteria of veracity stipulated by one of the disputants:

> They are clearly assumed and feigned, inasmuch as the first one, according to its date of one hundred and sixty years of antiquity and the second supposedly being made by Don Pedro Pastas, the eldest son, as it is said, of Don Gomes Pastas, who wrote the first one. [But] it is less than one

hundred years old, according to the ink and the paper and the handwriting, which was quite different in those days. This patently indicates that they are not, nor could they be, of the antiquity that is supposed, but instead are false and fabricated by some forger. This being the case, according to the rule of law, once wrong, always presumed wrong [and] what is wrong with the first testaments must be presumed for the third one presented by opposing party, that is, that it is assumed and false. (AHBC/Q 1748, 138r–40v)[24]

Such differences were common in legal disputes, as Karen Powers (1998, 193) records for a battle over chiefly wills in eighteenth-century Riobamba, Ecuador, where a seventeenth-century testament was disputed in court because its handwriting did not appear similar enough to other documents prepared by the same notary; in this case, however, the Spanish judge decided, after a careful study of the evidence, that the discrepancies were not great enough to invalidate the evidence, thus demonstrating that notions of falsity were highly subjective and were wielded as weapons in such paper battles.

Let us return to the Guachucal case, in which allegations of fraudulence led us on a brief detour into the implications of forgery. The lengthy dispute over the cacicazgo continued after the initial confrontation between Puenambás and Nembepud; it was layered with numerous other written documents framed by oral memory, sometimes recounted in the "mother tongue" (*lengua materna*) of Pasto and mediated by interpreters and Spanish scribes. Some of these later documents are reproduced in the record, such as the 1691 will of Doña Micaela Puenambás (ANE/Q 1691a), and are noted as having been written in the community by indigenous scribes, attesting to the role of indigenous agency in creating the archive (ANE/Q 1695, 42r–43r).[25] As disputants were progressively recognized and unseated as hereditary chiefs, the ritual context in which the dispute unfolded was itself inscribed into the record. Thus, in 1627, when Don Diego Puenambás expired, his son, Don Joan Guachocal, was ritually invested, as is recorded:

And present the aforementioned and the governor and principals, [the royal governor] ordered Don Joan to sit on a beam with his lasso beside him and being seated, the governor and principals arrived and kissed his hand and said that they would receive him and received him as their cacique and natural lord and Don Joan flung away his hat and ordered them to return it to him and they gave it to him and they were ordered to carry him on the beam upon which he was seated and they carried him and carrying him brought him along a space of the plaza of said town, all of which was done as a sign of possession. (ANE/Q 1695, 21v)[26]

The legal process, encoded in alphabetic documents that themselves catalogue earlier writs interwoven with oral testimony, was thus embodied in a performance that itself became part of the written record.

These are indeed ambivalent documents, evidence of the evolution of a colonial culture that emerged not only at the interstices of the República de Indios and the República de Españoles, but also within the República de Indios itself. They cannot be read as simple examples of a neutral technology, as some theorists would have it, nor as raw data for historical reconstruction. Their Pasto authors were themselves involved in the writing of history, enmeshed within a system in which the asymmetrical exercise of power obeyed an ideology of linguistic primacy whose supreme apex was Latin-based alphabetic literacy. Literacy thus functioned as both a stage for the creation, transformation, and transmission of colonial culture and as the measure of the social hierarchy through which this culture operated. The documents we have described cannot be read as simple expressions of the conflict between a primordial indigenous culture and its European counterpart, but as vehicles for the transculturative process, expressed in its written form through the sedimentation of literate, oral, and performative practices from indigenous and Spanish positions of enunciation. Literacy was, indeed, a prime scenario for colonization in the Spanish American world.

Maps and Portraits in Colonial Peru

The literacy required to create documents sometimes exceeded the knowledge necessary to produce an alphabetic text or a written description of a performance. Frequently, the additional presentation of visual materials—such as maps, drawings, and occasionally paintings—was required to substantiate claims to land rights or titles of nobility. Documents such as *probanzas de méritos y servicios* (autobiographical and service narratives of an individual) called new images—like coats of arms—into being. In other words, the probanza served as a vehicle for generating new heraldry, which would be granted later through the creation of a document of yet another genre, the *ejecutorio*. Images like the coat of arms circulated in greater spheres of activity—on door lintels or as decoration on clothing—but surviving today only in archival documents, either as insertions or as textual descriptions.

Some of these images were surely kept over generations for the visual plea-sure and fascination they offered; they might, then, become detached from the documents they originally accompanied. Such isolated images distort our comprehension of how they were intended to be seen and understood, be they maps, coats of arms, or drawings.

The significance of these images lay in their validity as evidence in legal claims. For this reason, like the documents legitimizing cacicazgos, images also were copied into later documents, since in subsequent litigation they might be employed as evidence for other claims. This form of visual literacy must be understood within the context in which it appears: a legal document in which oral and visual knowledge is affirmed through its relationship to alphabetic writing and the strictly codified form in which such inscriptions are cast. This form makes such evidence useful in the present, as well as in future litigation. Just as the written word was accepted as a vehicle for tran-scribing oral testimony to faithfully convey the words of a witness, images were believed to express visually, and even substantiate, an eyewitness's ex-perience and knowledge (Cummins 1995). Therefore, images achieved evi-dentiary status once they were entered into a legal document.[27]

The transformation of images into legal evidence could take two forms. Images could be described by eyewitnesses who stood before them and re-ported orally what they saw. Alternately, the image itself was entered directly into the document as prima facie evidence (Cummins 1995). Sometimes, both forms appeared in a single document. In Mexico, even pre-Columbian "paintings" achieved such evidentiary status, because it was argued that they more faithfully presented the memory of ancient deeds and institutions than the mere oral testimony of witnesses.[28] Pre-Columbian "paintings," such as those of the late fifteenth-century *Bodley Codex*, were said to communicate knowledge of the past more faithfully because they were uncorrupted by present turmoil, thus permitting their presentation in court.[29] There were no such paintings in the Andes, and we find no pre-Columbian images or ob-jects, such as *khipus*, entered directly into the evidentiary record, only the in-formation they recorded. However, with the acquisition of the knowledge of European-style drawing and painting, framed by an understanding of how genres could operate in different contexts and carry distinct meanings in each arena of appearance, new images—decidedly colonial images—could be made and used for legal purposes.

Perhaps the most famous example of such images from the Andean region appears in the set of legal documents that were first generated in the 1590s by Felipe Guaman Poma de Ayala, author of the *Nueva corónica*. The document, published under the title of *Y no ay remedio . . .* (1991 [1594–1646]), details Guaman Poma's legal struggles as the hereditary lord, Spanish-appointed governor of indios, and administrator of the province of Lucanas, highlighting in particular his claim to lands in the village of Chupas, near Huamanga (present-day Ayacucho; Adorno 1993). As in some documents concerning litigation over land claims, a map is included (figures 36 and 37). The type of map attached to this document is pictorially descriptive of the Spanish city of Huamanga in relation to its surrounding territories. That is, the map is not truly Euclidian: it did not employ an overarching grid through which relationships of distance could be represented geometrically and according to scale (Mundy 1996, XIII; Padrón 2004, 35). Rather, it portrays the city of Huamanga pictorially by means of elevated views of its buildings arranged around a central plaza within a vast territory. In this sense Guaman Poma's map is visually similar to the maps presented in Spain by the cacique of Turmequé in his petitions for rights and privileges in the New Kingdom of Granada (figures 1 and 2). Guaman Poma's map functions in much the same way as those presented by Don Diego de Torres.

Guaman Poma's map visually establishes the place of contention named in the text—Chupas—and its relationship to the principal city of Huamanga. This relationship is pictorially conveyed according to both Andean and Spanish criteria. First of all, the viewer is offered a bird's-eye view of the surrounding territory and a schematic vista of the city of Huamanga. The territory defined by the city limits as they were first imposed by the Spanish founders is marked by two parallel lines that form a rectangle around the city, with architectural boundary markers at each of the four corners. Thus, we can simultaneously observe the legal dimensions of the city as it was first laid out as an urban grid and note its specific jurisdiction as defined by boundary markers. The foundational importance of the image is asserted by the phrase written next to it: "The City of Huamanga, laid out in a grid and delimited by boundary-markers by the first founding citizens."[30] The text, while supplemental to the image, is critical to conveying its meaning, because it situates the image in time, pointing to Huamanga's "first founders," whose actions established the sociopolitical space that is both drawn and verbally described in the phrase. The conjunction of time and space is visually difficult to convey within the economy of the pictorial conventions used for this map, but as a map with legal implications it is imperative that it estab-

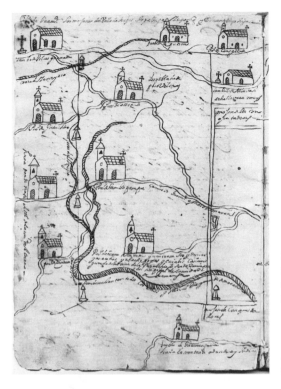

FIGURE 36 Half of the map of Ayacucho area after Guaman Poma, legal actions regarding land titles in the valley of Chupas near Huamanga, Peru, ca. 1560–1640, Tello Prado ms. known as *Y no ay remedio*, ca. 1640, f. 52v. Courtesy of Juan Ossio.

FIGURE 37 Half of the map of Ayacucho area after Guaman Poma, legal actions regarding land titles in the valley of Chupas near Huamanga, Peru, ca. 1560–1640, Tello Prado ms. known as *Y no ay remedio*, ca. 1640, f. 53r. Courtesy of Juan Ossio.

lish *a terminus a quo*, a starting point, for the legal boundaries and cityscape, so that claims could be made.

Above and outside the boundary markers of Huamanga is Chupas, the village whose lands are under dispute. Rendered in a smaller scale, Chupas is presented in schematic form similar to Huamanga, with a few defining buildings arranged around a central plaza. All other communities are emblematically represented through a single structure: the church. The pictorial conventions of place, be they schematic or emblematic, convey here the Spanish legal concerns as outlined in the text. Not only are the two important urban centers depicted differently from the others, but the scale used to depict Huamanga and Chupas expresses their relationship within a Spanish geopolitical hierarchy, rather than a spatially proportional one. That is, the distance between the two entities is not based on any rational system of reduced measurement, but on their structural position in the administrative hierarchy. The existence of these two towns on the map is crucial for what is argued in the litigation: the map confirms spatially what is textually recounted.

However, the relationship that Guaman Poma details between Chupas and Huamanga in the map is not only about Spanish legal jurisdiction and how it can be depicted pictorially. As in the case of the considerably more numerous maps produced in Mexico in response to a royal questionnaire in the 1570s (Mundy 1996), Guaman Poma's map depicts a native Andean sensibility toward the landscape through his placement of Chupas within a specific topographic feature. He places the town at the headwaters of the Guatata River, in the very midst of a series of small streams that meet at the boundary line of Huamanga. There, the streams converge into the Guatata River, which is identified in an alphabetic caption as the source of power for Huamanga's many mills. Rivers are, in fact, the only topographical features in the map. This is not accidental, as rivers and their flow of water are key topographical features in the mythic and social Andean world (Salomon 1991, 14–16). The sociopolitical connection between Chupas and Huamanga is, therefore, to be understood as being something more than the socioeconomic power of a river as it enters into the Spanish district (Adorno 1993, 61). Instead, the river must be understood as carrying an Andean cultural meaning.

The orientation of the map itself is altered to call this relationship into view. The west is at the top of the map, with the south on the viewer's left. This is a very odd orientation for a European map. In the few extant maps from the colonial Andes, the usual orientation is with either east or north at the top, following normal conventions (MacCormack 1991, fig. 23, and Salomon 1998, fig. 5). Even the maps that Guaman Poma creates for Martín de Murúa's 1590 "Historia del origen y genealogía real de los reyes Incas del Perú" and his own *Nueva corónica*, circa 1615, are either oriented north or east, when a direction can be deduced. His view of the city of Huamanga in the *Nueva corónica* has no indication of cardinal directions. Only by comparison with his 1590s map of Huamanga contained in the litigation over Chupas, does it become apparent that he has maintained the same orientation in the *Nueva corónica*.[31] In fact, the unusual orientation is really only significant in the 1590s map, as it allows the viewer to perceive Chupas as being above Huamanga. In other words, mapping conventions of orientation are superseded in order to use pictorial conventions on the flat picture plane. This creates the illusion of receding space: Chupas is depicted as smaller than Huamanga and is placed above it, so as to demonstrate its distance. This suggests that it lies at a higher altitude and that the waters flow downward toward Huamanga and the imagined place of the viewer. Because the rivers are necessary to the image's meaning from an Andean perspective, what seems a rather odd feature becomes comprehensible. Although this native artist understood European pictorial and cartographic conventions, the artist's rendering suggests that he was able to manipulate those conventions to his own advantage to present his case visually.

Equally important are the three small figures placed standing above the town of Chupas, arranged in a triangular composition. The middle figure clearly represents an Inca, specifically, Topa Inga Yupanqui. This figure is critical, as it represents the concept of time immemorial, which, as we described in relation to Pasto documents, was also known as the "time of the Inca." This is a Spanish legal category through which rights of inheritance to lands and titles of nobility were calculated. In the lawsuit, it is claimed that it was Topa Inga Yupanqui who conquered the territory and recognized the authority of Guaman Poma's ancestor. On either side of Topa Inga Yupanqui are the figures of Don Juan Tingo and Don Domingo Guaman Malque (who is also called Don Martín de Ayala); it is through them that Guaman Poma and his co-litigant, Dõna Juana Chuquitinta, claim descent and their right to the lands of Chupas. Dõna Juana was the oldest legitimate heir to Don Juan Tingo; Guaman Poma de Ayala was the legal descendant and heir to Don Martin de Ayala. The map therefore serves a double legal purpose: it not only demonstrates visually the legal and topographic relations of Chupas and Huamanga with its boundaries and lines of territorial jurisdiction, but it also presents the three major historical characters who preceded the Spaniards' arrival in the region, and whose existence is the legal basis on which the claims were made. That is, the Spanish legal categories of time ("time of the Inca" and direct descent) and space (an area constituted by a city and its marked boundaries) are compressed into a single composition. This map is, then, a complex visual argument that was meant to stand as an "eyewitness" to the claims of Guaman Poma and his co-defendant.

The concept of time and descent are reified through a second visual genre introduced into the document. Pen-and-ink full-length portraits of the two ancestors through whom title is claimed, Don Juan Tingo and Don Martin de Ayala, precede the map (figures 38 and 39). They are the same two figures that flank Topa Inga Yupanqui in the map. Here, however, they are not schematic figures, but fully developed portraits, with distinct physiognomies, as well as very different dress and attributes, such as weapons and bracelets. The distinguishing iconographic features in their costumes are repeated in their schematic images in the map, insuring the identification of the individual portraits with the figures in the map. But one must ask: Why does Guaman Poma include these portraits? What is the task that they visually perform? We can understand the role of a map in delineating territory, but portraits, as a genre, usually appear in a different context, as we will consider in the next two chapters. To answer these questions, it is important to point out that these are not idealized portraits. There is an attempt to render the figures as individuals, as if drawn from life. Don Domingo Guaman Malque de Ayala, as he is titled in the portrait, has a more rounded and heavier face than Don Juan Tingo; his lips are pursed and turned down, giving him a more severe appearance; he also has a broad nose with flared nostrils, while the nose of Juan Tingo is more aquiline. These are all distinguishing features that create the image of an individual, a historical subject.

This effort at individual likeness is not simply an aesthetic exercise, but like the genre of the map, it has a precise purpose within the context of the document. In a very real sense, the two portraits make visible the legal claim of time immemorial. These are images of individuals who were alive and held title at the time of the Inca. They are not mere illustrations of illustrious ancestors. As a genre within painting, portraiture is understood to make the past present or, as Alberti claimed, the portrait has the divine force to make "the dead seem almost alive" (Alberti 1991 [1435–36], 60). In the context of this document, divine force allows the past to be present, visually substanti-

FIGURE 38 Portrait of Don
Martin de Ayala Guaman
after Guaman Poma, legal
actions regarding land titles
in the valley of Chupas near
Huamanga, Peru, ca. 1560–
1640, Tello Prado ms. known
as *Y no ay remedio*, ca. 1640,
f. 49r. Courtesy of Juan Ossio.

FIGURE 39 Portrait of Juan
Tingo Guaman after Guaman
Poma, legal actions regarding
land titles in the valley of
Chupas near Huamanga,
Peru, ca. 1560–1640, Tello
Prado ms. known as *Y no
ay remedio*, ca. 1640, f. 51r.
Courtesy of Juan Ossio.

ating the claims of the living. In other words, for the portrait to be made in the likeness of someone means that a person existed from whom the likeness could be extracted.

Surprisingly, the text does not make reference to the accompanying drawings, neither the map nor the portraits. Why it might be asked, if the witnesses, lawyers, and notary do not overtly acknowledge them, should we pay so much descriptive and analytical attention to these images? One response is to suggest that they stand autonomously, as if to convey their significance independently in the visual channel. The portraits and map are in and of themselves necessary and sufficient for what they depict. Of course, they reference the text through the names and captions included in each image. They are sufficient, nonetheless, because their existence is not acknowledged in the textual document; they are necessary because they are placed in the document. Finally, we understand that they were not considered incidental, but integral to the document for a very telling reason. The map and portraits we have been discussing are not the original images; nor is the document in which they appear the original document: they are all copies. We can rest assured, therefore, that the original images did, in fact, carry enough visual weight in the document to be copied in a later redaction made for a dispute that occurred, more or less, in 1640. Although the original drawings by Guaman Poma are unknown to us, we can be sure that what we do have are very faithful copies made by a artist or a notary skilled in drawing (Adorno 1993, 56).

That they are copies, and precise copies at that, is clear for three reasons. First, the images appear within a complete signature, either on the verso or recto sides of a folio.[32] This means that we can be sure that they were integral to the copy and have not been added to it. What we cannot be sure of is their placement in the original document, or whether they were loose-leaf inserts or drawn directly into the document, as they appear in the copy. The former is probably the case, since they are not mentioned in the text. Second, the figures appear standing above what might at first glance seem to be a ground line, but is, in fact, the rubric of the notary marking the fidelity of his copy. Third, the drawings do not exactly follow stylistically the known drawings of Guaman Poma. Some differences are very noticeable, such as the cross-hatching used in the copies to give greater volume to the figure. Nonetheless, the copyist has been quite faithful to the originals. We know this because Guaman Poma uses the image of Don Domingo to depict his grandfather, Don Martin, in the *Nueva corónica* (1980 [1615], 165 [167]); the figures are almost identical in pose and iconography. The only radical stylistic difference is the bracelet (*chipana*) worn on the right arm.[33] Why is this small detail so important? It demonstrates the intervention of the copyist at the level of style, although his addition does not affect the intent of the images. In other words, apart from a few stylistic changes, the copyist places as much effort in re-creating the drawings as the notary—who may very well be one and the same person—does in retranscribing the document.

Writing Heraldry

The inclusion of the portrait drawings in the Chupas document is a rarity that adds an unusual degree of visual concreteness to the claims of legitimacy of the disputants. But in a very real sense, they are analogous to the much more prevalent donor portraits of caciques, such as those at Sutatausa (figure 26; plates 4 and plate 5), which we will consider in detail in chapter 6. Similarly, the map, a much more common image in legal disputes, is analogous to the frescos and paintings of the stations of the cross as in Sutatausa (figure 24), which depict the historical landscape of the central narrative of Christian salvation, giving place to text just as the map does. A second genre of documents establishes legitimacy through a different, more symbolic form. Here, we refer to documents granting a coat of arms to caciques in recognition of their noble lineage and service to the Crown. The design for the coats of arms was usually either painted, drawn, or verbally described. Such legal papers established its holder's right to display his coat of arms publicly and to pass it down to his descendants, thereby further ensuring proper genealogical succession.

Such documents were not without dispute. For example, in the 1550s several of the bilingual sons of Wanka lords from Huánuco traveled to Spain with their own notaries to petition the Royal Court for coats of arms, which they were granted (AGI/s 1555b, 107v–8r). In the coat of arms granted to one of these nobles, Felipe Guacar Paucar, he is depicted in the upper left-hand quadrant in an Andean tunic and mace that he argued commemorated in perpetuity the services rendered to the Crown (Cummins 1998b, 112–13). However, less than ten years later, Viceroy Francisco de Toledo, in an attempt to gain control over these newly enfranchised local lords, ordered that the probanzas de méritos and the ejecutorios—the documents requesting and granting such coats of arms—that had been granted by Charles V and Phillip II, be gathered and burned in the plaza of Jauja (AGI/s 1573). These alphabetic documents and the images they granted were powerful instruments for asserting and displaying authority, as many caciques understood. They were important enough to be faked; native elites sometimes invented their own coats of arms without going through the established procedure of submitting a probanza de méritos to be approved in Spain. For example, Martín de Murúa depicts a coat of arms for each one of the Inca dynastic families in both of his two illustrated manuscripts. In the earlier one, "Historia del origen y genealogía real de los reyes incas del Perú" (ca. 1600), the coats of arms are associated with the portraits of the *coyas*, or Inca queens (Murúa 1600, 22v, 24v, 25v, 26v, 27v, 28v, 29v, 31v). In the second manuscript, *Historia general del Pirú, origen y descendencia de los Incas* (1616), the same coats of arms are associated with portraits of the Inca kings (Murúa 1616, 21v, 23v, 26v, 28v, 30v, 32v). That is, Murúa alters the association of the coat of arms from female descent to male descent or from Andean rule to European ones (Cummins 2008). Whether or not these coats of arms were invented by Murúa or someone else is not important; rather, it is significant that within them, indigenous symbols (such as the *mascapaicha*, or Inca crown) are pictorially inserted into a Spanish heraldic escutcheon, just as they were for the Wanka lords. That is, local elements of symbolic importance were used to create both official and unofficial coats of arms, often in relation to events mentioned in the probanza de méritos. These documents were kept in family archives and handed down with other important papers from generation to generation. Their importance in documenting legitimate authority both within the colonial regime and within the indigenous communities is evident in the fact that Toledo had them burned in Jauja in front of the indigenous community to whom they had been granted. Such a bonfire was suggested, again, 200 years later. In 1761, Eusebio de Llano Zapata suggested that no greater service to the king of Spain could be offered than to create a genealogical book that dealt only with family of the caciques, their coats of arms, and their family trees. One would then be able to establish those who falsely claimed to be descendants of the Inca and who displayed fraudulent coats of arms.[34] Less than twenty years later and following the rebellion of Tupac Amaru in 1780, the *visitador* Areche was sent to evaluate the situation in the highlands. He found that many local elites still demonstrated their authority through both portraits of the Inca and by displaying coats of arms, many of which he claimed were not even legitimate. He instructed that the coats of arms, along with portraits of the Incas, be gathered up and burned in order to end such pretensions (Rowe 1954, 30).

Despite such occasional punitive actions, coats of arms were accepted visual symbols that were much sought after by local elites throughout the Andes, as elsewhere in the Americas. One such escutcheon was granted to Don Sancho Hacho de Velasco, *cacique mayor* of Latacunga (a province south of Quito).[35] In 1559, Don Sancho sent a letter to the king of Spain, Philip II. This was the beginning of a series of documents presented before the Council of the Indies by his lawyer, Juan de la Peña. The process was long, stretching on for more than twenty years; however, this was not all that unusual a time frame. Don Sancho was making several requests, based on his status and the assistance he had given the Spanish Crown. For his community, he asked that the tribute they paid to the Crown be reduced and that usurped lands be returned to them. He also requested he be paid a salary of 1,000 pesos from the tribute paid by the natives of Latacunga; if that could not be granted, he asked, as an alternative, for a royal decree giving him control over the collection of the tribute of a group of indigenous tributaries (a *repartimiento de indios*). He requested that the Crown bestow upon him the right to bear Spanish arms—a sword, a lance, and a musket—and that he be allowed to be accompanied by two African slaves (Oberem 1993, 27). He also asked for a coat of arms, for which he provided a sketch.

It is the coat of arms and how Don Sancho imagined it, in relation to how he recounted his merits and services to the Crown, that are important to us here, because the example displays a different sensibility about how such an image should appear and be understood. We shall first recount the narrative of the important events that Don Sancho wanted to set before the king, because it is the relationship between this text and the design of the coat of arms that is unusual for its degree of literalness. As one finds in all such documents, Don Sancho prepared a list of questions to be asked of the witnesses he called in support of his request. Among other things, these questions elicited accounts of his various efforts to assist in pacifying the natives of Quijos. The witnesses testified that they knew of the aid and loyalty that Don Sancho had shown the king and his representatives. All was in place for the petition to be entered.

Here is Don Sancho, cacique and señor principal, as presented through the voice of his attorney, Juan de la Peña: "Say that since the Spanish had entered this province until now, I have been and am a God-fearing Christian and follower of His holy commandments and as such I have offered to serve Your Majesty with his person and goods and horses and indios from the towns of which I am cacique and always as a good and loyal vassal, offering comfort and aid to your viceroys and others who have come to these parts in the name of Your Majesty" (AGI/S 1559, 47 r).[36] Among other things, Don Sancho recounted that he aided Viceroy Núñez y Velasco in the civil war against Gonzalo Pizarro, by taking 200 men to battle at his own cost.

Don Sancho's statement, is of course, similar to other probanzas de méritos y servicios, such as the ones presented by the Wanka lords, all of whom attempted to insert themselves into the documentary record with the aim of obtaining recognition as historical protagonists and gaining the rights and privileges of nobility. However, indigenous heraldry, unlike the more symbolic heraldry of Spaniards, does not refer to ancient foundational events or to genealogy, but to more immediate events accountable by eyewitnesses. Native American coats of arms were often more literal and narrative in nature, reproducing in imagery the key elements of the probanzas de méritos, the foundational events that would henceforth validate the noble lineage. In the northern Andes, the reference is much more literal than in the Wanka example: Don Sancho pictorializes the written genre of the probanza. Once the coat of arms was granted, his narrative would be made public through its exhibition on house lintels and on clothing. Indigenous heraldry thus functioned as a visual companion to the notion of "time immemorial."

Let us then look at Don Sancho Hacho's own description of his coat of arms, which appears first in his petition and then again in a second presentation as both a drawing and a description by his agent, Estevan Pretel. In the second presentation, the coat of arms is drawn with its description below (figure 40). (Note that the description is not written from the vantage point of the viewer, but from that of the escutcheon itself):

> A coat of arms divided in four parts, which in the upper right-hand quadrant shows an armed man with a royal standard of blue and gold in his hand, and in white armor within a red background. On the left-hand side indios with their bows and arrows going to war against a green background. And in the lower right-hand quadrant, a white horse, saddled and bridled, with a lance placed in the pummel of the saddle with a golden staff and a silver spear point, with an indio of natural color, who holds the reigns. And in the fourth quadrant, a rampant lion of natural color, with a sword in its hand, against a golden background. And above the shield, a closed helmet with a lion's arm holding a sword in its hand and blue and gold foliage. (AGI/S 1568, 50v)[37]

The heraldry Don Sancho describes reproduces the narrative of his probanza, rather than including native symbolic objects, as in Wanka and Inca

Below the drawing, handwritten caption text:

*Vnescudo partido engualp partes que enla vnr alla sela mano decci huest
vn hombre armado con vna bandera Real enlamano deagul colob licen
y las buinas blancas encofso ailando- zenlastzaparle de lamano y aquei via
vnos mdtro con tus flethis y yro sundefue ra en campiss vuite que n'lastraparle
de abazo dela mano dy zebra maiba le blanco entillada y enfuendo con Vna
lancon zruh aerparry tonge El buelos decro zel buisos de plata con vngnin de su
elar y la tuenest vuenta y enelbm grauth miaenvelmusta puel hconfella con
masspada enlamans Perencampssfoza y farhines, se bsu vn colona de carmido
con vn braço de leon convna es pala inlamans y fillazes de aquel y ses*

FIGURE 40
Coat of arms
of Don Sancho
Hacho de Velasco,
cacique and
governor of the
town of Tacunga,
province of Quito,
1568, AGI/S, MP
Escudos 216,
f. 50v. Courtesy of
Archivo General
de Indias, Seville.

coats of arms. Don Sancho appears in the upper right-hand corner, armed in defense of the Crown, just as he claims in his account. To his left are the native troops at his command. Below, he depicts the horse he claims to have ridden into battle. Next to his horse is the only emblematic image in the coat of arms: a sword-wielding rampant lion, representing Don Sancho's bravery and fealty. The coat of arms thus mixes two types of images, emblematic and pictorial. In so doing, it makes transparent the historical acts for which the coat of arms was to be awarded, acts that are narrated in the alphabetic channel. We cannot refer to this as intertextuality, a term that refers to how texts relate to one another. In the Spanish case, such texts encoded in alphabetic and visual documents would circulate within the myriad archives that comprised the colonial legal system. In contrast, Don Sancho's coat of arms moves beyond the legal archive into other spheres of activity and representation, appearing as architectural ornamentation, on tapestries and banners, and in decorations on clothing; these are not necessarily part of the legal, or even the alphabetic domain, indicating that when literate genres enter into action, they address a whole range of audiences through a multiplicity of channels and vehicles.

Don Sancho's coat of arms came with a bundle of obligations, in addition to the rights it bestowed on its owner. The cacique of Latacunga was responsible for catechizing his community, a role that involved building and adorning churches, as well as supporting priests (Oberem 1993, 27–35). He was required to support Spanish economic interests by sending subjects to distant provinces as miners (ibid., 27). He served as a broker in peace negotiations between the Crown and native groups in the lowlands (ibid., 25–26). He owned a textile workshop that produced hats for the market (ibid., 130). In other words, he was a responsible member of colonial society, who defended both the interests of his own community and of the Crown. Don Sancho's coat of arms is the tangible result of these efforts.

Indigenous Elites and the Creation of Colonial Culture

We commonly misconstrue colonial hybridity as a product of the imposition of Spanish cultural representations upon indigenous people, and not the conscious adoption by native elites of a range of foreign cultural forms in an effort to bring a cosmopolitan ambiance to their localities, thus enhancing their own status and that of their communities in the colonial world. The acquisition of alphabetic literacy was but one facet of this elite project. We tend to think of reading and writing as solely a critical form of instrumental knowledge, a means to getting things done within a colonial system administered by the Spaniards. At one level, as we have shown, this is true. However, the songbook and drums that Don Diego Guachocal Aza included in his will, which we described in the previous chapter, move beyond the purely instrumental needs of a bureaucracy. Reading and writing formed part of a broader universe of literacy that included music and art. The creation of the colonial cultural order was not only enacted through administrative exigencies, but perhaps even more, through these other channels, whose production culminated in the celebration of the Catholic cult: the ornamentation of churches, the donation of musical instruments to local sanctuaries, the sponsorship of indigenous students in schools for caciques, where music and painting were part of the curriculum. In short, indigenous elites were involved in the production of a new colonial ethos.

On 31 December, 1582 Don Pedro de Henao initiated a probanza de méritos petitioning to be named governor of the natives of Ipiales and Potosí in the Pasto Province. He submitted a series of nine questions concerning his capacity to hold office. Significantly, the second question did not concern his administrative experience, but rather, his cultural knowledge base. Witnesses were asked to testify to his participation as a *cantor de canto de órgano*, a singer, in his community's church (AGI/S 1582, 1r). One of them added to his testimony that Don Pedro had also composed a musical work for the mass (ibid., 5v). Clearly, Don Pedro's authority rested on a number of qualities of leadership, including participation in the creation of musical texts, as well as administrative documents, which were deemed sufficiently important as to be included in his petition.

Much of what the caciques created grew out of the new desires that had developed among them, their willingness to engage with an expanding world, including both the acquisition of objects and techniques from abroad, and the inclination to visit distant realms. Don Diego de Torres was not the only cacique to visit Spain. In fact, sixteenth-century Spain hosted a significant number of indigenous visitors (de la Puente Luna 2010): as well as the visit by Wanka lords, an embassy of Tlaxcalans arrived at the court of Philip II (Muñoz Camargo 1981 [1585]). Mestizos who identified themselves with natives, such as Garcilaso de la Vega and the cacique of Turmequé, even settled in Spain. Generally, such voyages were made at the Crown's expense, after years of petitioning. The Pasto cacique Don Pedro de Henao spent three years obtaining the wherewithal for his trip to Spain (AGI/S 1583, 1584a, 1584b, 1584c, 1586a). Don Pedro traveled to Spain in 1584 with the intent of gaining privileges for his people in the form of royal decrees. He was successful in terms of readjusting the amount for which they should be taxed. At the same time, however, he pressed his own personal legal claims before the Crown. Among other things, he petitioned to bring back to Ipiales from Seville a master tile-maker and an organist, as well as their wives and children (AGI/S 1578–88, 117r); he also requested funding to pay for ornaments for his church (1578–88, 113r, 155r–56v).

What we are arguing, then, is that the indigenous participants in the literate world—particularly the native nobility with whom we have been largely concerned—cannot be understood as simple pawns of it. They participated actively in colonial culture, engaging new technologies of literacy, both alphabetic and visual, and new forms of expression. Like the Spaniards whose representational systems they emulated, the literate indigenous nobility was thoroughly familiar with how different genres of alphabetic documents and visual evidence intersected in practice, and they used this knowledge to their own ends. However, as we have also demonstrated, they subtly transformed these genres, infusing them with indigenous content, thereby creating new representations that were colonial in nature. But the creativity of native elites is only part of the story. The colonial ethos that they fostered, which engaged literacy in myriad ways, was also experienced by common people, those who had less access to the written word and who never imagined developing coats of arms. To comprehend the experience of literacy by commoners, however, means that we must go beyond the production and manipulation of literate forms, to search out how the ethos of literacy infused everyday life: we must look at how literate metaphors were incorporated into public ceremony and spectacle, how Catholic ritual became a stage upon which the ideology of literacy was taught to nonliterates, how the grid plan of the indigenous town projected literate values and concepts. To these issues we will now turn in an effort to understand how Andean commoners came to be exposed to the literate ethos that their cosmopolitan caciques espoused.

On 30 May 1613, two Muisca caciques, Don Francisco and Don Diego, wrote to King Philip II from their communities of Tuna and Suba, just a few leagues from Bogotá (AGI/s 1613). They informed the king that their lands had been taken over by outsiders and that their fields were being destroyed by grazing cattle. If these activities continued, they would soon be unable to sustain themselves. As they state in the opening to their letter, Don Francisco and Don Diego sought the mercy of His Majesty, being aware of the particular affection and love that the king had for the natives, who lived so distant and removed from his royal person.

Unlike the cacique of Turmequé and other indigenous nobles, these local caciques could not travel to Spain to present their plea in person. Consequently, they resorted to a letter, as did so many of their counterparts throughout the Americas, presenting themselves and their petitions in writing. In their missive, they acknowledge the physical distance between his royal Majesty and themselves, "because we cannot appear in person before your Royal Majesty our pleas are made through letters" (AGI/s 1613, 1r–v).[1] What is of interest here is not the political or economic needs that the missive would assuage; instead, we need to focus in on the capacity of the letter to represent not only words and thoughts, but also the absent speaker. Letters were understood to bridge the distance between king and his American subjects—"we live so removed and remote from your royal person."[2] The nature of a letter is distilled in the imagined dialogue it projects across space, a desire for communication that Guaman Poma described in his illustrations. Generally, we take this as a given, how a thing—a letter—can represent its authors. As a thing, the missive of Don Francisco and Don Diego, stands for their persons before the king. This is an aspect of the written word that transcends alphabetic literacy as a technology. Here, it is the phenomenology of the object bearing the graphic inscription that makes the absent present and, therefore, precedes and authorizes any decoding of the written word. This phenomenon expands our notion of literacy to include those who cannot read, because the power of the written word does not merely adhere to the act of deciphering it.

Thus, we move beyond our focus on how northern Andean literates—as readers, writers, and artists—appropriated the technologies of alphabetic and visual literacy. For the most part, literate colonial actors were members of the indigenous elite, caciques and cacicas, such as Don Francisco and Don Diego, who either had been trained in literate communication or had access to those who were. But what of the majority of the indigenous population—those who did not write wills, did not engage in extended land litigation, had not been educated in the erudite intricacies of artistic expression or in the conventions of map making, those who did not speak Spanish and could not sign their names? How did they participate in the colonial literate world? The intertextuality of the visual with the alphabetic is traceable, on the one hand, in the educated appreciation of these two channels of expression, and, on the other, can be pursued through the interpretation of how literacy intersects with performative activity. Following the analysis by Paul Connerton (1989) of the primacy of ritual and bodily habit in the construction of memory, linked to Michel Foucault's (1979) theory of the role of bodily discipline in the constitution of power, we will dedicate the remainder of this book to interpreting how colonial northern Andeans absorbed the ideology of literacy through the ritual manipulation of objects and the experience of space. That is, we will take a step back to examine how the workings of literacy permeated society at large, creating what can be called a "paraliterate" society, composed of people who, though they could not read or write, entered into literacy from its margins: by listening to sermons on Christian ritual practice illustrated through pictures, or by participating in the myriad administrative rituals of both the secular and sacred lettered cities.

In this chapter, we will focus our attention on the varied meanings that inhere in a ceremony that confirmed divine and secular authority through the physical manipulation of the document as a sign and as the written word: the ritual of swearing obedience to a royal decree. The same attitudes, postures, and gestures toward alphabetic documents associated with the acknowledgment of the authority of secular rule were employed in the affirmation of divine supremacy conveyed in the visual realm. Hence, this example furnishes a crucial link between alphabetic and visual literacy. Moreover, a look at colonial sermons demonstrates that these practices and objects were perceived as intimately connected. The intertextuality of alphabetic and visual literacy in the colonial Andean world was frequently grounded in ritual, which might profitably be thought of as a kind of "performative literacy," the embodiment of the notion of literacy in an ephemeral performance. Thus, we prefer to understand literacy as not exclusively a symbolic technology of encoding and decoding, but as something enacted in space and amongst people, linking several fields of discourse. As William Hanks points out in relation to the production of colonial Maya documents, the texts produced by native officials manifest "the rapid emergence of language use, new types of action in colonial society." "In describing such discourse," he notes, "one is led to treat genres as historically specific elements of social practice, whose defining features link them to situated communicative acts" (2000, 133). Although documents are grounded in concrete spheres of activity and practice as texts, they also enter these scenarios as objects.

We do not refer here exclusively to discourse encapsulated in writing and image, but to the acts of production themselves, which emerge as critically important. That is, writing and image-making have their own histories and associations; they have social meaning in and of themselves. The medium constitutes a message that is different from the information it contains, one that is, moreover, more powerful. The appropriation of literacy by those who theoretically had no knowledgeable access to it has the effect of bringing the medium itself to the fore, making it visible as a technology that both transmits and embodies power. When literacy is placed on display, its appropriation becomes a significant gesture, apart from whatever is contained in the text or image. Yet the display of literacy as an action is already often an articulated gesture. Understanding the origins of such gestures means weaving together the message of the medium with the rituals of literacy (Justice 1994, 25).

The King's Signature

The ceremonial display of obedience paid to documents containing the king's seal—which is the king's image—and the signature of his royal court

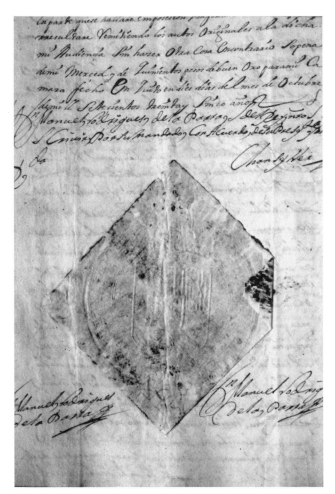

FIGURE 41
Real provisión,
with royal seal
and Audiencia
signatures, 1635,
ANE/Q, *Indígenas*,
caja 3.

by colonial officials (figure 41) took place repeatedly in the course of disputes and was witnessed by indigenous spectators, recorded in the documentary record, and subsequently singled out as significant by future generations of indigenous readers. The document that was the focus of this ceremony, the *real provisión*, or royal decree, was a formality in a series of legal interactions between two parties in conflict. By acquiring a real provisión in a dispute over lands or chiefly succession, a party to a suit was able to ensure that the king's orders would be obeyed and that the case would be procedurally suitable for consideration before the Audiencia (Díaz Rementería 1977, 137). In order to ensure compliance, however, the document had to be first presented to the official responsible for the case, before he could continue the process.

But it is an object contained in the real provisión that was the focus of this ceremonial presentation: the royal seal. The real provisión carried an image of the royal coat of arms embossed in wax onto a separate piece of paper, which was affixed to the end of the document (*Recopilación* 1973 [1681], libro II, título XXI, ley iii, 243v). It therefore appears as something apart from the specific document, yet integral to conveying its author's supreme authority. Moreover, it is the visual nature of the seal, the coat of arms literally pressed into the material of the document, rather than any written words it contained, that was first recognized as conveying this authority—the authority that the local official had to ceremonially accept. Let's look at an example of this from the Ecuadorian coast.

In the hot and humid coastal mangrove of Ecuador, a chain of verbal, visual, and textual exchanges took place in 1577 between Miguel Cabello de Balboa, a priest, and Alonso de Illescas, an African, bringing King Philip II before them. Cabello de Balboa, writing sometime later, recounts that he stood on the shore where he had built a chapel the night before in order to celebrate the Nativity of the Virgin. Shifting his account to reported speech, he writes that he addressed Alonso, saying "Come sir, Lord Alonso Illescas, partake of the goodness and the mercy that God our Lord and His Majesty the King offer to you this day" (Cabello Balboa 1945 [1589], 37).[3] Alonso responded from the prow of his canoe: "I call myself Alonso and I don't have [the title] Don" (ibid., 37).[4] Cabello de Balboa replied to Alonso, saying "The King can give and confer the [the title] Don, as you will come to understand, be that you come to land" (ibid., 37).[5] Later that day, King Philip II did grant Alonso the title of Don, making him governor of the territory. This was accomplished by virtue of the fact that Cabello de Balboa carried with him a real provisión that not only pardoned Alonso de Illescas of past transgressions; he made him governor of the area. The document was read *de vervo ad verbum*, after which Cabello de Balboa took the hand of the "the new and black Governor" (nuevo y el negro Gobernador) and, holding the real provisión, they both focused their eyes on the King's image (mirando el sello) and said, "This is the coat of arms of my lord the King that you well know" (ibid., 37).[6] Taking the document in his hands, Don Alonso kissed it and placed it over his head, saying "Lord vicar, I commend to you as to the Lord Father my head and those of my children and companions, and I give to you my obedience and that of the mulattos who are in my charge (who live within nine or ten leagues of my house)" (ibid., 37).[7]

The acts and dialogues recorded here were the result of political expediency, as we will describe presently. First, however, let us simply conjure up the space in which this transformative looking transpired. Envision two men, distrustful of one another yet pressed fairly closely together in the hot and humid air of the Pacific coast, joined by clasped hands. Their eyes and gaze are so differently embodied, but mutually concentrated on the same embossed image that emitted the presence and the power of Philip II, king of Spain. The image, attached to the words of the king, conferred the title of "Don," a gift that only the king could bestow, and in return for which the newly titled Don Alonso was forced to acknowledge the presence and power of the monarch, as well as the subservience of himself and his community to the king. This he accomplished by literally placing himself below the king—embodied in his image upon the seal—after first kissing him by kissing the seal. The image impressed upon a surface has, of course, a long tradition in Western art of making the invisible present. Moreover, those images created by touch have a particular agency, such as the shroud of Turin, or the Veil of Veronica (Belting 1994, 49–57). The king's embossed image, although mechanically rather than miraculously impressed upon the surface, also had agency and could transform the political and social state of things. In colonial America, a place in which the king would never appear in person, this image became the lynchpin in a syntagmatic chain of Spanish colonial political and religious images. It was not just the seal that made the distant presence of the monarch immediate. Above the seal came the signatures of the royal officials of the Audiencia. The almost undecipherable flourish of these marks provides a kind of visual transition between the imagery of the seal itself and the scribal text of the document: even someone who could not read could, at the very least, recognize these different elements of the document by their form.

The Ritual Kiss

Inscribed repeatedly in the record each time a royal decree was presented, an act that could occur at numerous points in a dispute, was the same ceremony that Cabello de Balboa and Don Alonso Illescas enacted: the ritual kissing of the document, which was placed on the head of the colonial authority to symbolize his intent to obey the orders inscribed therein. While the performance of this ritual in and of itself left no tangible traces, its memory was formulaically inscribed by the notary who witnessed the proceedings, as can be noted in the following document from Cumbal, in the Pasto Province:

In the town of Cumbal, within the limits and jurisdiction of the city of Pasto, twenty-eighth of the month of April of the year sixteen hundred and fifty-six, before the Maestre de Campo Miguel de Caizedo, Lieutenant Governor, High Justice, Magistrate of Natives, and High Mayor of Mines of the city of Pasto for Your Majesty in its limits and jurisdiction, this royal decree and petition therein contained was presented for its compliance and inspection by the Lieutenant Governor, [who] received the royal decree in his hands and kissed it and placed it over his head, which was bare, and he obeyed it with the respect due to a letter and royal decree from his king and natural lord, whom the divine lord should protect for many years by increasing his dominions as Christianity wishes. And he ordered it be executed and preserved as is stated therein, and he is prepared to supervise personally its execution according to the letter of said royal decree. Then, without delay he signed it with himself as witness, there being present in said town neither public nor royal notary: Miguel Caizedo. (ANE/Q 1656, 9v–10r)[8]

This act of placing a document on the head, probably a ritual of Roman or Byzantine origin, was also incorporated into Islamic political culture. In Arabic, for example, the best term for obedience is "On my eye and on my head," and in twentieth-century Iran, the receipt of writing issuing from the shah was acknowledged by placing the document on the eyes and on the head (Mehdi Abedi, personal communication).[9] The roots of this act in Spain are unclear. It could have arisen from either Christian or Muslim political culture, but most likely it was a ritual common to both and mutually recognizable. This act was, moreover, not restricted solely to political documents. The same ceremony of obedience was enacted by Spanish ecclesiastical authorities at the close of the fifteenth century, when investigators into the authenticity of miracles placed orders by the archbishop on their heads, just as secular authorities did in civil disputes (Christian 1981a 125–26). It is recorded in the acts of receipt of apostolic briefs, such as papal pronouncements, where ecclesiastical judges engaged in similar ritual acts (Cook and Cook 1991, 116–17).

While the kissing of the real provisión and its placement on the head of the royal official confirmed that its recipient recognized the king's authority and was bound to respect his orders, it did not necessarily entail carrying out those orders, as is expressed in the formula "obey but do not comply" (obedézcase pero no se cumpla), which legal scholars have interpreted as a means in the medieval era of preserving municipal law in the face of the expansion of royal jurisdiction (González Alonso 1980). On a deeper, less legalistic level, Rama interprets the formula as a manifestation of the quasi-sacred nature of writing in a society in which the rule of law was incomplete:

> The exclusive place of writing in Latin American societies made it so revered as to take on a aura of sacredness. The letter was always "obeyed," even when that obedience did not translate into action, whether in the case of royal directives to the colonies or later republican constitutions. Written documents seemed not to spring from social life but rather to be imposed upon it and to force it into a mold not at all made to measure. There was a wide and enduring gap between the prescriptive detail of the law codes and the anarchic confusion of the social realities toward which the letrados directed their legislation. The gap did not reduce the coercive force applied to enforce the legal requirements pertaining to persons and property. Still, the inefficacy of those requirements becomes clear in the monotonous reiteration of identical proclamations or prohibitions in similar edicts issued year after year. Considerable portions of society were somehow able to ignore the legal dispositions of the letrados. (1996, 29–30)

It is precisely for this reason that we must look beyond the technologies of colonial literacy, to the ritualized contexts in which their meaning was diffused, in order to comprehend what literacy meant to colonial-era native Andeans.

What sort of meaning might the European and Islamic ritual of kissing a real provisión have had for native Andean peoples? We have little information available to answer this question for the northern Andes, although there are significant clues in the Inca area. Given the Spanish propensity for describing northern Andean cultural practices in Incaic terms and for introducing colonized Incaic cultural forms in the north, the following Peruvian example provides a glimpse, at least, of how we might read colonial literate ritual from an indigenous point of view. In Incaic ritual conventions, practicants made kissing sounds at *huacas* (shrines), an act communicated by the Quechua word *muchana*.[10] Andean observers, then, might have read the act of kissing the real provisión ambiguously, from both Andean and European perspectives. We know, however, that by the middle of the sixteenth century, the act of muchana acquired new meanings that brought the act of kissing the royal decree and the reverential Andean kiss into a new approximation, as the following document illustrates.

Between 1550 and 1552, a document was generated for lands in the valley of Yucay, Peru, produced as a part of the response to a real provisión concerning the possible redistribution of vacant plots to the Spanish residents of Cuzco. As we already observed in documents relating to coastal Ecuador and highland Cumbal, in this instance, as well, the *corregidor* greeted the royal decree with the appropriate ceremony of raising it over his head (Villanueva Urteaga 1971 [1970], 32). He then traveled from Cuzco to Yucay to make a personal inspection, which involved questioning the hereditary lords of the area in reference to a map made of the region in 1551. Their testimony and its truth content were transcribed into the document as follows:

> And then the indio caciques Incas of the above declared by translation of Pedro Delgado native interpreter from this valley under the oath that they made to tell the truth, by which they all swore in the following form according to their law, *mochando* the sun and the earth and the *guaca* as is their custom, promising to tell the truth and responding to what they were questioned by the interpreter they said, having the said painting [map] before them, the following. (ibid., 32)[11]

The map referred to in this quotation was an image made on the ground using dirt, rocks, and other items so as to register (*pintar*) the topographical features of the valley, to indicate (*señalar*) lands dedicated to cultivation, and to verify the indigenous testimony (1971, 40).

The visual nature of the map—or perhaps, the painting—is unclear. When it was shown to Don Francisco Chilche, the principal cacique of the valley, it was described as "figure and painting" (*figura y pintura*). Whatever forms were seen by Don Francisco, he recognized them as faithful to what was known to be true, acknowledging his general agreement through an interpreter and correcting a few fields that were depicted in the wrong location. A month later, in Cuzco, when the final draft of the document to be sent to Lima was being drawn up, the corregidor, who had gone to Yucay and had seen the image, asked that it be now painted on cloth and appended to the document. He ordered, however, that it be glossed with written text, so that what was depicted could be clearly understood.

What is important here is how Inca forms of representation melded with European ones, bringing them into commensurability with the formal necessities of the document. That is, the participants agreed to gloss a local sort of image as a "map" bearing certain information that could be agreed upon and sworn to. Once the "map" left the immediate space of the participants, however, it had to be copied and glossed so that external viewers could agree to see the same. But the act signifying the truthfulness of the Incas' Quechua testimony was not the sign of the cross that normally accompanied European legal procedures. Rather, they made a commensurate reverential act, kissing and blowing across their hands—muchana.

In González Holguín's Quechua dictionary, *muchaycupuni* is translated as follows: "To return to the status of subject, when the loser or rebel pays obedience, or to ask forgiveness of one's senior, or to reconcile with one's senior or with God" (1989 [1608], 246).[12] In other words, by this time *muchana* acquired the meaning of subordination to both secular and Christian authority.[13] This new, political use of muchana as an expression that negotiates the relations of colonial authority becomes clear in a Quechua phrase of salutation and subservience appearing at the end of a 1600 letter by the hereditary lords and Inca nobility of Cuzco to King Philip III concerning the need for Jesuits to found schools in Peru. The letter opens in Spanish with the stock salutation of subservience: "The hereditary lords and Inca nobility, natives of this city of Cuzco, capital of this kingdom, vassals of your Majesty, we humbly kiss your royal feet and hands. . . ." (Egaña and Fernández 1981, 221–23).[14] Here, the written word performs the conventional ritual act conducted for an audience before the king, as in any letter addressed to him. At the end, however, just before the signatures, is written: "Ten by ten, I thank you, Great Lord. Give, o give your hands and feet, even the last toe/finger to [us] Incas" (Chunca chunca muchai coscaiqui capac apo sulcaruciqui[man] yanaiqui[man] chaquiqui[cta] maquiqui[cta] cui cui, yngacona[man]).[15] This is, seemingly, a stock phrase employed to express in Quechua the same act of subordination toward royal authority as the Spanish phrase that opens the letter. The institutionalization of this phrase and the muchana ritual as an act of subordination are revealed by González Holguín, whose dictionary was published seven years after the letter was written: "Ten by ten, I kiss your feet and hands, or I thank you" (Chunca chunca muchascayqui chaquiyquicta maquiyquicta, o muchay cusccayqui), which he translates into Spanish as "Beso las manos de vuesa merced que es saludar" (I kiss the hands of your Majesty, greeting you) (González Holguín 1989 [1608], 121). This phrase is incorporated into the ending of the letter and made more subservient by addressing the king as *capac apo*, or high lord, and the Inca as his son. Clearly, the Jesuits in Cuzco understood how to turn Quechua terms into phrases that expressed the humility and subordination of the native community. It is in such ritual acts, situated at the interstices of the two cultures, that we can begin to decipher a specifically colonial iconology, captured in writing and image.

The Experience of Writing

For many native observers, especially those living in the first century after the Spanish invasion and those who were not members of chiefly families or officeholders, the act of obeying the royal decree was one of the few direct encounters they would have with alphabetic and visual literacy and its relation to ultimate authority.[16] Whether they could read the documents in question is immaterial, because the royal decrees were inspected by participants and then read aloud (in Spanish) to the spectators (ANE/Q 1771, 5v; AGI/S 1639, 6r; Cabello Balboa 1945 [1589], 36–37). More importantly, while they may not always have conveyed the content of the particular decree in question, such engagements with image and writing imparted the system of values attached to literacy and language.

Once committed to paper, the memory of this ritual was transferred from the space and time of performance to the space of the inscribed page. The orality and rituality captured by colonial scribes would acquire significance over time, as indigenous readers from later periods perused the documentary record for legal purposes — such as land claims — observing the presence of annotations describing such ceremonies, appended to the end of copies (or sometimes originals) of royal decrees, usually in a different handwriting. The best example we have of the assignation of meaning to this ritual by contemporary people comes from Cumbal, Colombia, where the mid-twentieth-century descendants of the Pastos use the metaphor of a crown to refer to their land title (itself a real provisión) and to the lands it encompasses. The rings on the staffs of office that symbolize the authority of indigenous officeholders are also called crowns (Rappaport 1994, 80–83). In a 1950 letter from the elected authorities of Cumbal to the Ministry of Mines, the author Agustín Colimba, secretary of the community council, invokes a colonial moment at which the Spanish authority officiating in the land transfer, Mauricio Muñoz de Ayala, bestowed title upon Cumbal's forebears:

PATIENTLY ACCOMPLISHED the boundary-marking to which the other towns were invited, the Spanish Infantry Captain knelt on the plain and then, placing on his head the golden crown of his king, his natural lord, in a loud voice he handed over the land in its tenancy, possession, its very dominion, to the hereditary chiefs, the genuine representatives of the town of CUMBAL. (ACIGC/N 1950, 5)[17]

Embedded in this brief narrative is a very clear reference to the act of obeying a royal decree, when that document—here, represented by a crown—is placed on the head of the authority named to obey it—here, through the bestowal of land rights.

Essential for constituting the authority of the real provisión are the seal and signatures it bears, which authenticate the contents of the decree and ensure its juridical force in perpetuity (Fraenkel 1992, 88). The royal signature "like its counterpart, the seal, and its medieval antecedent, the subscription, connected a monarch's individual and corporate bodies" (Aram 1998, 335), endowing "the page with strength (*firmeza*)" (ibid., 347). Sebastián de Covarrubias (1995 [1611], 548) defines *firma* as, "the rubric, inscription, and written name in one's own hand, which makes firm all that contained and written above the signature."[18] This sense of signature comes from the position of scribes as urban officials who appear "in documents on the basis of the strength of their testimonial capability," which was described as "firm" and "stable" (Thierry 1850–70, vol. 1, 146 in Bedos-Rezak 1993). For example, the thirteenth-century custumal of Amiens states: "Thus, the trustworthy testimony of the aldermen of the town of Amiens. First of all, when two aldermen testify and it is recorded, *it is firm and established*, and henceforth no one can speak against nor do anything against it" (1850–70, vol. 1, 146; italics ours).[19] It is both the royal seal and the signature of the royal court, which stood in for the king (*Recopilación* 1973, libro II, título VI, ley 23, 163r), that was the object of the brief ritual recorded in the documents.[20]

But what might a signature be for colonial-era native peoples, many of whom could not sign their names, as is repeatedly noted in the documentary record, or if they could write, were not necessarily schooled in the intricacies of notarial rhetoric? Hereditary lords, who were educated in special schools (ANE/Q 1695, 67r; Cárdenas 1975–76; Galdo 1970; Hartmann and Oberem 1981; Jaramillo Uribe 1989; R. Wood 1986), comprehended the rationale behind signatures, as did native scribes. An eighteenth-century cacica from the town of Pastás, for instance, demonstrated her familiarity with notarial conventions by pointing out in her arguments in favor of granting the chiefly succession to her son, that a will she had submitted as proof that the title ran in her family was legitimate because it contained the signatures of seven witnesses (AHBC/Q 1748, 214r).

Other parties to documented disputes, however, did not necessarily view signatures as connected to specific individuals (Fraenkel 1992, 9). This is evident in the confusion of the signatures of Pasto hereditary lords, who might sign their names in one document, while in another, the same men might swear that they did not know how to make a signature (ANE/Q 1695, 98r–v; ANE/Q 1760, 1v, 4v). In other cases, signatures and rubrics of multiple signatories are so similar as to suggest that they were created by a single hand (ANE/Q 1634a, 136r–v; ANE/Q 1716, 2v), contrary to Spanish legal usage that required that witnesses confirm in writing their act of signing for an illiterate. In one document we consulted, a real provisión was invalidated when it was proven that the caciques who had requested it and affixed their signatures to the petition had never really signed it at all, because they could not afford to accompany the only real signatory to Quito to make the request (ANE/Q 1656, 12v, 13v–14r).

In a society that had been without writing until the advent of the Spaniards, it is not clear that a signature would have carried the same meaning for the Pastos as it did for Europeans. In eighteenth-century Bolivia, indigenous commoners wrote a petition against the abuses of their priest, signed in the name of their community, with the names of local kin and residential units instead of those of individuals (Penry 2000, 225). This suggests an alternative explanation for the interchangeability of Pasto signatures, given that their communities were organized into a hierarchy of sections, whose nobility frequently carried the same name as the residential unit.

The Quechua term for a signed document acknowledges the specificity of an individual's hand by employing the word *maqui*, or hand: "Escriptura firmada y signada. Maqui yoc vnanchayoc qquellca" (González Holguín 1989 [1608], 514). The Quechua translates as "*quillca* [writ] including a hand, including a sign," while the Spanish is "a writ, signed and marked."[21] The reference here may be to the notary or *quellcaycamayoc* who, as a member of the *cabildo* (council), validated the document, not to the individual signatories. This is what Hanks (2000, 106) reports for the Maya area, where colonial notaries wrote the signatures of the noble signatories whose letters they penned.

Vicente Rafael suggests that signatures acquired a similar ambiguity in the Spanish-ruled Philippines. The pre-Spanish Tagalog script, *baybayin*, was not perceived by the Europeans as adequate for rendering sound in alphabetic writing, because the Spaniards could not link one sound with one letter with any certainty (Rafael 1988, 47–51). Signatures were accordingly ambiguous; some groups of signatures appeared to have been inscribed by a single hand:

> The question then arises: What would a "signature" be which perpetually postponed the definitive location of name and person? In the case of *baybayin*, it was a series of marks that called forth sounds but whose referent had to be "guessed"—perhaps with a little help from God: "With respect to the inscriptions [*letreros*] [of the documents] we have transcribed them as God has given us to understand them," Santamaría explains. (ibid., 49–50)

The ambiguity of native signatures across the Spanish empire suggests that the meaning of other acts, such as the ritual elevation of a document bearing bureaucratic signatures and the royal seal above the head of a European official, were similarly ambivalent. But if we look at the signature as a trace left by an activity, as opposed to the sign of an individual, as graphic ceremonial space replacing physical ceremonial space (Fraenkel 1992, 9), the ritual acquiescence to a royal decree becomes more comprehensible. In this sense, it would be better to interpret the recognition of signatures as the intersection of indigenous and Spanish forms of commensurability that operated through an analogy based on ritual practices, creating a space in which these actions and marks could be mutually interpreted.

Signature, Seal, and Image

That the ceremony and the signature sustaining it were relevant to native northern Andean peoples is clear from Spanish references that emphasize the importance of visual literacy and its relationship with alphabetic literacy. Although pictorial images were often termed "books of the illiterate" (Acosta 1940 [1950]), we tend to forget how much writing intersected with pictorial images in the colonial period. Writing often appears in paintings themselves, thereby calling forth the notion of document. For example, the series of portraits of Spanish kings and queens, possibly painted by the native Andean artist Andrés Sánchez Gallque in the late sixteenth century, are depicted as if they stand before a background on which are written their names. That is, there is a physicality or substance given to both the text and figure, such that they occupy different points in the imagined space of the painting (figure 42). And while the vast majority of viewers may have not been able to read the words nor fully understand the intricacies of European iconography, the relationship between alphabetic text and pictorial image was continually on display. Paintings formed a site of dialogue between priest and catechumen, or native informants and colonial officials (Cummins 1995). Moreover, as documents of biblical or secular history, their artifice is sometimes marked in the same way as a written document, through the signature of whomever produced it (figures 43 and 44). This follows from developments in late fifteenth century and early sixteenth, where personal style—as well as signatures, monograms, or initials—functioned to guard against artistic forgery, hence equating artist with scribe (C. Wood 1993).

Pictorial images, especially prints, carried signatures in the form of initials, just as the document carried the rubric of the notary or author. It is here that the meaning of signature might be expanded in unexpected ways. The introduction and copying in the Americas of prints from northern Europe were extremely important, given that the prints served as models for paintings and drawings made by both creole and native artists. It is easy to identify the native artist's difficulties in reproducing correctly many of the conventions used in these models. For example, the misinterpretation of the rules of perspective are immediately recognizable in the paintings of Spanish kings by Sánchez Gallque, the native artist working in Quito at the end of the sixteenth century, whom we discussed early in this book. But it is also clear that the division between the written and the pictorial was not always apprehended when European models were copied. For instance, we might look at a depiction by a native artist of the art of Aztec gold-working within a European architectural setting, contained in Bernardino de Sahagún's *Florentine Codex* (figure 45). The source for the European elements in this image may have come from an architectural treatise, possibly by Serlio, in which the pictorial architectural forms are keyed to the text by letters. In the illustration contained in Sahagún the indigenous artist copies not only the image, but also the letter *A* of the European prototype, which appears at the base of the depicted column (Ellen Baird, personal communication). Here, however, the letter is no longer an index of something exterior to the image (either another image or a text). Rather, it becomes a virtual part of the image, a trace of something other than what it was originally intended to signify, suggesting that Spaniard and native understood such conventions differently.

FIGURE 42 Portrait of King Sancho of Castile, attributed to Andrés Sánchez Gallque, ca. 1600, Museo del Convento de San Francisco, Quito. Oil on canvas.

FIGURE 43 The Passion of Christ, signed and dated in lower right-hand corner by Francisco Quispe, 1688, Museo del Convento de San Francisco, Quito. Oil on canvas. Courtesy of Carmen Fernández.

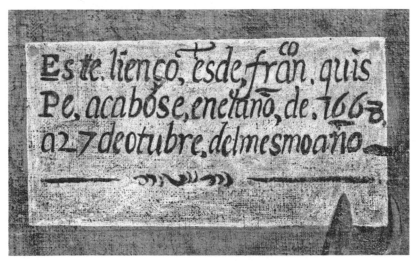

FIGURE 44 Detail of the Passion of Christ, signature of Francisco Quispe, 1668, Museo del Convento de San Francisco, Quito.

FIGURE 45 Chapter on goldsmiths, middle illustration showing the letter A inserted at the base of column, Bernardino de Sahagún, *Historia general de las cosas de Nueva España*, book 9 folio 53, 1579. Laurentian Library, Florence.

In this sense, the signature and the pictorial image might not always be so easily distinguished. This becomes even more disconcerting in the sense that over time a signature could acquire almost the same status as a pictorial portrait. As we cited in chapter 4, Alberti had written in the fifteenth century that "painting possess a truly divine power in that not only does it make the absent present (as they say of friendship) but it also represents the dead to the living many centuries later, so that they are recognized by the spectators with great pleasure" (Alberti 1991 [1435–36], 60). This sentiment is invoked in the eighth sermon of the Third Catechism of Lima, in which the role of saints is to be explained to native Andeans:

> And now all those saints, which are innumerable, are in heaven, enjoying the presence of God, and they pray for us and are our mediators. And for this reason we honor them and implore them in their names and *we keep their images in Churches, so that they can remind us of those parents and teachers.* (Lima, Concilio de, 1990 [1585], 690; italics ours)[22]

Signatures also came to bestow the same sentiment, especially in relation to painting. Fray Pedro Bedón was, among other things, one of the principal founders of the Quiteño school of painting. In fact, the earliest extant signed portrait from South America was painted by one of his students, Sánchez Gallque. Bedón's own signed work survives in the form of both documents and paintings (figure 46). It is the signature on both that came to stand for his continued, almost saintly, presence in the eighteenth century:

> At the very beginning of the Provincialship of Rm. P. Mro. Fr. Pedro Martyr, this province hosted the Venerable P.M. Fr. Pedro Bedón, whose signatures in his books are venerated as relics. They are found there, as a Depositary of those years, and in the Refectory in the year 1594, whose painting is the product of his hands. (Zamora 1701, 143)[23]

The character of Bedón's signature was transformed over time, nearly taking on the properties of a holy relic, and the object (the book or painting) on which it appears, a reliquary. His signature therefore became disembodied from the sense of the written word and took on the materiality of the body. It no longer merely testified to the authenticity of the document of which it is a part; it visually manifested the presence of someone who cannot be physically present, but whose trace transcends time and space, just as a painted image might—or even more so, since it became almost incarnate in the sense of a relic.

FIGURE 46 Detail of initials of Fray Pedro Bedón in an illuminated letter from a choral painted by Bedón, 1613, Biblioteca del Convento de Santo Domingo, Quito. Paint, ink, and gold leaf on vellum.

Quillca

This mingling of signature and painting as a trace of something is a crucial aspect in the indoctrination of native Andeans, as enunciated in the nineteenth sermon from the Third Catechism:

> And thus the heart must be entrusted to heaven where Jesus Christ and his Saints abide; and hope and will placed in Jesus Christ. And if they revere images, and [if] they kiss them and bare their heads before them and kneel and beat their chests, it is for what those images represent, and not for what they are in themselves. As the Magistrate kisses the royal decree and seal and puts it over his head, not because it is wax or paper, but because it is the King's quillca. (Lima, Concilio de, 1990 [1585], 653)[24]

Invoking the secular ritual pertaining to a real provisión, the identity of writing and image in the colonial Andes is most clearly expressed in the use of the term *quillca*, which is used in the sermon to represent the seal on the royal decree. A colonial Quechua neologism, *quillca* refers to writing and the recording of statistics, on the one hand, and to sculpting and painting, on the other (González Holguín 1989 [1608], 301, 513; Santo Tomás 1951 [1560], 357), indicating the ambiguities of alphabetic script in a society that did not know alphabetic writing, but whose system of recording—the khipu, or knot record—was transmitted as much through the tactile channel as through the visual one.[25] In northern Andean languages, the commonality of the alphabetic and the visual is also the rule. In Muisca, *bchihisqua* means both "to write" (Anonymous 1987 [1607–20], 260) and "to paint" (ibid., 295).[26] In the Nasa language, *fis* (in modern usage, *f'i'ya*) means both "to read" and "to paint" (Castillo y Orozco 1877 [1755], 50), although the Quechua borrowing *quillca* is used for "paper," "book," and "letter" (ibid., 76). It must be remembered here, however, that the use of a common word for these very different practices is the product of colonial language planning, the institutionalized standardization of language through the creation of grammars, dictionaries, and educational policy; the homologies we cite do not necessarily stem from pre-Columbian usages, of which we know nothing.

In González Holguín's Quechua dictionary, there is yet another meaning of *quillca*: "Quellcar payachispa yachachimi. Enseñar la theologia dictandola" (1989 [1608], 301). An English translation of the Quechua might be: "To teach by having something written down continuously," or possibly, as the Spanish gloss conveys, to teach theology by dictation.[27] This suggests, as is implicit in the passage from the Third Catechism, that more than simply referring to writing or painting, *quillca* refers to a particular pedagogical technique for conveying a body of knowledge and practice. This acknowledgment of the ideological matrix within which colonial literacy was understood and practiced can also be seen in yet another meaning of *fis* (in Nasa Yuwe, "to read" or "to paint"): "persignarse," or to make the sign of the cross (Castillo y Orozco 1877 [1755], 50). The writing on one's body of the Christian doctrine (de Certeau 1984) conjoins literacy as writing with literacy as depiction in an efficacious and ritualized movement.[28]

The sermons of the Third Catechism were highly explicit in their teaching of this symbolic gesture, which they bifurcated into two distinct movements:

And you must also make the sign of the cross frequently, especially when you arise, when you leave your house, when the devil brings you temptations, when you find yourself in danger or working, because the sign of the cross conquers the enemy and causes him to flee from Christians. We make this sign on the forehead, on the mouth, and on the breast when we persignar, so that God our Lord frees our understanding from evil thoughts, our mouths from evil words, our hearts from evil desires and evil works.

When we *santiguar*, we make the sign of the holy cross on our entire body, from the forehead to the waist and from one shoulder to the other, invoking and acclaiming and confessing the name of the Holy Trinity, Father and Son and Holy Spirit, who is one God, so that we receive its blessing and grace and we are saved from all evil. (Lima, Concilio de, 1990 [1585], 729–30)[29]

A slightly earlier colonial catechism written in Bogotá is even more specific so as to enforce strict uniformity:

It is ordered that the form of persignar be the following: a cross made with the thumb of the right hand placed over the index (by) moving the thumb from the forehead to the tip of the nose, you must say, "by the sign"; and then crossing [it] from the left temple to the right one, you must say, "of the cross"; and taking said thumb from the point of the nose to the chin, you must say, "of our"; and crossing it from left to right, you must say, "enemies"; and crossing the said finger from the chin to the middle of the belly, you must say, "deliver us Lord"; and crossing the breast from left to right, you must say, "our God." And similarly when you santiguar there should be uniformity, placing the thumb next to the two closest fingers of the right hands, and the other two pulled in, placing the points of the extended ones flat on the forehead, you must say, "In the name of the Father"; and lowering [them] to the middle of the belly, you must say, "and the Son"; and raising the hand and placing it on the left shoulder and carrying it [across] to place it on the right one, you must say, "and the Holy Spirit"; and folding the hands and crossing the thumbs and kissing the cross with these thumbs done, you must say, "Amen, Jesus." (Zapata de Cárdenas 1988 [1576], 45)[30]

This is a very conscious inscription of the Christian doctrine upon the native body.

The sign of the cross, traced upon the body, was, however, more than the act of the Christian faithful. It was linked to speech acts transcribed into mundane documents as a mnemonic for the gesture and its meaning (Clanchy 1989, 174), such as "juramos a dios nuestro señor y vna señal de cruz + no çer de maliçia etc.," or "we swear by God our lord and the sign of the cross + that we proceed without malice, etc." It was also inscribed into the landscape as a boundary marker (ANE/Q 1767, 11r; Fray Pedro de la Peña 1995 [1570], 470). Just as importantly, the relationship between text and image is formed in this part of the document. The words "en señal de cruz" (in the sign of the cross) are interpolated with the graphic image of the cross, similar to the relation between the gesture of making the cross while reciting the prayer.[31]

This relationship between text and image and its bodily ritual enactment are crucial in the passage from the nineteenth sermon of the Third Lima Council that equates the ritual of obeying a real provisión with the act of revering a religious image. The ritual is evoked so as to conflate alphabetic and visual literacy, calling both of them quillca. What is raised over the head of the corregidor is the king's quillca, while images are God's quillca. In the Pasto Province and beyond to the north, Quechua was not spoken; hence, the term *quillca* could not be used in this sense in catechisms or sermons. Nevertheless, the identity between painting and writing is also evident in documents from the northern Andes, as in the following excerpt from the 1570 *Laws for caciques of the indios of the Synod of Quito*: "And if they have crucifixes, images of our Lady or of the saints, lead them to understand that such images are a form of writing that represents and leads to the understanding of that which it represents" (Peña 1995 [1570], 471).[32] As we have already illustrated, moreover, the colonial meaning of quillca had its equivalents in various northern Andean languages.

The analogy being traced here arises out of Catholic doctrine on images that was first articulated in the Council of Trent as discussed in chapter 2. Subsequently, it was rearticulated in the Third Council of Lima in order to give Andean specificity to the interpretation of the first commandment and the distinction between idolatry (adoration) and representation (veneration). If, on the one hand, an image is taken to be in and of itself as that which is worshipped, then that is idolatry. If, on the other, an image is understood to refer through its form to that which is adored—the Holy Family and the saints—then it is properly venerated. Thus, reference is always directed at that which is represented, rather than at the representation itself. Image can never be literally what it refers to, and this is true for both writing and picture, which is why both are termed *quillca* in colonial Quechua. This relationship is based, in part, upon a pedagogical analogy between writing and the pictorial that can only be made concrete by the Quechua word *quillca*, as it encompasses both without really signifying either in a traditional Andean sense. So even in the Spanish version of the bilingual sermon from the Third Council of Lima, the Quechua term *quillca* is used. It is one of the very few Quechua terms that appears in the Spanish version of the sermons, other than names that identify certain Andean titles, such as *curaca* (hereditary lord), and Andean "idols," such as guaca.

Standing in for the King

But *quillca* is deployed differently than these other Quechua terms. *Quillca* is necessary because only by using Quechua can the early Christian analogy be so explicitly expressed in the Andes: that the king's seal stands for the absent king, just as the image of Christ stands for Him while not actually being Him.[33] Yet, honors and rituals are accorded to the image as if it were the king or Christ. The ceremony of kissing the king's quillca—with its accompanying seal—and raising it above the head was preceded by the ritual entrance of the seal itself into the Real Audiencia as stipulated by a royal decree in 1559:

> It is just and advantageous that, when our Royal Seal enters one of our Royal Courts, *it be received with the authority that, if our royal person were entering, would be given in [the courts] of those Kingdoms of Castile.* Therefore we order that when our Royal [Seal] arrives at any of the Courts of the Indies, our Presidents and Judges, and the justices and Government of the City must depart a good distance from there to receive it, and from wherever it should be encountered, it should be carried to the Town on the back of a horse or a mule, with respectable harnesses, and the President and the most senior Judge must carry it between them, with due veneration as is required and as is customary in the Royal Courts of these Kingdoms of Castile, to the headquarters of the Royal Court, where it should be kept, so that it can be cared for by the person who serves the office of the Chancellor of the seal, to seal decrees dispatched by the Chancellery. (*Recopilación* 1973 [1681], libro II, título XXI, 243; italics ours)[34]

The entrance of the royal seal was to be treated just as if the royal person were entering the colonial city.

This ceremony follows from medieval political theology as analyzed by Ernst Kantorowicz (1957) and which, as Louis Marin (1988) has demonstrated, also permeated the discursive formation of royal absolutism in seventeenth-century France. But in the colonial Andes, royal representation took a different turn as it passed through the gates of the city in the guise of the king's seal. Here, the seal appeared on documents distributed to and manipulated by natives, an experience that was conjured by sermons where the metaphysics of Catholicism was interpreted for Andeans. For example, sermons implored Andeans to recall their personal experiences with administrative documents and the potential benefits of such decrees as a conceptual bridge to the explanation of the mysteries of divine grace achieved through the sacraments:

> Sacraments are what we call the signs and ceremony ordered by Jesus Christ, by which we honor God and share his grace. Just as the Viceroy or the Court makes a decree or quillca to free you from tribute and moreover, orders you to be paid one hundred pesos from the King's treasury, you must take the quillca and save it, and by virtue of it you will remain free of tribute and even wealthy. Similarly, the sacraments of the Holy Church function so that those who take them remain free from sin, although wealthy in grace. (Lima, Concilio de, 1990 [1585], 657)[35]

It is not through the sacrament that the king's representation is understood. Rather, it is just the opposite: it is the power of that representation in the form of a bureaucratic document that is most immediate and real in the colonial interaction between Spaniards and natives.

The king's written person in the form of his seal and portrait is the same, and at times the two versions can be combined in a single composition such that the corporeality of the figure and the authority of the word reinforce each other. For example, the royal *cédula* (decree) of Charles V granting Cortés a coat of arms in 1525 (plate 8) begins with the illuminated letter *D* initiating the title *Don*, followed by the other titles of the emperor. The *D* is filled with no less than a profile portrait of the emperor himself, such that Charles V appears both in name and figure.[36] The king's portrait was, in fact, understood to mark his presence, even though he was not corporeally present. In the 1666 celebration in Lima of the crowning of the new Spanish king, Charles II, after the death of Philip IV, the king's portrait acted as the surrogate for the presence of the absent physical body.[37] Mugaburu writes in his diary:

> The throne where the portrait of our king and lord was placed was impressive. It was set up next to the door of the palace, on the left as one enters the plaza. There was much to see in the tableau, where there were many large figures in the round, and the Inca and [his queen, the] Coya

offering our king and lord, with great reverence, an imperial crown. . . . In the plaza there was a large formation of Spaniards made up of more than a thousand men with twelve captains and eight cavalry companies with their captains, the four of the city and the four of the rural states, and another two squadrons of Indians. . . .

A simultaneous charge (of artillery and muskets) was fired at the same time that the portrait appeared in the plaza, which caused great admiration. The shouts and acclamations were, "Long live the king our lord!"

The king at arms . . . requested silence three times, then the royal ensign repeated in a loud voice . . . , "Castile, Leon, and Peru for the king our lord Don Carlos II, may he live many years!" The squadron rendered the same musket and artillery salute. This ceremony on the stage being over, the due reverences having been paid to His Majesty, all descended and mounted their horses, and the royal ensign returned with the flag to face the portrait of our king. . . . Upon lowering the portrait of His Majesty, the last artillery and musket salute was given, and the portrait was placed in the room from which they took it. (1975 [1686], 105–06)

Here, the painted image stands in for a king who will never set foot in the New World. More importantly, as Mugaburu narrates it, the subject of representation in the portrait — the king — is not addressed through the medium itself. Rather, the distance between the representation and the represented is imagined to be momentarily collapsed, so that a kind of political transubstantiation takes place and the object to which the oaths are sworn in Lima is addressed directly. The term "portrait of the King" becomes briefly and simply "the King."

The secular ritual celebrating the king through his portrait can also be conflated with the celebration of the Christian mysteries through Catholicism's most important representation. One can see how this meaning of the king's portrait is closely related to the spiritual realm of colonial power in one of the paintings from the circa 1680 series of eighteen works depicting Cuzco's Corpus Christi procession (Dean 1999). The festival celebrates the ineffable presence of Christ through the only Catholic symbol that is, in and of itself, what it represents: the Eucharistic wafer, or Christ's body. Consecrated in the Cathedral, the host was processed through the streets, where ephemeral altars were built in celebration, until it returned to the place of its transubstantiation. Each of the paintings is a kind of mise-en-scène that localizes the universality of the ritual by depicting various social constitu-

FIGURE 47 Corpus Christi series, Dominican friars processing before the altar dedicated to the Holy Host, portrait of Charles II hanging over the entrance to Cuzco's Cabildo, anonymous, ca. 1680, private collection, Santiago, Chile. Oil on canvas.

encies in front of specific buildings. In one painting (figure 47), members of the Augustinian order process into the picture plane from the viewer's right as they pass through an ephemeral arch.[38] A mirrored altar is dedicated to the consecrated host that stands atop it, encased in a golden monstrance. The altar is placed before the building housing the cabildo, Cuzco's secular political power. From the cabildo's wall behind the altar are hung the portraits of the Old Testament prophets who foretold the birth of Christ. To the right of these portraits is the only secular painting depicted in the entire series, the portrait of Charles II, hung over the entrance into the building. Like the consecrated host, the portrait of the king marks his presence, despite his corporeal absence; he becomes present through his portrait. The Host and the king's portrait—and, also, the king's seal—are therefore more than representations; they both refer to and are.[39] This simultaneity of the Host and the king's portrait is registered in the painting as its theme. They stand out as unique, as signs of presence, in comparison to the portraits of the prophets, which only recall them.

It can also be suggested that just as religious and secular images stood in for those they represented, alphabetic writing "stood in" for the physical presence of people as ritual participants and as the makers of documents.

Sometimes, a document could stand for a ritual. In 1693 and 1735, documentary evidence of the performance of a ritual granting possession of lands in Cumbal to the community's hereditary caciques was presented as evidence in a dispute over chiefly succession (ANE/Q 1735a, 30r). Likewise, paper could replace a writer. When a witness in the mid-eighteenth century, Magdalena Mallama, could not appear in person to give testimony in a dispute over the succession to the cacicazgo of Pastás, she sent a written document, stating "I appear before Your Grace with this brief" (AHBC/Q 1748, 243v).[40] And in the late seventeenth century, when the new cacica of Guachucal was awarded the succession to her chiefdom, she ceremonially received census data from the Spanish officials: "And Your Grace took her by the hand and gave her the census of this said town, all acts which were said to have been done as signs of possession" (ANE/Q 1695, 37r).[41] In this case, a document "stood for" an entire community, which was itself present at the succession ritual. Similarly, a royal seal stood for the king (Fraenkel 1992, 83), as did his signature, which took the place of the king in the brief ritual of acceptance of a royal decree (Aram 1998, 346–47).

Literacy and Performance

What our small example demonstrates is that literacy is a strategy intrinsic to the Spanish colonization of the Americas, one that goes well beyond the physical written page or the painted canvass to encompass performative activities that promote and sustain colonial ideologies and social arrangements. What is to be found in the legacy of writing, the myriad of documents, is not therefore a neutral gathering of data to be ordered and analyzed. Documents, visual as well as textual, and the technologies used to produce them, are social and cultural forms that are enacted and experienced, not only by those who know how to decipher their contents. Although their meanings inhere in the words or images they bear, they are conveyed as well through forms of activity, such as ritual, that bestow upon them a legitimacy that transcends their contents. To think of a signature as a relic or the king's seal as a quillca suggests that much more is at stake than the neutral transcription or rendering of something. What is at stake is much larger than the concrete purpose of each individual document. Not only are the contents of the catechism conveyed through a painting, or the political aims of a disputant cemented by a real provisión, but the surrounding rituals make these documents part of the sacred domain through which the Spanish Crown maintained and justified its presence in the Americas. Documents are crucial props for enacting and sustaining the colonial social formation.

The sacred character lent to documents by rituals such as the kissing of the royal seal, make public the power of the Crown. Clearly, the caciques and other indigenous nobility who enacted such ceremonies were made doubly aware of the presence of colonial power. They already knew of their subservience to the Crown from the contents, which were read or explained to them. Through the rituals surrounding the presentation and creation of documents, they were more completely implicated in the colonial project, particularly the Christianized caciques who knew what a Christian oath meant and hence were aware of how ritual bound them to the colonial administration. But ceremony also fulfilled a purpose for the nonnoble subjects of these caciques, the tributaries and their families, who could not read and perhaps did not completely understand what a royal decree was for. They vicariously participated in literacy when they observed these rituals, cementing their own acceptance of their place in the colonial scheme of things. When the corregidor kissed a royal decree emanating from a dispute in a native community and placed it above his head, indigenous commoners may not have been able to decipher its contents, but as viewers, they were initiated into a political system in which the spectacle of writing solidified colonial power through a particular blending of the sacred and the profane. In the process, documents became *things* in the colonial world, things that were both transformed and transforming. This gave documents and paintings—indeed, literacy in general—a certain agency or efficacy that exceeded the intentions of their authors. Even those for whom colonial culture was a distant second language, the colonial was made tangible, not through the technology of literacy, but through the ritual that encompassed it.

SPACE AND THE IMPOSITION OF LITERACY

L iteracy, whether alphabetic or visual, is an intimately physi
cal practice that involves the human body in a series of learned,
though largely unconscious, activities: the position in which the reader
or writer sits, grasping the book or the pen; the distance at which one
must stand to view artwork; the act of crossing oneself when approach-
ing certain images or when swearing as a signatory to a document "in
the name of the cross." The ideological edifice which the Spaniards
sought to inculcate in Native Americans through the teaching of the
Christian doctrine, alphabetic literacy, and the Castilian language, was
built upon a complex of bodily habits which, as Bogotá archbishop
Fray Luis Zapata de Cárdenas (1988 [1576], 28) admonished, "serve[d]
as a ladder toward spirituality and [took] advantage of the ascent to
another higher rung" (sirve de escalón para lo espiritual y aprovecha
a la subida de otro grado mas alto). In the previous chapter, we saw
how such bodily experience was enforced through the participation in
or observation of the rituals surrounding literacy, how even nonliterates were implicated within the social formation that literacy helped
to spawn. In this chapter, we will move more deeply into the bodily
experience of literacy to inquire into how it constituted a fundamental facet of the physical world in which colonial native peoples lived.

Archbishop Zapata of Bogotá advises that all natives should live in
well-kept houses and towns, much as people did in Spain (Zapata de
Cárdenas 1988 [1576], 31–33):

Item, because the cleanliness of the town is necessary so that they live healthy and with cleanliness, it is ordered that the priest take care over how clean the town is, each one cleaning his own property and weeding it, and the same with the houses, and they must be well organized, and they must have platforms and clean beds to sleep on, and the priest must make visits with the alcaldes and with the cacique, or with the captain of each capitanía [Muisca political division] to whom the given houses belong, to see if they have complied with the above . . . and he must order that the kitchens and pantries be [constructed] apart from where they live and sleep.[1]

Architectonic and urban space must be clean and ordered according to Archbishop Zapata's strictures; moreover, the very bodies of the natives must be clothed, the men in shirts and breeches, the women in high blouses and mantles reaching down to their feet, all with their hair tied back in an orderly fashion (Zapata de Cárdenas 1988 [1576], 33). In short, this was a comprehensive reworking of the spatial order, beginning with the indigenous body and extending out to the home, the town, the administrative domain, and the spiritual universe, all traversed by the inscribed page and the painted canvas (Castañeda Vargas 2000; López Rodríguez 2001).

The spatial order—be it the human body, topographic space, community organization, pictorial composition, or the surface of the written page—is a social creation and therefore never fixed. In the northern Andes, the colonial spatial order reworked Spanish and indigenous structures in new ways, by recasting civic space, producing a resonating chamber in which political ritual and organization of sacred precincts took on distinctly literary and pictorial tones. Nonalphabetic spaces, like the streets of an indigenous village or its main square were, simultaneously, reformulated on the written page in census documents, baptismal records, and legal papers. We will examine the intersection between these spatial genres, their social production, and their reconfiguration, in an effort to comprehend the interrelationships of visual and alphabetic literacy as they were inscribed upon indigenous bodies in the colonial era.

Visuality and literacy were intimately connected to colonial bodily practice. As we noted in the previous chapter, graphic symbols were simultaneously inscribed and enacted ritually, the most simple example being the making of the sign of the cross at the moment the cross was written or drawn into a document. Such literate patterns were, moreover, superimposed in both sacred and secular contexts upon the architectonic and topographic space within which people walked, the kinship networks by which they traced descent, and the sacred precincts where they worshiped. That is, just as alphabetic and visual texts were ceremonially manipulated, the categories and spatial dimensions of their organization were reproduced in nonliterate genres. In this sense, we must understand literacy as transcending the producer or the direct consumer of an alphabetic or pictorial text, to include a much broader range of participants. We must pay heed to the corporeal experience of a colonial culture that was inscribed both on paper and canvas, as well as upon the land, its buildings, and the bodies of its inhabitants.

The *Reducción*

Such multiple spaces physically overlapped discourses of power and were perceived as analogous by the Spaniards. The town grid, the church fresco, and the alphabetic document were all understood as bestowing order upon the chaos the Spaniards discovered when they arrived in the New World, a disorder which they considered to be diabolical. The Spanish term *reducir*, which was the metaphor used to refer to the civilizing process, meant "to order" or "to bring to reason" (Covarrubias 1995 [1611], 350, 854); it has mistakenly been translated as "to reduce," a gloss that obscures the ideology upon which the term was premised. For the Spaniards, Christianity was central to the ordering process: a Jesuit annual letter—written in Italian—from Bogotá (AGCG/R 1616, 116v) speaks of "reduc[ing the natives] to the true knowledge of the holy God" (ridurle alla uera cognitione di dio beneditto). Language, the symbolic system through which the Christian doctrine was taught, was susceptible to such ordering, through the generation of grammars of indigenous languages and the teaching of alphabetic literacy (AGCG/R 1606, 48r). Both grammar and literacy were measuring sticks of the universal hierarchy that placed the Muiscas and Pastos on considerably lower rungs than that occupied by Europeans; their languages, which were not based upon Latin and were unwritten, were seen as inferior to Spanish, and their speakers were, consequently, seen as in want of the structure that only Spanish could confer. This hierarchical model of language and society was implemented in various discursive contexts, most notably, through written law (González Echevarría 1990) and evangelization, whose performative force was clearly expressed in the grid pattern upon which all towns and cities in the New World were founded, duly recorded in acts of foundation authorized by legal officials, and written and validated by notaries.

The typical colonial Latin American city, town, or village is organized into a grid of parallel and intersecting streets that emerge from a central plaza, unlike the medieval towns of Spain, whose streets meander in a less perfect arrangement. The colonial grid was understood to be a kind of a *reducción*, a model for creating order in a world in which antisocial and wild chaos lurked in the countryside (Rama 1996 [1984]).[2] The order of the urban grid was a visual manifestation of the divine order of Augustine's City of God, as contrasted against the chaos of the *civitas diaboli*, the cities of the heathens. Thus, there existed a morphological relation between the material form of the terrestrial city and the celestial one. But while the grid pattern found its philosophical basis in medieval European writings, the plan of the Spanish medieval city was considerably more haphazard and labyrinthine than the recognizable mesh of parallel and perpendicular streets branching out from a central plaza that is ubiquitous to Spanish America; it is only unevenly and partially apparent in the Iberian urbanscape. The grid was very much an ideal in the Spanish mind, a plan which could only be physically enacted in the new colonial space, thus lending a tangible, corporeal aspect to the ideological notion of order (Cummins 2002b; Durston 1994; Foster 1960; Fraser 1990; Gutiérrez 1993; Herrera Ángel 2002; Kagan 2000; Kubler 1948; Rama 1996 [1984], 11).[3] As Valerie Fraser (1990, 41) states, the grid was both a demonstration of Spanish civility and an encouragement toward it for native people.

Before a space was ordered through architecture, however, it was carefully planned in the graphic space of a map, itself a classification of groups of people and of property that was only beginning to come into its own in the late medieval period in conjunction with a significant increment in notarial practice and in sales of properties (Smail 1999). In Latin America, unlike in the Marseille studied by Daniel Smail, streets were not identified in maps, although the names of new residents were written within the city blocks. This approach can be seen in the documentation of Pizarro's 1535 founding of Lima: "In order to found this city the Governor first ordered its plan be drawn on paper with the measurements of the streets and blocks and he signaled in the maps the lots given out to the settlers, writing the name of each one in the lot assigned to him" (Lima, Cabildo de 1935 [1535], 12–13).[4] The convention is also clear in the map that accompanied the establishment of the town of Paipa, in the Muisca area (figure 48). Fray Pedro de Aguado de-

FIGURE 48 Distribution of house plots for the town of Paipa in the New Kingdom of Granada, 1602, AGN/B, *Mapoteca* SMP4, ref. 311A. Courtesy of Archivo General de la Nación, Bogotá.

scribes how this procedure was implemented in the founding of the villa of Tudela, in what is today Boyacá:

> The plan of the town is then made in the manner and order in which the lots will be built, and according to the plan that is made all of the citizens [*vecinos*] are assigned their plots [*solares*] in order, giving the first to the church, and then to the captain, and then to the other principal personages, so that the town is founded according to the plan that was made; and in this way it is built by blocks [*cuadras*], which are square lots [*cuarteles*] divided into four equal parts, and in front of every lot there is a street, and the four parts of the lot are four solares, and these are given to four people or to two, as you like, and in this way the population of the town or district is spread or extended out from the plaza, which is also square, and it is a block of four solares with their streets issuing out from them, which are eight streets, two at each corner, by which the entire town

is very neatly governed, walked, and ordered. (Aguado 1957 [1575?], IV, 75; cf. Aprile-Gniset 1991, 193)[5]

Similar acts were drawn up for native communities, as occurred when the Muisca of Suta, Tausa, and Bobotá were resettled in a single town, which was appropriately called a reducción:

> In the aforementioned site of Bobota, the highest and most convenient spot will be chosen for the church, fifty-four varas long and twelve wide, with the substructure and foundations according to the plan and conditions drawn by Juan Gomez, builder, and laying out the front toward the direction of the sunrise and in front of the aforementioned church, seventy square varas should be apportioned or however many are appropriate for the site, for a plaza. At the sides of the church twenty-five varas square will be assigned for the priest's house and on the other side, the same for the home of the principal cacique and around the plaza, the houses of the capitanes, twenty varas square. By the same order, the rest of the indios must be apportioned houses in squares ordered in straight lines, where they will build their storeroom and kitchen and corral, and the streets must extend in straight lines, clean and weeded, six varas wide between every eighty [varas]. (AGN/B 1594–1600, 827r)[6]

Although there is no surviving map for the foundation of Bobotá, maps from what is today the Colombian department of Santander show indigenous towns with central squares and lots marked off for a church, the house of the cacique, and the homes of the general population (figure 49); these plans were drawn in the early seventeenth century, when Beltrán de Guevara established reducciones among the indigenous population of Tunja and Santander (Corradine Angulo 1993, 159–65).[7]

The physical act of creating order in space began with the construction of a church, because, as Jesuit Bernabé Cobo writes in 1639 (1956 [1639], 289–90), the plan's moral basis was in God and thus by necessity commenced with His church. Pizarro therefore began the plan of Lima with a church, then marked out the plaza on the grid, laid the first stone of the temple, and finally divided the city blocks among the citizens, in a ceremony called an "act of foundation."[8] The ritualization of the foundational process "demonstrates that towns depended less on their physical manifestation, or *urbs*, than their *civitas*, or community of citizens, organized into a republic, and therefore living in *policía* [civic order]" (Kagan 2000, 31). Urban space was

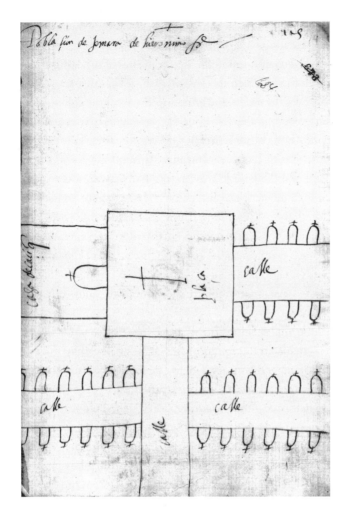

FIGURE 49 Map
of the *reducción*
of Gemara in the
New Kingdom of
Granada, 1602,
AGN/B, *Mapoteca*
SMP4, ref. 169A.
Courtesy of
Archivo General
de la Nación,
Bogotá.

thus the ritual and spatial enactment of a discourse of colonization that was
previously constituted through writing. In fact, while the grid emerged in-
stantly on the paper of maps drawn up at the founding of towns, its tangible
manifestation in architecture was a good deal more belated, slowly growing out from the church square under the careful supervision of colonial
authorities (Castañeda Vargas 2000; Fraser 1990, 69–73; López Rodríguez
2001).

The plaza of a reducción was filled by practices that made tangible the
power of the secular colonial order. Punishments were enacted at the *picota*,
the stone column in the plaza that symbolized a stake and stood as a reminder of the gallows (Nader 1990, 135–37) — the national prison in Bogotá

is called "La Picota," harking back to colonial usage. Community meetings were held at the same location or at the cross in the town square (ibid., 137). Caciques were carried on chairs around the square in rites of investiture. The plaza was also the scenario in which the *pregonero*, or town crier, translated into indigenous languages the orders and announcements of the colonial administration. Urban space was always a zone of interaction between native peoples and Spaniards, both metaphorically and corporeally, embodied in the presence of Europeans or caciques centralized around the plaza. It was the bringing of *civitas* and the *polis* to the Andean native, who was seen as occupying a state of incomplete social and cultural development, in need of the civilizing mission that the grid imposed. The spatial hierarchy thus had its analog in the social and political hierarchy. Furthermore, this hierarchical plan inserted indigenous people into the economic structure of the empire, given that plaza space was also provided as lodgings for traveling Spaniards, there to collect tribute or arrange labor corvées (Gutiérrez 1993, 27), and served as a market square.

Superimposed upon this secular grid was the space of practice of the church, from which emanated the sound of the church bell calling inhabitants to mass, to the saying of the rosary, and to catechism classes. The territory within which such a sound carried was constituted as a legal community, mapped onto provincial space—the *resguardos*, or indigenous communities, of the New Kingdom of Granada were built around this concept, with all native people living "a son de campana," within the sound of the church bell. Out of the church and into the plaza came processions of religious images. The populace congregated several times a week in the atrium of the church as the doctrinal priest directed sermons at them, instructing them in the mysteries of Christianity.

Although native Andean institutions and forms of territoriality persisted into the colonial period, they were reconfigured or "colonized" by European forms of order and control. Extending out of the plaza into the countryside was the very distinct organization of the native community. In the Pasto community of Cumbal, such sections radiated out of the town center in a hierarchy regulating the orderly transition of the periods of office of colonial governors (Rappaport 1988, 1994), a rotational system similar to the Muisca system, in which towns alternated in providing caciques for some communities (Simón 1981 [1627], 415). In Sutatausa, near Bogotá, Muisca *parcialidades*, or community sections, were (and still are) associated with chapels standing at the corners of the plaza—similar to and probably derived from the *posas* or chapels commonly found at the four corners of the courtyards in Mexican sixteenth-century missions (McAndrew 1965; cf. Fraser 1990). This constellation extended the conceptual structure of the plaza out into the (unordered) hinterland.[9]

The architectural volume of the plaza is conceptually a void. As a social space, though, the plaza was bounded by the architectural manifestations of sacred and secular institutions of power: in a reducción, the chapel and the cacique's house; in a city, the major administrative offices and the church.[10] The plaza was therefore constantly filled by a multiplicity of practices that were simultaneously inscribed aurally and ritually in urban space, as well as pictographically and alphabetically in paintings, murals, and written documentation. In this chapter we will probe this palimpsest by examining the spatiality of literate practice in colonial Muisca and Pasto communities.

Alphabetic Space

The space of the alphabetic document is constituted by more than its linguistic contents. Of equal importance in assigning meaning to alphabetic writing is the organization of the page (Messick 1993; Street 1984), the nature of validating seals and signatures (Clanchy 1993; Fraenkel 1992), and the deployment of illustrations and marginalia (Adorno 1986; Camille 1992; Dagenais 1994). In the Spanish American world, documents were readily recognizable by their form: the sometimes indecipherable scrawl of the notary, the hierarchical sequence of the *visita*, or tribute census, the seal at the end of the royal decree that stood in for the monarch in his royal court. Documents validated by a notary were sometimes signed with handwritten signatures accompanied by elaborate interwoven emblems — *rúbricas* — that were not easily falsified. Most often composed of complex designs fashioned out of Christian phrases, these emblems appeared on key pages of documents and in particular positions on the page (Luján Muñoz 1977, 58). Color was also a pertinent part of the semiotic system of the administrative document. Sebastián de Covarrubias (1995 [1611], 872) defines *rúbrica* as "the inscription of the titles of the law. It is called thus because it is written with red letters to distinguish it from other writing" (La inscripción de los títulos del derecho. Díjose así porque se escribe con letra colorada para diferenciarse de la demás escritura).

In native Andean communities there existed local notaries and scribes who were, of course, intimately acquainted with legal formulas and rhetoric

(AHBC/I 1654, 3r–v; ANE/Q 1634a, 125v; ANE/Q 1653; Mannheim 1991, 143–
44; Murra 1998; Spalding 1984, 217). But those who owned documents also
understood their meaning, whether or not they had command of the technology of literacy or the grammar and vocabulary of Castilian. The graphic
space demarcated by these different genres was constitutive of a social space
within which power could be contested, a fact well recognized by indigenous
people, literate and illiterate alike.

Baptismal records and tribute censuses were frequently referred to by native disputants in contests over political positions and lands (ANE/Q 1686,
1695, 1735a). Stored in the church or in portable desks (*escritorios*) owned by
caciques (ANE/Q 1681b), many of these records were readily accessible to native authorities.[11] The baptismal record is particularly interesting, because it
created a transmutable social space that was modified over time, as the priest
added marginal notes to update each entry. The visual form of these books
was considered of utmost importance to church authorities, who mandated
certain formats be followed by parish priests. Luis Zapata de Cárdenas (1988
[1576], 63–64) explains how such records were to be amended:

> Therefore the priest is ordered to take special care, which Your Lordship
> or another Prelate who succeeds him, or with his permission, will con-
> firm, to make visible in the Baptismal Book those who should be con-
> firmed . . . And he should place in the margin of the Book a cross in the
> following form, +, in front of the name of the person confirmed, to signal
> that the name with the cross is confirmed, and so that there is no confu-
> sion of godparents, there should be one or two chosen as godparents of
> all those confirmed in the town, and in the Book the godparents of those
> confirmed in a given year should be written. And likewise, the year of
> confirmation will be written in the margin with the aforementioned cross,
> in such a form as it is signaled in the margin.[12]

This passage, in which alphabetic writing is combined with an image, is accompanied as well by a marginal note in which a cross is drawn, reproducing graphically the form it mandates. The production of baptismal records
was therefore not seen as fixed or static. Rather, the records were modified
in relation to sacramental rituals performed in the town's sacred precincts,
ceremonies in which community members passed from one religious status
to another (Inclán Valdés 1910 [1681], 14; Peña 1995 [1570], 465–66). In other
words, the transmutability and glossing of the baptismal record betray a

colonial form of literacy quite different from our own, akin to the mutable manuscript culture described by John Dagenais (1994).[13]

Such ceremonies were enacted within architectonic spaces to which access was strictly limited by social category, emphasizing in particular the distinction between Christians and non-Christians, as the 1576 catechism of the archbishop of Bogotá, Fray Luis Zapata de Cárdenas (1988 [1576], 69–70), details in its dictates concerning the organization of the interior space of the church:

> It is ordered and commanded that be it known that this mystery [the Mass] is the most elevated of the holy sacraments and only the faithful deserve to enjoy it or see it. The priest should not tolerate that those who have not been baptized observe this divine sacrament, but that he reserve the right for the catechumens to be admitted only until the Creed is said in the mass, and not until the Gospel has been read, and before communion they should be taken outside from where they should not see it. For this effect there should be a part of the church in which the catechumens may remain, from the middle of the church to the back, and the Christians closer to the altar, so that between one and the other there is a space dividing them. And there should be a doorkeeper who takes care to admit them into the church and who takes them out at the appropriate time and those who are simple gentiles should not be tolerated to enter the church at any time.[14]

Difference—between the initiated, catechumens, and the unconverted—was thus inscribed in architectonic space, simultaneous with its inclusion in the graphic space of the baptismal record.

The *visita*—a detailed census of native tributaries that included a precise ethnographic description of the structure and customs of communities; orders to be implemented by colonial officials; and minute tabulations of the names, ages, and families of tributaries—was more than a written document.[15] It was also an elaborate performative act in which bureaucrats made "pilgrimages" across a vast terrain—to appropriate Benedict Anderson's expression—moving from town to town. In the course of his performance, the *visitador* (the Crown official charged with making the census) ritually enacted the colonial social order through the consultation of church records—such as the baptismal books—and the interviewing of all the tributaries of the town, who were congregated by their caciques in the plaza

FIGURE 50
Visita page from
the New Kingdom
of Granada, 1601,
AGN/B, *Visitas de
Cundinamarca*,
t. 13, f. 25r.
Courtesy of
Archivo General
de la Nación,
Bogotá.

of the reducción, paraded in long lines before the visitador and his huge reti-
nue (Guevara-Gil and Salomon 1994). So in the public space of the plaza,
the social space written into baptismal records and inscribed in the organization of the church, was reenacted in a secular ceremony and ultimately reinscribed on the pages of lengthy documents stored in official archives and
by hereditary lords.

Visitas have a characteristic design, readily recognizable by anyone initiated into the trappings of the colonial power structure, as we can see in the
layout of an early seventeenth-century folio from a visita compiled in Cundinamarca (figure 50). In general, the form of the visita appears as a long list of
individuals, organized into community segments. The Quechua word *ayllu*,
which denotes a kin group, or the Spanish term *parcialidad*, or section, are
employed alongside the names of political units in the Pasto Province and

the Popayán District, even though Quechua was not spoken (it was, however, in Pasto towns under the jurisdiction of the city of Ibarra); Muisca social units were labeled as *capitanías*, or captaincies (*uta*, in the Muisca language). Each parcialidad or capitanía is introduced with centered titles in bold print naming the section and the ethnic lord who commanded it, followed by tributaries, who are each accorded a paragraph. There is a characteristic hierarchical ordering of these entries, beginning with the principal cacique and his immediate family, moving to the other lords below him — his *principales*—followed by the male community members of tributary age and their families, and finally the *reservados*, those who were exempted from tribute due to age or illness, and the single women (sometimes, in the Bogotá area, listed with their mestizo or mulatto children). Thus, the visita page graphically reproduces the ritual procession that systematized data and the social hierarchy of the community; given that caciques lived in the town center, the page also reproduces in linear fashion the radial hierarchy constituted by the grid plan. Moreover, visita documents reproduce movement of the Spanish officials across the territory because their sequential listing of communities recapitulates the order in which they were visited.

In the Pasto area, cacicazgos were organized in territorial hierarchies that emanated out of town centers in radial or linear sequences and were divided into upper and lower moieties. Frequently, chiefly spokespersons or ethnic lords serving as governors took turns according to this hierarchy. In the cacicazgo of Cumbal, the hierarchical organization moved in descending order from northeast to southwest, following the path of the sun between the June and December solstices. While the territorial hierarchy may have resembled pre-Columbian forms of political organization, we are speaking here of a *colonial* structure, created through the colonial amalgamation of pre-Columbian cacicazgos into a single district in the face of population movements and land usurpations by the Spaniards. In an earlier article, Joanne Rappaport (1988) interprets the persistence of the formal structure of the territorial hierarchy of Cumbal by comparing the colonial structure of the component sections of the community with pre-Columbian iconographic motifs, in which figures are organized in a radial system that rotates around a central stellar symbol. We are not denying that aboriginal cultural forms were deployed in colonial settings. In fact, the very choice of a radial pattern suggests that indigenous concepts were, indeed, at play in colonial territorial formations. However, while the territorial organization of Cumbal must be interpreted as an *indigenous* cultural form, it is manifestly *colonial* in nature. Its pre-Columbian structures were "sedimented" over with distinct meanings during the course of the colonial process; our use of the concept of sedimentation follows the geological sense of the word, implying the breaking up of rock layers and the creation of overlays of heterogeneous matter, suggesting that these cultural strata were not homogeneous, but uneven and heterogeneous. The colonial territorial hierarchy of the Pastos was inscribed into visitas, given that the native authorities from each section were interviewed in strict hierarchical order. The space of the written page thus merged the Spanish rituality of the visita with colonial native forms of social hierarchy expressed through territorial structure, producing a document which appears as "the precipitate of a drama of colonial power" (Guevara-Gil and Salomon 1994, 24), constituting both the colonial and the native orders in rituality and in graphic form.

Such documents were reinscribed repeatedly into later manuscripts, produced as evidence for disputes, and rearticulated as ritual props. In 1695, for example, the ritual of installation of the cacique of Guachucal included the ceremonial acceptance of his community's census records, standing in for his subject population that was not present (ANE/Q 1695, 37r). In other words, the written word both reflected and constituted reality. As social, political, and ritual space was inscribed graphically, the written record became a central vehicle for the construction of the colonial order. In the process, certain elements of native memory, particularly those which lent meaning to topographic space, were effaced. Toponyms—which carried information on crop types, geographic features (such as rivers and plains), and architectonic forms (such as mounds and terraces)—were slowly simplified by Spanish-speaking scribes (Caillavet 1982b) in a process that paralleled the language loss that, by the eighteenth century, resulted in Spanish monolingualism among the Pasto. Place-names also lost their significance as the Pasto population fell precipitously in the first half of the colonial period (Padilla, López Arellano, and A. González 1977) and as lands were usurped by Spaniards. Given that historical memory depended upon topographical referents in the Andes, these related processes fostered a toponymic simplification which literally "reduced" the semantic load of place-names within the order of notarial practice and diminished their significance for later indigenous readers (Rappaport 1993, 120–21), forcing them to pay more heed to the European-framed models conveyed graphically in written documentation.

Architectonic and Urban Space

The space of public ritual was the plaza at the center of the reducción, the architectural void that became occupied by people engaged in social activity. The plaza was framed by surrounding buildings defining the civic space of political, social, and religious activities; however, it also reframed the reference of vision for Andeans. Passing through the entrances of the main roads leading to the plaza, the gateways defined the limits of the grid layout of orderly crisscrossing streets constituting straight lines meeting at right angles. The plaza was in itself a spatialization of the political or civic order. Here, an individual passed into a colonially configured space to become part of the Christian community, a membership that could never be complete in the sense that all natives were understood as perpetually in a social state of becoming. That is, although natives might mature physically, they did not psychically (Pagden 1982). Rather, they were suspended in a liminal state of social and spiritual development. One can thus think of the gateways of the reducción as forming an axis of this transitional state, marking the teleological movement from wilderness to civility. Only the priest standing in the sanctuary of the church represented the ultimate stage of Christian humility; he was ordained, the only sacrament denied natives by virtue of their arrested state of being. Still, on their way to their fields, natives passed in and out of the reducción and its representation of order and of their place in it. At times, activity among community members swelled as they gathered or were made to congregate to witness political rituals, to celebrate religious rites, or to enjoy games such as bullfights and *cañas*—a mock war-game, played on horseback—all taking place in the plaza.

The plaza's space of public ritual was framed materially by the buildings of colonial authority. Private residences were, for the most part, kept off the plaza, drawing a distinction between private property and the state. As Ross Jamieson suggests:

> There was more than beauty at stake. Conflicts between the authority of the Church and state and the desires of colonial vecinos [citizens] for more local power were manifested in the subordination of the architecture of urban private homes. The gridiron plan of the city meant that private house facades that were not on plazas were always seen at an angle, because an observer on the street could not step back any great distance to admire a large facade. (2002, 53)

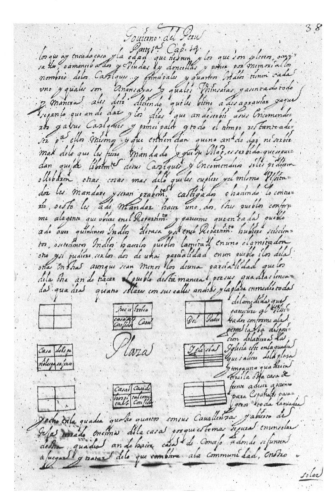

FIGURE 51 Plan for a *reducción*, Juan de Matienzo, *Gobierno del Perú*, 1567, Obadiah Rich Collection, NYPL, Astor Lenox and Tilden Foundations, Rich Ms 74, f. 38r. Ink on paper. New York Public Library.

At the same time, both the central space and buildings, and private residences, were linked conceptually to the other symbolic technologies of colonial knowledge and power. Most immediately, the plan of the city, town, or village could be and often was graphically rendered according to a line drawing of the grid, emanating from and around the central void as we can see in the plan of an ideal Andean native village, drawn by Juan de Matienzo in 1567 (Cummins 2002b, 203–5; figure 51). Such representations were legitimate in courts of law, metonymically standing for the social aggregate. But even when the reducción had been physically constructed and filled with bodies, the principal architectural elements were defined by multivalent terms, such as *portada* (portal), *frontispicio* (frontispiece), and *lienzo* (canvas). *Portada* and *frontispicio* were used interchangeably to refer to the main portals of important buildings, most of which faced onto the plaza. *Frontispicio* is defined by Covarrubias (1995 [1611], 560) as "the front of the house" (la delantera de la casa) and portada (ibid., 839) as "the front of the house, where the main door with its decoration is located" (la delantera de la casa, adonde está la puerta principal con adorno). *Portada* was also used to term the gates of a city, town, or reducción. Sometimes, such as in the reducción of Tiahuanaco, Bolivia, entry to the plaza from neighboring streets was broached by permanently constructed arches, thus architectonically converting the plaza into a sacred precinct. In the colonial Andes, arches were only employed for entrances to religious buildings; the doors of secular edifices being marked by lintels (Fraser 1990, 10). *Portada* was also used to refer to the ephemeral arches that were erected in the plaza, under which passed religious processions or the festive entrance of a distinguished visitor, such as a viceroy or new bishop (Esquivel y Navia 1980 [1749]; Mugaburu 1975 [1686]).

These two terms, however, conjured up more than visions of doorways, ephemeral arches, and passageways into reducciones. They also referred to writing, books, and painting. *Portada* and *frontispicio* were used interchangeably to name the fronts of books or manuscripts. This relationship was more than linguistic, however. Very often, the frontispiece of a book or illustrated manuscript from the sixteenth or seventeenth century imitated the architectural features of a doorway, depicting columns, lintels, and jambs in illusionist detail, suggesting a spatial entrance for the reader passing into the constructed world of the text, as we can see in two books concerning the history and indoctrination of natives and African slaves, that circulated in Quito and Bogotá (figures 52 and 53). The perspectival illusion of the drawing, engraving, or woodcut of the title page visually evoked more than a wordplay between page, architectonic image, and their positions in the manuscript. Both portada as frontispiece of a book and portada as architectural penetration framed a sense of being and transition by suggesting an entrance into knowledge, policía, and civitas. The text could only be penetrated by European alphabetic literacy, while the church could only be entered by the faithful. That is, the act of passing through a portada, whether it be a doorway or a page, was a point of liminal differentiation of time and place.

Conceptually, the portada of a book and of a building placed the reader/ viewer momentarily within the closed structure of a frame. In terms of the portada of a book, the observer occupied a constructed artificial world of images and conscious illusion laid out on the flat page. At the same time, he or she looked through this frame as though it were a door or window open-

FIGURE 52 Franciscan preaching to Indians, after Diego Valadés (1579), from copy in the library of Santo Domingo, Quito. Title page of Juan de Torquemada, *Monarquía indiana* (Seville: Matthias Clauso, 1616).

FIGURE 53 Frontispiece to Alonso de Sandoval, *Naturaleza, policia sagradas i profanas, costumbres i ritos i catechismo evangelico de todos etiopes* (Seville: Francisco de Lira, 1627).

ing onto a view of the world that was suggested without conscious reference to the artifice of painterly illusion, simply promising what lay beyond. There is, then, a wordplay between the page and image, and their position in the manuscript. Both the page as a frontispiece and the illusionist architectural structure that frames it are termed *portada*, and both suggest the entrance into something from someplace.

But only one sense of the term *portada* is intended as a physical passage, a gateway, arch, or door through which a body passes, materially, into another space. No less important a transition was the passing through the portada of the church of the *doctrina* into the nave of the (usually) single-aisle church of the reducción. Here, the sense of liminality was spiritually marked. Only those who had been baptized could remain within the church for communion, as Archbishop Zapata clearly wrote. The rest sat in the rear of the church and were asked to leave before the transubstantiation. The portada of the church marked this phenomenological differentiation. What is important is that this sense of enacted spatial liminality was clear within Catholic doctrine, in which the catechumens who left the church and died in that spiritual condition, as well as the souls of those who were never baptized, remained literally in a state of eternal liminality or limbo (Covarrubias 1995 [1611], 716). What is important to a sense of colonial phenomenology is that the body was integrated into this cross-referentiality. The terms for doorways were also related to the appearance of a person, such that *frontispicio* as doorway is understood by Covarrubias (ibid., 830) as "the most showy and spacious, as is the brow on the face; with this similarity the Italian calls the front of the house *fachata*."[16] Not only is the doorway likened to the forehead of a person, but a person's appearance can be defined by the term "a good bearing or presence" (buena portada de una persona, buena presencia).

It is crucial to recognize that Covarrubias's definitions are not dependent upon historical or true etymologies in the sense of the modern dictionary. Rather, he stresses the social and cultural meanings of words and their etymologies—though the longest definition of a word is found under the entry for *elephant*, one would be hard-pressed to recognize the animal by the characteristics that are listed. The tensions inherent in Covarrubias's definitions and characterizations of words pull them and their referents into various discursive realms of unsuspected social and cultural reifications. It is visual discourse that brings portada, frontispicio, and lienzo together, such that the final term, *lienzo*, unites the planar properties of architecture with the illusionary properties of painting in a way that underscores the ideological regime of vision and order.[17]

Painted Space

One of Covarrubias's (1995 [1611], 715) definitions for lienzo is "the continuing, upright wall" (la pared seguida y derecha). In a secondary definition of the word, however, he writes that "canvases frequently mean the pictures painted on canvases" (lienzos significan muchas veces los cuadros pintados en lienzo). That is, the flatness of the wall is equivalent in some ways to the surface of the painting. At one level, it is simply the property of the surface, which is flat and smooth. At the same time, in painting of the sixteenth and seventeenth centuries, that flatness is denied by the illusions of perspective. Depth, rather than flatness, operates such that the desired effect is recession into and penetration of the surface. This illusion is predicated on techniques of perspective as developed by Leon Battista Alberti and others. In the colonial Andean world of the lienzos of the reducciones, this illusion, based in part upon converging orthogonal lines drawn obliquely to the surface, had to be learned in order to be recognized by native people as a system that convincingly presented the here and now of the universal history of Catholicism. That is, the portadas through which the native community passed opened into churches whose walls were covered with paintings of the gospels.

For example, in Sutatausa, a Franciscan reducción in Cundinamarca located some eighty-eight kilometers north of Bogotá, a series of murals, based upon European prints, were painted on the lateral walls of the single-aisle nave church (Lara 1996, 263–68). All but one depict the events of Christ's passion; the final scene, the Last Judgment, was added slightly later. The scenes of Christ's passion are arranged into discrete units that are separated by illusionist architectural elements painted so as to suggest the division of the single-aisle nave into a more complex interior space. Each scene appears as though within a bay, defined by painted fluted columns and Corinthian columns supporting an entablature. The border of each scene is arched such that it mimics the actual arch that defines the transition from the nave to the choir. The painted architecture therefore gives the illusion that there are a series of side chapels into which the viewer can look and penetrate through the imagination. This technique affords a visual transition so that the narrative scene unfolds in an altogether more convincing illusionist space. The perspectival devices and composition combine to explode the rather confined narrow space of the nave and allow the "cultured" eye to see not the flat surface of the lienzo (wall), but the illusionist properties of the lienzo (painting), such that the historical places of Christ's passion become recognizable and almost physically experienced.

But how does this fiction play out in the reverse, in the physical environment of the reducción? If we think of the linear perspective traced onto the murals at Sutatausa with their converging orthogonal lines as more than an illusion or trick of the eye, but as a regularizing element in the system of ordered experience of the reducción itself, then the phenomenology of colonial visuality is already built into the plan of the town. Standing in the plaza and looking outward or down the sight line of one of the main roads toward the countryside, the lines formed by the road and framing walls (lienzos) are sight lines that lead the urban gaze to the edge of the grid and beyond. Fray Buenaventura de Salinas y Córdoba, standing in the plaza of mid-seventeenth-century Lima, gives just such a description of streets and walls converging into the distance:

> There is singular beauty in the plans and the proportions of the plazas and the streets, all the same. . . . The form and plan is a square of such order and harmony that all the streets are alike, wide enough to permit three coaches to move side by side . . . and so equal that standing in the central plaza one sees the limits of the whole city; because as from the center the lines move out to the circumference of the plaza, toward the edge of it there run long streets. . . . All are sightly for their uniformity and wideness and rectitude and also because the buildings that were built in this city at great cost . . . are very beautiful. (Salinas y Córdoba 1957 [1630], vol. 1, 108–9)[18]

This is the illusion that urban and architectural order provides, and which the orthogonal lines of the paintings try to create. Significantly, this illusion was meticulously reproduced, in city after city and reducción after reducción, with commissions appointed to supervise the ongoing construction of the urban grid, placing particular emphasis on the straightness of the streets (Fraser 1990, 73).

Ritual Space

It is important to stress that the intersecting elements of visuality existed prior to the formation of colonial reducciones. Sebastiano Serlio is quite explicit in his eight-book treatise (1537–75) on architecture and perspective in regard to the relation between perspective, theatrical scenes, and the architecture of the plaza, arches, and straight streets (Damisch 1995, 199–218; see especially Serlio 1537 1540, 44r; 1547).[19] However, in the New World, these elements come into play within a conceptual field of order that is meant to reformulate modes of social identity and being of the colonial subject. Thus, each entrance into the plaza is marked by a small chapel called a posa, indicating that it is a ritual staging-place within Catholic drama. Stopping at each chapel in a liturgical procession, one focused on the chapel and the ritual, yet one could see down the road and note the straight lines converging in the distance. So, too, one could sit, stand, or kneel in the church, listen to the gospels being read, and enter into the paintings on the walls.

Capillas posas are found in various towns in the Sabana de Bogotá and Boyacá, the territory inhabited in the colonial period by the Muiscas (Lara 1996, 260), as well as in other Andean and Mexican settings (Fraser 1990, 113) (figure 54). The four chapels originally located at the corners of the plaza of Sutatausa (of which three are still extant) mark the ritual space within which conversion took place. Processions moved from one chapel to the next in counterclockwise order during major feasts, such as the Nativity. Today, the children of the town reenact Christ's birth with visits to each chapel, where they ask for lodging. During Corpus Christi, the monstrance is carried from one chapel to another, in numerical order. Moreover, just as the colonial indigenous community was "reduced" into the space of a league in radius from the church (González 1979), ensuring that all were within earshot of the bell calling them to observance, the sacred space of the churchyard, framed by the four chapels, extended out into the rural hinterland surrounding the town center. The multiple sections (now called *veredas*) of Sutatausa were charged with the care of the chapels. If we divide the community into four quadrants radiating out of the plaza, the sections lying within each quadrant were responsible for the upkeep of their corresponding chapel, creating a superimposition of topographic and urban space. Wakes for the dead were also held in the chapels, such rites of passage duly inscribed into church records. The baptismal books, remember, contained images such as crosses and other marginalia that fleshed out the individual life cycle. Crosses also

FIGURE 54 Map of the town and lands of Sopó, 1758, AGN/B, *Mapoteca*, SMP4, Ref. 459a.
Courtesy of Archivo General de la Nación, Bogotá.

became boundary markers in the colonial period, extending documentary
and religious iconography out into a now-Christianized hinterland (for the
Pasto area, see ANE/Q 1767). Thus, topographic and urban space were superimposed upon ritual and graphic space in a palimpsest in which literacy,
rituality, and social organization mirrored one another.

At the door of the church, which was comparable to the frontispiece of
a book, both being portadas, the uninitiated were instructed in an open-air
chapel. Bishop Zapata of Bogotá mandated that such observance take place
in the following manner:

> And at the door (the town church) a (large) portal will be constructed,
> if possible, where there will be a pulpit for preaching to the infidels who
> have not yet entered into the ranks of the catechumens, because it is desir-
> able that they understand that they are still not worthy of using nor enter-
> ing that holy temple. (Zapata de Cárdenas 1988 [1576], 42)[20]

This open-air space of conversion was conceived of as a theater (Osorio
2004, 455), a concept sometimes carved into architectonic space. The Church
of San Francisco in Quito is entered by ascending a set of convex steps, fol-

FIGURE 55 Facade
and staircase of
San Francisco,
Quito, ca. 1600.

lowed by a similar set of concave ones, called a *teatro*, or theater (figure 55).
The design is, in fact, derived from Sebastian Serlio's plan of Bramante's Belvedere Theater (Serlio 1537, 1540, 119v–20r) (figures 56a and 56b). A similar
arrangement grants access to the altar of the Church of Santo Domingo in
the Colombian city of Popayán.

The church courtyard thus operated as a kind of stage upon which the
mysteries of Christianity were recounted within architectonic space, much
as they were on the murals inside the church (Lara 1996, 268–70). This is
where Muisca initiates were taught the doctrine, as one Jesuit observer
writes:

> Seven capitanías or parcialidades made seven circles in the plaza, each
> one in the following manner: the natives of a capitanía sat on the ground
> making a semicircle and then in front of them in another semicircle

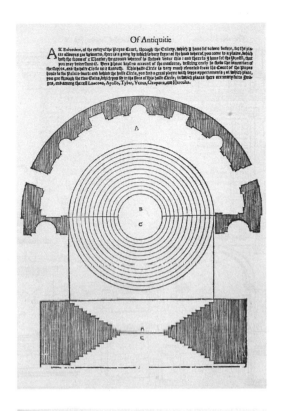

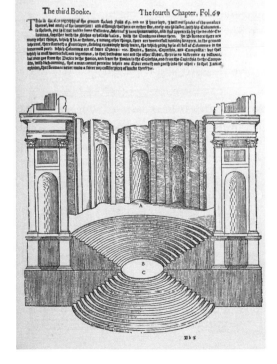

FIGURE 57 Franciscan teaching doctrine to the Chichimec, Diego Valadés, *Rhetorica christiana* (Perugia, 1579). Engraving.

were the women with their backs turned to the men and the space in the middle filled by the boys and girls [and] in the middle of all a child stood with a large cross in his hand and he began to recite the prayers, everyone responding, and once finished, another and another entered, for an hour and a half, and thus at the same time all seven circles were praying, then a father would bring them together and make a large circle in the same form where he would catechize them for the space of five quarters of an hour, then they entered the church to hear the mass sung with much music and there he preached to them. . . . In the afternoon there was a procession of Our Lady around the plaza, singing her litany. (AGCG/R 1608–9, 50v)[21]

A mestizo Franciscan, Diego Valadés, produced an image of such instruction of natives—in this case, Chichimecas from northern Mexico—in his 1579 *Rhetorica christiana* (figure 57). This method of teaching in a circle was etymologically related to the concept of the book, particularly to the idea of the encyclopedia. A genre employed by such Spanish authors as Bernardino de Sahagún to classify and make sense of the cultural realities of the New World (Sahagún 1956–69 [1579]; Mignolo 1995, 187–200), the encyclopedia was more than a genre of written expression. It was also a pedagogical technique based upon the educational benefits of a particular body posture:

> Encyclopedia, then, brings us back to education and, consequently, to genres in the organization and transmission of knowledge. A secondary meaning of *enkyklios paideia* was "teaching in circle," applied to the physical setting in which the transmission of knowledge was performed rather than to the "well-rounded education" contemplated in the curriculum. (1995, 203)

In the urban space of the churchyard, the social and territorial organization of the community was transfigured or "reduced" through communal prayer and catechism.[22] The ideological relationship between bodily posture and the book clearly illustrates that in the Spanish value system, word, image, and space were perceived as superimposed, associated conceptually and in practice with the "ordering" of the Other through Christian indoctrination and through the rearrangement of physical space.

The Superimposition of Sacred and Secular Space

The entryway to the church was also a scenario for a very different performance of secular colonial power in which ceremonial objects, themselves the product of the sedimentation of various cultural traditions, became polysemic and symbolically ambiguous as they were juxtaposed in the colonial context. In the mid-eighteenth century, a teatro was erected at the doorway of the Church of Pastás (today, the town of Aldana) in preparation for the investiture of its new cacique, Don Manuel Nastar y Canchala. The teatro, probably consisting of triumphal arches of the sort that greeted the arrival of viceroys or other colonial officials in cities and towns (Espinosa 1995), set the scene for a ceremony in which Pasto, Incaic, and colonial Spanish elements interpenetrated:

> In the town of Pastas on the eighteenth day of the month of October of seventeen sixty one, General Don Gregorio Sanchez Parra, Lieutenant Governor, Corregidor [provincial governor], and High Justice of this province and its jurisdiction for Your Majesty, having come here in conformity with what was ordered in the previous decree, standing in the theater formed according to custom at the door of the church, accompanied by the R.P.M. Fr. Fernando Paredes, priest of the town of Carlo-

zama and this its annex, by various individuals, religious and secular, the Protector de Naturales [royal advocate for native people], the caciques of the province, the Alcalde Mayor [constable], and a great number of male and female indios, I ordered the previous writ and decree read in a clear voice and as its consequence, the anticipated investiture with the following formality and words: I, General Don Gregorio Sanchez Parexa, Lieutenant Governor, Corregidor, and High Justice of this province in the name of the King our lord, to you, Don Manuel Nasttar y Canchala I elevate you and place you in possession of the cacicazgo of the parcialidad of Nastar, one of those of the town of Pastas, and I order its governor, principales, heads, and leaders, indios and indias, boys and girls of the entire parcialidad to receive you and present themselves at your call, to have and obey you as their cacique and natural lord under the penalty of royal law against the disobedient. And as a sign of your possession I give you this staff of lordship and seated the cacique in his seat, the indios and indias, boys and girls of his parcialidad came and laid out their mantles, making [signs of] their obedience according to their uses and customs, they kissed his foot and his relatives embraced him as a sign of welcome and obedience and then he was carried on the shoulders of his principales and processed around the four sides of the plaza. (ANE/Q 1761, 4v–5r)[23]

In the Pasto area (ANE/Q 1694, 4v; 1695, 2r; 1735a, 41r, 54r–v; 1735a, 414, 54r–v; 1761; 1764; 1771,334v) and throughout the colonial Andes (Martínez Cereceda 1995), the investiture of caciques and other native authorities was marked by the seating of the ethnic lord on a wooden stool (sometimes covered by a rug), commonly called by the Quechua word *tiyana* or the Carib word *duo* (or *duho*). This was followed by an act of obedience in which the new ethnic lord was kissed by neighboring caciques or his subordinate principales; in Peruvian and Bolivian documents, this act is called by the Quechua term *mochar*, which, as we mentioned in the previous chapter, consisted in the pre-Columbian period in the making of a kissing sound in recognition of the sacred character of huacas (shrines), mummies, caciques, or the Inca himself (ibid.). In the colonial ceremony, the newly invested cacique was then carried on a litter around the plaza by his political subordinates or by neighboring caciques.

The similarities in terminology and in practice that this ceremony presents across the Andes, even in regions beyond Inca control such as the Pasto Province, suggest that it was standardized by the Spaniards, using an Incaic model. The eighteenth century witnessed further transformation when the ritual bestowal of staffs of office—an object of European origin—was introduced (Martínez Cereceda 1995; Rappaport 1990). Herein lies the derivation of the insignia received by Don Manuel Nastar y Canchala in the quotation, similar to those still carried by native authorities throughout the Andes (Rappaport 1994; Rasnake 1988). Despite the fact that this ceremony flourished under Spanish domination, its constituent elements probably resonated with Pasto tradition, given that ethnic lords in the Colombian Andes were processed on litters by their principales, as Cieza de León (1962 [1553], 58) records for what is now Antioquia and Pedro de Simón (1981 [1627], 391) describes for the Muisca of the Sabana de Bogotá; Muisca caciques were also seated in "chairs of authority" (ibid.).

The ritual of investiture thus interwove layers of Pasto, Incaic, and Spanish colonial practice. A variant was also employed by Pasto caciques in recognition of their Spanish encomenderos—holders of royal tribute grants—in an ironic inversion of the chiefly ritual (ANE/Q 1723, 1727a; Rappaport 1990, 17). Chiefly investiture therefore entailed numerous forms of "order." The public space in which the ceremony was held had been "reduced" by town planning. The pre-Columbian forms of authority were "ordered" within Spanish models of civil society. Elements of the rituals were transferred onto the legitimization of the encomendero, who "reduced" the natives to civilization through the control of their productive force and support of the Christian mission. Finally, the ceremony itself was then inscribed into the documentary record: it was "reduced" to writing. Like the repetitive recording of the messages of town criers into documents, the ceremony of chiefly investiture was repeatedly recorded in the documentation disputes over cacicazgos, documents that frequently covered the history of chiefly governance over two centuries or more. Hence, the ritual became a significant feature in written communication, reminding the indigenous readers of its symbolic continuity over time.

Woven Literacy

The Pasto ceremony of chiefly investiture, unlike recorded rituals from other Andean regions, also incorporated the ceremonial exchange of weavings, specifically, mantles, that were laid at the feet of the newly installed authority. Pedro de Simón (1981 [1627], 398) records a similar practice among the pre-Columbian Muisca upon the selection of the heir to a chiefdom: "[The selection] having ended, they also finished off great quantities of their wine in a great festivity for all the neighboring caciques, who received the returned folded presents [the heir] had made them of mantles, gold, arms, and other things."[24] The symbolic importance of weavings among the Pastos is evident in their presence in pre-Columbian burials (Cardale de Schrimpff 1977–78) and in the fact that they were acquired by caciques from status traders (*mindaláes*) who operated under chiefly control and bolstered chiefly authority (Salomon 1986, 105). As we detailed in chapter 3, native textiles were sometimes included in the wills of caciques (ANE/Q 1624, 87v; ANE/Q 1730a, 4v–5r). In an early will from the southern portion of the Pasto area that was briefly under Inca control (AHBC/I 1606, 1v), a cacica described an Incaic textile among her many possessions, suggesting that in the colonial order, the authority of Pasto chiefs was validated in part by Spanish recognition of their command of Incaic symbols of legitimacy (Rappaport and Cummins 1994). Here we note once again the superimposition of various cultural forms whose validation is made patent in the alphabetic record. The significance to the colonial Pastos of Andean textiles was further reconfigured as they came to represent an important form of tribute to the Spanish Crown, which annually exacted massive numbers of mantles from Pasto caciques (AGI/S 1570–71). For this reason, mantles were not only offered to newly installed ethnic lords, but also to new encomenderos, the latter act symbolizing the encomendero's crucial role in the transfer of tribute payments to the Crown and, by association, imparting a particularly colonial significance to their presence in the chiefly investiture.

In Andean society—where alphabetic, syllabic, and pictographic literacy were unknown before the Spanish invasion—weaving was an essential medium of inscription, bearing a meaning that was intimately tied into its very technology (Cardale de Schrimpff 1977–78; Frame 1994). Nonlinguistic systems of inscribing narrative, such as the khipu or knot record (Ascher and Ascher 1981; Conklin 1982; Urton 1994, 1998, 2003; Urton and Quilter 2002), continued to be relevant even under Spanish secular and religious administration in the northern Andes, as well as in Peru (Espinoza Soriano 1960, 223–24). Thus, it is not surprising that textiles, whose symbolic load among the colonial Pasto we can only guess at, were a meaningful addition to colonial secular ceremony.

Alphabetic literacy, however, is not the only channel through which the colonial significance of textiles was communicated. The reattribution of meaning to pre-Columbian iconographic motifs on painted Muisca textiles can be interpreted from the murals in the church at Sutatausa. Dating from the 1620s, these paintings depict the final events in the life of Christ (plate 9) and a Last Judgment scene (plate 7 and figure 30), as we have described above. Below the Last Judgment there is one of two portraits of a contemporary Andean male.[25] On each of two sides of the arch separating the nave and choir is a portrait of one of two caciques and a cacica (figures 23 and 26, and plate 4). A legend to the lower left of the Last Judgment provides the names of a cacique and four capitanes, and it can be assumed these are the individuals who appear in the murals (figure 9).[26] The three extant cacique portraits depicted them in Spanish dress, as befitted indigenous nobility in the colonial period. The cacica, however, is shown wearing an elaborate painted cotton mantle complete with complex geometric motifs, whose detail is such that quite clearly the colonial Muisca artist took great pains to convey the dense iconographic content of the weaving, which is considerably more detailed than the remainder of the painting. That such weavings continued to bear significance for the colonial Muisca is evident in wills of the sixteenth and seventeenth centuries that list *mantas pintadas de pincel* or hand-painted mantles (AGN/B 1576, 202r–v; 1609–10, 373v; 1630a, 47v; 1633a, 97r).

Painted cotton textiles were central to many pre-Columbian Muisca chiefly rituals (Simón 1981 [1627], 390), and weaving technology was one of the fundamental categories of knowledge that myth taught them was acquired from the deities (ibid., 375). Muisca priests, who spent several years in seclusion in preparation for the priesthood, devoted this period of isolation to weaving and painting mantles, among other tasks (AGCG/R 1608–9, 49v). The colonial chronicler Pedro de Simón read Muisca iconography as indicating their prior knowledge of Christianity, since crosses were among the motifs employed:

> Others called this man Nemterequeteba, others said Xué. He taught them to spin cotton and to weave mantles, because before, the Indians had only covered themselves with some sheets they made from raw cotton, bound with hemp cords, one to the other, all badly ordered and still like primitive people. When he left a town he would leave the looms painted on some smooth and polished stone, as one sees today in some places, in case they forgot what he had taught them. . . . He taught them to make crosses and use them in the paintings on the mantas they covered themselves with and perchance, declared their mysteries to them and those of the Incarnation and death of Christ. (Simón 1981 [1627], 375)[27]

The notion of the prefiguring of the Christian era in the Americas was a common motif in colonial writing (Adorno 1986, 58–62), sometimes depicted through the appearance of European-like emissaries in ancient times (Hazañero 1645, 214). While crosses are not depicted in the Sutatausa cacica's clothing, the Christian significance of indigenous weavings was part of the symbolic load carried by textiles in the colonial period.

Of more significance, however, is the meaning conveyed by the juxtaposition of women and men in the Sutatausa murals. The cacica, although wearing an aboriginal mantle—her blouse underneath the mantle is European—is portrayed holding a rosary, thus marking her membership in the Christian community. The men, who also carry rosaries, are marked as members of the colonial nobility by virtue of their exclusively European clothing. This gendered enactment of the complex and heterogeneous nature of Muisca colonial culture is embodied in the classification of textiles, both European and indigenous, and their use by men and women.[28] Thus, the use of native textiles presents a multilayered set of meanings: the memory of pre-Columbian symbolic motifs and ritual practices; the reattribution of meaning to weavings within a colonial system of legitimization that fostered the persistence of Incaic symbols of authority; the restructuring of hierarchical social relationships through colonial tribute payments; the recognition of the prefiguring of Christianity in textile designs; and finally, the gendered nature of colonial hybridity. These multiple significations, originating in a broad array of cultural formations, were articulated within a system that "reduced to order" oral and written communication, territorial organization, urban space, and the hearts and minds of native Andeans in overlapping and simultaneous circles of meaning that irrevocably altered northern Andean society, giving birth to a colonial reality.

Conclusion

In one of the early seventeenth-century Jesuit annual letters, a Muisca woman recounts a telling vision to her confessor. Twenty years earlier she had been seriously ill and sought the services of a shaman (*jeque*) who asked her to make an offering of a parrot and a monkey to a temple that the local encomendero had destroyed:

> Already at the end, a woman whom he visited and knew sent for a jeque, a priest of idolatry. The evil old man entered the house of the sick woman, bringing what he needed for his task. He chewed coca, drank tobacco, and began in a low voice to intone certain chants that are like *consevios* [?]. He called the demons by name, spoke with them, and when he finished all of his ceremonies in the presence of the sick woman he then informed her, telling her, "You should know that the ancestors of this native woman made in a certain place a temple of idolatry that was destroyed by the cursed encomendero of that town and for this great sin the gods punished the innocent native woman. But there is an easy remedy if she obeys what the idol demands, which is that the sick woman buys a parrot and a monkey and raises them during two years and at the end takes them to the jeque to offer in that temple. And if she promises this, she will not only get well but will be very rich and of good fortune." (AGCG/R 1611–12, 67v–68r)[1]

When the woman refused to comply with the jeque's demands, he became furious. Suddenly, she fell into a deathlike state and was placed in a shroud for burial. However, she had not died, but lived to recount the following vision to a Jesuit:

> She seemed to be in bed, very quiet and still, but sick, and being awake, the most serene of the angels, Our Lady of the Rosary, entered her hut seated in a golden chair with the Christ Child in her arms, who was beautiful to an extreme. The child did not say a word to the sick woman but looked at her with a very happy and smiling face. The Virgin had a face that undid the good native woman in her efforts to appreciate its beauty, and she finally said that she lacked the words to explain how from her head and her tresses emanated rays and a brilliance like that of the sun when it comes out in the morning, and her clothing was like sheets of gold. The Virgin, in all her majesty, neared the bed and very affably touched her on the head, saying that soon two Dominican fathers would visit her and she would be cured. Having said this the vision disappeared and then she saw two small children of hers who had died once baptized, dressed in golden cloth with their hair like Nazarenes and four angels much more beautiful than them, also clothed to the knees very richly with beautiful golden crosses on their foreheads. Behind the angels the two Dominican friars arrived and placed their hands on her head. And praying for her they left in procession, as when they entered, and they appeared no more. The sick woman woke out of a sweet sleep and when she realized she was enshrouded, began to make noise and scream, at which point the householders undid and removed the shroud, very frightened by the event, which they perceived as miraculous, and although they asked her many things she never wanted to say anything from then on, living her life in a new manner. (ibid., 68r)[2]

In fact, it is the vision that cured the woman, bringing her out of her death-like state and into a sweet sleep from which she awoke.

The woman's dream image is predicated on a well-known iconography, the image of the Virgin of the Rosary holding the infant Jesus. This comes from the miraculous image of the Virgin of Chiquinquirá (plate 2), a devotional painting that restored itself after falling into disrepair (the first miracle associated with the painting). Soon afterward, numerous other miracles were attributed to the image, including the curing of the sick and bringing an end to a drought (Cummins 1999). The Church of Chiquinquirá soon became a major pilgrimage shrine in the region. In the painting, the Virgin stands, holding a rosary, with the Christ Child in her arms. Today, she is crowned with a silver halo, as is Christ, both recent additions to the canvas. However, in copies of the painting she is surrounded by a *mandorla*, an oval flamelike aura, which is precisely what the Muisca woman described in her vision. The vision is not a precise match with the painting: the visionary only recounts the central figure of the Virgin, who is always flanked in paintings by Saints Andrew and Anthony of Padua; she has her seated in a golden chair, while she stands in the canvas. But in the vision, the Virgin promised that the woman would be visited by two Dominicans, who would cure her, thus conflating the pastoral work of the Dominicans in Chiquinquirá with the principal figures of their most miraculous image.

This is a striking example of the internalization of a new visual culture in the psyche of a native woman. Her dream experience was shaped by a painting, before which she may very well have prayed but whose iconography she probably did not fully comprehend. Nevertheless, in her vision the canvas becomes a vehicle mediating between her pagan past and her Christian future; the former is literally represented by the jeque, and the latter by the Dominicans who would cure her. In this instance, the structures of the new civil and religious order are manifest in the woman's accessing of a particular form of colonial literacy over which her command was only partial. This literacy was, nevertheless, deeply ingrained in her imagination, a dramatic example of how literate conventions touched the lives of even the most marginal of folk in the New Kingdom of Granada. The exemplary nature of her tale is what caused it to be cast in writing, to enter into an epistolary genre and to be forwarded to the Jesuit General in Rome, where the letter is now stored. As a result, the traces of visual literacy that impacted the vision are recast in alphabetic form.

This is the interplay that we have tried to articulate in the course of this book. To accomplish this we have gone beyond the usual boundaries of literacy as normally constituted by scholars. We see literacy as much more than the technology of alphabetic writing and reading. We treat documents as more than transparent repositories of data. We attempt to access literacy among those who would be considered the least literate. In other words, we seek to expand the notion of the lettered city to include a broader range of participants than that envisioned by Ángel Rama and a wider scope of practices than that posited by Jack Goody, or even M. T. Clanchy. Our argument is that perhaps the most fertile ground for comprehending how literacy works can be found in stories like that of the Muisca visionary with which we opened this chapter, as well as in others we introduced in chapter 2.

Few of the protagonists in this book were men of letters, or even able to manipulate the written word at all. Even fewer were painters or notaries, professions that were not open to the vast majority of native people in the northern Andes. Moreover, the indigenous communities of the Andes did not know narrative pictorial representation or alphabetic or hieroglyphic literacy before the arrival of the Spaniards, and to enter into such literate conventions they needed to learn not only a new set of technologies, but they had to come to understand that what was represented was not embodied in the image or symbol, but referred to something outside of it—what can be called deferred referentiality. In other words, native peoples entering the Spanish literate world were forced to undergo cognitive and philosophical transformations, requiring an active engagement with European symbolic systems.

What our statement implies is that to understand indigenous literacy, we need to go beyond the written word. It is precisely in the learning of perspective by walking the streets of a reducción, the observation of a corregidor kissing a royal decree, the recounting of a dream sequence that mirrors a painting, the introduction of Spanish tilework in a wattle-and-daub Andean village, that we can begin to perceive the process through which such cognitive transformation occurred. Only after that can we fully comprehend what it meant for a native artist such as Andrés Sánchez Gallque to paint a portrait of the three mulatto gentlemen, or for Muisca cacique Don Diego de Torres to pen his petitions to the king. Their control of literate conventions was predicated on an acceptance and understanding of the importance of the philosophy of literacy by a wider indigenous constituency. That is to say, Don Diego's writing issued both out of a European ethos, and out of a colonial indigenous one.

Documents, whether alphabetic or visual, have a social life that transcends the information they carry. In some cases the document or the painting, as a physical object, takes on the aura of a precious thing, regardless of whether those who own it can decipher its contents. In other cases, it is more in the assemblage of documentary series, in their arrangement in social and political space, or in the ways that they are read across time, that such texts acquire significance. And in still other instances, it is in the enacting of the contents of a document—such as in the construction of a town whose plan has been already inscribed in a drawing—that the information contained in the text becomes real. In other words, although the document is not entirely meaningless without the accompanying acts that validate it, it also becomes meaningful from the acts that convert it into lived experience.

For instance, we can think of a last will and testament as a record of the possessions of an individual. But the will is predicated on a number of social relations, including an acceptance of the Christian form of death; European forms of ownership and of transmitting property; the colonial legal system in which the wishes of the dead were recorded, copied, contested, disputed, and remembered; and the ritual enacted in masses said on behalf of the dead. What makes the will important as a form of literacy is, therefore, not just what it records but the social formation that the writing and reading of the will generates. For this reason, we argue in this book that literacy must go beyond texts to encompass the world.

When the word *literacy* is used, one normally thinks of reading and writing. We have stressed here that the literate world is constituted by intersecting literacies that individually cannot stand alone. The literate world is thus multifaceted and often recursive. It is, moreover, specific to a given social and historical context, and is something that must be learned and transmitted. Let us provide a hypothetical example. An indigenous worshipper in the Church of Sutatausa listens to a sermon delivered by the parish priest. The sermon was previously written in alphabetic form, and is read aloud to the congregation. In the liturgy, the written word—in the form of the Bible—is treated as a sacred object, as well as being read. In fact, the interior of the church is understood to be divided into two sides with a central axis; this spatial division represents the New and Old Testaments, as enacted by the liturgical readings from the Gospels and the Psalms. Within the fullness of the mass, they are read sequentially and together they form the unity of the sacred word of the Bible. Also, the priest's sermon sometimes referred directly to one of the paintings on the church wall, such as the Last Judgment, in which natives carrying painted gourds containing beer are being led to hell. The male members of the congregation face the altar, sitting on the left-hand side of the church, where the reading of the gospel is conducted; the women, in their painted mantles, sit on the right side. It is, however, the altar that determines where one sits and where the different parts of the Bible are read. The males are therefore to be understood as sitting on the right, or "elect," side of this ritual space. But not everyone was allowed to enact this ritual experience that was at once phenomenological and symbolic. Only those who have received the catechism were allowed inside; the others had to stand in the plaza. The catechistic teachings are based on published texts, which, it must be remembered, begin with syllabaries. The building of the church and the naming of the parish priest are encoded in legal documents, as well as in portraits of the donors. Our point here is that literacy is constituted by the interaction of these multiple alphabetic genres, visual representations, architectural forms, and legal conventions within a single physical space. However, not everyone in the church has the same proficiency in any one of these literate forms, yet they all accept the forms' legitimacy and understand their interrelationships.

We have examined literacy in a specifically colonial situation, restricting it historically and geographically. The Andean context is particularly revelatory though highly specific. On the one hand, such literate forms were completely alien to native peoples. On the other hand, the process was part of a wider project in which the Spaniards erected in tangible form those early modern ideals that had only been imagined, not effected, in Europe: notions such as the grid plan or the massive social planning that created a new order in the Americas. This could not be accomplished in quite the same fashion anywhere else in the world, because Europeans in this period had not penetrated or did not have sufficient control over other regions, except for part of the western coast of Africa. The Spaniards had no choice but to engage literacy to create the sort of bureaucratic colonial state that they envisioned. They needed administrative documents, doctrinal texts, city plans, grammars and lexicons, and devotional and miraculous images to create and sustain a far-flung colonial society. They also needed a layer of literate native people, trained in newly created institutions—such as schools for caciques—to negotiate the colonial administration and to move between the colonies and Spain. Finally, they needed a native populace that was conversant enough in this new system to fuel its operations. In this sense, the lettered city could not have existed, if not for the participation in it of people who were considered to be nonliterates.

This process was lodged in a particular historical moment. The conversion of Native Americans to Catholicism was interpreted within Counter-Reformation theology. The entry of indigenous people into Christendom would offset the loss of northern Europeans to Protestantism. The complete conversion of the natives of America to Christianity was therefore more than a political project; it was also a messianic necessity that would hasten the Last Judgment and the end of the world. But conversion was only possible if the world was imagined according to a social hierarchy based upon language and literacy, and if the Christian doctrine could be adequately explained, which could only be effected through the expansion of literate technologies and accompanying social formations. Yet for Don Diego de Torres, the cacique of Turmequé, and others like him, who were caught within this merging of cultural worlds, theology was not as important as were more instrumental considerations. Access to literacy allowed him to negotiate the ways in which he and his constituents would exist in and impact upon this new world order. His legacy—of documents, maps, church buildings—would help to define what being American meant for people of every ethnicity. Thus, it is no accident that the first maps we know for Colombia were drawn by this Muisca cacique.

The vast majority of the most influential works on literacy focus on Europe, tracing the genealogy of the technology back to ancient Greece, Rome, and the Middle East. What we attempt in this book is to draw readers' attention toward the colonial periphery, the place where Iberian modernity was conceived and experimented on, and where literate conventions combined with Andean forms of inscription in novel ways.

It was in the Americas, for example, where literate discourses were incorporated into a new urban landscape based on the grid pattern, a template that redirected the eye and the mind at the same time that it reoriented the body, a guide to Christian living that altered native forms of memory and recast them in the form of the book and the pictorial image. In this sense, the Spanish colonial city was not only lettered in its dependence on the written word and the educated European letrados whose laws provided the foundations of the lettered city, as Ángel Rama would have it. It was lettered in its very building blocks: the frontispieces of its doorways, the canvases of its walls, arranged in such a way as to encourage the development of an architectural sense of perspective and the emergence of a distinct social hierarchy based both on social status or economic power, and on ethnic difference.

It was in the Americas that the rise of a literate layer of native people and mestizos—like Don Diego de Torres—challenged the lettered city by creating a lettered city of its own. It was not an autonomous social structure, nor one whose component parts displayed a consistent sense of cultural alterity. Literate discourses merged with Andean means of encoding history in the landscape, frequently in subtle manners whose nuances cannot be explored thoroughly if we cling to the romantic but unrealistic and ahistorical notion of the "indigenous voice." In fact, many of the European practices that touched the hearts and minds of native people, providing the

broad contours of their participation in the lettered city—such as, for instance, the ceremony of obedience to the king through the ritualistic manipulation of his royal decrees—ultimately came to define what is "indigenous" in the twentieth and twenty-first centuries. Indigenous testators and
mestizo authors of denunciations of the abuses of the encomenderos, the
artisans of barniz de Pasto writing desks and the muralists of Sutatausa, all
the members of the "indigenous lettered city," were colonial subjects who
lived in historical time, attended Catholic mass, and created new forms of
expression whose character can only be discerned in its dialogue with European expressive forms and technologies of inscription.

It is in this sense that it is worth the effort to explore the nuances of the
spread of alphabetic and visual literacy in the Americas. As we have demonstrated, the study of the indigenous lettered city involves taking into account
not only the pen but also the paintbrush; it involves not only the notary but
the mason; its audience is not only the man of letters who reads erudite
manuscripts but the native witness who inscribes on his body the sign of
the cross. The intricate interdependency of letter and image in the colonial
Americas forces us to go beyond the technology (or even the social organization) of the written word, which has so dominated the study of literacy in
Europe. The Americas presented Spain with an opportunity to create a new
kind of society whose foundations were firmly premised on the structures
and metaphors of literate expression, both alphabetic and visual. In turn, the
Americas provide us with the challenge of tracing both the maintenance and
the subversion of this new society by indigenous actors, with all of the complexity and ambivalence that the indigenous lettered city produced.

Glossary

aquilla	Silver drinking vessel.
Audiencia	Representatives of the Royal Court in the Americas; after the viceroyalty, the most inclusive administrative unit in the New World.
cabildo	Town council or the council governing an indigenous *resguardo*.
cacica	Female hereditary chief, a member of the indigenous nobility.
cacicazgo	Hereditary chiefdom.
cacique	Male hereditary chief, a member of the indigenous nobility.
capilla posa	One of four chapels located at the corners of the church courtyard in some Latin American locations; see *posa*.
capitanía	Section of a Muisca community; see also *parcialidad*.
casta	Ethnic category used, in the colonial period, primarily to refer to those of mixed descent.
cédula	Royal decree.
criollo	Settler of Spanish descent, born in the New World.
curaca	Hereditary chief in southern Andean Quechua.
doctrina	Village-level structure of Christian indoctrination.
encomendero/a	Holder of a royal tribute grant.
encomienda	Royal tribute grant given to individuals who performed service to the Crown.

frontispicio	Frontispiece of a book or the portal of a door.
indio/a	Indigenous person.
khipu	Andean knot record.
ladino/a	Indigenous person who could speak Spanish.
letrado	A man of letters.
lienzo	Canvas or the walls of a colonial town.
limbiquiro	See *quero*.
lliclla	Woman's mantle. Also called *líquida* in some colonial documents.
mestizo/a	Individual identified or self-identifying as of mixed indigenous and European descent.
muchana, mochar	The making of a kissing sound in recognition of the sacred character of *huacas* (shrines), mummies, curacas, or the Inca himself.
oidor	Judge of the Audiencia.
parcialidad	Section of an indigenous community.
portada	Portal to a building or frontispiece of a book.
posa	Small chapel, serving as a staging place for Catholic ritual.
principal	A member of the indigenous nobility occupying a rank lower than that of *cacique*.
probanza de méritos	Report on services rendered to the king. Includes a list of questions (*interrogatorio*) and depositions by witnesses.
qompi	Fine Andean textile.
quero	Lacquered wooden drinking vessel.
quillca	To write or to draw in Quechua.
real provisión	Royal decree.
Reconquista	The conquest of Muslim Spain by the Catholic kings.
reducción	Planned indigenous town, organized in a grid pattern.
reducir	To bring to order.
relación	Colonial written genre used for reports, frequently written as responses to questions.
República de Españoles	Administrative and judicial division covering Africans, *castas*, and Spaniards.

República de Indios	Administrative and judicial division covering native people.
requerimiento	Proclamation read to military rivals requiring them to submit to Christianity or die in war.
resguardo	An indigenous community in the New Kingdom of Granada, holding royal title to communal lands, administered by a cacique.
teatro	Site of Catholic ritual, sometimes marked by the church steps and sometimes by triumphal arches.
visita	A detailed census of native tributaries that included precise ethnographic description of the structures and customs of communities, orders to be implemented by colonial officials, and minute tabulations of the names, ages, and families of tributaries.
visitador	Crown official charged with compiling a *visita*.

Notes

INTRODUCTION

A note on transcriptions and translations of colonial documents: Our transcriptions attempt to preserve the orthography and punctuation of the original documents, while at the same time making them comprehensible to twenty first century readers. Thus, we spell out most abbreviations and generally (but not always) convert the letter "u" to "v" and the "f" to "s," but we do not convert "y" to "i" or add the letter "h" where it is missing. We do not include accent marks in our transcriptions, as they were not used in the colonial period; for this reason, names like "Popayán" will appear with an accent mark in the text, but without an accent in documentary citations. We do not attempt to translate punctuation into our modern system; for example, we retain the equal sign (=) for distinguishing members of a list. We do not reconcile divergent spellings of a word or a proper name, which might be spelled in different ways, even in the same document; this is particularly true for toponyms and anthroponyms in native languages, which Spanish scribes struggled to grasp using Castillian phonological conventions, although they were not proficient in the language in question. Our English translations sometimes omit the constant use of legal terms such as *dicho* and *dicha* ("said" or "aforementioned") in an effort to make the quotations more readable. Colonial documentary writing frequently has run-on sentences. In the interests of making quotations in translation more readable, we have opted for dividing some run-on sentences into more coherent phrases; the Spanish originals contained in the notes preserve the run-on quality of these quotes. In the citations to the Archivo General de Indias (AGI), l. stands for *legajo* (file, docket), n. for *número* (number), and r. for *ramo* (section, division, department).

1. He is called "Don Diego de la Torre" in documents, but since most publications refer to him as Don Diego de Torres (Gálvez Piñal 1974; Rojas 1965) and he is remembered with this name in popular memory in Colombia, we will also call

him thus in the following pages. In the early colonial period Muisca cacicazgos passed through the female line, that is, from a maternal uncle to his nephew.

2. For example, Torres cites Charles V's New Laws, proclaimed in 1542, in his 1586 report, or *relación*, "De como son mui mal tradados los pueblos" (About how the *pueblos* are very mistreated):"Your Majesty also orders through the New Law and royal ordinance that the *pueblo* or *pueblos de indios* must be better treated and conserved" (Tambien manda Vuestra Magestad por ley nueva y hordenança real que el pueblo o pueblos de yndios . . . sean major tratados y conservados) (AGI/S 1586b, 229r). The report is twenty-two chapters long.

3. Don Diego de Torres's life is chronicled in minute detail, including transcriptions of his immense corpus of petitions and accusations held at the Archivo General de Indias, by Ulíses Rojas (1965). Esperanza Gálvez Piñal (1974) focuses on the role of Don Diego in motivating the Crown to order a *visita*, or royal inspection, to investigate abuses committed against the indigenous population of Santafé and Tunja in the second half of the sixteenth century. Hoyos García (2002, part III) analyzes in detail a number of documents relating to the mestizo cacique, with an eye to comprehending his relationship with legal writing. The New Kingdom of Granada (Nuevo Reino de Granada) was the name given the jurisdiction of the Audiencia based in Santafé; in the eighteenth century, after becoming a viceroyalty, its name was changed to New Granada (Nueva Granada).

4. For letters and petitions to the Crown, written in Spanish and Latin by Mexican nobility, see Emma Pérez-Rocha and Rafael Tena (2000, 95–404).

5. Although the two volumes of Inca Garcilaso de la Vega are not illustrated, his understanding of the value of pictorial images is expressed at the end of his work, where he describes himself in Spain during March of 1604, having received a set a of documents composed by the descendants of the Inca ruling families to be presented at the court. Along with the written documents and "for clearer proof and demonstration, they [the Inca descendants] included a genealogical tree showing the royal line from Manco Capac to Huyana Capac painted on a Vara [unit of measurement of cloth] and a half of white China Silk. The Incas were depicted in their ancient dress, wearing the scarlet fringe on their heads and their ear ornaments in their ears; only their busts were shown." (1723 [1609], lib. 9, cap. 40).

6. As Gary Urton (2003, chap. 1) has very astutely pointed out, we would do well to consider numeracy alongside alphabetic literacy. Unfortunately, Urton's suggestion opens issues that cannot be explored with the archival material we have at hand, which is largely alphabetic and only marginally numeric. Music, something intellectually related in Western thought to numbers as expressed in the quadrivium (arithmetic, geometry, music, and astronomy), is an even more important part of the concept of literacy in its broadest understanding, but which, unfortunately, cannot be treated here.

7. Valadés's *Rhetorica christiana* circulated in the Andes as copies, which are listed in the inventories of several libraries, including that made by Francisco de Ávila in 1648 (Hampe Martínez 1996, 162).

8. "Pronunciar con palabras lo que por letras está escrito" and "enseñar alguna disciplina públicamente."

9. Located in the highlands of Carchi Province in northernmost Ecuador, Puntal is now called Bolívar. Tuza, immediately to the north of Puntal, is now called San Gabriel.

10. Most paper for books printed in the viceroyalties, as well as the paper used for all official documents, was brought to the Americas. There were attempts to produce paper in Mexico and sometimes this autochthonous paper was used to complete a printing, but it was not used as a first resort (personal communication, Marina Garone).

11. In the Pasto region, "mother tongue" denotes use of the Pasto language, as opposed to Quechua, which some indigenous litigants knew as a second language; Quechua is called the "language of the Inca."

12. The nondifferentiation between drawing and writing in the Andes as imaged by Guaman Poma finds linguistic corroboration in Quechua. The word *quillca*, for which we do not have a precise pre-Columbian definition, is used as a colonial neologism in various contexts to express the concept of paper, pen, writing, and drawing (see chapter 5).

13. We employ the Spanish term *india*—indigenous woman—in an effort to achieve the classificatory precision denoted by the terminology, which would not necessarily be reflected by the English word "Indian," whose meanings have been reified by British colonialism, by United States policy, and most recently, by Native American identity politics.

14. The aura of manuscript documents is still central to indigenous appreciations of the past in Colombia. Rappaport observed secretaries of late twentieth-century community councils among the Cumbales, descendants of the Pasto, copying land documents by hand because their constituents did not place credence in photocopies. Similarly, when she gave Nasa university students a handwritten (but published) history written by a Bolivian Aymara author (Mamani Quispe 1988), her interlocutors felt it was more "authentic" and more "autonomous" because it was written by hand (Rappaport 2000).

15. The Pasto language, which belonged to the Macro-Chibchan family, has not been spoken since the early nineteenth century and we know little of its grammar or lexicon. In 1594, two Mercedarian fathers were directed to produce a Pasto catechism and confessionary (López de Solís 1995 [1594], 473), but if this document was ever prepared it has not been uncovered by historians. On the use of Quechua, Muisca, and other aboriginal languages as a lingua franca by the Spaniards, see Humberto Triana y Antorveza (1987, 162–72).

16. Differences in access to notarial literacy were only exacerbated by the fact that

Chibcha, the common language of the Muiscas, was understood to be the lingua franca—the *lengua general*—through which the Christian doctrine was to be conveyed and legal interpretation was to be conducted in the area around Bogotá (AGI/S 1608). Spanish or Quechua, a southern Andean language spoken by the Inca and only recently introduced into the Quito area, served as the mediating languages for the communities near Pasto.

17. We thank Carolina Castañeda, Mercedes López, and Marta Zambrano for underscoring these differences and offering possible explanations and documentation, including the suggestion that the lack of Muisca literacy owes to the greater levels of repression by the corrupt colonial apparatus in Santafé. Castañeda, López, and Zambrano told us that there are only three instances of Muisca chiefly signatures in the extensive documentary record they have studied, in addition to the literary production of the cacique of Turmequé; two of these signatures are by the cacique of Machetá, Don Andrés, confirming his testimony in a case (AGN/B 1619b, 703r) and in his will (AGN/B 1633a, 92v).

18. We will come back to the notion of "time immemorial" in chapter 4.

19. Juan Felipe Hoyos also argues that the verity of a witness's statement could only be confirmed if he had been administered a Christian oath that included swearing on the cross. Clearly, only Christianized natives were in a position to take such an oath, but as Hoyos argues, colonial officials were sometimes reticent to administer such oaths to indigenous witnesses who did not speak Spanish, because of the difficulties of determining if they adequately comprehended the significance of this ritualized act. In many cases, such witnesses' testimony was ensured, instead, by the threat of punishment (2002, 127–30). The ambivalent passage between native vernaculars and Castilian Spanish indeed impinged to a significant degree upon the collective production of truth in writing.

20. Serge Gruzinski (1993 [1988]; 2001 [1990]) has explored the introduction of both European visual and alphabetic literacy in colonial Mexico. However, he considers the two modes in separate volumes, only focusing on the relation between them in his interpretation of hybrid documentation merging alphabetic writing with hieroglyphs.

21. The command of literacy skills eventually came to work both ways in the interaction between native peoples and Spaniards, affording indigenous communities a measure of control over European interlopers. This is demonstrated in a 1761 Inquisition record from Lima, in which a literate sacristan caught an imposter who was attempting to pass as a priest, after noticing that he could not read the mass nor distinguish between the various versions of it available to priests (Anonymous 1761).

22. A good example of this ekphrasis is a bilingual sermon of Francisco de Ávila, in which the sky is equated with an Andean weaving through its depiction as a cloth of blue background with the heavenly bodies set upon it; this was an at-

tempt to disprove the Andean belief that the sun and stars were animate beings that moved of their own volition (Ávila 1648, 102).

23. In the *Catecismo breve para los rudos y occupados*, printed in Lima in 1584 and used throughout the northern Andes, a syllabary appears on the first page (Lima, Concilio de 1584, 24r). For how syllabaries were used to teach reading and writing in relation to prayers, see Emelio Valtion (1947). Two interconnected problems arose from the introduction of Western images, especially prints: the irreverent use of sacred images and the spread of profane images that found their way into native communities and that seemed to have been given the same status and understanding as sacred images (see the 1570 *Constituciones para curacas de indios* of the Synod of Quito [Peña 1995, 471]).

24. The concept of the portrait presupposes the existence of the individual on which it is based; the subsequent reappearance of the portraits in Guaman Poma's map, just above the contested territory, condenses and summarizes the historical narrative, and is at the same time inscribed within the legal testimony.

1. IMAGINING COLONIAL CULTURE

1. In quotations and period terminologies where *indio* appears in the Spanish original, we employ *native* ("native man" / "native woman") or retain the Spanish term indio/india, to refer to indigenous people, with the intention of privileging the colonial category instead of relying on the slippery English glosses, "Indian" or "indigenous" (the latter is prominent in nineteenth-century usage but does not reflect the language of the colonial period, while the former's pejorative English undertones interfere with its colonial meaning).

2. On petitions to change ethnic identity, generally from indio to a mixed category in order to avoid tribute payments, see ANE/Q (1732, 1743, 1746). On the fluidity of the classification of children according to legitimacy or illegitimacy, see Ann Twinam (1999). On the possibility of gaining official recognition of an individual's desire to project a gender identity different from the one with which he or she was born, see Mary Elizabeth Perry (1999).

3. Caste—or in Spanish, *casta*—should not be confused with the hierarchical system of India. Nor should it be confused with race. As Laura Lewis explains, "Colonial Mexicanists who write in English tend to translate casta as 'race' and to base their analyses of the caste system (*sistema de castas*) prevalent in the colony on caste as a stratified set of sociolegal rankings. Yet while race was produced through taxonomies developed to exclude from power individuals Western science construed as essentially different due to blood, ancestry, or color, caste constituted a more ambiguous and flexible set of qualities that combined social affiliations, kinship, and inherent differences as it worked to facilitate incorporation into systems of power. Ultimately, caste was something of a capacity, elaborated through the genealogical, moral, and operational aspects of a person's place in relation to other persons." (2003, 4–5).

4. Lewis also shows that these opposed systems of power—that of law and that of witchcraft—were gendered, so that women belonging to different categories worked the system differently from men.

5. For an interpretation of the Victorian-era British colonial context in which the notion of hybridity came to be applied to human populations, see Robert Young (1995). Young's research situates the notion of hybridity in space and in time, arguing forcefully against its application to colonial Latin America. Nevertheless, there will be moments in this book when, for a loss of an alternate terminology, we will be forced to use the word *hybrid*.

6. "The terms of cultural engagement, whether antagonistic or affiliative, are produced performatively. The representation of difference must not be hastily read as the reflection of *pre-given* ethnic or cultural traits set in the fixed tablet of tradition. The social articulation of difference, from the minority perspective, is a complex, ongoing negotiation that seeks to authorize cultural hybridities that emerge from moments of historical transformation. The 'right' to signify from the periphery of authorized power and privilege does not depend on the persistence of tradition; it is resourced by the power of tradition to be re-inscribed through the conditions of contingency and contradictoriness that attend upon the lives of those who are in the 'minority'" (Bhabha 1994, 2).

7. Although indigenous nobility of the southern Andes was most properly called by the Quechua term *curaca*, not the Carib word *cacique*, in the interests of consistency we will use the northern Andean terminology throughout this book.

8. "Si saben que el dicho Don Fernando Chinchi en mas de treinta años que sirvio el dicho officio de gobernador del dicho pueblo de Copoata acudio en la forma rreferida al enterar de la mita de las tassas . . . fue persona que con su industria solicitud y diligencia por ser mui celoso del servicio de Dios se hizo y edifico en el pueblo de Pocoata una de las mas ssumptuossas y mejores yglesias que hay en todas las provincias para cuia fabrica dio de su parte mucha summa de pesos por que fue buen cristiano temorosos de dios obedientes a los mandatos de las Justicias de buen entendimiento y much capacidad y que siempre se trato con mucho lustre y adorno de su persona y como tal andaba siempre en abito de español y trujo armas ofensivas y defensives con permicion y licencia del señor de Monteclaros Virrey que fue de estos rreinos."

9. In the late colonial period, the blurred boundaries of Spanish, mestizo, mulatto, and indio were compounded by the adoption by criollos of the ideas of native peoples. In particular, criollos of the eighteenth century and early nineteenth appropriated, out of rebellion against the Crown, indigenous utopian notions revolving around the return of the Inca monarch to assert the criollos' own alterity in relation to Spain (Flores Galindo 1988).

10. In the case of the Andes, only two such series of *castas* paintings are known to exist, and at least one was produced for export. Commissioned by Viceroy Amat y Junyent in 1770 (Majluf 2000), it was sent immediately to Spain with an ac-

companying explanatory letter addressed to Julián de Arriaga, secretary of the Council of the Indies. The letter stated that the series of twenty paintings "represent different aspects proceeding from the mixture of [female] indias and [male] blacks" (AGI/S 1770, 236–38) (representan distintas figuras dimanadas de la mezcla de yndias y negros). The objective was to contribute to "the formation of a natural history room upon which our revered Prince of Austria is bent" (la formación del gabinete de historia natural en que se halla empeñado nuestro reverendisimo Principe de las Austrias).

11. "Por parecerle Vuestra Magestad gustaria ver aquellos barbaros retratados (que hasta agora an sido invensibles) y ser cossa muy extraordinaria los embio con su carta y este memorial a Vuestra Magestad. . . . Van todos retradados mui al propio como son y andan de ordinario—excepto el vestido que luego que dieron la paz y obedencia a Vuestra Magestad y dellos se tomo la possession y fueron puestos en vuestra real corona se les dio como de sus retratos lo uno y lo otro parece. Porque no son gente politica y en su tierra que es caliente no traen mas que mantas y camisetas como los demas yndios. Tienen buen entendimiento y son muy astutos y sagaces entienden la lengua española aunque hablan torpemente. An sido grandes guerreros contra yndios de otras provincias ynfieles. Temenlos mucho porque matan muchos y dellos que cautivan se sirven como esclavos con gran señorio y son terribles determinados y crueles en el castigo. Jamas an podido ser sujetados de españoles."

12. Gutiérrez de Pineda and Pineda Giraldo worked on the basis of census material which, needless to say, reflect not the biological mixing of populations but the identities that respondents assumed (or which were assumed for them by census takers). In this sense, they do not sufficiently problematize their data. Nevertheless, their identifications are highly significant in a comparative sense, suggesting that caste identification differed across the landscape of New Granada. In the viceroyalty as a whole, only 20 percent of the population was classified as indigenous, while in the territory surrounding Bogotá, as well as in the Andean cities of Popayán and Pasto, the vast majority of the population was classed as "indio" or "blanco" (1999, 89, 107, 110). The Pinedas' analysis is based upon data from the late eighteenth century. However, they also illustrate how the proportion of the population of the Bogotá area classed as indio fell across the colonial period (1999, 127–32), leading us to assume that mestizos were, indeed, even less typical in Don Diego's time. Presumably, most mestizo commoners living in rural areas were reabsorbed into the indigenous population, as occurred with *métis* in colonial Canada (White 1991, 14–215).

13. "Barchilon: Di ya, Tito, que cierto admirado de tu habilidad y lengua, y como hablas la mia como si fuera la tuya propia, aunque segun lo que has de tu vida contado, no es de maravillar, pero ¡qué dissmulado andas entre nosotros con habito de indio; quien pensara tal de ti si te vee entre otros indios!"

14. "Y es el mayor mal que a los pobres indios que llevan a alquilar les hacen la

paga en latón o alquimia, o menos el tercio del jornal que ganan usando con ellos como miserables y faltos de quien vuelva por ellos y para recoger el dicho alquiler hay otra mayor vejación y es que envían para cada pueblo muchos alguaciles indios ladinos y algunos españoles que no tienen oficios con vara de justicia, que con achaque de recogerlos los roban y cohechan y les hacen otros mil desafueros dignos de gran castigo y remedio en ello."

15. For a North American analysis of how colonial Euro-Americans constructed an identity in relation to subordinated groups, see Michael Zuckerman (1977).

16. "Al morisco y al extranjero que aprendió nuestra lengua, con tanto cuidado que apenas le diferenciamos de nosotros, también le llamamos ladino."

17. A related term, *monfí*, was used in early modern Spain to refer specifically to Moors or Moriscos who had learned Castilian (Burshatin 1999, 437–38). Sebastián de Covarrubias Orozco (1995 [1611], 761) notes that *monfí* comes from the Arabic term for *ladino*.

18. Jaime Lara (2008) suggests that Valadés may not have been biologically a mestizo. Be that as it may, his self-presentation is that of someone who is of both worlds and hence can be considered similar to the position of Muñoz Camargo, Inca Garcilaso de la Vega, and Diego de Torres.

19. "Entenderian que por ser hijo de español y crisptiano los dichos vuestro Presidente y oydores me quitan el dicho mi caçicazgo y que me uviera valido mas ser hijo de yndio ydolatra y no de crisptiano entendiendo ellos que en ser hijo de español y crisptiano como lo soy abia de ser mejor anparado por ser de tan buena sangre proçedida de españoles y crisptianos por lo qual todos los caciques deste reyno me quieren y aman."

20. Although we draw upon Carlos Espinosa's account in article form, a more extensive narrative and commentary are contained in his dissertation (1990).

21. The inclusion of Native Americans in royal pageantry seems to have extended far beyond the Americas. Michael Wintroub (1998) describes the erection of a Brazilian indigenous village along the route of Henri II of France, in the course of his 1550 royal entry into Rouen, following his anointing as king. This representation of American savagery was linked, through the royal procession, to other *tableaux vivants* depicting classical mythic episodes and meant to serve as allegories (1998, 470–71).

2. GENRE/GENDER/*GÉNERO*

1. "Pintura es el arte que enseña a imitar con lineas y colores. Esta es la definición. Para explicación de la cual se a de saber que toda la definición debe constar de género y diferencia. El género, según los lógicos, es una razón común que se dize de muchos diferentes en especie; diferencia es todo aquello por lo cual un especie se distingue de cualesquier otras del mismo género."

2. In the last two books of his treatise, Giovanni Paolo Lomazzo (1584) details the

proper genres and where they should be seen. Burckhardt (2005) is fundamental for the study of genre and its importance in the orgniztion of painting.

3. "Esta pintura está cargada en género de pinturas de devoción y allí vale y aquí no" (Sánchez Cantón 1958 [1599]). The second half of the transcription of this document is found in Sánchez Cantón (1960 [1599]).

4. See Checa (1992, 440).

5. "Lo mejor de lo que ha pasado á Indias, se nos olvidava, que son los Españoles, y los Negros, que despues acá han llevado por Esclavos, para servirse dellos, que tampoco los avia antes en aquella mi Tierra. Destas dos naciones se han hecho allá otras, mezcladas de todas maneras, y para las diferenciar, les llaman por diversos nombres, para entenderse por ellos diferenciar. . . . A los Hijos de Español, y de Española nacidos allá, dicen Criollo, ó Criolla, por decir, que son nacidos en Indias. Es Nombre, que lo inventaron los Negros, y asi lo muestra la obra. Quiere decir entre ellos, Negro nacido en Indias: inventaronlo para diferenciar los que van de acá, nacidos en Guinea, de los que nacen allá, porque se tienen por mas honrados, y mas calidad, por aver nascidos en la Patria, que nos sus Hijos, por que nascieron en la agena, y los Padres se ofenden si les llaman Criollos. Los Españoles, por la semejança, han introducido este Nombre en su Lenguage, para nombrar los nacidos allá. De manera, que al Español; y al Guineo, nascidos allá, les llaman Criollos, Y Criollas. Al Negro, que va de acá, llanamente le llaman Negro, ó Guineo. Al hijo de Negro, y de India, ó de Indio, y de Negra, dicen Mulato o Mulata. A los hijos de estos llaman Cholo, es vocablo de las Islas Barlovento, quiere decir Perro. . . . A los Hijos de Español, y de India ó de Indio y Española, nos llaman Mestiços, por decir, somos mezclados de ambas Naciones: fue impuesto por los primeros Españoles, que tuvieron hijos en Indias; y por ser nombre impuesto por nuestros Padres, y por su significación, me lo llamo Yo á boca llena, y me honrro con él. Aunque en Indias, si á uno dellos le dicen, sois un Mestiço, o es un Mestiço, lo toman por menosprecio. . . . A hijos de Español, y de Mestiça, ó de Mestiço y Española, llaman Quatrralvos por decir que tienen Quarta parte de Indio, tres de Español. A Hijos de Mestiço y de India o de Indio y de Mestiça llaman Tresaluos por decir que tiene tres partes de Indio y una de Español. Todos estos nombres, y otros, que por escusar hastio dejamos de decir, se han inventado en mi Tierra, para nombrar las Generaciones, que ha avido, despues de los Españoles fueron á ella, y podemos decir, que ellos los llevaron con las demás cossas, que no avia antes."

6. Garcilaso de la Vega's claim to the newness of difference in the Americas is critical to the concept of "racial" awareness in the Americas: that there were never before experienced categories of human beings. Thus, even though Spain of the sixteenth century and seventeenth century was a multiethnic and racially diverse nation (despite expulsions and forced conversions), and had been for centuries, something new and different was produced in the Americas.

7. Paul Julian Smith (1989, 8, 9), in his study of Spanish literature and sexuality, points to this figure as articulating his thesis "that the bundle of practices and discourses we call 'sex' has been subject to a wholly discontinuous development: that each age considers its articulation of sexuality to be natural and each is deluded." We would agree with this thesis, but we would expand it beyond sexuality and its representation to a much broader historical set of conditions, which encompass the colonial relationship between America and Europe and the notions of being as composed by race, ethnicity, and so on.

8. Brígida del Río de Peñaranda was someone well known in much of Spain. In the 1580s she made a tour throughout the peninsula during which time a number of portraits were made. Sánchez Cotán's portrait was painted in 1590 when she was at the Royal court in Madrid (Konečný 1994, 825).

9. By being a copy of a portrait, there is also a double play on the Spanish concept of portrait, as *retrato* is not only a portrait of someone but is a copy of a painting. Hence, one can have "un retrato de un retrato." That is, there is always implied in a retrato an original form, be it the sitter or the first painting to which all others are related by being copies.

10. In creating such an image, Covarrubias seems to contradict Stephen Greenblatt's assertion that "allegory, in attempting and always failing to present Reality, inevitably reveals the impossibility of this project" (1981, viii). The first emblem book in Spain was the 1549 translation into Spanish of Andrea Alciato's 1531 *Emblematum liber.*

11. We are referring to Pierce's notion of index and portrait here, but in fact this image complicates the distinctions Pierce makes (Pierce 1955).

12. "Le pertenece la nobleza moral, supuesto que tiene por motivo, y objeto la virtud y honestidad, pues por medio de la Pintura ha pretendido la Santa Madre Iglesia, se convierta la criatura a su Criador como de ha experimentado en conversiones hechas por medio de santas imágenes, y otros actos de devoción como lo refieren muchos Santos y los Concilios han mandado, se use deste Arte con este fin: y para resguardo desta parte solo refiere las palabras del santo Concilio Tridentino, de que se sacará plenaria satisfacción dize asi; De todas las sacras imágenes se saca fruto, no solo porque se amonestan al pueblo los beneficios, dones, y gracias que Cristo le ha hecho: más también porque los milagros de Dios, obrados por medio de los Santos, y exemplos saludables a los ojos de los Fieles, se representan para que por ellos den gracia a Dios, y compongan la vida y costumbres suyas, a imitación de los Santos y se exerciten en adorar a Dios y abrazar la piedad."

13. Hypostasis as used by Aristotle and the Neoplatonists, refers to the objective reality (as opposed to outer form or illusion) of a thing, its inner reality. However, as it is used in the Second Council of Nicaea, hypostasis refers to the doctrine of the two natures (divine and human) which are united in one person (existence or reality, "hypostasis") of Christ, as declared in the Council of Chalcedon of 451.

14. Also: "We define with all certainty and care that both the figure of the sacred and life-giving Cross, as also the venerable and holy images, whether made in colors or mosaic or other materials, are to be placed suitably in the holy churches of God, on sacred vessels and vestments, on walls and pictures, in houses and by roads; that is to say, the images of our Lord God and Savior Jesus Christ, of our immaculate Lady the holy Mother of God, of the honorable angels and all saints and holy men. For as often as they are seen in their pictorial representations, people who look at them are ardently lifted up to the memory and love of the originals and induced to give them respect and worshipful honor (*aspasmon kai timetiken proskynesin*) but not real adoration (*alethinen latreian*) which according to our faith is due only to the Divine Nature. So that offerings of incense and lights are to be given to these as to the figure of the sacred and life-giving Cross, to the holy Gospel-books and other sacred objects in order to do them honor, as was the pious custom of ancient times. For honor paid to an image passes on to its prototype; he who worships (*ho proskynon*) an image worships the reality of him who is painted in it."

15. In late seventeenth-century Quito, for example, one can see both types of paintings created by the same artist, Miguel de Santiago. His series of paintings "Doctrina Cristiana," which personifies the virtues (Faith, Hope Charity, etc.) for the cloister of San Francisco, express these doctrinal teachings through a complex arrangement of interacting allegorical and biblical figures, whereas his series of paintings concerning the local miraculous image of the Virgin of Guápulo are straightforward narrative renderings of the main events of the image's history and set within a specific Andean landscape.

16. Relics constitute a different category of Christian sign. According to the Council of Trent, they are "the holy bodies of holy martyrs and of others now living with Christ—which bodies were the living members of Christ and 'the temple of the Holy Ghost' (1 Corinthians 6:19) and which are by Him to be raised to eternal life and to be glorified and are to be venerated by the faithful, for through these [bodies] many benefits are bestowed by God on men, so that they who affirm that veneration and honor are not due to the relics of the saints, or that these and other sacred monuments are uselessly honored by the faithful, and that the places dedicated to the memories of the saints are in vain visited with the view of obtaining their aid, are wholly to be condemned, as the Church has already long since condemned, and also now condemns them" (Schroeder 1978 [1564], 217).

17. Copies of the Covarrubias's *Emblemas morales* were sold in the Americas. For example, the Lima bookseller Miguel Méndez received two copies to sell in the City of The Kings in 1606, *Protócolos de Francisco Dávalos*, 1606, Archivo Nacional, Lima, 315v–37v, as cited in Irving Leonard (1992, 394–95).

18. For example, José de Acosta makes the following analogy, in discussing Inca deities: "They (the Inca) also worshipped the earth, which they called Pacha-

mama, just as the ancients celebrated the goddess Tellus, and the sea, which they called Mamacocha, just as the ancients called it Thetis or Neptune." Acosta also makes comparisons between specific buildings, saying that the Coricancha (the Inca temple of the Sun) was like the Pantheon in Rome (Acosta 1940, 355, 380). Bernardino de Sahagún (1979 [1579]) begins his four volume *Historia General* with a comparison of the Aztec deities with the Roman ones.

19. Acosta is here also refuting Bartolomé de Las Casas's paralleling of Antiquity and the New World, a strategy through which Las Casas attempted to demonstrate the rationality of the Indians (Las Casas 1967 [1559]).

20. "En muchas partes de la Cristiandad, por el poco, ó ningun peligro, que ay de la Ydolatria se conservan, especialmente en Roma, la estatuas antiguas de los Ydolos, celebrando en ellas solo el primor de sus artifices, y la antiguedad de sus marmoles, porque como la fé, por gracias de dios, esta tan arraygada en las coracones de los fieles, ya no corre aquel peligro, de persumir, que ay diuinidad en piedras: y assi con ellas los palacios, y los jardines, y Galerias. Pero en las Yndias, como los Yndios originarios de aquellas paises, todavia son recien convertidos a la Fé, y esta tiene tan pocos años de possession, en los corazones de los descendientes de su Antigua gentilidad, aunque ay muy Buenos Christianos entre ellos, todavia ay muchos flacos, y porque siendo todos generalmente de naturales facilamos de mudarse, ó ya fea de malicia, ó de flaqueza suele suceder, que se buelven a los idolos, y á sus ritos, ceremonias antiguas, no se permitan guardar, ni conferbar sus idolos, ni sus huacas, ni por raçon de memoria, y demostración de la antiguedad. Assi se tiene mandado, que no solo en las yglesias, sino que en ninguna parte, ni publica, ni secreto de los pueblos de los Yndios, se pinte el Sol, La Luna, ni las estrellas; y en muchas partes, ni animales terrestres, volatiles, ni marinos, especialmente algunas especies de ellos, por quitarlos la ocasion de bolver . . . á sus antiguos delirios, y deparates."

21. "Esto hazen los Predicatores y maestros de la ley evangelica, que no tiendo la consideracion que devan, mas excediendo de la capacidad y necesidad de los oyentes se ponen a predicar a indios cosas exquisitas o en estilo levantado, como si preicassen en alguna corte o universidad, y en lugar de hazer provecho hazen gran daño porque offuscan y confunden los cortos y tiernos entendimientos de los indios."

22. As Durston points out, "the demand for an *estilo llano* or 'plain style' is associated with the restricted range of genres produced by the Third Council [of Lima], and especially with its emphasis on catechetical at the expense of liturgical discourse" (Durston 2007, 94). Different styles of preaching depending upon the social class and intellectual capacity of the congregation have a long tradition in the Catholic Church, see Lara (2008, 41–43).

23. We stress Andean painting in native churches because some of the early mural painting in native Mexican churches have a rich allegorical content, such as at

Ixmiquilpan and Malinalco. These precede the Third Council of Lima and the idea that a plain style of sermon was needed.

24. For example, in the thirtieth sermon from the Third Council of Lima's sermons, which deals with Psychostasis, the authors write in Spanish: "Y por estos aveys visto pintando a sant Miguel glorioso Archangel con un pesso que esta pessando animas que significa y quiere dezir que en la otra vida se mira el bien, y el mal que han hecho las almas, y se conforme a eso reciben sentencia" (Lima, Concilio de 1585, 196r).

25. At least one series was also taken back to Spain at the end of the seventeenth century by José Velasco and his wife and placed in the chapel that they founded in 1710 in the Rioja town of Ezcaray (Merino Urrutia 1958, 248–49).

26. Gamboa Hinestrosa (1996, 27), makes the case that the paintings were originally made for the Dominican monastery in Bogotá after it burned in 1671 and were transferred to Sopó after either the damaging earthquake of 1743, or the one in 1785. The Dominicans were given charge of the indoctrination of Sopó, so their placement of the paintings there is certainly possible. There are two other series known in Colombia, a complete one in the Church of Santa Clara in Bogotá and another consisting of only nine of the original twelve, in the Church of Santa Bárbara in Tunja. See also Mejía Gutiérrez (1994) and Ortega Ricaurte (1935) for the history of the church and the paintings.

27. "Los primeros, que padecieron grandissimos trabajos, por fundar la Fè, y procurar la conversion de almas, apartandolas de los errores, con que el demonio las tenia engañadas: principalmente con aquel tan pernicioso, como, que el alma muere con el cuerpo, que destruye todo genero de Religion, y edifica toda especie de abominacion, y pecado. De aqui passaron a quitar los idolos à los naturales, y a quemarlos en su presencia, para confirmacion de lo que les predicaban, que tales figuras no eran, ni podian ser dioses, pues se dexauan consumir, y acabar, sino estatuas de metal, oro, plata, cobre, palo, hilo, algodon, meramente instrumentos del demonio, con que los tenia engañados. . . ."

28. Le llebò tambien a una cueva, a la qual se bajaba por unos despeñaderos muy peligrosos, que tenia doze pies de largo, seis de ancho, y estaba entolada, con muchas mantas pintadas con figuras de demonios muy horrendas de diferentes hechuras, conforme el demonio se aparece a los sacerdotes, y el Padre sacò della tantos Ydolos, que pudo cargar dellos hasta veinte Yndios, y entre ellos vino de la estatura de un Yndio, y este hizo, que el Sacerdote le cargasse" (Meléndez 1681, I: 420).

29. "No solo procuraruan los Padres quitar los idolos, con peligro de sus vidas, sino qualquier otro rito, y ceremonias, como lo hizo Padre fray Pedro Martir de Cardenas, dotrinando en Suezca, que teniendo noticia de una Cueva donde los Yndios hazian sus idolatrias, y enterrauan los cuerpos de *uchos*, que morian en su gentilidad, se fue alla con un mulatto, que se llamaua Martin Cauallero. Qui-

taron la losa de la puerta de la Cueva, y entrando dentro hallaron mas de ciento y cinquebnta cuerpos sentados en rueda al uso de sus antepasados, y en medio de todos estaua el Señor, o Cazique, que se diferenciaua de los demas en el adorno, de cuentas en los braços, y cuello, y una tocado, ò turbante en la cabeza, y junto a el cantidad de telas pequeñas, que los Yndios ofrecian. Hizole sacar, y con el todos los demas cuerpos, y trayendolos en rastras a la plaza del pueblo, adonde les pegò fuego, con general sentimiento de todo el pueblo."

30. Eighteenth-century accounts of idolatry among the Nasa also point to the significance of balls of thread in their ceremonial practice (Rappaport 1980–81). Fray Juan de Santa Gertrudis (1970, chap. 5) describes the tombs of Tierradentro and the wealth that was to be found in them in the late eighteenth century in the following: "Este pueblo fue muy rico antes de la Conquista, y advierto que los indios entonces los enterraban con todo cuanto tenían. Y estos entierros o sepulcros llaman guacas; y cuando moría algún cacique, todos los del pueblo le tributaban oro, ya labrado o sin labrar, y lo echaban en la guaca; y como había indios ricos y pobres, de aquí es que hay guacas ricas donde se halla mucho oro, y guacas pobres donde no se hallan sino juguetes como son platillos, ollitas, jarras, muñequitos y varios pájaros y animales. Pero todo de un barro muy fino y las figuras con una total perfección. El día que fui en La Plata al trapiche de doña Manuela Flóres, junto al trapiche había cavado una guaca. Era una concavidad hecha de propósito en una peña, con una boca por donde la fabricaron y después se cayó. Yo la vi, y según lo grande y primoroso que está, hubo de ser guaca de algún cacique. Así llamaban a los que gobernaban los pueblos, o de algún indio de gran nombre. La guaca se descubrió por las llamas que echaba de noche. La cavaron y no hallaron sino tiestos y muñecos. Lo que digo que arden las guacas es cosa cierta, especialmente los viernes y en los cuartos de luna. Y por estas llamas se han descubierto muchísimas. En el Pedregal hay muchísimas guacas y las estaban cavando el cura por una parte, y por otra el doctor Caycedo de quien hablaré en llegando a Popayán. Este cura me contó que de unos años a esta parte habían descubierto que había en las guacas mucho oro menudo, y que hacían catear la tierra que sacaban y hallaban bastante oro. El año anterior el doctor Caycedo encontró una guaca tan rica que las alhajas que sacaron de oro, tigres, monos, sapos, culebras, etc., puesto en una batea un negro con toda su fuerza no lo pudo levantar. Y que el mismo año había encontrado otra con un indio seco y entero, rebosado con un capote de oro, que pesó más de cuatro quintales. Ello los dos en esto de cavar guacas se habían hecho muy ricos y poderosos. El pueblo tendrá unas 50 familias, y es lugar muy rígido, tierra fría todo el año."

31. "Estando el Padre Fray Diego Mancera sirviendo la doctrina del Pueblo del Quiqui jurisdiccion de la Ciudad de Tunxa, tuvo noticia, que los Indios del dicho pueblo, los demas comarcanos tenian un santuario general, donde todos, a ciertos tiempos, a haser sus ofrecimientos de oro, Esmeraldas, y otras cosas,

con todas las ceremonias de su idolatria: Este santuario estaba en una peña, en que auian hecho, y abierto una concauidad en forma de una sala muy grande, adonde se entrava por una puerta muy angosta, y esta cerrauan con una losa tan ajustada, que no se diferenciaba, por la parte de afuera, de la misma peña. Dentro de la sala tenian un pajaro de madera, todo cuerpo de pluma, de grandeza des proporcionada. A este tomaba el demonio por instrumento para hablarles, y hacerles practicas contra la Doctrina santa del Evangelio, que los Religiosos les predicaban, pronosticandoles cosas por venir, con que à vueltas de una verdad les hazia creer muchas mentiras. Pero los simples a todo le dauan tanto credito, y hacian del tanta estima, que auia mas de quatrocientos años, que en aquel lugar le adoraban, y obedecian, sacrificandole, entre los demas ofrecimientos muchos, niños inocentes, assitiendo en la sala de noche, cantidad de donzellas, que tenian dedicadas a su culto, que se mudaban a cierto tiempo Diòle al Padre Fray Diego noticia deste santuario una India vieja Buena Christiana, y de las grandes torpezas, y abominaciones, que en ofensa de Dios nuestro Señor en aquela lugar se cometian todas vezes, que se juntaban."

32. The veneration of bird images may have a time depth and geographic expanse that dates to around 500 BC and as far south as the present day Ecuadorian coast. In the ceramic corpus of figurines of the Jama-Coaque culture, there is a group of human figures placed together within a fence; the central figure is often a large parrot toward which all other figures are directed.

33. "Había juntamente en Santa Rosa un loro tan hablador que no he visto otro semejante jamás; y remedaba con tal gracia cuanto oía, que el Padre Urrea, viendo que a pocos días remedaba ya cuanto nosotros hablábamos, lo odió y decía: Este loro tiene algún demonio en el cuerpo."

34. "Dió el Señor liciencia al demonio en esta sazon liciencia para hablar, y comenzó à dar grandes vozes en el paxaaro: *Echad, echad aqui al Frayle*. Alborotòse la gente, y a grandes voces entre ellos se comenzaron a preguntar, que a donde estava del Frayle para matarle. El Religioso sintendose conocido del demonio, y la gente inquieta, y conciderando, y que si alli se dejaba matar, no se conseguia el fin, que pretendia en quitar aquellos sacrificios del demonio, determinò de salirse de la Cueva, y no fue conocido por el habito de yndio, con que deffimulaba."

35. "Sacando el paxaro, y muchos otros idolos de hilo, y de Madera en figura de hombre y mujeres, que en contorno del pajaro tenian puestos, lo truxeron todo a la plaza del pueblo y lo quemaron. Acudió a ver el incendio gran numero de yndios, por un parte admirados que una cosa tan Antigua, y tan oculta a los Españoles, hubiesse sabido, y por otra parte indignados de ver quemar lo que ellos estimauan."

36. *Guacamayo* is translated today as "macaw," which refers to the parrots of Central and South America. "Y paraque los yndios conociessen su engaño hizo el padre, que se manifestasse en la figura, que solia hablar a los Yndios, y al punto

tomò la forma de una Guacamaya, que a su parecer era la misma que habia
visto comer el pollo. Y en presencia de los Españoles que alli estaban, y toda la
gente de su casa y mucho indio, le hablò la Guacamayo, y el Padre la desterrò
al infierno, cosa que el demonio sentia mucho, y con mil ofrecimientos de oro,
y plata, perlas, y joyas, y otros bienes temporales le pedia que le senalasse otro
lugar. Pero como el padre no admitiesse estas ofertas, le mando de Nuevo ir al
infierno; Y haciendo grandes amenazas al Padre, se desapareciò en la forma del
pajaro que habia tomado."

37. "Que de el oro que sacò de los Ydolos hizo una Ymagen de bulto del Apos-
tol Santiago, y una corona para nuestra señora, y fue el artifice destas obras el
mismo Yndio que hacia Ydolos. Lo propio le sucedio al padre Fray Pedro de
Quiñones, dotrinando en Guacheta, que entregandole los Yndios por sus sermons los Ydolos de oro bajo, y se los truxeron un dia de fiesta a la Ygelsia, paraque hiziesse dellos a su gusto, el Padre fundiò el oro, que monutaria quatrocientos pesos, de a ocho quilates, que despues de purificado, y pagados quintos
a su Majestad, quedaron ciento y quarenta pesos, dèlos quales se comprò una
Imagen de Christo."

38. A cast-bronze liturgical bell with allegorical images in low relief that comes
from the same parish church of Pasca has an inscription "Me fecit Johannes a
fine Año 1553" (see Fajardo de Rueda 1990: 6–7, 54–55).

39. The totuma as a native object used to represent native drunkenness in Last
Judgment scenes has a counterpart in southern Andean Last Judgment scenes,
where it is replaced by the *quero*, or wooden drinking cup of the Inca (see
Cummins 2002a). As with the quero, the totuma was not in and of itself a demonic object. As such, we find the totuma listed along with religious images
in a number of wills of the native elite. For example, in the 1633 testament
of Francisco Tejar (AGN/B 1633e, 82v), he lists a pair of totumas immediately
after images of saints: "a large painting of Saint Francis, two paper engravings
[deleted: one] bound in wood = two *totumas* from Urabá" (vn quadro de San
Francisco grande, dos estanpas de papel [tachado: vna] guarnecidas en madera
= dos totumas de Vraba). This is also the case in the 1668 will of Pasquala de
Cotrina (AGN/B 1668b, 56r), "yndia ladina," who lists among her belongings
the following: "Item, a statue of Holy Mary Mayor and another of Our Lady of
Chiquinquirá and a Saint Christopher. Item, two linen sheets and five totumas
from Urabá, [both] new and old" (Yten vna hechura de Santa Maria la Mayor
y otra de Nuestra Señora de Chiquinquira y vn santo Cristobal de bulto. Yten
mas dos sauanas [sabanas] de lienzo y cinco totumas de Vraua nueuas y viejas).
And from another will of the same year by Don Juan, cacique de Cajicá (AGN/B
1668c, 201r), lists the following: "Item I also have three paintings, one of Our
Lady of Chiquinquirá and the other of San Onofrio and another of Christ, with
another small one of Saint Anthony and of these, I give the one of San Ono-

frio to Melchor, my son, and that of Our Lady to my son, Bartolomé, and the other two to my wife. Item I also have an axe, a crowbar. Item I also have a silver *totuma* weighing two and a half *marcos*, more or less, I order it be sold" (Yten mas tengo tres quadros el vno de Nuestra Señora de Chiquinquira y el otro de San Onofrio y otro de vn santo Christo con mas otro pequeñito de San Antonio y destos doy el de San Onofrio a Melchor mi hijo y el de Nuestra Señora a mi hijo Bartolome y los otros dos a mi muger. Yten mas tengo vna hacha vna barra. Yten mas tengo vna totuma de plata que pesa dos marcos y medio poco mas o menos mando se benda). Please see our explanation of colonial-era orthography and punctuation at the beginning of the endnotes for a clarification on the use of the equal sign (=) in colonial lists.

40. The depiction of natives within such Last Judgment scenes was common throughout the Americas. For Mexico, see Jaime Lara (2008, 54–56); for Peru, see Gisbert (2004).

41. The text has been restored to read as follows "This Judgment was painted for the devotion of the town of Suta, the cacique being don Domingo and the *capitanes* don Lázaro, don Neaetariguia, don Corula, and don And[rés] . . . year 16 . . ." (PINTOSE ESTE IVIZIO A DEVOCION DEL PUEBLO DE ŠUTA SIENDO CACIQUE DON DOMINGO Y CAPITANES DON LAZARO don Neaetariguia don Corula y don And[res] . . . año 16 . . .).

42. "Tengo por bienes mios un quadro que es ecce homo = otro de un cristo del altar de una tercia = otro de nuestra señora del rosario de una tercia, – otro de nuestra señora del rosario de una tercia de alto con el niño de bulto = otro de nuestra señora del rosario en lienso, en que estoy yo y mi muger retratados, este quiero que se ponga por mi devoción en la yglesia de mi parrochia en el altar de señora santa barbara y alli me an de enterrar donde esta mi madre Catalina."

43. For a social history of the contract see Mercedes López Rodríguez (2002).

44. "Un lienzo de ánimas de San Nicolás de Tolentino en el milagro de cuando habiendo muerto su amigo fray Peregrino se envió al purgatorio por su procurador para rogase a San Nicolás dijese aquella semana en la misa por las ánimas el cual lienzo costó de manos de Gaspar de Figueroa ochenta pesos." Segundo Libro Parroquial de Cómbita, folio 14, as cited in López Rodríguez (2002).

45. The image of Saint Gregory celebrating mass is based on two elements—one historical and the other miraculous. Saint Gregory (AD 540–604) is credited as being the compiler of the liturgy of the mass, which he is shown celebrating in this image. The miraculous element is the appearance of Christ on the Altar with the instruments of the passion as Gregory says mass. Christ appears in response to Gregory's prayer for a sign to demonstrate the doctrine of transubstantiation to one of his clerics who doubts that the mass can transform the bread and wine into the body and blood of Jesus Christ. Stoichita's (1994) analysis of the depiction of the intersection between the miraculous and the mun-

dane in Golden Age Spanish and New World painting is critical to an understanding of how these paintings were composed by artists and understood by the public.

46. Gaspar de Figueroa's son, Baltasar Vargas de Figueroa, is assumed to have copied the Cómbita composition for a painting commissioned by the Church of Santa Clara in Bogotá. In the copy, he eliminates the middle-ground figures of indigenous elites and the Augustinian San Nicolás and in doing so, removes the elements specific to the devotion of the confraternity (Restrepo Uribe 1986, 42).

47. "I wish to be buried in the church of Our Lady of the Snows, where I am a parishioner, in the sepulcre chosen by my executors and that I be accompanied by a priest and sacristan with a large cross and that a mass be sung over my body and a response over my grave. Item I wish that a mass be said by the priest of this parish to the souls of purgatory and it be paid with a peso of ordinary silver, I wish it to be charged. Item, I declare that Juan Romero, indio ladino, owes me a new mantle of six . . . that is worth and cost me four pesos of ordinary gold, I wish it to be charged" (Quiero ser enterrado en la yglesia de Nuestra Señora de las Nieves de donde soy parroquiano en la sepultura que a mis albaceas pareciere y me acompañe cura y sacristan con cruz alta y se me diga una misa cantada de cuerpo presente con responso sobre mi sepultura. Ytem mando se diga una misa rezada por el cura de esta parroquia a las animas del purgatorio y por ella se le de un peso de plata corriente mando se cobren del. Ytem declaro que Juan Romero yndio ladino me debe una manta nueva de seis . . . que vale y me costo quatro pesos de oro corriente mando se cobren del).

48. The black-and-white geometric design of the cacica's manta is not unlike the mural painting in the carved caves of Tierradentro, even though they are chronologically separated by almost a thousand years.

49. Lara (2008, 83) insists that in Mexico there is no evidence that "brute force was used or justified in the baptism of Mesoamericans . . . and that attendance at catechism classes was enforced by the Indian *fiscales* (church wardens) themselves." While this may have been the case in Mesoamerica, brutal punishment and mandatory fines were demanded by the church in the Andes: "El estilo de que han de tenido de y tienen nuestros frailes en doctrinar los indios ha sido (palabras del revrendíssimo Gonzaga) 'que los niños y niñas, en todos los pueblos y doctrinas que están a cuenta de la Religión, todos los días son obligados a assistir al sacrificio santo de la missa y a acudir a las vísperas en le iglesia. Allí, en alta voz y de memoria repiten la doctrina cristiana. Empero los domingos y días festivos son obligados a hacer lo mesmo los indios adultos, assí católicos como gentiles, con esta prefacio, se salen de la iglesia y no vuelven a entrar en ella hasta que se acaba la missa. Entonces el sacerdote llama todos por la memoria y padrón, que tiene en las manos, y les propone alguna cosa del Santo evangelio, de la doctrina cristiana y de la necessidad de los santos sacramentos, y al fin les obliga a que repitan la doctrina cristiana. Mas si alguno,

cualquiera que sea falta sin legítimo impedimento, assí él como el cacique, es azotado del religioso en las espaldas y es multado en alguna limosna para fabricar y adorno de la iglesia. Todo lo cual se hace con suma diligencia y sumo estudio de parte de los religiosos; y los yndios cada uno en los tiempos señalados acuden a la iglesia y trabajan para retener la doctrina que se les enseña."

50. The image appears on p. 599 of Guaman Poma de Ayala (1980 [1616]); see also 596, 605, 608, 657, 661, 684, 720, 796, 882, 936.

51. "Llegando a la iglesia mayor, subieron en un tablado grande ocho indios niños de la Residencia de Fontibón con muy lindas libreas, y danzaron un buen rato cantando ellos mismos a canto de órgano a tres coros, respondiéndoles la música con admiración de todos, echando toda la ciudad mil bendiciones a nuestros Padres por el cuidado que habian puesto y ponian en doctrinar y enseñar a los indios no solo la ley de dios sino música de voces e instrumentos en lo cual son ya muy diestros y se van cada dia enseñando y facilitando más."

52. Claver was aided by interpreters, among whom were Domingo Folupo, Andrés Sacabuche, José Monzola, and Ignacio Soso, who were themselves bought by the Jesuits. They are among the few Africans named in the book.

53. "En los patios, ó lugares espacioso armava el Altar, donde se pudiese gozar de todos partes. En èl hacia frente un lienço devotisimo de Christo Crucificado, q dava de todos su heridas otros tâtos golpes de sangre a una pila; de dôde la cogia un Sacerdote, para bautizar a un Negro, que de rodillas a sus pies esperava el beneficio de aquel preciofo baño. Autorizavan la accion retratos de Pontifices, Reyes, y Cardinales, afiftiendola; y adorando la misericordia de aquel Dios en Cruz que derramò sangre para todos. A un parte de el lienço se veìan Negros hermofamente afeados, reprefentacion de los que avian recebido el Bautismo; otros feroces los que lo reufavan; y entre infernales monsstros, que abrian horribles bocas para hacer prefa en ellos. Esta pintura vista de los negros, valìa por largas perfuafiones, al temor de la calamidad eterna; al defeo de huìrla, en virtud de aquella Divina Sangre mezclada al aqua de el Sacramento, a la eftimacion de este, onrada de las Dignidadas Supremas de la tierra; al amor de un Dios, en quien el amor de los ombres abrìo tantas fuentes de misericordia. Es la pintura viva, callada eloquencia; pero introducida por los ojos al alma de eficaz, y pronto imperio fobre sus afectos."

54. "Las pieças pues, ó zahurdas, en que jacen estos pobres Negros, para el V. Padre eran jardines; las llagas flores, los manantiales de postemas, fuentes de dulçura, los vapores ediondos, exalaciones de ambara, no porque lo dexáse de sentir; sino porque a fuerça de mortificacion llegó a hacer gusto del tormento."

55. "Declaro fui casado con Ynes de Costillo yndia que ya es difunta = de la qual me quedaron seis hijos y an muerto los quatro de ellos y yo tengo dos viuos que son Hilarion de Costilla y Felipa de Costilla [tachado: que oy viuen] declarolos por mis hijos legitimos. Declaro que quando nos casamos eramos ambos pobres y durante nuestro matrimonio adquirimos por bienes nuestros vn texar y dos solares y

medio en que esta edificado que contara por los titulos que tengo. Ytem tengo vna
caxa ordinaria = vn bufete = quatro silletas de nuestro vso = dos azadones buenos
y dos viejos gastados = tres palas = vna barra de hierro = vna angarilla de hazer
texa buena y otra quebrada = quatro machetillos de cortar rama vn cauallo rucio
= vn capote de pano nuebo vn uestido de xergueta de la palma = dos camisas dos
calçones, vn sombrero vn quadro de San Francisco grande dos estampas de papel
[tachado: vna] guarnecidas en madera = dos totumas de Vraba."

56. "Ytem que la suso dicha hizo por su deuocion vn lienso de nuestra señora del
Socorro a su costa que sola la pintura le costo quarrenta patacones que los pago
a Gaspar de Figueroa y la guarnicion treze patacones y de oro y dorarla otros
treze que son que son [*sic*] sesenta y seis patacones y el lienso esta puesto en
vn altar en la yglesia de señora Santa Barbara pegado al arco toral al lado de la
epistola y el doctor Bernardino del Castillo Carcamo cura de la dicha yglesia
dio el altar para que pasiesse en el la dicha ymagen sin llebarle cosa alguna por
el sino solo por fomentar su deuocion y que la ymagen estuuiesse en parte de-
cente y a tratado con el dicho cura le de sepultura junto al dicho altar y aunque
no se ha hecho precio de la limosna de ella quiere que muriendo la dicha Ana
Coro se sepulte su cuerpo alli y se conuierte la limosna de ella y se pague de sus
bienes para que quede por suya conocedamente y que se digan los responsos
sobre ella y quando se vuiere de dezir misa por su intencion y se encendieren
candelas sea alli y no en otra sepoltura que tiene en la dicha yglesia mas abaxo
de aquella que es de su marido y hijos que tiene pagado la limosna de ella y no
se le a dado titulo manda se cobre y el de la sepultura que agora elige y que la
ymagen se conserue en la dicha yglesia y altar perpetuamente porque para eso
la tiene dada y a dicho las misas de su deuocion en el dicho altar y que lo que a
gastado en el lienso a sido ganado con su mesma industria y trabajo sin que su
marido hijos ni hiernas le ayan dado cosa alguna para ello."

57. Cf. note 39.

58. For example, Meléndez tells of the cacique in Trujillo on the coast of northern
Peru, who commissioned a painting of Mary Queen of the Angels and had a
small chapel built and dedicated to her cult. The natives of the area went there
to pray for the salvation of their souls. The chapel and image became a site of
supernatural disputation, when an old woman cursed the image as representing the destruction of the old ways and the ruination of Andean people. Before
the faithful could respond to her blasphemy, "no podian sufrir, ni tolerar los
insultos, que la endiablada yndia pronunciaba," it became unnecessary because
of divine intervention, "pero no fue nessario por que dispuso Dios, antes que
ellos abriessen las bocas en defensa de su abogada, y amparo Maria, quitar de
repente á aquella infeliz la habla por medio de un demonio, que se apoderó de
ella, y la començo á tormentar, de manera, que entre gestos, visages feyissimos
con ansias, y movimientos del cuerpo, que significauan bien lo que padecia la

miserable, preludios de infierno, que la esperaba, bomitó frozada el tras las blas-femias" (Meléndez 1681, 2, 41–42).

59. "De aqui procedò, que un Yndio en el pueblo de Suezca, en tiempo, que le ad-ministrauan el Padre Fray Luys Colmenares, y el Padre Fray Luys Gaspar su compañero, sintiendose muy fatigado con visiones horribles y espantosas, con que el demonio le afligia muy de ordinario, haziendole grandes fieros, y ame-nazas porque los oya, y creya las cosas de nuestra santa Fee, acudiò a rezar el Rosario cada dia, y se librò de tan fieras fantasmas, y por assegurar su casa, pinto en ella mas de dozientos Cruzes de differentes colores, aunque este rremedio contra el demonio dixo, que se le auia dado el padre Fray Bartolome Nuñez antecessor de los dichos Padres. Usò tambien del un Yndio de Chipaça-qui, segun refirio al Padre Fray Angelo Serafino, llegandole a pedir Confession muy turbado, y decolorido, diziendole, que estando a media noche solo en su casa mazcando Ayo [coca], llego a su puerta (que por ser de canãs se via lo que estaua fuera) el demonic en figura de carnero, con unos cuernos muy largos, y despropocionados [*sic*], y el cuerpo de lana. Y de la cinta abaxo de cabra: y sen-tandose a la dicha su puerta le pedia con alagos y mucha instancia le abriesse y le dexasse entrar. Resitiòlo el Yndio con mucho temor, y el demonio le dixo: *Pues como; nos somos amigos? Como no me dexas entrar? Ya parece que me has olvidado, y no hazes caso de mi. Respondia el Yndio: Que se fuesse de alli, que ni la queria abrir, ni verle porque le decia, que era mentiroso, y engañador, y queria hazer mas lo que el padre le mandaua, que no lo que el, como demonio, le dezia.* A esto respondiò el enemigo. *Pues aunque el Padre y tu no quieras, mal de vues-tro grado no tengo de entrar:* diziendo esto se entrò, y le embistiò, y anduvieron los dos luchando un gran rato, y traya el demonio al Yndio tan apretado, que no sabiendo que hazese, porque ya le saltaua el aliento, dixo: *Iesus* y en el mismo punto desapareciò el demonio, y el hombre quedò desmayado, por muy gran rato. Boluiò en si, y temiendo que bolueria el demonio a hazerle algun gran mal, porque le auia amenaçado, acordó de hazer una Cruz de los primerros palos que hallò, y pusola a la entrada de la puerta, y estando desuelado, y te-moroso no boluiesse el demonio, acabo de muy gran rato boluiò el enimigo y le dixo: *Abreme que quiero entrar a verte, pues somos amigos.* Y el Yndio le dixo, que no queria, sino que se fuesse. El demonio repitiò. *Pues aunque te pese tengo de entrar, y me tengo de vengar de ti, pues siendo amigos me echas de tu casa.* El Yndio dixo, que no queria su amistad, sino hazer, lo que el Padre le enseñaua, y el demonio le dixo: *Agracedelo tu à estos malos palos, que has puesto al entrada (por la cruz) que sino yo entrara, y me vengara de ti:* hizole grandes amenaças, y con tantos ruydo como un trueno se desaparacio, y el Yndio se quedò toda la noche en vela junta a la cruz, y al manana contò todo lo succedido al Padre Fray Luys Colmenares, que de Nuevo le bolviò a instruir la Fè."

60. The process of learning sculpture was slightly different, as the mode of trans-

mission was more direct. The apprentice copied from works that were either brought from Europe or had been created in the New World.

61. "E quando os padres se forão delle despedir, lhes deu algumes peças devotas da sua recamara para o Monomatopa se sé convertesse. Entre as quais era hum Ecce Homo tamanho como hum quarto de papel de marca mayor de estranho feito e materia. Era de penas de passaros tão finas nas cores e por tal ordem postas que ficarão matizando muy do natural a imagem de Christo naquelle pasto. Esta imagem foi mandada em grande presente a S.A. das Indias de Cast.a Tambem um crucifixo de Marfim de mediocre grandura m.to proporcionado" (Bibliothèque Nationale de France 1561, 241r). We thank Cecile Fromont for bringing this document to our attention.

62. Mexican objects, including feather paintings, quickly made their way to South America. For example, a seventeenth-century feather painting of "The Virgin of the Immaculate Conception" from Mexico belongs to the Church of San Agustín in Bogotá (Cummins 2002a, 213–14; Fajardo de Rueda 1999, 83–84).

63. Leopold Ignaz Joseph Balthasar Felician was born in Vienna and became Leopold I, Holy Roman emperor, in 1658. His maternal grandparents were Philip III of Spain and Margarita of Austria, and his brother-in-law was Philip IV, who married Mariana of Austria in 1646. In 1666, the year the portrait was made, he married his cousin Margaret Theresa, daughter of Philip IV. Although no mention is made of the event, the feather portrait must be understood as being made in that royal context.

64. "Para la Cesárea Majestad del Emperador mi carta, la cual remito Vuestra Paternidad Reverenda abierta, para que la lea primero antes de enviársela con mayor maravilla con el pasmo mayor que esta tierra jamás fabricó humano primor, con su retrato de pluma que varias veces he escrito a Vuestra Paternidad Reverenda del; cosa de asombro y de admiración y espanto que no hay lengua para decir ni cantar ni exagerar, la perfección y hermosura con que aquellos bárbaros hicieron una obra tan bella y tan peregrina, gracias a la infinita sabiduría de Dios que quiso darles tal gracia cual que no la pueda haber en todas las naciones del mundo, para obrar una maravilla tan admirable que no pienso ha sido otra cosa sino que la Majestad de dios ha cooperado a ello. . . . Es tan grande la belleza y hermosura con que quedó esta pintura acabada, que todos allá en Mechoacan confiesan que no se ha hecho jamás allí cosa tan admirable y tan primorosa . . . y [en la casa de Pedroza y Zúñiga] cura de la ciudad de Pázcuaro en cuya presencia se hizo, trayendo a ella, diez maestros pintores que más de tres meses continuos trabajaban en ella."

65. Latin original: "Pretiosum illud donum plumeun quad omnes hic roma amirantur" (letter from Athanasius Kirchner to Alejander Favián, Rome, 1665, cited in Osorio Romero 1993, 85).

66. The first mention of armorial tapestries concerns those commissioned by Viceroy Toledo and Rodríguez de Figueroa (Cummins 1991).

67. Mopa mopa is a resin excreted from the leaf of the *Elavagia pastoensis Mora* tree, found in the warmer lands of the east. For a good description of mopa mopa production on *queros* (Andean wooden ritual vessels and other objects), see Howe et al. (1999) and Codding (2006, 106–7).

68. "Un valle . . . a quien los naturales llamaron Mocoa, y es el mismo de donde salieron después las primeras pinturas nombradas de Mocoa, que vienen de Indias en tabaqueros, cofrecillos, y diferentes vasos de madera, bien estimadas en estas partes de Europa por el primor con que se labran ya en la villa de Pasto, donde se ha pasado el comercio de género tan apetecido de los hombres de buen gusto." This passage has been misinterpreted by Nina de Friedemann (1990, 44) and Mitchell Codding (2006, 106) to mean that the reference to the objects is from the sixteenth century. If read correctly, it is clear that it is Fernández de Piedrahita who is speaking here, and he is referring to objects of the seventeenth century. To be fair, Codding cites Friedemann as his source for this reading.

69. "Vi también en casa del cura un aparador que tenía como vajilla de plata, y entre ella tenía también mucha loza que me pareció china muy primorosa. Y admirando que en tal paraje estuviesen alhajas tan preciosas, díjeles: Padre cura, más valdrá aquella loza de china en este paraje, que aquella de plata; porque a más de ser por sí muy preciosa, la conducción de una cosa tan frágil ha de ser muy costosa. El se echó a reír, y después me dijo: No es el primero que se ha engañado Vuestra Paternidad. Aquella no es loza de china, es de madera y está embarnizada con un barniz que le da este lustre. De allí adonde van ahora Vuestras Paternidades lo sacan los indios, que es la pepita de una fruta que hay en estos montes, y los indios de Pasto lo componen y con ello embarnizan la loza de madera con tal primor, que imitan al vivo la loza de china. Abrió el aparador, y hasta que lo tuve en las manos estuve creyendo que era china. Mas al tomarlo, con el poco peso, conocí que era madera embarnizada, porque hasta cocos, pilches y cucharas tenía del mismo modo. Y este embarnizado, por más que lo usen y refrieguen para limpiarlo, jamás se envejece ni pierde el lustre. Los encharolados que hacen en España algo le parece; mas aquello es más lustroso. En adelante diré el puesto en donde hay dicho barniz, y en llegando a Pasto diré el modo como lo van los indios beneficiando."

70. "Llegamos por fin a la quebrada, y junto a ella vi unos árboles que los llaman galanes, y es cierto que quien le puso el nombre acertó. Es árbol el galán muy alto, grueso y coposo. Su hoja es parecida a la que en España llaman toronjil, sólo que tiene algo de más cuerpo, y de la raíz de cada hoja le sale una cinta carmesí de 3 cuartas de largo a modo de un listoncito. Como estaban todos cuajados y llenos de tantas cintas con lo verde de la hoja es cosa que admira y provoca al mismo tiempo con su belleza y hermosura a alabar al Creador. A mano izquierda de Junguilla hay una partida de cerros, y por entre ellos pasa un río que llaman Condagua. En esta serranía es que se cría la fruta de que embarni-

zan en Pasto la loza de madera, como advertí en el Cáp. VI, y de que hablaré cuando llegue a Pasto" (Santa Gertrudis 1956 [ca. 1775], I, 164).

71. "En este tiempo que me detuve en Pasto vinieron un día de Sibundoy unos indios y yo los encontré en la plaza. Ellos me conocieron y me vinieron a hablar. Yo les pregunté a qué habían venido y ellos me respondieron que habían traído espingo y barniz de Condagua. Yo les dije que quería ver el barniz, y ellos dijeron que ya lo habían vendido. Con esto fui con ellos a la casa de los indios que con ello labran aquella losa de madera que noto en el Tomo Primero, capitulo VI, y en donde prometí explicar este punto en llegando a la ciudad de Pasto. Es pues este barniz la almendra de una fruta que dan unos árboles que hay en toda aquella serranía del río llamado Condagua. Es esta pepita un poco más gruesa que una almendra. Su color natural es entre amarillo y verde muy amortiguado. Estas pepitas son vizcosas, y para beneficiarlas las mascan como quien se pusiera a mascar cera blanda. De estas mascadas las juntan y hacen unas pelotas medianas. Estas las tiñen del color que quieren.

"Mandan pues estos hombres labrar a los carpinteros varias piezas de cedro, platos, platones, fuentes, vasos, cucharas, pozuelos, cocos, vasos comunes, etc. La pieza la dibujan a cincel, y lo que quieren que salga dorado o plateado se lo ponen. Ya aparejada la pieza toman una pelotita de este barniz, aplastándola, la cantean a cuatro cantos, y al calor del fuego tiran de los cantos entre dos, y se va el barniz dejándose estirar y adelgazar, hasta hacerse del canto más delgado que un papel. Calientan entonces la pieza y la abrigan con este barniz, y al instante queda pegado. Sácanle de pronto el dibujo que tiene, y después se lo ponen de barniz del color que quieren, y asimismo descubren lo plateado o dorado. Pero con la advertencia que la pieza que labran no se llegue a enfriar, porque al enfriarse, el barniz que una vez se pegó ya no hay remedio de quitarlo, y por esto tienen allí siempre la candela los que labran, y de rato en rato calientan la pieza, y queda tan lustrosa como la loza de China, y China parece al que no lo sabe. Yo mandé labrar para mi uso varias piezas, y cuando volví a entrar a la misión me las llevé, y aun cuando me subí para Lima, para venirme para España, traía algunas, pero en el camino unas repartí y otras me las hurtaron, y sólo me ha quedado mi cajeta que también mandé embarnizar."

72. See Friedemann (1990, 41) for a description and illustration.

73. William Christian (1981a, 1981b) discusses the need to bring miraculous images and the accounts of apparitions under the orthodox power of the church hierarchy and away from the local control of the peasantry of small towns. Similar stories abound throughout the Americas. Santa Gertrudis (1956, [ca. 1775], II, 165–66) recounts how the Indians who went to Condagua to collect the mopa mopa were moved by a Dominican priest to a new town located in a healthier place. The old town had a church in which there was a sculpture of Christ, which they took with them and placed in the new church. For three nights in a row the sculpture appeared back in the old church. The natives, thinking that

someone was carrying it back, waited on the road armed with clubs so as to punish the people doing it. All of a sudden they saw the sculpture walking on the road, and thereupon one of the natives gave the sculpture a tremendous blow on the leg with his club. The sculpture returned to the new church obeying the Indians. Upon hearing this story, the priest told his superior, who had the sculpture removed to Quito, where it was held in high veneration and because it was dark was called "El Zambo." All the narrative elements are close to those discussed by Christian except for the name of the dark sculpture, which in America takes on the name "Zambo."

3. THE INDIGENOUS LETTERED CITY

1. For example, Quechua served as a lingua franca in communications between ethnic lords and Spanish courts in the southern portion of the Pasto area, that is, Tuza (today San Gabriel), Guaca, and Tulcán, now part of the northernmost Ecuadorian province of Carchi. The scant ten years of Inca control of this region did not produce such bilingualism; it was, instead, the result of Spanish language policy, which sought to bring the numerous ethnic groups of what is today Ecuador under a common lingua franca.

2. On the colonial creation of literary Quechua, called the General Language of the Inca (la lengua general del inca), see Bruce Mannheim (1991), Frank Salomon (1991), and Alan Durston (2006); for works in literary Quechua, see Frank Salomon and George Urioste (1991). On the development of Classical Nahuatl, see Shirley Heath (1972) and Jorge Klor de Alva (1989); for literature in Classical Nahuatl, see Louise Burkhart (1996). Among the many scholars working on Mesoamerican vernacular literacy in the colonial era, the best known include Serge Gruzinski (1993 [1988]), Frances Karttunen and James Lockhart (1976), and Lockhart (1992) for Nahuatl-language writing in central Mexico; Kevin Terraciano (2001) for Mixtec notarial writing; and William Hanks (2000) and Matthew Restall (1997) for Yucatec Maya administrative literacy. The Maya area is known for its books of prophecy, collectively known as the Chilam Balam and written in alphabetic form in the colonial period (Roys 1967 [1933]). Arthur Miller (1991) and David Tavárez (1999) have studied the ritual applications of Zapotec alphabetic writing. Numerous collections and analyses of Mesoamerican wills provide an extensive corpus of everyday materials penned by native notaries in the colonial era (Cline and León-Portilla 1984; Hill 1989; Kellogg and Restall 1998; Restall 1995). Also significant are central Mexican indigenous maps, in which Nahuatl and Spanish alphabetic literacy, Nahuatl hieroglyphic writing, and European and American graphic conventions for representing space and time are juxtaposed (Gruzinski 1987; Leibsohn 1994, 2000).

3. There is precious little in the way of legal documents written by or for indigenous commoners, forcing us to turn the bulk of our attentions to the native nobility's participation in alphabetic literacy. Nevertheless, we will consider

a corpus of testaments from colonial Bogotá that includes commoners' wills. This corpus has recently been expanded by the publication of transcriptions of ninety-one indigenous testaments from Santafé de Bogotá (Rodríguez Jiménez 2002).

4. The fact that the Spaniards permitted vernacular legal literacy in Mexico is not all that singular when we remember that early modern European countries were multilingual, with developed literacies in a panoply of languages. In the Iberian Peninsula, for example, Catalonian and Galician writing coexisted with Castilian literacy.

5. Students of these complex historical texts include Roberto González Echevarría (1990) for Garcilaso, Rolena Adorno (1986) for Guaman Poma, and Regina Harrison (1989) for Pachacuti Yamqui. Colonial-era Quechua-language theater, unlike the Mesoamerican vernacular genres, was not authored by native people, but by Spaniards (Burga 1988, 319).

6. Denise Arnold (2006) persuasively argues, however, that visual genres emerging out of textile production—including, but not confined to khipus—have always mediated between Spanish literacy and Andean orality.

7. We have no evidence of the use of khipus in the Sabana de Bogotá and, in fact, the chronicler Pedro de Simón (1981 [1627], 363) expressly states that they were not used by the Muisca. Sixteenth-century *visitas* (tributary censuses) of Muisca towns report that the counting of tributaries by indigenous authorities was accomplished through the use of kernels of maize (AGN/B 1561–65, 476v). The maize-kernel record was incorporated into alphabetic documents to stand in for quantities of people and objects not present at the moment they were recorded by colonial notaries (Hoyos García 2002, 61–63), fulfilling a function similar to that of southern Andean khipus. The colonial Nasa, in contrast, did use some kind of textile record, according to a eighteenth-century bilingual dictionary: "*Quint*, sarta, v.g., *vite quint*, una sarta o hilo con cuentas, o sin ellas" (Castillo y Orozco 1877 [1755], 76); in English, "*Quint*, string, v.g. *vite quint*, a string or thread with accounts, or without them." Note here that the Spanish term *cuenta* might also be translated as "bead"; the same bilingual dictionary (ibid., 83–84) expressly defines *vite* as "otro" (other), *vitepazac* as "un ciento" (one hundred), and *vitech* as "uno, principio para contar" (one, the beginning of a count), suggesting that we might be speaking here of records inscribed either into a knot record or perhaps into the beadwork which was both a ubiquitous trade item and tributary currency in the colonial period (AGI/S 1558–59, 1570–71; López Medel 1989 [1558–59]). Ethnographic observation among the Nasa and their Guambiano neighbors indicates, however, that very simple khipus were in use fifty years ago; however, we do not know if they were in common use at the time of the Spanish invasion or if, perhaps, they were introduced by the Spaniards during the colonial period, as were so many other Incaic cultural forms.

8. M. T. Clanchy (1989) describes a similar state of affairs in medieval England, where objects and rituals were never wholly supplanted by the written word, but, instead, bestowed legitimacy upon written documents. See also Adam Fox (2000).

9. Town criers operated in a similar manner among the Pastos, as much in cases of land sales as in the settlement of disputes over hereditary chiefdoms (ANE/Q 1650, 1686, 1691b). Hevia Bolaños (1761), who authored a manual of legal practice, specifies in great detail when and how such announcements were to be made, depending upon the nature of the transaction in question. Note that the Quillacingas inhabited the territory surrounding the city of Pasto, while the Pastos lived to the south of the Quillacingas, around the city of Ipiales.

10. "Por virtud del qual dicho mandamiento, fulano Alguazil metio en la possession al dicho fulano, o el juez por su persona tomádole por la mano le metio en la heredad, o casa, y se passeo por ella, y cerro las puertas (si fuere casa) y echò fuera della a los que dentro estauan, è tomó las llaues de la dicha casa, è metio de su mano por inquilino a fulano, lo qual todo hizo en señal de possession." Lorenço de Niebla (1565, 85) urges a similar practice in his guide for scribes. We thank Kathryn Burns for bringing these two manuals to our attention.

11. "En nuebe dias del mes de otubre de mil y seiscientos y quarenta y siete abiendo bisto el auto de el General Don Antonio de Santillana y Oyos a pedimiento de Don Marcos Taques governador de los yndios de el pueblo de Tulcan yo Esteban Berdugo rrecidente de el dicho pueblo di posecion al dicho Don Marcos Taques en virtud de el auto a mi cometido tome por la mano a Don Marcos Taques le di posesion en las tierras llamadas Chunes y la loma de Chucanbut hasta la puente que baja al rrio yendo por el camino rreal hasta el pueblo a mano isquierda hasta la loma de Tugteta y la loma de Tainguaput que dibide la juridicion de Guaca y arrancando algunas matillas y yerbas tomo poscecion el dicho Don Marcos Taques de las dichas tierras sin contradicion alguna y yo ce la di judicialmente en nombre de Su Magestad en presencia del Rreberendo Padre Fr. Josef de Rribera siendo cura y vicario de el dicho pueblo y en presencia de el Sargento Bernardo Carballo y de Alonso Baes y Don Melchor G. Tulcanaza alcalde ordinario de el dicho pueblo y por verdad lo firme de mi nombre."

12. Such practices are mirrored in ancient Roman and rabbinical law, in which possession of real estate was marked by painting something onto the property (personal communication, Kalman Bland).

13. Some of these zanjas had toponyms assigned to them (ANE/Q n.d.b, 5v).

14. Note that other types of property were also susceptible to such ritual treatment, as is the case in a late seventeenth-century possession ceremony for a water source near the town of Mira, granted to the Jesuits. Here, water was poured over the hands of the procurator of the convent, who was then asked to drink and to scatter drops across the land (ANE/Q 1696, 4v).

15. "Y en esta conformidad el dicho jues y bista la utilidad que a el dicho casique

se le sigue de dejarle en posecion de dichas casas y corales mando se sesen en el deribarlas y traiiendo de las manos a el dicho Don Sebastian Guaman y le entro en las dichas tres casas y dixo que le daua y dio posecion dellas por aberse edificado en tieras suyas para que lo posea."

16. For example, see the notarial entries of Blas Rubio de Pereira in the Pasto area, from 15 July to 8 August 1691 (AHBC/I 1691–92).

17. As we will argue in the next chapter, legal documentation was also constructed for use by future generations. That is, legal genres point toward future legal challenges.

18. Not all of these testaments are included in the sample that will be analyzed in the discussion of the contents of wills, for lack of copies clear enough for transcription.

19. Among the notarial records, there were also 3 entries for sales of property other than land, 7 for complaints of abuses, and 28 miscellaneous entries.

20. The names of the two scribes are quite similar, suggesting that there may have been families of lesser nobility that assumed such office among the Pastos. A 1769 land sale in Tuza was signed by Don Sebastian Guamialamag (ANE/Q 1792b, cuaderno 11, no pagination), hinting at the inheritance of notarial positions.

21. The appointment of men who were not letrados to fill judicial functions and the informal naming of notaries was the rule in some frontier areas, as Charles Cutter (1995) documents in his study of Texas and New Mexico. However, in that region such posts were held by creoles, not by indigenous people.

22. For the northern Andes, dictionaries include Anonymous (1987 [1607–20]) and Eugenio Castillo y Orozco (1877 [1755]); for Peru, see Fray Domingo de Santo Tomás (1951 [1560]). An important sixteenth-century catechism and collection of sermons used throughout the Andes is that of the Third Council of Lima (Lima 1990 [1585]), although earlier catechisms, such as that of Archbishop Luis Zapata de Cárdenas of Bogotá (1988 [1576]), provide a window into more localized evangelization projects in the northern Andes.

23. For example, the contents and organization of indigenous testaments were described and classified in Juan Pérez de Bocanegra's *Ritual formulario* (1631) and Alonso de la Peña Montenegro's *Itinerario para parochos de indios* (1995 [1668]). Not only native peoples, but Spaniards and criollos as well, employed manuals when writing wills (Lara Valdés and Vidaurri Aréchiga 1998 [1810]).

24. "Entre las virtudes que los ladinos estudian es, una, cómo sabrán poner pleito y hacer una petición para mover una acusación: para el cual fin un indio ladino de un pueblo llamado Andamarca en una provincia de las Carangas compró un Monterroso y en otro pueblo llamado Coquemarca otro ladino compró Las Partidas del Rey don Alonso, que le costaron 40 pesos. Para conocer su indignado [sic. = indigno, ¿malintencionado?] intento no es menester mirar más que al indio—que quiere ser letrado para poner pleitos, sin haber estudiado que pren-

tende. Y que, si lo examinasen, no sabría la ley de Dios; y si sabe la doctrina, no la sabe entender ni declarar. Y si le preguntan quién es su padre y a su padre le examinan, se hallará que no sabe palabra de la dotrina cristiana ni cree si hay Dios; y trata de criar un hijo ladino que no sepa leer y escribir y trastonará [a] Monterroso y las leyes de Las Partidas para solo hacer mal."

25. This book appears in the inventories of a number of Lima booksellers of the sixteenth century and the seventeenth. For example, in 1583 the Lima book dealer Juan Ximénez del Río contracted with Francisco de la Hoz to bring twelve volumes of *Práctica civil y criminal y instrucción de escribanos* from Seville for sale in the viceroyalty (Monterroso y Alvarado 1603 [1563]). They also contracted to acquire two copies of the *Siete partidas, glosadas por Gregorio López de Tovar* in 1566–1583 (Archivo Nacional del Perú, Lima, Protocolos de Alonso Hernández, 1419r–22v, cited in Leonard 1992, 218–25, 350–58). These may very well have been the copies purchased by the two native lords mentioned by Bartolomé Álvarez. Again in 1606, the Lima book merchant Miguel Méndez acknowledged receipt of another copy of Monterroso y Alvarado, valued at twenty-four reales each. This was the same price as the first volume of *Don Quixote* (Protocolos de Francisco Dávalos, 1606, Archivo Nacional del Perú, Lima, 315v 37v, cited in Leonard 1992, 394–95).

26. "En la villa de San Miguel de Ybarra a dies y seis dias del mes de diziembre de mill seis sienttos y noventta y dos años ante mi el escriuano de cauilldo publico y testigos Doña Magdalena Guachan casica del pueblo de Guaca residente en esta uilla que doy fee conosco = ottorga que por si y en nombre de sus herederos y subsesores vende y da en ventta rreal por juro de heredadado donde aora para siempre xamas a Sebastian Galindes que esta presentte para el y sus herederos y subsesores vn pedasso de ttierra que tiene y posee en therminos del pueblo de Punttal en el sittio nombrado Mumiar de ocho quadras de tierra algo mas o meno que huuo y heredo de Doña Juana Guachan su madre difuntta que linda por la partte de arriba y la de abajo con ttierras de Don Francisco Paspuel casique del pueblo de Tussa a un lado con ttierras de Doña Maria Guachan y al otro con las de Doña Francisca Guachan primas hermanas de la otorgantte, con todas sus entradas y salidas vssos costumbres derechos y seruidumbres y segun y en la forma que las a poseydo y que las poseyo la dha su madre y demas sus anttecesores por libres de censso enpeño e ypotteca en precio y quanttia de settentta y dos patacones que el dho comprador exsiuio en tabla en rreales de a dos y sensillos que despues de conttados se los lleuo y passo a su poder la otorgantte en mi presencia y de los testigos de que yo el presentte escriuano doy fee."

27. "El testamento es un acto religiosísimo y de muy católicos ánimos porque mira el que lo hace a destituirse de las cosas terrenas, encaminando el objeto a su salvación, y como es parte (y no pequeña) la de quietar la conciencia cumpliendo sus obligaciones, pagar sus deudas y restituir lo ajeno, mandas forzosas y demás cosas que en los testamentos se incurre es menester solicitar medio tan impor-

tante con todo cuidado, puesto que es una memoria o recuerdo medicinal de la salud eterna y se presume así en el derecho."

28. Don Alonso de Torres, the cacique of Turmequé who traveled on two occasions to Spain to press for a solution to the abuses against native people in the New Kingdom of Granada, served as executor to the will of Alonso de Atagualpa, the last Inca emperor Atahualpa's grandson, whom he met in Madrid (Rojas 1965, 484). As we will detail below, native Andeans living in urban areas were more likely to write wills, regardless of their social status, than were rural indigenous commoners.

29. Sometimes these analyses exoticize what was fairly standard Christian procedure. For example, in her analysis of the 1598 testament of Panzaleo cacique, Don Diego Collín, the historian Chantal Caillavet (1983, 10) reads the provision for reserving six sheep to be offered on the day of burial and a year after the testator's death as a continuation of pre-Columbian structures of belief, although it is more probable that such "offerings" were meant to pay for masses and other Catholic rituals.

30. The encomendero received a tribute grant (encomienda) from the Crown and the right to indigenous labor in recognition of his military or administrative contributions to the colonization effort. In return he was obliged to support the doctrinal priest in the community assigned him, among other responsibilities. Encomiendas were inherited for a stipulated number of generations, depending upon the grant.

31. We have worked with thirty-nine Pasto wills, all but three by caciques or other members of the Pasto nobility (AHBC/I 1592, 1606, 1654 [contains two wills], 1674, 1713, 1739, 1748; AHBC/Q n.d., 1588, 1709, 1710, 1720; ANE/Q n.d.a, n.d.b, n.d.c, n.d.e, n.d.f, 1585, 1589, 1624, 1634b, 1653, 1661, 1681a, 1681b, 1689, 1691a, 1697, 1700, 1709, 1711, 1720b, 1729, 1730a, 1730b, 1733–, 1759). Note that when wills are embedded within other documents, they are identified separately in the bibliography. The Pasto testaments turn up as evidence in later lawsuits, sometimes as originals and sometimes as copies, many of them never registered with notaries.

32. Those wills registered in the notarial record of Ibarra were validated by an official notary months or years after their inscription; in one case, this occurred more than forty years after the will was prepared (AHBC/Q 1748, 4v). In most cases, we have no idea who wrote the documents, although in at least one will (ANE/Q 1691a), a cacique did the writing for his aunt.

33. "Comunmente entre Indios pobres, que hazen testamento de la miseria que tienen, se está à las memorias que dexan hechas por mano de qualquiera que sabe escribir, y como es tan poco lo que tienen; raras vezes, ò nunca hay ocasion de pleytos, ni discordias, ni de que parezcan en juizio; pero en algunas partes ay Indios ricos, y entre ellos viven Españoles, que tienen caudal, y en los pueblos apartados no siempre es posible hazer el testamento con las solemni-

dades del Derecho, por falta de Escrivano, y para estos casos se pone la duda presente, y antes de la resolucion supongo, que aunque el testamento sea nulo para el fuero exterior, es muy probable, que en el fuero interior es valido." When Peña Montenegro refers to "external" and "internal" law, he is delimiting the jurisdictions of the two republics, and is not referring to indigenous customary law.

34. Twenty-five of the wills were consulted in manuscript form and sixty-three were published in Rodríguez Jiménez 2002; the following wills, which were consulted in manuscript form, are also transcribed in Rodríguez Jiménez 2002: ABN/B 1567, 1617a, 1617b, 1619a, 1630b, 1630c, 1633a, 1633c, 1633d, 1633e, 1633f, 1633g, 1655, 1665a, 1668b, 1668c. The Muisca wills we consulted were written for the most part by urban commoners, with only eleven by caciques or other members of the nobility (AGN/B 1567, 1609–10, 1617b, 1617c, 1619a, 1629a, 1629b, 1629c, 1630a, 1630b, 1630c, 1633a, 1633b, 1633c, 1633d, 1633e, 1633f, 1633g, 1655a, 1665a, 1665b, 1668a, 1668b, 1668c, 1758–59; Rodríguez Jiménez 2002, 48–51, 79–81. 194–96, 208–10, 294–98).

35. Jacques Poloni (1992), working with notarial documents from Cuenca recording transactions in which native Andeans were involved, found that an unusually high number of purchases and sales of land were by women. He surmised that a sexual division of labor was operating, in which indigenous women resided in the city and worked as traders, while native men farmed in rural districts. José Ramón Jouvé-Martín (2005) discovered, similarly, that the majority of notarial documents produced for African and mulatto residents of Lima in the seventeenth century recorded documents requested by women. Jouvé reasons that black women were more active than men in notarial transactions because as house slaves they were more likely to acquire their freedom and thus have the opportunity to engage notaries. What is consistent across Bogotá, Cuenca, and Lima is the urban nature of their notarial arenas, suggesting that women — particularly unattached women — had more freedom of movement in the urban legal context than in rural areas.

36. Of course, some of the most striking differences between the corpus of testaments from Bogotá and Pasto may have a great deal to do with the fact that the former were collected from notarial archives and the latter from court records, where they had been inserted as evidence. The early colonial notarial archives from Pasto were not available during any of the field trips made there. A longer list drawn up by Mercedes López of 112 indigenous wills registered by Santafé notaries between 1567 and 1751 shows that only 10 were by caciques or other indigenous officials and 2 by mestizos (one of these, AGN/B 1617a, was the son of a Spaniard and an indigenous woman from Quito, a man who served as interpreter for the Audiencia).

37. The 1556 Synod of Bogotá found the large number of testators who neglected to leave bequests to the church extremely perturbing, as it cut into their revenue.

Thus, they ordered priests and notaries to remind testators of their spiritual obligations (Romero 1960, 546–47).

38. At least one Muisca testator had a pressing spiritual reason to prepare a will—and perhaps was pressured by the colonial administration—as he was about to be executed by the Crown (AGN/B 1617c).

39. "Alli suelo acudir a misa cuando voy a mis chacaras."

40. "Porque dios los traiga a verdadero conocimiento."

41. "Consejo de ejemplo las cosas de dios recibiendo los tributos y acudiendo con tributo a la casa del cacique."

42. Notwithstanding the paucity of pious bequests among the Pasto nobility, indigenous testators in other areas appear to have been prone to cede too much of their property to the church. Given that so many native testators prepared their wills at home in the company of the parish priest who thus had the opportunity to influence the nature of the pious bequests, the church fathers were concerned that rightful heirs not be cheated out of their inheritances by greedy prelates. They advised that only a portion of indigenous estates be dedicated to masses and other pious bequests. This concern is evident in manuals written for priests (Peña Montenegro 1995 [1668], 346, 350–51; Pérez de Bocanegra 1631, 278). In 1681, the *visitador* Don Diego Inclán Valdés (1910 [1681], 15) went so far as to order that priests not participate in the composition of indigenous wills, in order to ensure that estates were left to heirs and not to pay for masses. The church also ruled that in cases of people dying intestate, only a fifth of their estates were to be spent on masses (Romero 1960, 547; Zapata de Cárdenas 1988 [1576], 133). This was particularly important, given that by the end of the sixteenth century so many masses were being ordered by testators in the Spanish world that priests could not possibly fulfill all of their requests (Eire 1995, 216). The Synod of Bogotá attempted at midcentury to audit parish records to this end (Romero 1960, 547).

43. The paucity in Muisca wills of indigenous luxury items conferring status upon their owners can be chalked up to the fact that the overwhelming majority of the testaments consulted from Santafé were of poor urban migrants.

44. The Pasto area on the Colombia-Ecuador border was only controlled by the Incas for some ten years before the Spanish invasion. Nevertheless, Pasto caciques listed Inca objects in their wills in their bids to legitimacy under the Spanish system.

45. In particular, the will of Doña Pascuala Tainbupas of Tuza includes numerous textiles, both indigenous and European, identified by their use, as well as by textile type, color, and design (ANE/Q 1730a).

46. This is evident in almost all of the female wills published by Rodríguez Jiménez (2002), which constitute the vast majority of the testaments he found in the notarial archives in Bogotá.

47. "Y si tuvieren crucifixos, ymagenes de nuestra Señora o de los sanctos, les den a

entender que aquellas ymagenes es una manera de escriptura que rrepresenta y da a entender a quien representa."

48. "Recaudos que tengo de mis antepasados."

49. "Recaudos de amparo del señor Alcalde Ordinario de la ciudad de San Francisco de Quito el dicho alcalde ordinario que se llamaba Torivio de Cortiguera y otra escriptura de Don Christoval Tusa . . . a Don Francisco Tuspas principal del dicho pueblo de Tusa por otras quatro quadras de tierras."

50. On the resguardo in colonial Colombia, see Margarita González (1979); on the resguardo among the Nasa, and for an extended analysis of this document, see Joanne Rappaport (1998).

51. "Hijo de las estrellas de la dicha Quebrada de Tama."

52. Both the titles to Pitayó and Vitoncó also include documentation of nineteenth-century legal moves to register their contents, thus expanding their sedimentary character, but here we are referring exclusively to the colonial portions of the documents. Note that Don Juan Tama's assertion of such far-ranging boundaries in the title to Vitoncó cuts into his territorial claims for Pitayó, as well as into the pretensions of other ethnic communities nearer to Popayán.

53. Rappaport arrived at this conclusion during a collective reading of the title, which she directed in 1998 with Nasa university students in a community pedagogy program directed by the Regional Indigenous Council of Cauca, a Colombian indigenous organization. The students emphasized the secrecy of the document and the fact that its impenetrable cosmological referents hindered intellectual access to it by outsiders. The document, which is kept in the departmental archives in Popayán, is itself a copy that was in the hands of the nineteenth-century caciques who presented it to the Colombian administration.

54. For example, in Tama's account of his triumph against Calambás, there are passages that look like they could have written by a nonnative speaker of Spanish (although they might also be colonial Spanish). Abelardo Ramos, a Nasa linguist, assisted me in identifying these phrases, which are italicized in what follows: "Y dice que les estubieron aciendo guerra y perjuicios *á los otros yndios de Don Juan Tama* que se pucieron en guerra y los dichos yndios de Don Juan Tama se paso a defenderse con sus yndios y les gano la cavesa al dicho Calambas y que se quedaron sin el dicho Calambas dice Don Juan Tama que por acudir á conquistar *se alsaron contra á Don Juan Tama el dicho cacique Calambas y sus yndios de Don Juan Tama se defendio y les gano la guerra con sus yndios de Calambas se quedaron sin cacique* y los a desterrado Don Juan Tama" (ACC/P 1883 [1708], 2183v–84r). (And he says that they made war on him and caused harm to Don Juan Tama's other indios who rose up in war. And Don Juan Tama's indios defended themselves and he won the head of Calambás. And they were without Calambás. Don Juan Tama says that hoping to conquer him, they rose up against Don Juan Tama [who] defended himself and won the war. Calambás's indios were without a cacique and Don Juan Tama exiled them.)

4. GENRES IN ACTION

1. The attribution of retrospective significance is the centerpiece of Greg Dening's *History's Anthropology* (1988), a fascinating excursion into how different actors, including the professional historian, make history out of an encounter between memories and historical referents, on the one hand, and the exigencies of the context within which they work, on the other.

2. The profoundly literate character of postcolonial native Andean society is, appropriately, the focus of the research of Bolivian Aymara historians (Ari Chachaki 1994; Condori Chura and Ticona Alejo 1992; Fernández O. 2000; Mamani Condori 1991) and their nonindigenous collaborators (Rivera Cusicanqui 1992). Unlike Western historians, these scholars emphasize the contexts in which the Aymara appropriated literacy as a weapon for political struggle and identity production; on the copyright page of the publications of the Andean Oral History Workshop, an Aymara historical institute, literacy is identified as forming part of the "genealogy of knowledge," or *el tronco de saberes*, of the Aymara.

3. The notarial archive in Ibarra includes numerous transactions in which the Tuza nobility purchased, sold, mortgaged, or donated Puntal lands (AHBC/I 1593, 1634a, 1639, 1649, 1656, 1671, 1673, 1680, 1688, 1691a, 1691b, 1699, 1703, 1707, 1727a, 1727b, 1727c, 1727d, 1732, 1736, 1768, 1783, 1791). Puntal is the focus of the plurality of land transactions in the archives, with documentation not only relating to Tuzas, but to Spaniards and to the chiefly families of Carlosama, Guaca, and Tulcán.

4. "Pues lo que han echo los yndios de Tusa ha sido adquirir por justo y legitimo titulo qual es el de compra y venta aquellos retazos de tierra y mantenerse en ellos desde tiempo larguisimo y aun inmemorial de forma que aun quando no hubieran tenido el titulo de compra y venta por el qual adquirieron verdadero dominio es preciso confesar que en el dia pasados mas de cien años de posecion con su buena fee y el justo titulo que han manifestado, habian de ser dueños de ellas por solo el titulo de prescripcion."

5. In this particular label, the attribution of ownership of the documents is in a different hand from the listing of the contents of the packet. Spanish original: "Contiene este quaderno los ynstrumentos antiquisimos desde el año de [mil] quinientos ochenta y [mil] seiscientos veinte y nueve, con una Real Provision y otros mandamientos de amparo y possecion de las tierras de Mumiar en fabor de Don Diego y Don Francisco Paspueles Casiques Principales de todos tres pueblos de Tusa, Puntal y El Angel. Esta en posesion Don Agustin Don Manuel Tussa = onse folios."

6. "Este quaderno contiene la escriptura de venta que otorgo Doña Magdalena Guachan, casica del pueblo de Guaca, en fabor de Sebastian Galindes Cuerta vn pedaso de tierra de ocho quadras que heredo de su madre Doña Juana Guachan, en terminos del pueblo del Puntal, en el sitio nombrado Mumiar y en

el precio de setenta y dos patacones = Yten contiene el litis que sobre las mismas ocho quadras de tierras siguio Doña Maria Tuquer, desendienta de Don Dionicio Paspuel Tusa y de Doña Paula Cogollo contra Doña Petrona Mainbas, muger de Don Matheo Garcia Paspueltusa, sobre que se declaro en fabor de la dicha Doña Maria Tuquer las que pretende quitarles los yndios del Puntal Don Santiago y Don Jasinto Guachagmiras y Don Cas. Paspuel en nombre del comun de dichos yndios a los descendientes de la dicha Doña Paula Cogollo: Son instrumentos del año de seiscientos noventa y dos = de Doña Maria Tuquer catorse folios." The paper trail of this particular plot of land can be followed in other archives (ANE/Q 1727b).

7. "Digo que esta yndia me a ynformado que por muerte del dicho Don Carlos Paspuel su padre quedo vn pedaso de tierra de pan sembrar en el citio de Mumiar por yndiuiso entre Don Fernando Paspuel y Don Nicolas Paspuel sus hermanos los quales son difuntos y por auer quedado los papeles de las dichas tierras y testamento del dicho Don Carlos padre de la dicha mi parte en poder del dicho Don Fernando Paspuel como en hermano mayor por fallecimiento del suso dicho Don Carlos Paspuel hijo del dicho Don Fernando su hermano se a apropiado de dichos papeles y tierras y no consiente que asi dicha mi parte como los hijos del dicho Don Nicolas las ocupen ni gosen y para que se haga justicia de ella y que cada parte vse de su derecho que le pertenese en lo que le cupiere de ellas por tener como tiene dicha mi parte hijos tributarios que estan pagando tributos conbiene se haga diuision de dicho pedaso de tierras."

8. "Que dicho Don Carlos . . . no salga de [Ibarra] . . . hasta manifestar ante Vmd el testamento del dicho Don Carlos Paspuel padre de dicho mi parte."

9. "Contiene este cuaderno los ynstrumentos de venta judicial que hacen Don Vicente Garcia Paspuel Tusa y Don Dionicio Paspuel, *caciques* del pueblo de Tusa, a Josef Vsuay yndio natural de dicho pueblo, tres quadras de tierra que possehian en el citio de Mumiar jurisdicion del Puntal, las que hubieron y posehieron por herencia y reparticion que se hizo de otras muchas tierras, assi en dicha jurisdiccion del Puntal como en la del Valle [de Apaqui], segun todo consta y parece de los ynstrumentos de amparos y posseciones librados por las justicias que estan incertos en este Quaderno cuia antiguedad es tanta que hay algunos de mas de docientos años y otros de siento y cinquenta como se puede ver."

10. "Que por otro nonbre se llamaba Don Diego Guachocal Asa el qual gouerno mas tiempo de çinquenta años por auerle heredado y subçedido en el dicho caçicazgo por fin y muerte de Doña Françisca Asiachin su madre ligitima verdadera caçica y señora que fue del caçique y señor que fue del dicho pueblo abra tiempo ynmemorial por auer muerto sin herederos a mano de los españoles primeros que conquistaron esta tierra por ser como hera su hermana ligitima segun su ley y asi justamente heredo el dicho casçicazgo de la suso dicha el dicho Don Diego Moran Guambas."

11. "Porque el dicho Don Diego Guacal padre de mi parte fue el berdadero ca-

çique y señor natural del dicho pueblo de Guachocal y por el ofiçio y dignidad de caçique fue llamado comunmente Don Diego Guachocal Aça que es el apellido del mismo pueblo como es vso y costumbre en toda la prouinçia de los Pastos tomar los caçiques los apellidos de los pueblos y dezir que Don Diego Mueranbanpaz es lo mesmo que Don Diego Guachocal Aça no pudo usurpar el nonbre sino por ser gouernador del dicho pueblo mas son distintas y diferentes personas y lo fueron Don Diego Guachocal Aça o Don Diego Guacal que es lo mismo padre de mi parte y Don Diego Mueranbuenpaz que fue yndio particular y por ser ladino fue puesto por gouernador como esta puesto en la demanda y Tarauchaycalguascalaza que fue caçique prinçipal del dicho pueblo quando entraron los espanoles a esta tierra hera hermano mayor del dicho Don Diego Guachal padre de mi parte que por auer muerto sin hijos se subçedio su hermano y la que es llamada Doña Françisca de quien pretenden derecho fue una yndia particular de su servizio. . . . Hera mi parte como hijo de hermano del dicho Taraochayncal y que subçede por bia de baron que tubieron y por ser eran todos sus antepasados el dicho caçicasgo y señorio." Note that the Spanish scribes struggled to make sense of Pasto names, which are transcribed with different orthographies from one page to the next in the documents we consider in depth in this chapter.

12. "Don Diego [Guacal] no fue casado ni belado con Joana Chalacan alegada en su pedimiento sino ella fue su mançeba con otras muchas que tubo ni menos fue xpiano baptizado por aber naçido antes que obiese doctrina ni baptizmo entre los yndios y el nombre de Don Diego fue postizo por su amo Esquibel de donde se ynfiere no ser capaz al dicho cacicazgo ni tener derecho alguno lo otro por costumre ynbiolable y ley antigua entre nuestros antecesores los hijos no suceden a sus padres en los caçicazgos sino los hermanos auiendolos y a falta los sobrinos hijos de hermanas o los primos y demas parientes del poseedor como se berifico en Don Diego Moran Guanpas mi suegro y anteçesor el qual por la dicha ley suçedio en el caçicazgo al llamado Don Diego padre de la parte contraria por ser su primo . . . y agora tenemos a Josephe que es derecho y ligitimo sucesor al caçicasgo y conforme a la ley christiana en que agora biuimos."

13. The Third Council of Lima, in contrast, lauded *indios ladinos* for their participation in the Christian sacraments and their rejection of idolatry (Lima, Concilio de 1990 [1585], 669, 688).

14. "Para esto es de saber, que tiempo es una mudança breve, o larga de las cosas movibles, è inmemorial, que no ay memoria de lo contrario . . . y en este caso se entiende del principio de començar a posseer una cosa; y porque según ello se requiere discurso de tiempo, a que no se vea llegar ninguno, esta proveido de derecho, que se prevee de cinco cosas. La una diziendo los testigos que quarenta años de vista. La otra, que lo oyeron a otros antes que ellos, que lo avia visto en los suyos, que llaman primeras oidas. La otra que essos dixessen que lo avian oido a otros antes que ellos, que llaman segundas oidas."

15. This final phrase may be a literal response to a question asked a witness. However, Pasto witnesses also learned such conventions from their Spanish overlords, just as they included Incaic power objects in their wills, as we describe in chapter 3.

16. "El dicho mi marido estuuo en pocecion de muchos años a esta parte en continuacion de las que tuuieron sus padres y antepasados desde el tienpo ynmemorial."

17. Ypialpud argues in his brief that he was Don Diego Puenambás's nephew, first cousin of Doña Ursula García, Doña Micaela, and Don Agustín Puenambás (ANE/Q 1695, 1r).

18. The doctrinal obligations of indigenous governors are detailed in ANE/Q (1707). Participation of other community members in doctrinal activity is discussed in ANE/Q (1716).

19. Covarrubias (1995 [1611], 839) defines *publicar* as, "to manifest something in public" (manifestar en público alguna cosa).

20. "Estando en la plasa deste pueblo de Tussa auiendo salido de missa por ser lugar destinado para la dotrina y estando la jente deste pueblo congregado desde Don Tomatias [*sic*] Quatinpas gouernador y demas caciques y principales con asistencia de Miguel Rodrigues Moran protector nombrado para esta visita por mando de su merced el dicho teniente general de corregidor que se hallo presente por vos de Diego de Santa Maria quien hiso oficio de pregonero hise publicar la dicha Real Prouision de Proclama segun y como en ella se contiene explicandola yo el dicho escribano en la lengua general del Ynga."

21. "Que para fundar se yntento la parte contraria en rrazon de que nonbrahan a mi parte por hijo dize en su fecha que se otorgo en diez y ocho de agosto de mil e quinientos y ochenta y nuebe años y la prouision que se dio por esta Rreal Audiençia para aberiguar como el dicho mi parte hera hijo legitimo del dicho Don Diego Guachocal Asa fue el ano de mill e quinientos y ochenta y seis en la qual dicha rreal prouision se haze minçion auer muerto mucho tiempo antes el dicho su padre y que por auer quedado niño de poca hedad el dicho mi parte auia entrado en el gouierno del dicho caçicasgo Don Diego Mueranbanpaz. . . . y siendo esto ansi como consta de los autos esta notoria falçedad de la parte contraria y del dicho llamado testamento."

22. "Ante mi el capitan Don Josep de Simon y Belasco theniente de gobernador justicia maior y corregidor de naturales de la dicha ciudad y sus prouinsias Don Andres Garcia Yaputa exsiuio el testamento de Don Sebastian Yaputa su padre difunto gobernador y casique prinsipal de la parsialidad de Yaputa cuio testamento parese estar escripto en quatro ffoxas de papel comun sin autoridad de escribano ni jues y solo parese estar firmado de quatro testigos y la del dicho difunto."

23. "Llebo el dicho Don Luis al jues comissionario y a los yndios a mostrarles los linderos que le pertenesian a la hazienda de El Salado segun desia que contaba

de los titulos que llebo y manifesto al dicho jues de tierras quien haviendolos visto dijo que no hallaba los linderos por la parte de arriba y que no entendia la letra por ser mui antigua y que hisiese copiar los titulos para poderlos entender." This particular case is fascinating, because in the course of determining the limits of the plot, its boundaries were surveyed and walked by the parties to the dispute and all of the previous titles to the territory were read to those assembled (ANE/Q 1753), suggesting that the intertextuality of written and non-literate modes of inscription were appreciated by both Pastos and Spaniards through its oral performance, regardless of whether or not their relationship was understood in the same way by both sides.

24. The argument continues with further allegations of the fraudulence of the evidence, based on the lack of a signature or of the proper number of witnesses to one of the wills (AHBC/Q 1748, 140v). "Son manifiestamente supuestos y fingidos pues siendo el primero segun su fecha de siento y sesenta años de antiguedad y deuiendo ser el segundo que supone hecho por Don Pedro Pastas hijo maior como se dize de Don Gomes Pastas que hizo el primero quando menos de cien años de antiguedad hasi la tinta como el papel y la formacion de las letras que era muy distinta en aquellos tiempos muestra palmariamente que no son ni pueden ser de la antiguedad que supone sino que son fingidos y supuestos por algun falsario y siendo assi que segun reglas del derecho el que vna bes es malo siempre se presume malo lo mismo que de los primeros testamentos se deben presumir del terser testamento que presenta la parte contraria esto es que es supuesto y falzo."

25. The will is reproduced in the 1695 dispute, with community authorities acting as witnesses and attesting to the testatrix's identity, given that she could not sign her name; it is signed by its writer, Don Juan Bautista Ypialpud, one of the parties to the dispute.

26. For further reflections upon this ceremony, see chapter 6 and Martínez Cereceda (1995). "Y estando presentes el suso dicho y los dichos gobernador y prinçipales mando sentar en una tranga al dicho Don Joan i su lasso a contiguo y estando sentado llegaron el dicho gobernador y prinçipales y le besaron la mano y dijeron que le reçiben y reçibieron por su caçique y señor natural y el dicho Don Joan arojo su sonbrero y mando se bolviesen a dar y se lo dieron y les mando le cargassen en la tranga en que estaua ssentado y lo cargaron y trujeron cargado vn espaçio por la plaça del dicho pueblo todo lo qual se hizo en señal de la dicha poseçion."

27. This is the other side of the coin of our discussion in chapter 2, where we described how miraculous paintings generated a set of authenticating documents, structured as lists of prepared questions and responses based on eyewitness testimony, such as occurred with the image of the Virgin of Chiquinquirá.

28. We have used the English word *painting* to translate the Spanish word *pinturas* used in colonial documents to refer to the images painted on Mexican codices.

They are, in fact, categorically closer to manuscript illuminations, as they appear in screen-fold books or loose-leaf folios.

29. We are paraphrasing here the testimony by Don Felipe de Austria, governor of the indigenous community of Tilantongo in the Mexican Mixteca Alta. On 30 March 1568 he presented a series of paintings known as the *Bodley Codex* to demonstrate native rules of succession in a Spanish court of law. His testimony has been partially transcribed and translated by Amos Megged (2010, 45–46), in an extremely insightful study of the relationships among alphabetic text, memory, and indigenous painting in Mexico. We cite here the pertinent English translation of the testimony that was transcribed, translated, and kindly shared with us by Megged: "In accordance with the primordial founding of this rule, a painting had been made by the first founder and the inhabitants of those communities for the sake of memory and script of this foundation and primordial institution and the order in which one was to proceed in the above succession. . . . [The painting] should serve as a proof of the ancient deeds and of things which would have required writing. . . . Only to that [painting] should faith and credit be granted, for the above paintings serve as a form of writing, that, in the same manner as a written manuscript was kept on guard where such writings [paintings] were customarily guarded. In the same way as [a written script], they would consult the kept records of successions from time immemorial until these very days." The testimony goes on to argue that because knowledge of the custom of succession, as well as the custom itself, had been interrupted in the last forty years, evidence of succession as seen in the paintings should be measured against oral testimony. Painted slightly before the conquest, the *Bodley Codex* depicts Mixtec genealogical relationships and historical events spanning from AD 900 to 1521. See also Elizabeth Boone (2000, 100–106) for an analysis of the genealogical reading of the manuscript as it pertains to the "Family of 5 Crocodile" in the eleventh century and the rituals of succession.

30. "La Ciudad de Huamanga cuadrado y amojonado por los vecinos primeros fundadores."

31. In the text concerning Huamanga in the *Nueva corónica*, Guaman Poma (1980 [1616], 1050 [1058]) makes direct reference to the litigation over Chupas, writing that Don Martín de Ayala and Juan Tingo—two individuals whose portraits also accompany the document, as we will see presently—had houses and fields in Santa Catalina de Chupas and that they had served their king at the battle of Chupas, an event identified in the map accompanying the legal document. Hence, Guaman Poma clearly had this map and the view of Huamanga in mind when he created the city view of Huamanga in the *Nueva corónica*.

32. A signature is the proper term for a set of folded sheets that in printing usually numbers sixteen; in the documents we are using, the number varies.

33. Why Guaman Poma had Don Domingo wearing such an elaborate bracelet with a human head is impossible to know. There is nothing like it in the *Nueva*

corónica and the style of the profile head seems more like that of a miniaturist, decorating a choral book.

34. "Si se compusiese un libro genealógico que solo tratase de la familia de los caciques, sus escudos de armas y entroncamientos, se haría un grande servicio á la monarquía, sacando á muchos indios y á algunos provenidos de ellos del engaño en que viven, solo por los apellidos supuestos que han ursupado de los emperadores Incas, no pudiendo de ningún modo de ser hoy Inca el que así se apellidase, como se ha probado en esta disertación, que deben de tener muy presente todos los tribunales y jueces de Indias." (Llano Zapata 1904 [1761] 106).

35. The term *cacique mayor* was used in the northern Andes to refer to descendants of noble families who had led pre-Inca confederations of native groups and occupied a colonial status that lay between that of the descendants of the Inca and that of *caciques principales*, the local leaders of a community (Oberem 1993, 15–19).

36. "Digo que desde que entra gente española en aquella provinzia asta agora a seydo y es christiano themeroso de Dios y obidiente a sus sanctos mandamientos y como tal en todo lo que se a ofrezido y serbido a vuestra magestad con su persona y azienda y caballos y yndios de los pueblos cuyo cazique el es y sienpre en todo muy bien e lealamente e como buen y leal vasallo dando favor y ayuda a los vuestros virreyes y a otras personas que han ydo aquellas partes en vuestro real nombre."

37. "Un escudo partido en quatro partes que en la una alta de la mano derecha este un hombre armado con un estandarte real en la mano de azul orlado de oro y las armas blancas en campo de colorado. En la otra parte de la mano yzquierda unos yndios con sus flechas que vinien de guerra en campo verde y en la otra parte de abaxo de la mano derecha un caballo blanco ensillado y enfrenado con una lanza puesta en el arzon que tenga el hasta de oro y el hierro de plata con yndio de su color que le tenga de rienda. Y en el otro quarto un leon de su color puesto en salta con una espada en la mano en campo de oro y por timble y debisa un yelmo cerrado con un braço de leon con una espada en la mano y follages de azul y oro."

5. KING'S *QUILLCA* AND THE RITUALITY OF LITERACY

1. "Ya que en persona no podamos manifestar a Vuestra Magestad nuestras deprecaciones sea por cartas."
2. "Vivimos tan apartados y rremotos de su real persona."
3. "Llegue señor don Alonso Illescas, goce del bien y merced que Dios Nuestro Señor y su majestad le hacen en este día."
4. "Alonso me llamo yo, y no tengo Don."
5. "El rey que puede dar y pone el Don como mas largamente entenderá, venido que sea a tierra."
6. "Estas son las Armas del rey mi señor que bien conozcas."

7. "Señor vicario, mi cabeza y las de mis hijos y compañeros os encomiendo como a Señor Padre; la tierra y cuanto en ella hay, es de su Majestad y desde luego, en su real nombre, os doy la obediencia mía y de los que están a mi cargo los mulatos (que residen nueve o diez leguas de mi casa)."

8. "En el pueblo de Cumbal a terminos y jurizdicion de la ciudad de Pasto a veinte y ocho dias del mes de abril año de mil y seiscientos y cinquenta y seis años ante el maese de campo Miguel de Caizedo teniente de gobernador justicia mayor corregidor de naturales y alcalde mayor de minas de la dicha ciudad de Pasto sus terminos y jurizdicion por su magestad prezentaron esta real prouision con peticion los contenidos en ella y pidieron su complimiento y bista por el dicho teniente de gobernador reciuio en sus manos la dicha rreal prouision y la bezo y puzo sobre su cauesa teniendola destocada y la obedecio con el acatamiento deuido a carta y prouicion real de su rey y señor natural la quien la diuina magestad guarde muchos años con aumento de mayores reinos y señorios como la cristiandad desea y mando que se cumpla y guarde como en ella se contiene y que esta puesto de uer perssonalmente a cumplir con el tenor de la dicha real prouicion luego y sin dilacion y lo firmo ante si por no auer al presente en este dicho pueblo escribano publico ni real: Miguel Caizedo."

9. Similarly, in Jewish ritual, the reading of the Torah is accompanied by the act of holding up the scrolls, which are also kissed.

10. We thank Bruno Mazzoldi for alerting us to the connection between this practice and colonial ritual. In the twenty-first century southern Andes, loud and wet kisses between men indicate relationships of respect (Bruce Mannheim, personal communication).

11. "Y luego los dichos indios caciques Incas de suso declarados por lengua de Pedro Delgado interprete indio natural de este dicho valle debajo de juramento que para ello hizo de declarar la verdad de lo que los dichos indios dijeren los cuales todos así mismo juraron en forma según su ley mochando el sol y la tierra y la guaca como lo tienen de costumbre prometieron decir verdad y respondiendo a lo que les es preguntando por la dicha lengua dijeron teniendo delante la dicha pintura lo siguiente."

12. "Tornarse a sujetar, a dar la obediencia el reñido o alçado, o, pedir perdon al mayor, o reconciliarse con su mayor, o con Dios."

13. Implicit in the notion of subordination to royal authority was subordination to God, since the king was God's ordained and anointed ruler on earth (Michael Gerli, personal communication; Alfonso X 1992 [1555], Partida II, título I, leyes 1–10; Nieto Soria 1988, 51–55; see also Kantorowicz 1957, 193–272). While Teófilo Ruiz (1985) argues that the Spanish monarchy was characterized by a paucity or absence of ritual, this does not mean that the monarch himself was "unsacred" (see also Nieto Soria's [1993] critique of the Ruiz thesis).

14. "Los curacas y principales ingas naturales desta ciudad de Cuzco, caveça destos Reinos, vasallos de V. Magestad, humildemente besamos Sus reales pies y

manos." The document comes originally from the Archivo Generale della Compagnia di Gesù, Rome (ACGC/R), "Carta anua de la provincia del Perú del año de 1599. P. Rodrigo de Cabredo to P. Claudio Aquaviva, Lima, April 20, 1600."

15. We thank Frank Salomon for providing us with this English translation and the following one, as well as for signaling the appropriate suffixes left out of the original, which are marked in square brackets.

16. Another important example of native Andeans' simplest experiences with the written word was the receipt of *cédulas de confesión*, certificates verifying that the bearer had confessed and was able to receive holy communion (AGCG/R 1605, 3v; AGCG/R 1608–9, 46r); we do not know what these cédulas looked like, however. Such cédulas refer not only to the sacramental act of confession, but also to communion, the only sacrament in which a Christian ritual image—the Host—*is* what it represents and makes present the ultimate authority of Christianity (Marin 1988).

17. "HECHO lo cual pacientemente de la linderación a que fueron llamados los demás pueblos, el Capitán de Infantería española se puso de rodilla en la pampa y luego, ciniéndose la corona de oro de su rey, su señor natural, en alta voz hizo entrega de la tierra en su tenencia, en su posesión, en su mismo dominio a los caciques, representantes genuinos de sus pueblos de CUMBAL."

18. "La rúbrica, inscripción y nombre escrito de propia mano, que haze firme todo lo contenido y escrito encima de la firma."

19. "Ci parole de testmoinage d'eskievins de le chité d'Amiens. Derechief, tout quanque doi eskieven tesmoignent et recordant, *est ferm et estable*, et passe sans che que nus puist dire ne faire reins encontre." A customal is a written collection of the customs of a monastery or a town.

20. In the Arab world, script was seen as conveying "the qualities of the human witness," thus converting writing in general into a kind of signature (Messick 1993, 34).

21. We thank Frank Salomon for assisting us with the translation from the Quechua.

22. "Y ahora todos estos santos que son innumerables están en el cielo gozando de ver a Dios, y ruegan por nosotros y son nuestros abogados. Y por eso los honramos y llamamos sus nombres y *tenemos sus imágenes en las Iglesias, para que nos recuerden estos padres y maestros.*"

23. "Muy a los principios del Provinciato de Rm. P. Mro. fray Pedro Martyr tuvo esta provincia el Venerable P.M. fray Pedro Bedón, cuyas firmas se veneran en sus libros como reliquias. En ellos se hallan, como Depositario en estos años, y en el Refectorio en el año 1594, cuya pintura se debe a sus manos."

24. "Y así su corazón pónenlo en el cielo donde está Jesucristo y sus Santos; y en Jesucristo ponen su esperanza y su voluntad. Y si reverencian las imágenes, y las besan y se descubren delante de ellas, e hincan las rodillas y hieren los pechos, es por lo que aquellas imágenes representan, y no por lo que en sí son.

Como el corregidor besa la provisión y sello real, y lo pone sobre su cabeza, no por aquella cera ni el papel, sino porque es quillca del rey." The Third Catechism and its accompanying sermons were issued from the Third Lima Provincial Council (1582–83) and remained in use until the Plenary Council of Latin America in 1899 (Barnes 1992, 67). This material was intended to be used throughout the viceroyalty. Fray Pedro Bedón was consulted on the translation and the variations with the Quechua of the Quito area (ibid., 71). This catechism was also used in Bogotá, translated into Muisca (Romero Rey 1988, 22). A complete copy of the Third Catechism can be found in the Biblioteca del Colegio San Ignacio de Loyola, Cotocollao, Ecuador.

25. The tactile aspect of Andean methods of inscription is clear in a 1602 annual letter from the province of Peru, in which a blind man is described as basing his confession on a khipu: "This Indian made it from six varas of spun cord and from place to place, a thread that crossed it and some signs [made out] of stones or bones or feathers, depending upon the type of sin that he needed to confess, without which in the four days he took to confess, he forgot anything and by feeling the quipo and the signs placed in it, he confessed with such distinction and certainty as though he had eyes and a great understanding, crying for his sins and detesting the idolatries with which the devil had tricked him, satisfying all with his great penitence and pain" (Fernández 1986, 214–15). The Spanish original reads as follows: "Hízolo este indio de seis varas de cordel torcido y de trecho en trecho un hilo que lo atravesava y algunas señales de piedras o güesos o plumas, conforme a la materia del peccado que avía de confessar, sin que en quatro días que gastó en confesarse, dudasse en cosa alguna y por el tiento del quipo y de las señales puestas en él, se confessó con tanta distinción y puntualidad como si tuviera ojos y muy grande entendimiento, llorando sus peccados y detestando las idolatrías con que el demonio le avía engañado, satisfaciendo por todo con gran penitencia y dolor."

26. Interestingly, however, the Muisca translation of "to read" is *ioquec zecubunsuca*, literally "paper memory" (Anonymous 1987 [1607–20], 273, 287), whereas in Quechua, *quillca* is an integral component of "to read." According to González Holguín (1989 [1608], 561), "To read" is *qquellccactam ricuni*, which would translate literally as, "I see the quillca."

27. We thank Frank Salomon for the Quechua translation.

28. The branding of slaves—both indigenous and African—with letters on their foreheads, breasts, and arms, might be considered the secular antithesis to the symbolic marking of the Christian body through the sign of the cross. That is, the physical marking of property by the slave owner is the inverse of the symbolic self-marking of Christian metaphysics. Moreover, a narrative of the history of the slave's owners was visually displayed on the slave's body by the sequence of brands which marked each new "property owner." In addition to private marks of owners, which were dutifully entered into any legal document

of sale, African slaves in the seventeenth century were branded on the right breast with a royal brand using a capital *R* (for *real*, or "royal"), surmounted by a crown to mark that they had been legally imported (Bowser 1974, 82–83). For the branding of indigenous slaves with the letter *C* (probably standing for *caribe* or "Carib") in the sixteenth century, see Jack Forbes (1988, 34).

29. "Y también os señalad muchas veces con la señal de la cruz, especialmente cuando os levantáis, cuando salís de la casa, cuando el demonio os trae malas tentaciones, cuando os veis en algún peligro o trabajo, porque por la señal de cruz es vencido el enemigo y huye de los cristianos. Esta señal hacemos cuando nos persignamos en la frente y en la boca y en el pecho, para que Dios nuestro Señor libre nuestro entendimiento de malos pensamientos, nuestra boca de malas palabras, nuestro corazón de malos deseos y de malas obras" and "Cuando nos santiguamos, hacemos la señal de la santa cruz en todo el cuerpo, desde la frente hasta la cinta y desde el un hombro al otro, invocando y llamando y confesando el nombre de la Santísima Trinidad, Padre e Hijo y Espíritu Santo, que es un solo Dios, para que nos dé su bendición y gracia y nos libre de todo mal." There is no easy way to distinguish between *persignar* and *santiguar* in English, as both would be rendered "crossing oneself" or "making the sign of the cross." Indeed, although theologians like the authors of the sermons of the Third Council of Lima and the Bogotá archbishop Zapata de Cárdenas (see note 30) make a careful distinction between the two acts, by contrasting both the prayers they involve and the bodily movements that accompany them—practices which take place, moreover, at different points in the Catholic mass—in common usage the two words were interchangeable as is attested to by the 1726 definition of *santiguar* in the Royal Academy of Language's *Diccionario de Autoridades*: "Make the sign of the Cross on oneself, or the same as persignarse" (Real Academia Española 1990 [1726], vol. III, 43) or "Hacer sobre sí la señal de la Cruz, ò lo mismo que persignarse."

30. "Se manda que el modo de persignar sea y se guarde en esta forma: que hecha una cruz con el dedo pulgar de la mano derecha sobre el índex traigan el pulgar desde la frente hasta la punta de la nariz diciendo 'por la señal'; y luego cruzando desde la sien izquierda a la derecha diga 'de la cruz,' y trayendo el dicho dedo pulgar desde la punta de la nariz a la barba diga 'de nuestros': y cruzando por la boca del lado izquierdo al derecho, diga, 'enemigos'; y cruzando el dedo dicho hasta en medio del vientre desde la barba, diga 'líbranos Señor'; y cruzando por el pecho del lado izquierdo al derecho, diga 'Dios nuestro.' Y asimismo en el santiguar se guardará la uniformidad, juntando el dedo pulgar con los otros dos dél vecinos de la mano derecha, y encogidos los otros dos, y poniendo la punta de los extendidos en la frente de plano, dirán 'En el nombre del Padre'; y descendiendo hasta en medio del vientre, dirán 'y del hijo'; y levantando la mano y poniéndola en el hombro izquierdo y trayéndola hasta ponerla en el derecho, dirán 'y del Espíritu Santo'; y juntando las manos y cruzando

los dedos pulgares y besando la cruz con estos pulgares hecha, dirán, 'Amén, Jesús.'"

31. In the southern Andes, the making of the sign of the cross is first equated to, and then replaces, the act of *muchana*, in some documents, converted into the Spanish-style verb "mochar"—blowing a wet kiss across cupped hands—as a sign of reverence and blessing in relation to speaking or writing the truth. Hanks (2000, 283–98) traces the multiple intertextual trajectories of the sign of the cross in colonial vernacular documents among the Maya of Yucatán, presenting a broad range of semantic values inscribed in physical space, in alphabetic documents, and on indigenous bodies. While each of these instances operates in its own semantic context, they relate, ultimately, to the original cross upon which Christ was crucified: "There is a three-way relation established among the crosses: the *Cruz* (wooden) is the instrument of Christ's passion; the *cilich Cruz* (Maltese) is the sign of a Christian; and the *cilich Cruz* (verbal) is the sign of the *Cruz* (wooden). In terms of the system of Christianity, the original, material cross is the core of the series, with the two other versions standing as signs of it. Notice that only the wooden cross is properly described as *uahom che* 'erect wood.' It is not presented as a sign of anything other than itself. . . . It is the real thing, of which the others are signs. . . . This may explain why we find only the Spanish term *Cruz* in the *Doctrina*: the priests needed to tie together what was in fact a whole range of semantic values clustered around the cross, and to do this, it was more efficient to retain a single term" (ibid., 291).

32. "Y si tuvieren crucifixos, ymagenes de nuestra Señora o de los sanctos, les den a entender que aquellas ymagenes es una manera de escriptura que rrepresenta y da a entender a quien representa."

33. Hans Belting—citing the eighth-century theologian, Theodore of Studion— writes that "every image, no matter of what kind, originated in a prototype, in which it was contained in essence (by *dynamis*) from the outset. An impression belongs to a seal and a shadow or reflection to a body, so a likeness belonged to a model" (1994, 153). As Rachel Fulton points out, "seals and their marked cousins, had . . . a long history as metaphors for the relationship between God and the individual soul" (2002, 254–65). The relationship between being marked by a seal and the baptismal marking of the cross on the forehead is found in the Pauline epistles (2 Corinthians 1:21–22 and Ephesians 1:13–14, 4:30). In the Viceroyalty of Peru, the use of the term *quillca* succinctly and economically links the role of the Catholic theology of the *Corpus Mysticum* with the theory of royalty and of the royal crown and dignity as outlined by Ernst Kantorowicz (1957).

34. "Es justo y conveniente, que cuando nuestro sello Real entrare en alguna de nuestras Reales Audiencias, *sea recevido con la autoridad, que si entrasse nuestra real persona, como se haze en las de estos Reynos de Castilla. Por tanto mandamos, que llegando nuestro Real á qualquiera de las Audiencias de las Indias,*

nuestros Presidentes y Oidores, y la justica y Regimiento de la Ciudad salgan un buen trecho fuera de ella á recevirle, y desde donde estuviere, hasta el Pueblo sea llevado encima de un cavallo, ó mula, con adereços muy decentes, y el Presidente y Oidor mas antiguo le llevan en medio, con toda la veneracion, que se requiere, segun y como se acostumbra en las Audiencias Reales de estos Reynos de Castillo, por esta orden vayan hasta ponerle en la casa de la Real Audiencia Real, donde esté, para que en ella le tenga á cargo la persona que sirviere el oficio de Chanciller del sello, y de sellar las provisiones, que en las Chancillerias se despacharen."

35. "Sacramentos llamamos unas señales y ceremonia ordenadas por Jesucristo con las cuales honramos a Dios y participamos de su gracia. Así como si el Virrey o la Audiencia os da una provisión o quillca con que os hace libre de tributo, y más, os manda dar de la caja del Rey cien pesos, tomáis la quillca y guardáisla, y por ella que dáis libre del tributo y aun rico. Así también los sacramentos de la Santa Iglesia hacen que los que los toman, quedan libre de pecado, aún quedan ricos de gracia."

36. Patents of nobility (*cartas ejecutorias de hidalguía*) often carried the portrait of the king. The first known printed example was granted to Juan de los Olivios in 1597, produced on vellum and painted with a portrait of Philip II on the penultimate folio. Such documents were stored in the private archives of Pasto caciques and were willed by them to their descendants (ANE/Q 1695, 38r).

37. For an excellent discussion of the political and social role of portraiture in the seventeenth century, see Espinosa (1990, 1995), whose work is discussed more extensively in chapter 1.

38. See chapter 6 for a discussion of ephemeral arches as *portadas*, or portals.

39. The relationship between the image of Christ and the image of the ruler has a long history in Christian theology. While transubstantiation means that the host literally becomes the blood and flesh of Christ, it must be remembered that the body of Christ is the image of God made visible. Basil the Great (ca. 330–79) argues that the resemblance that inheres to an image by virtue of its form was brought about—in the relation of the Son and the Father—by divine nature (Belting 1994, 152–53). To demonstrate his meaning, he refers to the imperial image that received honors on behalf of the emperor, just as the portrait of Charles II receives honors on behalf of the king. Similarly, the imperial portrait presided over judicial proceedings. Basil writes: "Just as no one looks at the imperial image in the market place and acknowledges the emperor would deduce the existence of two emperors, first the *image* and then the real emperor, that is the situation here, too. If the image and the emperor can be one (for the image does not cause a multiplication of the emperor), the same holds true of the divine *Logos* and God" (ibid., 152–53). Belting further notes that Athanasius (295–373) takes this argument further: "In the image the features of the emperor have been preserved unchanged, so that anyone who looks at it recognizes him

in the image. . . . Thus the image could say 'I and the emperor are one.' He who honors the imperial icon, therefore honors in it the emperor himself" (ibid., 152–53).

40. "Ante Vuesa Mersed paresco con este memorial."

41. "Y Su Mersed la cogio por la mano y la entrego la numeracion deste dicho pueblo todos agtos que dijo hacia en señal de posesion."

6. REORIENTING THE COLONIAL BODY

1. "Item, porque la limpieza del pueblo es necesaria para vivir sanos y con limpieza, mándase al sacerdote que tenga cuidado cómo el pueblo esté limpio, limpiando cada uno su pertenencia y desherbándola, y ansí mismo sus casas, y las tengan bien compuestas, y para dormir tengan barbacoas y camas limpias, y el sacerdote visite con los alcaldes y con el cacique, o con el capitán de la tal capitanía a quien las tales casas competen, para ver si cumplen lo arriba dicho . . . y mande que las cocinas y despensas están apartadas de donde habitan y duermen."

2. During the Reconquest, towns served as vanguards of Christian civilization against the Moors, indicating that although they were not yet planned in grids, the ideological basis of urban life was already critical in the medieval era (Kagan 2000, 26–27). The emphasis on life in cities and towns was, later, characteristic of the European baroque in general and of the Spanish baroque in particular, a product of significant demographic shifts taking place in Europe (Maravall 1986 [1975], chap. 4).

3. Setha Low (2000, 86), in contrast, seeks to discover the roots of the grid pattern "in a multiplicity of architectural and cultural traditions" found throughout the world, including in pre-Columbian America. She suggests that the existing indigenous urban plans upon which the Spanish colonial city was superimposed were equally significant models for colonial city builders. Valerie Fraser (1990, 114), in another contrasting view, argues that colonial sources do not acknowledge such borrowings and that the grid was more in keeping with Spanish notions of an orderly society. The two principal components of the grid are its parallel and intersecting streets, and its central plaza around which the major public buildings are arrayed. While the street plan only becomes ubiquitous in the New World, the central plaza was introduced in Spain in the twelfth and thirteenth centuries during the course of the Reconquest; the plaza was a reaction to existing Moorish city plans, which had no separate meeting places for secular activities, but employed the mosque for both secular and sacred purposes (Jamieson 2000, 49).

4. "Para fundar esta ciudad hizo primero el Gobernador dibujar su planta en papel con las medidas de las calles y cuadras y señaló en las cartas de los solares que repartían a los pobladores, escribiendo el nombre de cada uno en el solar que le cabía."

5. "Hace luego traza del pueblo de la manera y orden que ha de ser edificado, y conforme a la traza que se hace señalan a todos los vecinos por su orden solares, dando el primero a la iglesia y luégo al capitán y luégo a las otras personas principales, de suerte que conforme a la traza que se hace queda el pueblo fundado; y así se van edificando en él por sus cuadras, que son unos cuarteles cuadrados divididos en cuatro partes iguales, y por cada frente del cuartel queda una calle, y las cuatro partes del cuartel son cuatro solares, y éstos se dan a cuatro personas o a dos, como quieren, y así se van dilatando y extendiendo la poblazón del pueblo o comarca de la plaza, que también es cuadrada, y es una cuadra de cuatro solares con sus calles, que de ella salen, que son ocho calles, dos por cada esquina, por donde muy acomodadamente se gobierna y anda y manda todo el pueblo."

6. "Que en el dicho sitio de Bobota en la parte mas comoda y superior se señale para la yglesia cincuenta y cuatro varas de largo y doce de ancho con los cimientos y estribos con la traza y condiciones declaradas en la escritura otorgada por Juan Gomez albañil y trazando el testero a la parte del nacimiento del sol y por delante de la dicha iglesia se señalen setenta varas en quadro o las que convinieren conforme la comodidad del sitio para plaza y a los lados de la yglesia se señalen veinte y cinco varas en quadro para la casa del padre y al otro lado otras tantas para el cacique principal y a la redonda de la plaza las casas de los capitanes con veinte varas en quadro y por la misma orden se han de señalar a los demas indios sus casas linea recta cuadradas en que hagan su despensa y cocina y corral y las calles han de ir derechas limpias y desherbadas de seis varas de ancho entre cada ochenta."

7. Alberto Corradine Angulo (1993, 165) notes that the dimensions of the towns of Santander and Tunja differed in many respects from reducciones in the Bogotá area that were overseen by Beltrán's colleague, Luis Henríquez. Corradine suggests that these discrepancies indicate that there was a gap between the norms of town construction and the realities of the foundation of reducciones, due to the fact that the royal officials charged with the task had no previous experiences upon which to base their enterprise. In the Popayán region, reducciones were established some fifteen years earlier (Salcedo Salcedo 1993, 188) and among the Pasto and the Nasa, the plans of indigenous towns were not as regular as those laid out by Henríquez and Beltrán de Guevara (ibid., 190). See Chantal Caillavet (2000, 143) for a 1584 map of Quinchunchic, Otavalo (today, Ecuador).

8. The ritual of foundation is described by the archaeologist Ross Jamieson: "The Spanish foundation of an Andean city could only occur with the consent of the Crown. The Act of Foundation was a ritual that was not always the same, but had several key steps. At the founding of the city all would gather in the area of the future *plaza mayor*. The designated official would take possession of the area for the Crown, and then the *rollo y picota* (pillar and pillory/gibbet) would be

set up in the middle of the future plaza as the symbol of royal justice. A cross or several foundational stones would be erected on the site of the future church. This done, the municipal councilors, and other town officials would be named. Following this the solares, or city lots, could be measured out and assigned, the first to the church, the second to the founder of the town, and then the others for the principal citizens" (2000, 51–52). We would add here that the "act of foundation" simultaneously referred to the ritual itself and to the document that anteceded and recorded the ceremony.

9. In the New Kingdom of Granada, these chapels were not part of the original town plan, but were erected some fifty years later at the initiative of individual parish priests (Salcedo Salcedo 1993, 195–96). Note that the twenty-first-century inhabitants of Sutatausa are migrants from other areas and not native to the region (Rodolfo Vallín, personal communication).

10. Henri Lefebvre (1992 [1974], 151–52) suggests that political power is behind the production of the social space of the colonial reducción, a point with which we agree. However, he reduces the concept of political power to "violence in the service of economic goals." Such an equation is too mechanistic, allowing him to dismiss the issue in less than a page. We thank Alan Kolata for directing us to this passage and its inherent problems.

11. The 1556 decrees of the Synod of Bogotá specified that baptismal books were to be maintained in the parishes, emphasizing their importance in establishing the paternity of mestizos: "We have seen by experience in this land that many mestizo children are brought up with neither Fathers nor Mothers, and sometimes it is not clear whose children they are, and how old they are, and who their Godparents were, which is important to know because of the impediment of spiritual relationships; therefore, as approved by the Holy Synod, we order our Priests, under penalty of major excommunication, that in a book which in the last inspection we ordered they keep in the Sacrarium, they place the names of all the babies they baptize, with the day, month, and year, and the names of their Parents, and Godparents, and when such book is full they make another one, for the same purpose, and all should be carefully kept in the Sacrarium, to avoid difficulties, and to know who can marry" (Romero 1960, 490) (Avemos visto por experiencia en estas partes, que muchos niños mestizos se crian sin Padres, ni Madres, y se duda algunas veces, cuios hijos son, y de qué edad, y quienes fueron sus Padrinos, lo qual conviene se sepa por el impedimento de la cognacion espiritual; por tanto Santa Synodo aprobante, mandamos a nuestros Curas, so pena de excomunion maior, que en un libro que en la visita pasada les mandamos tengan en el Sagrario, asiente los nombres de todas las criaturas que baptizaren, con dia, mes y año, y los nombres de sus Padres, y Padrinos, y quando el tal libro se acabare de henchir se haga otro, para el mismo efecto, y todos se guarden con cuidado en el Sagrario, por evitar inconvenientes, y saber los que se pueden casar).

12. "Por tanto se manda que el sacerdote tenga cuidado especial cuando que Su Señoria u otro Prelado que le suceda o con licencia va a confirmar, de ver por el *Libro del Bautismo* los que deben confirmar . . . y que hará en el margen del *Libro* una cruz de esta forma, + , frontero del nombre del confirmado, para que sea señal que el nombre que tiene la cruz está confirmado, y para que no haya confusión en los padrinos tendrá en el pueblo uno o dos señalados para padrinos de todos los confirmados, y escribirse han en el *Libro* como son los padrinos de los que se confirmaron tal año. Y asimismo, se pondrán el año de la confirmación en el margen de la cruz dicha en esta forma que en el margen se señala."

13. In this sense, the nature of manuscript culture gives the lie to an argument of Jack Goody (1977, 1987) that the advent of literacy made historical and scientific thinking possible because it provided a permanent record in the place of an ever-changing oral register. In fact, manuscripts were by design not permanently fixed, but ever changing.

14. "Se ordena y manda que por cuanto este misterio [la Misa] es la más alto de los que contienen los santos sacramentos y no merecen gozarlo ni verlo sino solo los fieles, que no consienta el sacerdote que ninguno que no haya recibido agua de bautismo vea este divino sacramento, sino que se guarde el derecho que dispone que los catecúmenos sean admitidos no más de hasta el credo cuando se dice en la misa, y cuando no hasta dicho el Evangelio, y antes de la ofrenda sean echados fuera todos los catecúmenos dándoles a entender el sacerdote la razón porque los echan fuera . . . y donde ni desde afuera no lo vea. Para el cual efecto tendrá apartado lugar en la iglesia donde los catecúmenos estén como desde la mitad de la iglesia abajo, y los cristianos más cercanos al altar, de suerte que entre unos y otros haya algún espacio que los divida. Y habrá un portero que tenga cuidado de admitirlos a la iglesia y de echarlos a su tiempo fuera y los que son mero gentiles no los consentirán entrar a la iglesia en ningún tiempo."

15. The most well known visitas for southern Colombia were those of Tomás López for the district of Popayán (AGI/S 1558–59; published as Tomás López Medel 1989 [1558–59]) and of the licentiate García de Valverde for Pasto and Almaguer (AGI/S 1570–71), although numerous other census were performed throughout the Audiencia de Quito and the New Kingdom of Granada. For example, there are multiple holdings, spanning the entire colonial period, of visitas of Muisca towns, such as AGN/B (1586).

16. "Lo más vistoso y espacioso, como es en la cara la frente; que con esta similitud llama el italiano fachata a la delantera de la casa."

17. It is also important to note that the door of a church could represent such concepts as the door of a cathedral, called the "puerta de perdón," before which, among other things, prisoners were hanged.

18. "Tiene singular belleza en las plantas y proporción de las plazas y las calles iguales todos. . . . La figura y planta es quadrada con tal orden y concierto que

todas las calles son parejas tan anchas que pueden yr lado a lado tres carrozas
. . . y tan iguales que estando en la plaza central se ven los confines de toda la
ciudad; porque como del centro salen las lineas a la circunferencia assi de la
plaza hasta los fines della corren calles largas. . . . Todas por su igualdad y an-
chura y rectitud son vistosissimas y tambien porque los edifcios que por esta
ciudad se an labrado a mucha costa . . . son muy hermosos."

19. Serlio's treatise was translated into Spanish in 1552 using the same illustrations
as the original Italian edition.

20. "Y a la puerta (iglesia del pueblo) se hará si fuere posible un portal donde estará
un púlpito para predicar a los infieles que aún no han entrado en el número de
los catecúmenos, porque se desea que les den a entender que aún no son dignos
de tratar ni entrar en aquello santo templo."

21. "Siete capitanias o parçialidades hazen en la plaça siete çirculos que cada vno
es desta manera sientanse en el suelo los indios de vna capitania haziendo vna
media luna y luego delante dellos haziendo otra media luna se ponen las mu-
geres bueltas las espaldas a los hombres y el blanco de en medio hinchen los
niños y niñas ponese en medio de todos un niño en pie con vna cruz larga en
la mano y comiença a resar las oraçiones respondiendo todos y en acabando el
entra otro y otro por espaçio de ora y media y asi a un mismo tiempo estan re-
sando en todos siete çirculos luego un padre los junta todos y haze vn çirculo
grande en la mesma forma donde los cathequisa de espaçio por çinco quartos
de hora entran luego a la yglesia a oyr la misa cantada con mucha musica y alli
se les predica. . . . A la tarde tienen proçession de Nuestra Señora alrededor de
la plaça cantando su letania."

22. Similar acts were held when several communities came together on market days
(AGCG/R 1611–12, 68v; 1616, 117r). In the Museo Bedón of the Convent of Santo
Domingo in Quito, there is a painting of a similar semicircle of catechumens.
The painting depicts a single semicircle, however, because the catechumens are
angels, who have no gender.

23. "En el pueblo de Pasttas en dies y ocho dias de el mes de octtubre de mill sette-
cientos sesentta y un años el general Don Gregorio Sanchez Parra theniente de
gouernador corregidor y justticia mayor de esta provincia y su jurisdiccion por
su magestad hauiendo venido a el en conformidad de lo mandado por el autto
antesedentte estando en el teattro formado segun costumbre a la puerta de la
yglesia acompañado de el R.P.M. fr. Fernando Paredes cura proprio de el pueblo
de Carlozama y este su anexo de barias personas relixiosas y seculares el pro-
tecttor de natturales los casiques de la provincia alcalde mayor y mucho numero
de yndios e yndias hiso leer en voz clara el escritto y autto antesedentes y en su
consequensia dio la prebenida posesion con la formalidad y palabras siguientes:
Yo el general Don Gregorio Sanches Parexa theniente de gouernador corregidor y justticia mayor de esta provincia en nombre de el rey nuestro señor a voz
Don Manuel Nasttar y Canchala os also y pongo en posesion de el casicasgo de

la parcialidad de Nastar vna de las de el pueblo de Pasttas y mando al gouernador principales cauesones y mandones de ella a los yndios yndias muchachas y
muchachos de ttoda la parcialidad os resiban y acudan a vuestro llamamientto
os hayan tengan acauen y obedescan como a su casique y señor nattural baxo
las penas de la ley real contra los ynobedienttes y en señal de vuestra posesion
os entrego este baston de señorio y senttado dho casique en su silla fueron vi-
niendo los yndios, yndias, chinos y chinas de la dha su parcialidad y tendiendo
sus mantas hasiendo sus acattamientos a su vsansa y costumbre le vesaron el
pie y los parientes le abrasaron en señal de resepcion y obediensia y despues fue
cargado en ombros por sus principales y paseado por los quattro angulos de la
plasa."

24. "Lo cual acabado, acababan también con gran cantidad de su vino en una gran
fiesta que hacían a todos los caciques convecinos, a quien volvían los retor-
nos doblados de los presentes que a él le hacían, de mantas, oro, armas y otras
cosas."

25. Jaime Lara (1996, 263) gives a date of 1626 based on a barely legible inscription
below the Last Judgment. If this date is correct, then the paintings of the Passion series are even earlier, as the Last Judgment and portraits of the caciques
were added later.

26. "THIS JUDGMENT PAINTED FOR THE DEVOTION OF THE TOWN OF SUTA.
BEING CACIQUE DON DOMINGO AND CAPITANES DON LÁZARO, Don Neaeta-
riguia, Don Juan Corula and Doña Ana. Year 16[26])" (Lara 1996, 263) (PINTÓSE
ESTE JUICIO A DEVOCIÓN DE EL PUEBLO DE SUTA. SIENDO CACIQUE DON
DOMINGO Y CAPITANES DON LÁZARO, Don Neaetariguia, Don Juan Corula y
Doñana. Año 16[26]). Note that we have read the last name as "Don Andrés."

27. "Otros le llamaban a este hombre Nemterequeteba, otros le decían Xué. Este les
enseño hilar algodón y tejer mantas, porque antes de esto sólo se cubrían los
indios con unas planchas que hacían de algodón en rama, atadas con unas cor-
dezuelas de fique unas con otras, todo mal aliñado y aún como a gente ruda.
Cuando salía de un pueblo les dejaba los telares pintados en alguna piedra lisa y
bruñida, como hoy se ven en algunas partes, por si se les olvidaba lo que les en-
señaba. . . . Enseñóles a hacer cruces y usar de ellas en las pinturas de las mantas
con que se cubrían y por ventura, declarándoles sus misterios y los de la encar-
nación y muerte de Cristo."

28. The gendered character of native participation in the literate legal system of
Santa Fé de Bogotá is analyzed in Marta Zambrano Escovar (2008).

CONCLUSION

1. "Estando ya mui al cauo cierta mujer que la visitaua y conocia enbio por vn
jeque ques sacerdote de idolos entro el mal viejo en la casa de la enfermera
lleuando los riquisitos para su intento masco ayo veuio tabaco començo en vos
vaja a entonar ciertos cantisos que son como conzevios llamo los demonios por

sus nombres hablo con ellos y auiendo concluido con todas sus çeremonias en presencia de la enferma dio luego quenta del suçeso diciendo aueis de sauer que los antepasados parientes desta india hizieron en tal parte vn templo de ydolos el qual destruyo el maldito encomendero de aquel pueblo y por este tan grande peccado castigaron los dios a la inocente india pero con todo tiene facil remedio si obedece a lo que manda el idolo y es que conpre la enferma vn papagayo y vn mico los quales criara por espacio de dos años y al cavo lleuara a ofrecer aquel templo por manos del jeque y se esto promete no esolo estara luego buena sino que sera mui rica y de buenaventura."

2. "Pareciale que estaua en su cama mui sosegada y quieta aunque enferma y estando despierta entraua por su choça la serenisima de los angeles Nuestra Señora del Rosario venia asentada en una silla de oro con el Niño Jesus en los braços que hera hermosissimo por estremo. El niño no hablo palabra a la enferma pero estauala mirando con mui alegre y risueño senblante. La virgen tenia vn rostro que se queria deshazer la buena india para dar a entender su hermosura y al fin dixo que le faltaua palabras para splicarla de su caueça y cauellos dixo que le salian vnos rayos y vn resplandor scmejante al del sol quando sale por la mañana y sus vestidos era como planchas de oro. La Virgen pues con toda su magestad se allego a la cama y con mucha afauilidad la toco en la caueça diciendo que presto vendrian a visitarla dos padres de Sancto Domingo y quedaria sana. Dicho esto desaparecio la vision y luego vio venir dos niños hijos suyos pequeños que auian muerto receuido el sancto bautismo vestidos de tela de oro con sus cauellos de naçareos y quatro angeles mucho mas hermosos que ellos vestidos tanbien hasta la rrodilla mui ricamente con vnas hermosas cruces de oro en sus frentes tras de los angeles llegaron dos religiosos de Sancto Domingo y poniendole las manos sobre la caueça y aciendo oracion por ella se boluieron a salir en procesion como quando entraron no parecieron mas. Desperto la enferma luego como de vn dulce sueño y viendose amortajada començo a rebullirse y dar gritos conque acudiendo los de casa la descosieron y rasgaron la mortaja mui espantados del suceso pareciendoles que hera milagroso y aunque le preguntaron muchas cosas jamas quiso descubrir nada desde entonces mudo la vida procediendo mui de otra suerte."

References Cited

ARCHIVES

Archivio Generale della Compagnia di Gesù, Roma (AGCG/R). 1605. "Carta annua de la vice provincia del Nueuo Reyno y Quito en los Reynos del Peru." (por el padre Diego de Torres), *Novi Regni et Quitensis, Historia*, 12-I, 1r–23r.

———. 1606. "Decreto de don Juan de Borja, Presidente, Gouernador y Capitan General" (25 agosto). *Novi Regni et Quitensis* 14, doc. 6, 48r–50r.

———. 1608–9. "Letras annuas de la vice provincia de Quito y el Nueuo Reyno de los años de mil y seyscientos y ocho y seycientos y nuebe" (por el padre Gonçalo de López). *Novi Regni et Quitensis, Historia* 12-I, 36r–60v.

———. 1611–12. "Letras annuas de la Prouinçia del Nueuo Reyno del año de 1611 y 612" (por Gonzalo de Lyra), *Novi Regni et Quitensis*, 12-I, 61/2–108/9.

———. 1616. "Annua della Prouincia del Nuouo Regno di Granada dell anno 1615" (por Manuel di Arceo). *Novi Regni et Quitensis*, 12-II, 111–90.

Archivo Central del Cauca, Popayán (ACC/P). 1881 [1700]. "Titulo de las parcialidades de Pitayo, Quichaya, Caldono, Pueblo Nuevo y Jambalo." *Protocolos Notariales*, partida 843.

———. 1883 [1708]. "Titulo de resguardo de Vitoncó." *Protocolos Notariales*, partida 959.

Archivo del Cabildo Indígena del Gran Cumbal, Nariño (ACIGC/N). 1950. "Borradores de cartas del Cabildo al Ministerio de Minas, sobre los yacimientos de azufre del Cerro de Cumbal." *Asuntos Varios*.

Archivo General de Indias, Seville (AGI/S). 1555a. "Catechismo breve y muy sumario . . . ordenado por el muy reverendo Padre Donosio de Sanchez . . . de la orden de los predicatores y obispo de Cartagena." *Patronato* 196, r. 10, 1/2, 130v–62r.

———. 1555b. "Recomendación de los indios del Valle de Jauja." *Lima* 567,1. 8, 107v–108r.

———. 1558–59. "Traslado del libro de tassaciones quel muy magnifico señor licenciado Tomas Lopez hizo en la gobernacion e provincia de Popayan." *Quito* 60, 1.

———. 1559. "Información de méritos y servicios de Don Sancho, cacique y governador de la Tacunga, en solicitud de un escudo de armas, cuyo dibujo acompaña, y de otras mercedes." *Quito* 22, n. 16.3.

———. 1563. "Expediente de Guacar Paucar." *Contratación* 5537, l. 3.

———. 1568. "Probanza de Don Sancho de Velasco cacique y gobernador de la Tacunga." *Quito* 22, n. 16.1, r. 1.

———. 1570–71. "Tassacion de los tributos de los naturales de las ciudades de San Joan de Pasto y Almaguer de la governacion de Popayan hecha por el señor licenciado Garcia de Valverde . . ." *Quito* 60, 2.

———. 1573. "Residencias. Lima." *Justicia* 465.

———. 1574. "Descripcion de los yndios, todos de la provincia de Musso, por Don Francisco Guillen." *Patronato* 196, r. 15.

———. 1576. "Causa contra Diego de la Torre por el levantamiento que intentó en el Nuevo Granada." *Escribanía de Cámara* 825A.

———. 1577. "Carta de Juan de Cabrera a Su Magestad en que dice la necesidad de aislar a los niños indios en escuelas." *Quito* 82, n. 6.

———. 1578–88. "Real Cédula a los oficiales de la Casa de Contratación para que den licencia de pasajeros a Pedro de Henao, indio y a dos criados que trajo y que pueda lleva también un maestro de azulejos y un organista que pueden llevar a sus familias." *Quito* 211, l. 2.

———. 1579. "Permiso por Luis de Quero, natural de Ocaña, para ir al Nuevo Reino de Granada como criado de Don Diego de Torre." *Contratación* 5538, l. 1, 215r.

———. 1582. "Expediente de Pedro de Henao, indio principal de la provincia de Quito, gobernador de los pueblos de Ipiales y Potosí en el corregimiento de los Pastos, pidiendo confirmación de dicho título de gobernador." *Quito* 22, n. 38.

———. 1583. "Carta acordada del consejo a Antonio de Cartajena, su receptor, dándoles orden de pago de 100 reales a Pedro de Henao, indio principal de Quito." *Indiferente* 426, l. 27. 63v.

———. 1584a. "Carta acordada del consejo a Antonio de Cartagena, su receptor, dándoles orden de pago de 10 ducados a Pedro de Henao, cacique natural de la Provincia de Quito." *Indiferente* 426, l. 27, 73r–v.

———. 1584b. "Carta acordada del consejo a Antonio de Cartagena, su receptor, dándoles orden de pago de 3 ducados a Pedro de Henao, cacique natural de la Provincia de Quito." *Indiferente* 426, l. 27, 78v.

———. 1584c. "Carta acordada del consejo a Antonio de Cartagena, su receptor, dándoles orden de pago de 10 ducados a Pedro de Henao, cacique natural de la Provincia de Quito." *Indiferente* 426, l. 27, 91r–v.

———. 1586a. "Carta acordada del consejo a Antonio de Cartagena, su receptor, dándoles orden de pago de 100 ducados a Pedro de Henao, indio, para gastos del viaje hasta Sevilla." *Indiferente* 426, l. 27, 128r.

————. 1586b. "La relacion que Don Diego de la Torre, cacique, hizo a Su Magestad sobre los agravios que a los naturales del Nuevo Reyno de Granada se hazen por las personas en quien Su Magestad los tiene encomendados y de la manera que se consumen y acaban y el poco fruto que con ellos se ha hecho en su conversion." *Patronato* 196, r. 16, 226r–44v.

————. 1590. "Sentencia sobre el cacicazgo de Turmeque por Don Diego de Torre remitido por la Audiencia de Santafe de Nueva Granada." *Escribanía de Cámara* 953.

————. 1600. "Carta de Juan de Barrio y Sepulveda, oidor de la Audiencia de Quito, a Su Magestad." *Quito* 9, r. 3, n. 21.

————. 1604. "Real Cedula sobre un colegio de hijos de caciques que ha fundado en Quito." *Quito* 211, l. 3.

————. 1608. "Carta de Fray Gabriel Ramirez, Comisario General de la Orden de San Francisco de las Provincias de Santo Domingo, Caracas, Nuevo Reino de Granada y Quito a Su Magestad." *Quito* 85, n. 34.

————. 1613. "Carta de Francisco de Tuna y Diego de Suba." In "Expediente sobre la solicitud de Francisco y Diego, caciques de Tuna y Suba, de una real cedula para la restauracion de unas tierras que les habian arrebatadas en estas dos poblaciones." *Santa Fe* 165, n. 55, 4.

————. 1633. "Autos de bienes de los herederos de Juana de Oropesa, viuda de Diego de Torre, cacique de Turmeque, difunta en Madrid, con testamento y codicilio, por los corridos de anuales que tenía situados en indios vacos del partido de Soraca en el Nuevo Reino de Granada." *Contratación* 959, 1r–20v.

————. 1634. "Expediente de Fernando Ayra de Arritu, principal y gobernador de Copoatá." *Charcas* 56, 6r–71v.

————. 1770. "Carta numero 324 de Amat a Julian de Arriaga, Secretario de las Indias, remite 20 lienzo de la mezcla de yndios y negros." *Lima* 652, n. 57, 236r–38r.

————. 1755. "Real disposicion, carta a Don Juan Simon Vengel de la Cruz, cacique de Bogota, por haver concluido las dependencias a que vino a España." *Contratación* 5490, n. 4.

Archivo General de la Nación, Bogotá (AGN/B). 1561–65. "El licenciado Garcia de Valverde, fiscal de la Real Audiencia de Santa Fe, se queja de la visita que practico el oidor Angulo de Castejon." *Caciques e Indios*, t. 5, 456r–602v.

————. 1567. "Testamento de Juana, yndia ladina cristiana." *Notaría Primera*, t. 1, 202r–v.

————. 1574. "Diego de Torres y principales de Turmequé contra Pedro de Torres por la encomienda." *Encomiendas*, t. 21, 392–594.

————. 1576. "Acta de la fundación de un colegio para instruir a los indios en la doctrina cristiana y compra de una casa y solares contiguos al convento del Carmen, con tal objeto." *Conventos*, t. 78, 768r–70r.

————. 1586. "Censo de población indígena de Cucunubá y Simijaca . . ." *Visitas de Cundinamarca*, t. 1, no. 5, 808–73.

————. 1594–1600. "Visita a la iglesia de Sutatausa." *Visitas de Boyacá*, t. 2, 801v–27r.

————. 1602. "Mapa del pueblo de Gemara." *Mapoteca* SMP4, ref. 169A.

————. 1609–10. "Causa mortuoria de los herederos de don Juan, cacique de Guatavita." *Notaría Primera*, t. 31, 371v–80r.

————. 1617a. "Testamento de Juan Lara, lengua interprete de la Real Audiencia." *Notaría Segunda*, t. 17, 181–82.

————. 1617b. "Testamento de Juan de Quintanilla, yndio natural del pueblo de Ramiquiri." *Notaría Segunda*, t. 18, 42r–43v.

————. 1617c. "Testamento de Juan, yndio de Ontibon." *Notaría Segunda*, t. 18, 85v–87r.

————. 1619a. "Testamento de Diego, indio ladino de Duytama." *Notaría Primera*, t. 1, 667r–68v.

————. 1619b. "Testimonio a favor de Pedro, indio principal de Guesca, en un pleito sobre tierras." *Notaría Primera*, t. 36, 701r–4v.

————. 1629a. "Testamento de Catalina, yndia criolla de Suta." *Notaría Tercera*, t. 26, 1r–2r.

————. 1629b. "Testamento de Pedro Casua, capitán del pueblo de Tuna." *Notaría Tercera*, t. 26, 75r–77r.

————. 1629c. "Testamento de Don Juan, cacique del pueblo de Tinjaca." *Caciques e Indios*, t. 74, 730r–38v.

————. 1630a. "Testamento de Beatriz, yndia de Chipaque." *Notaría Tercera*, t. 26, 47v.

————. 1630b. "Testamento y codicilio de Ana de Coro, yndia ladina criolla de Santa Fe." *Notaría Tercera*, t. 26, 73r–74v and 79r–80v.

————. 1630c. "Testamento de Francisca, yndia vecina de Santa Fe." *Notaría Tercera*, t. 26, 40r–41v.

————. 1633a. "Testamento y codicilios de Don Andres, cacique de Macheta." *Notaria Tercera*, t. 38, 89r–94r and 96v–98v.

————. 1633b. "Testamento de Francisca Coro, yndia ladina yanacona vecina de Santa Fe." *Notaría Tercera*, t. 38, 80v–81v.

————. 1633c. "Testamento de Juana, yndia del pueblo de Guasca, vecina en la ciudad de Santa Fe." *Notaría Tercera*, t. 38, 99r–100v.

————. 1633d. "Testamento de Juana Sanguino, yndia vecina de Santafe." *Notaría Tercera*, t. 38, 142v–43v.

————. 1633e. "Testamento de Francisco Texar, yndio vecino de Santafe y natural del pueblo de Ubaque." *Notaría Tercera*, t. 38, 82v–83v.

————. 1633f. "Testamento de Ysabel, yndia criolla." *Notaría Tercera*, t. 38, 109r–10r.

————. 1633g. "Testamento de Luis Ximenez, yndio ladino de Santafe." *Notaria Tercera*, t. 37, 67v–68r.

———. 1655a. "Testamento de Maria Teues, yndia ladina de Santafe." *Notaría Primera*, t. 50, 97r–98v.

———. 1665b. "Testamento de Don Francisco Bojaca, indio gobernador de Tabio." *Notaría Primera*, t. 67, 368r–73r.

———. 1668a. "Codicilio al testamento de Catalina de Cespedes, yndia ladina." *Notaría Primera*, t. 72, 452r–v.

———. 1668b. "Testamento de Pasquala de Cotrina, yndia ladina." *Notaría Primera*, t. 73, 53r–56v.

———. 1668c. "Testamento de Don Juan, cacique de Caxicá." *Notaría Primera*, t. 73, 198r–204r.

———. 1758–59. "Testamento de Manuel Supativa." *Caciques e Indios*, t. 53, 316–35.

Archivo Histórico del Banco Central del Ecuador, Ibarra (AHBC/I). 1592 "Testamento de Christobal Cuatin, principal del pueblo de Tuza." 1339/244/1/M (transcription by Cristóbal Landázuri).

———. 1593. "Carta de venta que otorga Don Francisco Cuatin, principal del pueblo de Tusa, a favor de Don Andres Guachan, gobernador del pueblo de Puechuquin, una caballeria en terminos del pueblo de Puntal." *Protocolos Notariales*, 1593, 14r. 9/1/9/J.

———. 1606 "Testamento de Catalina Tuza, principal del pueblo de Tuza." 1335/295/1/M (transcription by Cristóbal Landázuri).

———. 1634a. "Escritura de donacion de tierras que otorga Don Diego Taques a su hijo, Marcos Taques." *Protocolos Notariales*, 1634, 52r–53r. 51/13/0/J.

———. 1634b. "Querella por despojo de tierras entre Don Diego Paspuel y Don Diego Guachagmira." *Protocolos Notariales*, 1634, 53v–54v. 51/13/0/J.

———. 1639. "Escritura de venta de tierras que otorga Pedro Baes de la Cruz a Cristobal Taquez." *Protocolos Notariales*, 1639–40, 858r–59r. 55/17/1/J.

———. 1649. "Censo. Don Clemente Cuatimpas, la capellania de Don Diego Paspuel." *Protocolos Notariales*, 1646–49, 550–52. 58/20/1/J.

———. 1654. "Protocolos y testamentos a cargo de Juan Francisco Guapastal, escribano nombrado de Tulcan." 1140/39/6/M.

———. 1656. "Venta de tierras que hace Joan Quatimpas, Felipe Tusa y Brigida Tusa, naturales de Tusa, a Doña Ana Tusa." *Protocolos Notariales*, 1656–59, 16v–17v. 63/25/0/J.

———. 1671. "Cristoval Garcia Paspuel, casique principal y gobernador de los pueblos de Puntal y Angel y Tusa y su mujer Doña Francisca Tusa e hijos Sebastian Garcia Paspuel Tusa y Cristoval Garcia Paspuel Tusa, venden a Juan del Castillo Jimenez, una estancia y tierras de pan sembrar de cuatro caballerias junto al pueblo del Puntal." *Protocolos Notariales*, 1770–74, 79r–80v. 113/75/0/J.

———. 1673. "Venta de dos pedazos de tierra que hacen Pedro y Manuel Yangara en favor de Paula Rosero." *Protocolos Notariales*, 1672–73, 304r–v. 68/30/0/J.

———. 1674. "Testamento de Don Sebastian Garcia Paspuel Tusa, cacique de Puntal, Tusa y El Angel." 1164/268/1/M.

————. 1680. "Ymposicion de capellania a Don Xptoual Garcia Paspuel Tusa, gobernador de los pueblos de Tusa, Puntal y Angel, residente en esta villa, en favor del primer capellan, Joan Duque de Estrada, de principal de 1000 p." *Protocolos Notariales*, 1680–83, 84r–85v. 74/36/0/J.

————. 1688. "El cacique de Tusa vende tierras a un yndio." *Protocolos Notariales*, 1759–64, 235r–v. 108/70/0/J.

————. 1691a. "Transacsion y conuenio de Don Xpobal Garcia Paspuel Tusa y Don Visente Paspuel, sobre el quinto." *Protocolos Notariales*, 1691–92, 130v–31r. 80/42/1/J.

————. 1691b. "Transaccion y conuenio de Don Juan Quatimpas y Don Phelipe Tuspas, sobre las tierras de Quezacahuel [terminos de Puntal]." *Protocolos Notariales*, 1691–92, 194r–95r. 80/42/1/J.

————. 1691–92. "Protocolos notariales a cargo de Blas Rubio de Pereira." *Protocolos Notariales*, 1691–92, 125v–95r. 80/42/1/J.

————. 1699. "Venta de cuatro cuadras de tierras en Mumiar, que hace Cristobal Garcia Paspuel Tusa, cacique principal de Puntal, Tusa y el Antel, en favor de Sebastian Galindes." *Protocolos Notariales*, 1699–1701, 143r–50r. 85/47/0/J.

————. 1703. "Convenio entre Don Phelipe Garcia Yapud y Don Simon Guaspiramag, su suegro, del pueblo de Tusa, y por la otra parte, Gabriel Vaez de la Cruz, hijo legitimo de Marcos Vaes de la Cruz, sobre tierras de Quesaca." *Protocolos Notariales*, 1702–3, fol. 241r. 87/49/0/J.

————. 1707. "Venta de tierras en Puntal que otorga Thomas Garcia Paspuel Tusa, cacique principal de Tusa, Puntal y el Angel, residente en la villa de Ibarra." *Protocolos Notariales*, 1707–12, 56r–57r. 90/52/0/J.

————. 1713. "Testamento de Don Ambrocio Fernandez Taquez." In AHBC/1, 1787, "Demanda que hace Pedro Ramon de Rueda, Protector Sustituto de los Naturales, en nombre de Bernardo Garcia Tulcanaza y otros, a Francisco Perez, quien se ha introducido en las tierras que estan a beneficio del comun de los indios." 979/232/3/J.

————. 1727a. "Venta de vn pedaso de tierras en terminos del pueblo del Puntal, Don Luis Guaspiramag, en fauor de Don Bartholome Quastusa, [cacique y] gouernador de Guaca, en 40 patacones de contado." *Protocolos Notariales*, 1725–28, 445r–v.

————. 1727b. "Venta de dos partes de los bienes de Don Matias Quatinpas, Bacelio Chacon, en fabor de Juan de Roxas." *Protocolos Notariales*, 1725–28, 496r–98r. 97/59/0/J.

————. 1727c. "Venta de los caballerias de tierras nombradas Calipud en therminos de el pueblo del Puntal, los herederos de Don Sebastian Ytamay, indio, en fauor de Xptobal Nay, yndio, en 50 p. de contado." *Protocolos Notariales*, 1725–28, 502r–3v. 97/59/0/J.

————. 1727d. "Data y señalamiento de herensia, Doña Marta de Santamaria, yndia, en unas tierras en Tuza, en fauor de los hijos de Doña Magdalena Santamaria, su hermana." *Protocolos Notariales*, 1725–28, 503v–5r. 97/59/0/J.

————. 1732. "Los indios Paspueles venden tierras a la cofradia de Tusa." *Protocolos Notariales*, 1724–36, 204r–7v. 99/61/0/J.

————. 1736. "Un cacique de Tusa hipoteca tierras por deuda." Protocolos Notariales, 266r–67v. 100/62/0/J.

————. 1739. "Testamento de Don Pablo Taques, cacique de Tulcan." In AHBC/I, 1787, "Demanda que hace Pedro Ramon de Rueda, Protector Sustituto de los Naturales, en nombre de Bernardo Garcia Tulcanaza y otros, a Francisco Perez, quien se ha introducido en las tierras que estan a beneficio del comun de los indios." 979/232/3/J.

————. 1748. "Testamento de Mateo Quatinpaz." 375/104/1/M.

————. 1768. "El gobernador de Tusa vende tierras a un yndio." *Protocolos Notariales*, 1765–68, 368r(a)–68v(a). 110/72/0/J.

————. 1783. "Venta que hace Don Francisco Xavier de Mena de una cuadra de tierras en el sitio de Mumiar, en favor de Don Calisto Paspuel Tusa." *Protocolos Notariales*, 1783, 101v–3r. 1660/76–b/4/J.

————. 1791. "Agustin Paspuel Tusa, principal de Tusa, sobre tierras heredadas en Mumiar, terminos de Puntal." *Protocolos Notariales*, 1771, 27r–28r. 1459/358/1/J.

Archivo Histórico del Banco Central del Ecuador, Quito (AHBC/Q). n.d. "Testamento de Don Pedro Pastas, casique principal del pueblo de Pastas." In AHBC/Q, 1748, "Autos seguidos por Don Gregorio Putag, casique del pueblo de San Juan de Pasto [*sic*] con Don Pedro Pastas y vna calumnia que falsamente le a atribuido." 19/2, 135v–37r.

————. 1588. "Testamento de Don Gomes Pastas, cacique principal del Pueblo de Pastas." In AHBC/Q, 1748, "Autos seguidos por Don Gregorio Putag, casique del pueblo de San Juan de Pasto [*sic*] con Don Pedro Pastas y vna calumnia que falsamente le a atribuido." 19/2, 134r–35v.

————. 1709. "Testamento de Don Juan Pastas y Sapuis Asa." In AHBC/Q, 1748, "Autos seguidos por Don Gregorio Putag, casique del pueblo de San Juan de Pasto [*sic*] con Don Pedro Pastas y vna calumnia que falsamente le a atribuido." 19/2, 137r–v.

————. 1710. "Testamento de Don Antonio Cumbal Quaical, casique principal de la parcialidad de Cumbal." In AHBC/Q, 1748, "Autos seguidos por Don Gregorio Putag, casique del pueblo de San Juan de Pasto [*sic*] con Don Pedro Pastas y vna calumnia que falsamente le a atribuido." 19/2, 250r–52r.

————. 1720. "Testamento de Don Francisco Pastas, cacique absoluto del pueblo de San Juan de Pastas." In AHBC/Q, 1748, "Autos seguidos por Don Gregorio Putag, casique del pueblo de San Juan de Pasto [*sic*] con Don Pedro Pastas y vna calumnia que falsamente le a atribuido." 19/2, 215r–16v.

————. 1739. "Autos seguidos por Don Ventura Assa, pidiendo se le posesione del cacicazgo de Guachocal en la provincia de los Pastos." Archivo Jijón y Caamaño 18/8, 212–23.

————. 1748. "Autos seguidos por Don Gregorio Putag, casique del pueblo de San

Juan de Pasto [*sic*] con Don Pedro Pastas y vna calumnia que falsamente le a atribuido." 19/2, 125–265.

Archivo Histórico de Tierradentro, Belalcázar (AHT/B). 1729. "Tierras de los ocho pueblos . . ."

Archivo Nacional del Ecuador, Quito (ANE/Q). n.d.a. "Testamento de Don Francisco Aza." In ANE/Q, 1735, "Autos de Don Reymundo Cuaycal sobre el casicasgo de Cumbal." *Popayán*, caja 55, 33r–v. NB: Note that the holdings of the Archivo Nacional del Ecuador have been reclassified several times since our data was collected. References to documents in this archive must, consequently, be sought by date, rather than by box number, and there are numerous boxes for each year. It is for this reason that we have opted for this lengthy form of reporting our references. We have also chosen to record our sources by identifying documents, such as wills, embedded in later documentation, instead of simply listing the compilation.

———. n.d.b. "Testamento de Don Sebastian Calisto, principal mayor de Carlosama de la parcialidad de Yaputa." In ANE/Q, 1747, "Autos de Don Visente Garcia Yaputa, gobernador, y el comun de yndios del pueblo de Carlosama, con Don Mariano Paredes, sobre las tierras nombradas Yapudquer y San Sevastian, en los Pastos." *Popayán*, caja 75, 3v–8v.

———. n.d.c. "Testamento de Don Christobal Garcia Carlosama, cacique principal del pueblo de Carlosama." In ANE/Q, 1735, "Autos de Don Reymundo Cuaical sobre el casicasgo de Cumbal." *Popayán*, caja 55, 55r–58r.

———. n.d.d. "Testamento de Jacoba Heznam." In ANE/Q, 1792, "Titulos y ynstrumentos de los yndios y casiques del pueblo de Tusa sobre la propiedad de vnas tierras." *Cacicazgos*, caja 3 (Carchi), Cuaderno 14.

———. n.d.e. "Testamento de Andres Tapued, principal y mandon cobrador de los tributos reales del ayllo de Tayan." In ANE/Q, 1772, "Autos de Don Juan Rosero, vecino de la Provincia de los Pastos, con los indios de Tulcan, sobre unas tierras indigenas." *Indigenas*, caja 97, 7v–9v.

———. n.d."Testamento de Andres Yazam." In ANE/Q, 1772, "Autos de Don Juan Rosero, vecino de la Provincia de los Pastos, con los indios de Tulcan, sobre unas tierras indigenas." *Indigenas*, caja 97, 3v–4v.

———. 1585 "Testamento de Don Fernando Titamuesnan, principal de Tuquerres." In ANE/Q, 1735, "Thomas Rodriguez de Herrera, con Fray Jose Pintado, sobre las tierras de Yanguel." *Popayán*, caja 55, 103v–5r.

———. 1589 "Testamento de Don Diego Guachaocal Aça, cacique principal del pueblo de Guachocal." In "Don Juan Ipialpud contra Rafael Assa, sobre el cacicazgo de Guachocal." ANE/Q, 1695, *Popayán*, caja 13, 48r–49v.

———. 1624. "Testamento de Doña Luisa Actasen." In ANE/Q, 1735, "Thomas Rodriguez de Herrera, con Fray Jose Pintado, sobre las tierras de Yanguel." *Popayán*, caja 55, 86r–88r.

———. 1634a. "Autos del señor licenciado Manuel Suarez de Poago fiscal de Su

Magestad en esta Real Audiencia por la defensa de los caciquez de Tuza, Puntal y Angel contra Alonso Yanez, Alonso Garcia Jatiua, Felipe Zamora y otros complices sobrel despojo de la tierra de los yndios de Tuça, Angel y Puntal." *Indígenas*, caja 3.

———. 1634b. "Testamento de Miguel Guaichar, natural del pueblo de Guachaves." In ANE/Q, 1765, "Autos de Esteuan Guaychan, yndio natural del pueblo de Guachaues, sobre las tierras de Ybilan." *Popayán*, caja 115.

———. 1647. "Don Marcos Taques, cacique del pueblo de Tulcan, contra su sobrino Garcia Tulcanaza, quien ha cedido las tierras de su tio a un español." *Indígenas*, caja 5.

———. 1650. "Traslado segundo de la numeracion, quenta y discrepcion de los yndios de los yndios [*sic*] del pueblo de Guaca de las parcialidades de Pu Chuquin de la Corona Real fecha por el capitan Diego de Alarcon Uribe, corregidor y justicia mayor de la villa de San Miguel de Yvarra." *Indígenas*, caja 6.

———. 1653. "Testamento de Doña Esperanza Carlosama, cacica principal del pueblo de Carlosama." In ANE/Q 1735, "Autos de Don Reymundo Quaycal sobre el casicasgo de Cumbal." *Popayán*, caja 55, 34r v.

———. 1656. "Don Gabriel Naçate, casique de Cumbal, contra Don Alonso Godoy, sobre tierras." *Indígenas*, caja 7.

———. 1661. "Testamento de Doña Esperansa Gauilan, natural de Puntal." In ANE/Q, 1792, "Titulos y ynstrumentos de los yndios y casiques del pueblo de Tusa sobre la propiedad de vnas tierras." *Cacicazgos*, caja 3 (Carchi), cuaderno 8.

———. 1669. "Proceso seguido por Salvador Marin Delgado con el capitan Andres de Espana, sobre unas tierras nombradas Chapaqual." *Popayán*, caja 4.

———. 1677. "Los gouernadores y casiques de Muellamues y Guachocal sobre visita de tierras." *Popayán*, caja 6.

———. 1680. "El presbitero Don Joseph Freyre de Bohorques con los casiques del Puntal, sobre unas tierras que son de las lomas de Quasmal, Pilpudis, Chalqualam, y Piartales." *Indígenas*, caja 8.

———. 1681a. "Testamento de Don Marcos Taques." In "Patricio Cisneros contra Maria Taques Garcia Tulcanasa, cacica principal de Tulban, por las tierras de Carampuer." ANE/Q, 1727, *Indigenas*, caja 46, 43r–45v.

———. 1681b. "Testamento de Don Sebastian Carlosama." In ANE/Q, 1736, "Don Domingo Garcia Yaputa, Gobernador del pueblo de Carlosama, sobre el cacicazgo de Carlosama." *Popayán*, caja 58, 4v–9v.

———. 1685. "Materia seguida por Lucas Falconi, cacique de Botana, sobre licencia de venta de tierras." *Popayán*, caja 8.

———. 1686. "Materia seguida por Esteban Velazquez de Obando con el Gobernador de Pasto, sobre arrendamientos de tierras y ganados." *Popayán*, caja 8.

———. 1689. "Testamento de Don Francisco Paspuel Guachan de Mendoza, cacique principal del Pueblo de Tuza." In ANE/Q, 1757, "Cuaderno de los instrumentos de la escritura de venta, otorgada por Don Pedro Guatinango a Don

Andres Gualsago y testamento de Don Francisco Pasquel Guachan en la causa que siguen Don Hernando de Cuatinpas y Don Pedro Garcia, principales del pueblo de Tusa, con Don Antonio Luna, sobre tierras." *Indigenas*, caja 77, 10r–21r.

———. 1691a. "Testamento de Doña Micaila Garsia Puenambas." In ANE/Q 1695, "Don Juan Bautista Ypialpud, casique de Guachocal, con Don Raphael Assa, sobre el cacicazgo de Guachocal." *Popayán*, caja 13, 38r–39r.

———. 1691b. "Remate de las tierras del Nuevo Mundo (Mira) en nombre del ayudante Geronimo Mantilla." *Tierras*, caja 17.

———. 1693. "Autos del Alferes Real Nicholas Gregorio Zambrano sobre el remate de un pedaso de tierra del pueblo de Quina, jurisdiccion de Pasto." *Popayán*, caja 12.

———. 1694. "Materia seguida por don Ambrosio de Prado y Sayalpud, sobre el cacicazgo de Cumbal." *Popayán*, caja 13.

———. 1695. "Don Juan Bautista Ypialpud, casique de Guachocal, con Don Raphael Assa, sobre el cacicazgo de Guachocal." *Popayán*, caja 13.

———. 1696. "Composicion de la hacienda y tierras del sitio de Pisquer, por Don Antonio de Ron." *Tierras*, caja 23.

———. 1697. "Testamento de Don Francisco Paspuel Guachag y Mendosa, cacique principal de San Pedro de Guaca." In ANE/Q, 1759, "Autos seguidos por el Protector General por la defensa del cacique gobernador y comun de indios del pueblo de Guaca." *Indígenas*, caja 80 (no pagination).

———. 1700. "Testamento de Lorenso Tarambis." In ANE/Q, 1772, "Autos de Don Juan Rosero, vecino de la Provincia de los Pastos, con los indios de Tulcan, sobre unas tierras indigenas." *Indígenas*, caja 97, 11v–13v.

———. 1707. "Diego Maita, Juan Guatimpas, Francisco Paspuel y los otros principales de los pueblos de Tusa y Puntal piden que se le quite al gobernador Vicente Paspuel Tuza el gobierno de esos pueblos." *Indígenas*, caja 33.

———. 1709. "Testamento de Don Mathias Quatimpas, principal del pueblo de Tusa."In ANE/Q, 1746, "Autos en favor de Miguel Garcia Paspuel Tuza por unas tierras que heredo de su abuela." *Indigenas*, caja 63, 7r–10v.

———. 1711. "Testamento de Don Feliz Quastuza, cacique principal del pueblo de Guaca." In ANE/Q, 1734, "Autos de Domingo Yaputa, Francisco Paspuel Tuza y demas caciques de Guaca, sobre las tierras nombradas San Bartolome." *Indígenas*, caja 53, 3r–7r.

———. 1716. "Autos de los yndios del pueblo de Cumbal en la Provincia de los Pastos, sobre los agrauios que a hecho el Maestre de Campo Don Bernardo de Erasso." *Popayán*, caja 36.

———. 1720b. "Testamento de Don Ambrosio Taques, cacique de la parcialidad de Taques." In ANE/Q, 1762, "Autos de Feliciano Hecher, gobernador de Taques, con Don Andres Garcia, cacique de Tulcan, sobre una caballeria de tierras nombradas Santiago." *Indígenas*, caja 85, 2v–3r.

———. 1723. "Autos de Doña Gertrudes Zambrano de Benavides sobre la encomienda de Muellamas." *Popayán*, caja 41.

———. 1727a. "Doña Juana de Basuri y Sanbursi sobre que se le entregue la encomienda de Buesaquillo en Pasto." *Popayán*, caja 45.

———. 1727b. "Paula Cogollo Tuza del pueblo de Tuza, contra el corregidor, por el embargo de unas tierras suyas y de su hija." *Indígenas*, caja 47.

———. 1729. "Testamento de Don Nicolas Garcia Paspuel Tusa, casique principal de los pueblos de Tusa, Puntal y Angel." In ANE/Q 1771 "Autos de proclama de Don Matheo Garcia Paspuel Tusa, casique principal de los pueblos del Angel, Puntal y Tusa, en la jurisdiccion de la Villa de San Miguel de Ibarra, para que le den posesion del dicho cacicazgo." *Cacicazgos -Volúmenes*, caja 35, vol. 62, 38v–43r.

———. 1730a. "Testamento de Doña Pascuala Tainbupas." In ANE/Q, 1746, "Autos en favor de Miguel Garcia Paspuel Tuza por unas tierras que heredo de su abuela." *Indigenas* 63, 3r–5v.

———. 1730b. "Testamento de Don Thoriuio Taquez, principal mayor del pueblo de Tulcan." In ANE/Q, 1727, "Patricio Cisneros contra Maria Taques Garcia Tulcanasa, cacica principal de Tulban, por las tierras de Carampuer." *Indígenas*, caja 46, 15r–v.

———. 1732. "Autos de Augustin de Ribera sobre que se le declare por montañes." *Popayán*, caja 52.

———. 1733. "Testamento de Don Celidonio Garcia Paspuel Tusa, caçique principal de los pueblos de Tusa, Puntal y Angel." In ANE/Q 1771 "Autos de proclama de Don Matheo Garcia Paspuel Tusa, casique principal de los pueblos del Angel, Puntal y Tusa, en la jurisdiccion de la Villa de San Miguel de Ibarra, para que le den posesion del dicho cacicazgo." *Cacicazgos -Volúmenes*, caja 35, vol. 62, 35r–38v.

———. 1735a. "Autos de Don Reymundo Guaycal sobre el casicasgo de Cumbal." *Popayán*, caja 55.

———. 1735b. "Thomas Rodriguez de Herrera, con Fray Jose Pintado, sobre las tierras de Yanguel." *Popayán*, caja 55.

———. 1736. "Don Domingo Garcia Yaputa, gobernador del pueblo de Carlosama, sobre el cacicazgo de Carlosama." *Popayán*, caja 58.

———. 1743. "Autos de Melchor Narvaes vesino de Tumaco, en que pide no le cobren tributos por montañes." *Popayán*, caja 66.

———. 1746. "Autos de Francisco Cobo, mulato, sobre que le exima de la paga de tributos." *Popayán*, caja 72.

———. 1753. "Don Francisco Prado con los indios de Pastas, sobre un salado." *Popayán*, caja 86.

———. 1757. "Don Joseph Cuatin y Don Manuel Caype, principales y gouernadores del pueblo de Mollamuez, con Antonio de la Ampudia, sobre el servicio en las haciendas." *Popayán*, caja 97.

———. 1759. "Testamento de Doña Luisa Chescued, natural del pueblo de Tusa." In ANE/Q, 1792, "Titulos y ynstrumentos de los yndios y casiques del pueblo de Tusa sobre la propiedad de vnas tierras." *Cacicazgos*, caja 3 (Carchi), cuaderno 6.

———. 1760. "Los yndios de Cumbal, sobre la substracsion de las campanas y ornamentos." *Popayán*, caja 101.

———. 1761. "Proclama de Don Benbenutio Nastar del pueblo de Pastas, sobre el cacicasgo de las parcialidades de Nastar y Canchala." *Popayán*, caja 103.

———. 1764. "Autos de Don Marthin Cumbal Aza, sobre el cacicazgo de Cumbal." *Popayán*, caja 111.

———. 1767. "Autos seguidos por Don Pedro Ordoñez de Lara con Don Sebastian Magdaleno Padron, sobre el despojo de las tierras de la hacienda de Quaspud." *Popayán*, caja 118.

———. 1771. "Autos de proclama de Don Matheo Garcia Paspuel Tusa, casique principal de los pueblos del Angel, Puntal y Tusa, en la jurisdiccion de la villa de San Miguel de Ibarra, para que le den posesion del dicho cacicazgo." *Cacicazgos (Volúmenes)*, caja 35, vol. 62.

———. 1791. "Expediente de los casiques y comun de yndios del pueblo del Puntal con los casiques del pueblo de Tusa sobre tierras." *Cacicazgos*, caja 3 (Carchi).

———. 1792a. "Expediente de Doña Maria Melchora Ygues, casica de Ypiales, sobre que el agente solicitador entregue unos papeles." *Popayán*, caja 213.

———. 1792b. "Titulos y ynstrumentos de los yndios y casiques del pueblo de Tusa sobre la propiedad de vnas tierras." *Cacicazgos*, caja 3 (Carchi).

Archivo del Palau, Barcelona (AP/B) 1548. "Inventario de las alhajas y muebles." *Marquesado del Zenete* 122c, 1–58.

Bibliothèque Nationale de France. 1561[?]. "Relacao da viagem." MS portugais 8, 241–65.

Notaría Primera de Pasto (NP/P). 1908 [1758]. "Expediente sobre los linderos del resguardo del Gran Cumbal." Escritura 228.

PUBLISHED AND MODERN SOURCES

Abercrombie, Thomas A. 1998a. *Pathways of Memory and Power: Ethnography and History among an Andean People*. Madison: University of Wisconsin Press.

———. 1998b. "Tributes to Bad Conscience: Charity, Restitution, and Inheritance in Cacique and Encomendero Testaments of Sixteenth-Century Charcas." In Susan Kellogg and Matthew Restall, eds., *Dead Giveaways: Indigenous Testaments of Colonial Mesoamerica and the Andes*, 249–89. Salt Lake City: University of Utah Press.

Acosta, José de. 1940 [1590]. *Historia natural y moral de las Indias*. Ed. Edmundo O'Gorman. Mexico City: Universidad Nacional Autónoma de México.

———. 1984 [1588]. *De procuranda Indorum salute*. Madrid: Consejo Superior de Investigaciones Científicas.

Acuña, René. 1981. "Introduction." In Diego Muñoz Camargo, *Descripción de la ciu-*

dad y provincia de Tlaxcala de las Indias del mar océano para el buen gobierno y ennoblecimiento dellas, 1–47. Mexico City: Universidad de Nacional Autónoma de México.

Adorno, Rolena. 1982. "On Pictorial Language and the Typology of Culture in a New World Chronicle." *Semiotica* 36(1–2): 51–106.

———. 1986. *Guaman Poma: Writing and Resistance in Colonial Peru.* Austin: University of Texas Press.

———. 1991. "Images of *Indios Ladinos* in Early Colonial Peru." In Kenneth J. Andrien and Rolena Adorno, eds., *Transatlantic Encounters: Europeans and Andeans in the Sixteenth Century*, 232–70. Berkeley: University of California Press.

———. 1993. "The Genesis of Felipe Guaman Poma de Ayala's Nueva corónica y buen gobierno." *Colonial Latin American Review* 2(1–2): 553–92.

Aguado, Fray Pedro de. 1957 [1575?]. *Recopilación historial.* 4 vols. Bogotá: Biblioteca de la Presidencia de Colombia.

Aguilar, José Hernán. 1990. "Escenario devocional: El barroco flamenco y la vida de la Virgen." In *Lecciones barrocas: Pinturas sobre la vida de la Virgen de la Ermita de Egipto*, 6–19. Bogotá: Banco de la República, Museo de Arte Religioso.

Alberti, Leon Battista. 1991 [1435–36]. *On Painting.* Trans. C. Grayson. London: Penguin Classics.

Alciato, Andrea. 1549. *Los emblemas de Alciato Traducidos en rhimas Efpañolas. Añadidos de figuras y nuevos emblemas. Dirigidos al Ilustre S. Juan Vazquez de Molina.* Lyon, France: Guillermo Rovillio.

Alfonso X, El Sabio. 1992 [1555]. *Las siete partidas.* Ed. Francisco López Estrada and María Teresa López Gracía-Berdoy. Madrid: Castalia.

Álvarez, Bartolomé. 1998 [1588]. *De las costumbres y conversión de los indios del Perú. Memorial a Felipe II.* Madrid: Ediciones Polifemo.

Anderson, Benedict. 1983. *Imagined Communities.* London: Verso.

Anonymous. 1761. *Relación de auto particular de fee, celebrado por el tribunal del Santo Oficio de la Inquisicion de Lima 6 de abril de 1761.* Lima: Impresea nueva de los Huerphanos.

Anonymous. 1987 [1607–20]. *Diccionario y gramática chibcha: Manuscrito anónimo de la Biblioteca Nacional de Colombia.* Transcribed by María Stella González de Pérez. Bogotá: Instituto Caro y Cuervo, Biblioteca "Ezequiel Uricoechea" 1.

Aprile-Gniset, Jacques. 1991. *La ciudad colombiana: Prehispánica, de conquista e indiana.* Bogotá: Biblioteca Banco Popular.

Aram, Bethany. 1998. "Juana 'The Mad's' Signature: The Problem of Invoking Royal Authority, 1505–1507." *Sixteenth Century Journal* 29(2): 331–58.

Ares Queija, Bertha. 1989. "Estudio preliminar: El Oidor Tomás López Medel, visitador de Popayán." In Tomás López Medel, *Visita de la Gobernación de Popayán: Libro de tributos (1558–1559)*, xv–lix, Bertha Ares Queija, ed. Madrid: Consejo Superior de Investigaciones Científicas, Centro de Estudios Históricos, Departamento de Historia de América.

Ari Chachaki, Waskar (Juan Félix Arias). 1994. *Historia de una esperanza: Los apoderados espiritualistas de Chuquisaca 1936–1964. Un estudio sobre milenarismo, rebelión, resistencia y conciencia campesino-indígena.* La Paz: Ediciones Aruwiyiri.

Ariès, Philippe. 1991. *The Hour of Our Death.* New York: Alfred A. Knopf.

Arnold, Denise (with Juan de Dios Yapita). 2006. *The Metamorphosis of Heads: Textual Struggles, Education, and Land in the Andes.* Pittsburgh: University of Pittsburgh Press.

Ascher, Marcia, and Robert Ascher. 1981. *Code of the Quipu.* Ann Arbor: University of Michigan Press.

Ávila, Francisco de. 1648. *Tratado de los Evangelios que nuestra Madre la iglesia propone en todo el año desde la primera domínica de adviento hasta la última missa de Difuntos, Santos de España y añadidas en el nuevo rezado . . .* 2 vols. Lima: Jerónimo de Contreras.

Bakhtin, M. M. 1981 [1975]. *The Dialogic Imagination.* Austin: University of Texas Press.

Barletta, Vincent. 1999. "'Por Ende Deuemos Creer': Knowledge and Social Practice in the *Libro del Cauallero de Dios.*" *La Corónica* 27(3): 13–34.

Barnes, Monica. 1992. "Catechisms and Confesionarios: Distorting Mirrors of Andean Societies." In R. Dover, K. Siebold, and J. McDowell, eds., *Andean Cosmologies through Time,* 67–94. Bloomington: Indiana University Press.

Baxandall, Michael. 1988. *Painting and Experience in Fifteenth Century Italy.* Oxford: Oxford University Press.

Bedos-Rezak, Brigitte. 1993. "Civic Liturgies and Urban Records in Northern France (Twelfth-Fourteenth Centuries)." In Barbara Hanawalt, ed., *Medieval City and Spectacle,* 35–55. Minneapolis: University of Minnesota Press.

Behar, Ruth. 1986. *Santa María del Monte: The Presence of the Past in a Spanish Village.* Princeton: Princeton University Press.

Belting, Hans. 1994. *Likeness and Presence: A History of the Image before the Era of Art.* Trans. E. Jephott. Chicago: University of Chicago Press.

Bernand, Carmen. 2001. "Mestizos, mulatos y ladinos en Hispano-América: Un enfoque antropológico y un proceso histórico." In Miguel León Portilla, ed., *Motivos de la antropología americanista,* 105–33. Mexico City: Fondo de Cultura Económica.

Bhabha, Homi. 1994. *The Location of Culture.* New York: Routledge.

Bonnett, Diana. 1992. *El protector de naturales en la Audiencia de Quito, siglos XVII y XVIII.* Quito: Facultad Latinoamericana de Ciencias Sociales.

Boone Elizabeth. 2000. *Stories in Red and Black: Pictorial Histories of the Aztecs and Mixtexc.* Austin: University of Texas Press.

Boone, Elizabeth Hill, and Walter D. Mignolo, eds. 1994. *Writing without Words: Alternative Literacies in Mesoamerica and the Andes.* Durham: Duke University Press.

Bourdieu, Pierre. 1993. *The Field of Cultural Production*. New York: Columbia University Press.

Bowen, John. 1991. *Sumatran Politics and Poetics: Gayo History, 1900–1989*. New Haven: Yale University Press.

Bowser, Fredrick P. 1974. *The African Slave in Colonial Peru 1524–1650*. Stanford: Stanford University Press.

Bryson, Norman. 1988. "The Gaze in the Expanded Field." In Hal Foster, ed., *Vision and Visuality: Discussions in Contemporary Culture*, 87–108. New York: Dia Art Foundation.

Burckhardt, Jacob. 2005. *Italian Renaissance Painting according to Genres*. Trans. D. Britt and C. Beamish. Los Angeles: Getty Research Institute.

Burga, Manuel. 1988. *Nacimiento de una utopía: Muerte y resurrección de los incas*. Lima: Instituto de Apoyo Agrario.

Burgos Guevara, ed. 1995. *Primeras doctrinas en la Real Audiencia de Quito, 1570–1640: Estudio preliminar y transcripción de las relaciones eclesiales y misionales de los siglos XVI y XVII*. Quito: Abya-Yala.

Burkhart, Louise M. 1996. *Holy Wednesday: A Nahua Drama from Early Colonial Mexico*. Philadelphia: University of Pennsylvania Press.

Burns, Kathryn. 2005. "Notaries, Truth, and Consequences." *American Historical Review* 110(2): 350–79.

Burshatin, Israel. 1999. "Written on the Body: Slave or Hermaphrodite in Sixteenth-Century Spain." In Josiah Blackmore and Gregory S. Hutcheson, eds., *Queer Iberia: Sexualities, Cultures, and Crossings from the Middle Ages to the Renaissance*, 420–56. Durham: Duke University Press.

Cabello Balboa, Miguel. 1945 [1589]. "Verdadera descripción y relación larga de la Provincia y Tierra de las Esmeraldas. . . ." In *Obras*. Vol. 1, 1–76. Quito: Ecuatoriana.

Caillavet, Chantal. 1982a. "Caciques de Otavalo en el siglo XVI: Don Alonso Maldonado y su esposa." *Miscelánea Antropológica Ecuatoriana* 2: 38–55 (Quito).

———. 1982b. "Toponimia histórica, arqueológica y formas prehispánicas de agricultura en la región de Otavalo—Ecuador." *Bulletin de l'Institut Français des Études Andines* 12 (3–4): 1–21 (Lima).

———. 1983. "Ethno-histoire équatorienne: Un testament indien inédit du XVIᵉ siècle." *Caravelle* 41: 5–23 (Toulouse).

———. 2000. *Etnias del norte: Etnohistoria e historia del Ecuador*. Quito: Ediciones Abya-Yala.

Calero, Luis F. 1997. *Chiefdoms under Siege: Spain's Rule and Native Adaptation in the Southern Colombian Andes, 1535–1700*. Albuquerque: University of New Mexico Press.

Camille, Michael. 1989. "Visual Signs of the Sacred Page: Books in the *Bible moralisée*." *Word & Image* 5(1): 111–30.

————. 1992. *Image on the Edge: The Margins of Medieval Art*. Cambridge: Harvard University Press.

Cañeque, Alejandro. 2004. *The King's Living Image: The Culture and Politics of Viceregal Power in Colonial Mexico*. New York: Routledge.

Cardale de Schrimpff, Marianne. 1977–78. "Textiles arqueológicos de Nariño." *Revista Colombiana de Antropología* 21: 245–82 (Bogotá).

Cárdenas Ayaipoma, Mario. 1975–76. "El Colegio de Caciques y el sometimiento ideológico de los residuos de la nobleza aborigen." *Revista del Archivo General de la Nación* 4/5: 5–24 (Lima).

Carducho, Vincencio. 1633. *Dialogos de la pintura: Su defensa, origen, essencia, definicion, modos y diferencias*. Madrid: Impresso con licencia por Francisco Martinez.

Carruthers, Mary J. 1990. *The Book of Memory: A Study of Memory in Medieval Culture*. Cambridge: Cambridge University Press.

————.1998. *The Craft of Thought: Meditation, Rhetoric, and the Making of Images, 400–1200*. Cambridge: Cambridge University Press.

Castañeda Vargas, Ana Carolina. 2000. *La vida en pulicía: El escalón para lo espiritual. Control moral, público y privado de los muiscas en el siglo XVI*. Tesis de Grado en Antropología, Universidad Nacional de Colombia, Bogotá.

Castillo y Orozco, Eugenio. 1877 [1755]. *Diccionario páez-castellano* . . . Transcribed by Ezequiel Uricoechea. Paris: Collection Linguistique Américaine, no. 2.

Chandler, Nahum Dimitri. 2000. "Originary Displacement." *Boundary 2* 27(3): 249–86.

Checa, Fernando. 1992. *Felipe II: Mecenas de las Artes*. Madrid: Editorial Nerea.

Christian, William A., Jr. 1981a. *Apparitions in Late Medieval and Renaissance Spain*. Princeton: Princeton University Press.

————. 1981b. *Local Religion in Sixteenth-Century Spain*. Princeton: Princeton University Press.

Cieza de León, Pedro de. 1962 [1553]. *La crónica del Perú (primera parte)*. Madrid: Espasa-Calpe.

Clanchy, M. T. 1989. "Reading the Signs at Durham Cathedral." In K. Shousboe and M. T. Larsen, eds., *Literacy and society*, 171–82. Copenhagen: Akademisk Forlag.

————. 1993. *From Memory to Written Record: England, 1066–1307*. Oxford: Blackwell.

Cline, S. L., and Miguel León-Portilla, eds. 1984. *The Testaments of Culhuacán*. Los Angeles: UCLA Latin American Center Publications, Special Studies, vol. 2, Nahuatl Series, vol. 1.

Cobo, Bernabe. 1956 [1639]. "Fundación de Lima." In *Biblioteca de Autores Españoles*. Vol. 92, 280–476. Madrid: Gráficas Orbe.

Codding, Mitchell. 2006. "The Decorative Arts in Latin America, 1492–1820." In Joseph J. Rischel, ed., *The Arts in Latin America, 1492–1820*, 98–143. New Haven: Yale University Press.

Condori Chura, Leandro, and Esteban Ticona Alejo. 1992. *El escribano de los caciques apoderados / Kasikinakan purirarunakan qillqiripa*. La Paz: Hisbol.

Conklin, William J. 1982. "The Information System of Middle Horizon Quipus." *Annals of the New York Academy of Sciences* 385: 261–81.

Connerton, Paul. 1989. *How Societies Remember*. Cambridge: Cambridge University Press.

Cook, Alexandra, and Noble Cook. 1991. *Good Faith and Truthful Ignorance: A Case of Transatlantic Bigamy*. Durham: Duke University Press.

Córdova Salinas, Fray Diego de. 1957 [1651]. *Crónica franciscana de las Provincias del Perú*. Ed. Lio Gómez Canedo. Washington, D.C.: Academy of American Franciscan History.

Cornejo-Polar, Antonio. 1996. "Una heterogeneidad no dialéctica: Sujeto y discurso migrantes en el Perú moderno." *Revista Iberoamericana* 62(176–77): 837–44.

Coronil, Fernando. 1995. "Transculturation and the Politics of Theory: Countering the Center, Cuban Counterpoint." In Fernando Ortiz, *Cuban Counterpoint: Tobacco and Sugar*, ix–lvi. Durham: Duke University Press.

Corradine Angulo, Alberto. 1993. "Urbanismo español en Colombia: Los pueblos de indios." In Gutiérrez, Ramón, ed., *Pueblos de indios: Otro urbanismo en la región andina*, 157–78. Quito: Ediciones Abya Yala.

Cortés, Hernán. 1986 [1520]. *Letters from Mexico*. Trans. and ed. Anthony Pagden. New Haven: Yale University Press.

Covarrubias Orozco, Sebastián de. 1610. *Emblemas morales*. Madrid: L. Sánchez.

———. 1995 [1611]. *Tesoro de la lengua castellana o española*. Felipe C. R. Maldonado, ed. Madrid: Editorial Castalia.

Cummins, Tom. 1991. "We Are the Other: Peruvian Portraits of Colonial Kurakacuna." In Rolena Adorno and Kenneth Andrien, eds., *Transatlantic Encounters: The History of Early Colonial Peru*, 203–31 Berkeley: University of California Press.

———. 1994. "Representation in the Sixteenth Century and the Colonial Image of the Inca." In Elizabeth Hill Boone and Walter Mignolo, eds., *Writing Without Words: Alternative Literacies in Mesoamerica and the Andes*, 188–219. Durham: Duke University Press.

———. 1995. "From Lies to Truth: Colonial Ekphrasis and the Act of Crosscultural Translation." In Claire Farago, ed., *Reframing the Renaissance: Visual Culture in Europe and Latin America 1450–1650*, 152–74. London: Yale University Press.

———. 1998a. "El lenguaje del arte colonial: Imagen, ekfrasis, e idolatría." *I Encuentro Internacional de Peruanistas: Estado de estudios histórico-sociales sobre el Perú a fines del siglo XX*, 23–45. Lima: Universidad de Lima.

———. 1998b. "Let Me See! Reading Is for Them: Colonial Andean Images and Objects 'como es costumbre tener los caciques Señores.'" In Elizabeth Hill Boone and Tom Cummins, eds., *Native Traditions in the Postconquest World*, 91–148. Washington, D.C.: Dumbarton Oaks Research Library and Collection.

————. 1999. "On the Colonial Formation of Comparison: The Virgin of Chiquinquirá, the Virgin of Guadalupe, and Cloth." *Anales del Instituto de Investigaciones Estéticas* 74–75:51–77.

————. 2002a. *Toasts with the Inca: Andean Abstraction and Colonial Images on Quero Vessels*. Ann Arbor: University of Michigan Press.

————. 2002b. "Town Planning, Marriage, and Free Will in the Colonial Andes." In Claire Lyons and John Papadopoulos, eds., *The Archaeology of Colonialism*, 199–240. Los Angeles: Getty Press, Issues and Debates Series.

————. 2005. "La fábula y el retrato: Imágenes tempranas del Inca." In Tom Cummins, *Los incas, reyes del Perú*, 1–41. Lima: Banco de Crédito.

————. 2008. "The Images in Murúa's *Historia general del Piru*: An Art Historical Study." In Thomas B. F. Cummins and Barbara Anderson, eds., *The Getty Murúa: Essays on the Making of Martín de Murúa's "Historia General del Piru."* pp. 143–69. Los Angeles: Getty Research Institute.

————. 2011 "The Indulgent Image: Prints in the New World" In Ilona Katzew ed., *Contested Vision*, 201–223, 289–292. Los Angeles: LACMA.

Cutter, Charles R. 1995. *The Legal Culture of Northern New Spain, 1700–1810*. Albuquerque: University of New Mexico Press.

Dagenais, John. 1994. *The Ethics of Reading in Manuscript Culture: Glossing the Libro de buen amor*. Princeton: Princeton University Press.

Damisch, Hubert. 1995. *The Origins of Perspective*. Trans. J. Goodman. Cambridge: MIT Press.

Dean, Carolyn. 1999. *Inka Bodies and the Body of Christ: Corpus Christi in Colonial Cuzco, Peru*. Durham: Duke University Press.

Dean, Carolyn, and Dana Leibsohn. 2003. "Hybridity and Its Discontents: Considering Visual Culture in Colonial Spanish America." *Colonial Latin American Review* 12(1): 5–35.

de Certeau, Michel. 1984. *The Practice of Everyday Life*. Trans. Steven Rendall. Berkeley: University of California Press.

————. 1988. *The Writing of History*. Trans. Tom Conley. New York: Columbia University Press.

de la Cadena, Marisol. 2005. "Are *Mestizos* Hybrids? The Conceptual Politics of Andean Identities." *Journal of Latin American Studies* 37: 259–84.

de la Puente Luna, José Carlos. 2010. "Into the Heart of the Empire: Indian Journeys to the Habsburg Royal Court," Ph.D. diss. in History, Texas Christian University, Ft. Worth.

del Río, Mercedes. 1990. "Simbolismo y poder en Tapacarí." *Revista Andina* 8(1): 77–113 (Cuzco).

Dening, Greg. 1988. *History's Anthropology: The Death of William Gooch*. Lanham, Md.: University Press of America.

Derrida, Jacques. 1981. "The Law of Genre." In W. J. T. Mitchell, ed., *On Narrative*, 51–78. Chicago: University of Chicago Press.

———. 1987. *The Truth in Painting*. Trans. G. Bennigton and I MacLeod. Chicago: University of Chicago Press.

Díaz Rementería, Carlos J. 1977. *El cacique en el Virreinato del Perú: Estudio histórico-jurídico*. Seville: Publicaciones del Seminario de Antropología Americana, Universidad de Sevilla, 15.

Du Bois, W. E. B. 1989 [1903]. *The Souls of Black Folk*. New York: Bantam.

Durston, Alan. 1994. "Un régimen urbanístico en la América hispana colonial: El trazado en Damero durante los siglos XVI y XVII." *Historia* 28: 59–115 (Santiago de Chile).

———. 2007. *Pastoral Quechua: The History of Christian Translation in Peru, 1550–1650*. Notre Dame: University of Notre Dame Press.

Egaña, Antonio de and Enrique Fernández, S.J., eds. 1981. *Monumenta peruana (1600–1602)*. Rome: Institutum Historicum Societatis Iesu, vol. 7.

Eire, Carlos M. N. 1995. *From Madrid to Purgatory: The Art and Craft of Dying in Sixteenth-Century Spain*. Cambridge: Cambridge University Press.

Elliott, John. 1970. *Imperial Spain, 1469–1716*. Harmondsworth: Penguin.

Espinosa, Carlos. 1990. *Portrait of the Inca*. Ph.D. diss. in History, University of Chicago.

———. 1995. "Colonial Visions: Drama, Art, and Legitimation in Peru and Ecuador." In Emily Umberger and Tom Cummins, eds., *Native Artists and Patrons in Colonial Latin America*, a special issue of *Phoebus: A Journal of Art History* 7: 84–106. (Tempe, Ariz.).

Espinoza Soriano, Waldemar. 1960. "El alcalde mayor indígena en el Virreinato del Perú." *Anuario de Estudios Americanos* 17: 183–300 (Seville).

Esquivel y Navia, Diego de. 1980 [1749]. *Noticias cronológicas de la gran ciudad del Cuzco*. 2 vols. Lima: Fundación Augusto N. Wiese, Banco Wiese Ltd.

Estupiñán Freile, Tamara. 1988. "Testamento de Don Francisco Atagualpa." *Miscelánea Histórica Ecuatoriana* 1: 8–67 (Quito).

Fajardo de Rueda, Marta. 1990. *Oribes y plateros en la Nueva Granada*. Bogotá: Banco de la República, Museo de Arte Religioso.

———. 1999. *El arte colonial neogranadino a la luz del estudio iconográfico e iconológico*. Bogotá: Convenio Andrés Bello.

Fernández, Enrique, S. J., ed. 1986. *Monumenta peruana VIII (1603–1604)*. Rome: Institutum Historicum Societatis Iesu. Monumenta Historica Societatis Iesu, vol. 128.

Fernández, José. 1666. *Apostólica, y penitente vida de el V.P. Pedro Claver, de la Compañía de Jesús. Sacada principalmente de informaciones jurídicas hechas ante el Ordinario de la Ciudad de Cartagena de las Indias . . .* Zaragoza: Diego Dormer.

Fernández de Piedrahita, Lucas. 1973 [1688]. *Noticia historial de las conquistas del Nuevo Reino de Granada*. Bogotá: Editorial Kelly.

Fernández Osco, Marcelo. 2000. *La ley del* ayllu: *Práctica de* jach'a *justicia y* jisk'a *justicia (justicia mayor y justicia menor) en comunidades aymaras*. La Paz: Fundación PIEB.

Fletcher, Richard. 1992. *Moorish Spain*. Berkeley: University of California Press.

Flores Galindo, Alberto. 1988. *Buscando un Inca*. Lima: Editorial Horizonte.

Forbes, Jack D. 1988. *Black Africans and Native Americans: Color, Race and Caste in the Evolution of Red-Black Peoples*. Oxford: Basil Blackwell Ltd.

Foster, George M. 1960. *Culture and Conquest: The American Spanish Heritage*. New York: Viking Fund Publications in Anthropology.

Foucault, Michel. 1979. *Discipline and Punish: The Birth of the Prison*. Trans. Alan Sheridan. New York: Vintage.

Fox, Adam. 2000. *Oral and Literate Culture in England, 1500-1700*. Oxford: Clarendon.

Fraenkel, Béatrice. 1992. *La signature: Genèse d'un signe*. Paris: Gallimard.

Frame, Mary. 1994. "Las imágenes visuales de estructuras textiles en el arte del antiguo Perú." *Revista Andina* 12(2): 295-372 (Cuzco).

Fraser, Valerie. 1990. *The Architecture of Conquest: Building in the Viceroyalty of Peru, 1535-1635*. Cambridge: Cambridge University Press.

Frezier, Amédée. 1716. *Relation du voyage de la Mer du Sud, aux côtes du Chili, et du Pérou, fait pendant les annees, 1712, 1713, et 1714*. Paris: Chez Jean-Geoffroy Nyon, Etienne Ganneau et Jacques Quillau.

Friedemann, Nina S. de. 1990. "Mopa-mopa o barniz de Pasto: Los marcos de la Iglesia de Egipto." In *Lecciones barrocas: Pinturas sobre la vida de la Virgen de la Ermita de Egipto*, 40-53. Bogotá: Banco de la República, Museo de Arte Religioso.

Fulton, Rachel. 2002. *From Judgment to Passion: Devotion to Christ and the Virgin Mary, 800-1200*. New York: Columbia University Press.

Galdo Gutiérrez, Virgilio. 1970. "Colegios de curacas: Frente a dos mundos." *Educación: Revista del Maestro Peruano* 3: 30-38.

Gálvez Piñal, Esperanza. 1974. *La visita de Monzón y Prieto de Orellana al Nuevo Reino de Granada*. Sevilla: Escuela de Estudios Hispano-Americanos de Sevilla, vol. 225.

Gamboa Hinestrosa, Pablo. 1996. *La pintura apócrifa en el arte colonial: Los doce arcángeles de Sopó*. Bogotá: Editorial Universidad Nacional.

García Canclini, Néstor. 1989. *Culturas híbridas: Estrategias para entrar y salir de la modernidad*. Mexico City: Grijalbo.

Garcilaso de la Vega, El Inca. 1723 [1609]. *Primera parte de los comentarios reales de los Incas*. Madrid: Nicolas Rodrigues Franco.

Garrido Aranda, Antonio. 1980. *Moriscos e indios: Precedentes hispánicos de la evangelización en México*. Mexico City: Universidad Nacional Autónoma de México.

Gee, James Paul. 1988. "The Legacies of Literacy: From Plato to Freire through Harvey Graff." *Harvard Educational Review* 58(2): 195-212.

Gerli, E. Michael. 1996. "Performing Nobility: Mosén Diego de Valera and the Poetics of *Converso* Identity." *La Corónica* 25(1): 19-36.

Gheyn, Jacob de. 1608. *Maniement d'armes, d'arqvebuses, movsqvetz, et piqves. En conformite de l'ordre de monseigneur le prince Maurice, prince d'Orange . . . representé par figures, par Jaques de Gheijn. Ensemble les enseignemes par escrit a l'utilite de tous amateurs des armes, et ausi pour tous capitaines & commandeurs, pour par cecy pouvoir plus facillement enseigner a leurs soldatz inexperimentez l'entier et parfait maniement dicelles armes.* Amsterdam: Imprimé a Amsterdam chez R. de Baudous; on les vend ausi a Amsterdam chez Henrij Laurens.

Ginsburg, Carlos. 1983. *The Night Battles: Witchcraft and Agrarian Cults in the Sixteenth and Seventeenth Centuries.* Trans. John and Anne Tedeschi. Baltimore: Johns Hopkins University Press.

Gisbert, Teresa. 1986. "The Angels." In *Gloria in Excelsis: The Virgin and Angels in Viceregal Painting of Peru and Bolivia,* 58–63. New York: Center for Inter-American Relations.

———. 2004. *El cielo y el infierno en el mundo virreinal del sur andino.* La Paz: n.p.

Goodman, Nelson. 1976. *The Languages of Art.* Cambridge: Harvard University.

González, Margarita. 1979. *El resguardo en el Nuevo Reino de Granada.* Bogotá: La Carreta.

González Alonso, Benjamín. 1980. "La fórmula 'obedézcase, pero no se cumpla' en el derecho castellano de la baja edad media." *Anuario de Historia del Derecho Español* 50: 469–87.

González de Torneo, Francisco. 1614. *Practica de escrivanos. Que contiene la judicial, i ordé de examinar testigos en causas civiles, y hidalguias, y causas criminales, y escrituras en estilo estenso, y quentas, y particiones de bienes, y exccuciones de cartas executorias.* No publisher or place of publication (held in the Biblioteca Nacional de Colombia).

González Echevarría, Roberto. 1990. *Myth and Archive: A Theory of Latin American Narrative.* Cambridge: Cambridge University Press.

González Holguín, Diego. 1989 [1608]. *Vocabulario de la lengua general de todo el Peru llamada lengua qquichua o del inca.* Lima: Editorial de la Universidad Nacional Mayor de San Marcos.

Goody, Jack. 1977. *The Domestication of the Savage Mind.* Cambridge: Cambridge University Press.

———. 1987. *The Interface between the Written and the Oral.* Cambridge: Cambridge University Press.

Goody, Jack, Brian Stock, Jerome Bruner, Roger Shattuck, Carol Fleisher Feldman, David R. Rolson, Rolena Adorno, and Christopher Miller. 1988. "Selections from the Symposium 'Literacy, Reading, and Power,' Whitney Humanities Center, November 14, 1987." *The Yale Journal of Criticism* 2(1): 193–222.

Graff, H. G. 1987. *The Legacies of Literacy: Continuities and Contradictions in Western Culture and Society.* Bloomington: Indiana University Press.

Greenblatt, Stephen, ed. 1981. *Allegory and Representation.* Baltimore: Johns Hopkins University Press.

Gregory the Great. 2004. *The Letters of Gregory the Great*. 2 vols. Trans. John R. C. Martyn. Toronto: Pontifical Institute of Medieval Studies.

Grijalva, Carlos E. 1937. *La expedición de Max Uhle a Cuasmal, o sea, la protohistoria de Imbabura y Carchi*. Quito: Editorial Chimborazo.

Gruzinski, Serge. 1987. "Colonial Maps in Sixteenth-Century Mexico." *Res* 13: 46–61.

———. 1993 [1988]. *The Conquest of Mexico: The Incorporation of Indian Societies into the Western World, 16th-18th Centuries*. Trans. Eileen Corrigan. Cambridge: Polity Press.

———. 1999. *La pensée métisse*. Paris: Fayard.

———. 2001 [1990]. *Images at War: Mexico from Columbus to Blade Runner (1492–2019)*. Trans. Heather MacLean. Durham: Duke University Press.

Guaman Poma de Ayala, Felipe. 1980 [1616]. *El primer nueva corónica y buen gobierno*. John Murra and Rolena Adorno, eds. Mexico City: Siglo XXI.

———. 1991 [1594–1646]. *Y no ay remedio*. Msgr. Elías Prado Tello and Alfredo Prado Prado, eds. Lima: Centro de Investigación y Promoción Amazónica.

Guevara, Pedro de. 1788 [1560]. *Comentarios de la pintura . . . se publican por la primera vez con un discurso preliminar y algunas notas de Antonio Ponz, quien ofrece su trabajo al Excelentisimo Señor Conde de Florida-Blanca, protector de las nobles artes (1560)*. Madrid: Don Geronimo Ortega: Hijos de Ibarra y Compañía.

Guevara-Gil, Armando and Frank Salomon. 1994. "A 'Personal Visit': Colonial Political Ritual and the Making of Indians in the Andes." *Colonial Latin American Review* 3 (1–2): 3–36.

Gutiérrez, Ramón. 1993. "Las reducciones indígenas en el urbanismo colonial: Integración cultural y persistencias." In Ramón Gutiérrez, ed. *Pueblos de indios: Otro urbanismo en la región andina*, 11–63. Quito: Ediciones Abya-Yala.

Gutiérrez de Pineda, Virginia, and Roberto Pineda Giraldo. 1999. *Miscegenación y cultura en la Colombia colonial, 1750-1810*. 2 vols. Bogotá: Colciencias.

Hampe Martínez, Teodoro. 1996. *Cultura barroca y extirpación de idolatrías: La biblioteca de Francisco de Ávila—1648*. Cuzco: Centro de Estudios Regionales Andinos, Bartolomé de las Casas.

Hanks, William F. 2000. *Intertexts: Writings on Language, Utterance, and Context*. Lanham, Md.: Rowman and Littlefield.

Hardman, Martha. 1988. "Jaqi aru: La lengua humana." In Xavier Albó, ed., *Raíces de América: El mundo aymara*, 155–205. Madrid: Alianza.

Harrison, Regina. 1989. *Signs, Songs, and Memory in the Andes: Translating Quechua Language and Culture*. Austin: University of Texas Press.

———. 1995. "The Language and Rhetoric of Conversion in the Viceroyalty of Peru." *Poetics Today* 16(1): 1–27.

Hartmann, Roswith, and Udo Oberem. 1981. "Quito: Un centro de educación de indígenas en el siglo XVI." In Thekla Hartmann and Vera Penteado Coelho, eds., *Contribuições à antropologia em homenagem aõ Professor Egon Schaden*, 105–27. São Paolo: Coleção Museu Paulista, Série Ensaios, vol. 14.

Havelock, Eric A. 1986. *The Muse Learns to Write: Reflections on Orality and Literacy from Antiquity to the Present*. New Haven: Yale University Press.

Hazañero, Fray Sebastián. 1645. *Letras anvas de la Compañía de Iesus de la Provincia del Nvevo Reyno de Granada desde el año de mil y seyscientos y treinta y ocho, hasta el año de mil y seyscientos y quarenta y tres*. Zaragoza.

Heath, Shirley Brice. 1972. *Telling Tongues: Language Policy in Mexico, Colony to Nation*. New York: Teachers College Press.

Herrera Ángel, Marta. 2002. *Ordenar para controlar: Ordenamiento espacial y control político en las llanuras del Caribe y en los Andes centrales neogranadinos, siglo XVIII*. Bogotá: Instituto Colombiano de Antropología e Historia.

Herzberg, Julia P. 1986. "Angels with Guns: Image and Interpretation." In *The Virgin and Angels in Viceregal Painting of Peru and Bolivia*, 64–75. New York: Center for Inter-American Relations.

Herzog, Tamar. 1996. *Mediación, archivos y ejercicio: Los escribanos de Quito (siglo XVIII)*. Frankfurt am Main: Vittorio Klosterman.

Hevia Bolaños, Juan de. 1761. *Curia philipica, primero, y segundo tomo*. Madrid: Imprenta de los Herederos de la Viuda de Juan García Infanzón.

Hill, Robert M. 1989. *The Pirir Papers and Other Colonial Period Cakchiquel Maya Testamentos*. Nashville: Vanderbilt University Publications in Anthropology, no. 37.

Howard-Malverde, Rosaleen 1990. *The Speaking of History: 'Willapaakushayki' or Quechua Ways of Telling the Past*. London: University of London, Institute of Latin American Studies, Research Papers 21.

Howe, Emily, Emily Kaplan, Judith Levinson, and Ellen Pearlstein. 1999. "Queros: Análisis técnicos de queros pintados de los períodos Inca y coloniales." *Iconos: Revista Peruana de Conservación, Arte y Arqueología* 2: 30–38.

Hoyos García, Juan Felipe. 2002. *El lenguaje y la escritura como herramientas coloniales: El caso de Santa Fé y Tunja, durante el siglo XVI*. Tesis de Grado en Antropología, Universidad Nacional de Colombia, Bogotá.

Huot, Sylvia. 1987. *From Song to Book: The Poetics of Writing in Old French Lyric and Lyrical Narrative Poetry*. Ithaca: Cornell University Press.

Inclán Valdés, Diego. 1910 [1681]. "Ordenanzas expedidas por don Diego Inclán Valdés, del Consejo de S.M., Oidor de la Real Audiencia, Visitador etc. etc., para el buen tratamiento de los naturales." Appendix to Antonio Olano, *Popayán en la Colonia*. Popayán: Imprenta Oficial.

Jackson, Jean. 1989. "Is There a Way to Talk about Making Culture without Making Enemies?" *Dialectical Anthropology* 14: 127–43.

Jamieson, Ross W. 2000. *Domestic Architecture and Power: The Historial Archaeology of Colonial Ecuador*. New York: Kluwer Academic.

Jaramillo Uribe, Jaime. 1989. "El proceso de la educación en el virreinato." In Álvaro Tirado Mejía, ed., *Nueva historia de Colombia*, vol. 1, 207–15. Bogotá: Planeta.

Jiménez Moreno, Wigberto, and Salvador Mateos Higuera, eds. 1940 [1545–50]. *Códice de Yanhuitlán*. Mexico City: Secretaría de Educación Pública.

Johns, Adrian. 1998. *The Nature of the Book: Print and Knowledge in the Making.* Chicago: University of Chicago Press.

Jourdan, C. 1991. "Pidgins and Creoles: The Blurring of Categories." *Annual Review of Anthropology* 20: 187–209.

Jouvé-Martín, José Ramón. 2005. *Esclavos de la ciudad letrada: Esclavos, escritura y colonialismo en Lima 1650–1700.* Lima: Instituto de Estudios Peruanos.

Justice, Steven. 1994. *Writing and Rebellion: England in 1381.* Berkeley: University of California Press.

Kagan, Richard L. 2000. *Urban Images of the Hispanic World, 1493–1793.* New Haven: Yale University Press.

Kantorowicz, Ernst H. 1957. *The King's Two Bodies: A Study in Medieval Political Theology.* Princeton: Princeton University Press.

Karttunen, Frances, and James Lockhart. 1976. *Nahuatl in the Middle Years: Language Contact Phenomena in Texts of the Colonial Period.* Berkeley: University of California Press.

Katzew, Ilona. 1996. "Casta Painting: Identity and Social Stratification in Colonial Mexico." In Ilona Katzew, ed., *New World Orders: Casta Painting and Colonial Latin America,* 8–29. New York: Americas Society Art Gallery.

Kellogg, Susan, and Matthew Restall, eds. 1998. *Dead Giveaways: Indigenous Testaments of Colonial Mesoamerica and the Andes.* Salt Lake City: University of Utah Press.

Klor de Alva, J. Jorge. 1989. "Language, Politics, and Translation: Colonial Discourse and Classic Nahuatl in New Spain." In Rosanna Warren, ed., *The Art of Translation: Voices from the Field,* 143–62. Boston: Northeastern University Press.

Klumpp, Kathleen. 1974. "El retorno del Inca: Una expresión ecuatoriana de la ideología mesiánica andina." *Cuadernos de Historia y de Arqueología del Guayas* 24(41): 99–136 (Guayaquil).

Konečný, Ludomir. 1994. "Una Pintura de Juan Sánchez Cotán, emblematizada por Sebastián de Covarrubias." *Actas del 1 Simposio Internacional de Emblemática, Teruel, 1 y 2 de Octubre 1991,* 823–34. Teruel: Instituto de Estudios Turolenses.

Kubler, George. 1948. *Mexican Architecture of the Sixteenth Century.* 2 vols. New Haven: Yale University Press.

Kuznesof, Elizabeth Anne. 1995. "Ethnic and Gender Influences on 'Spanish' Creole Society in Colonial Spanish America." *Colonial Latin American Review* 4(1): 153–76.

Landázuri, Cristóbal. 1995. *Los curacazgos pastos prehispánicos: Agricultura y comercio, siglo XVI.* Otavalo, Ecuador: Instituto Otavaleño de Antropología.

Lara, Jaime. 1996. "Los frescos recientemente descubiertos en Sutatausa, Cundinamarca." *Instituto de Investigaciones Estéticas Ensayos* 2: 257–70 (Bogotá).

———. 2008. *Christian Texts for Aztecs: Art and Liturgy in Colonial Mexico.* Notre Dame, Ind.: University of Notre Dame Press.

Lara Valdés, José Luis, and José Eduardo Vidaurri Aréchiga, eds. 1998 [1810]. *Com-*

pendio de escrituras, poderes, y testamentos con otras curiosidades para govierno de escribanos, alcaldes mayores, y notarios con el estilo forense y practica que se acostumbra. Guanajuato, Mexico City: Universidad de Guanajuato, Facultad de Derecho.

Las Casas, Fray Bartolomé de. 1967 [1559]. *Apologética historia sumaria.* Ed. E. O'Gorman. Mexico City: Universidad Nacional Autónoma de México.

Leal Curiel, Carole. 1990. *El discurso de la fidelidad: Construcción social del espacio como símbolo del poder regio (Venezuela, siglo XVIII).* Caracas: Academia Nacional de Historia.

Lefebvre, Henri. 1992 [1974]. *The Production of Space.* Trans. D. Nicholso-Smith. Oxford: Blackwell.

Leibsohn, Dana. 1994. "Primers for Memory: Cartographic Histories and Nahua Identity." In Elizabeth Hill Boone and Walter Mignolo, eds., *Writing without words: Alternative Literacies in Mesoamerica and the Andes,* 161–87. Durham: Duke University Press.

———. 2000. "Mapping after the Letter: Graphology and Indigenous Cartography in New Spain." In Ed Gray and Norman Fiering, eds., *The Language Encounter in the Americas, 1492–1800,* 119–51. Providence, R.I.: Berghahn.

Leonard, Irving A. 1992. *Books of the Brave: Being an Account of Books and of Men in the Spanish Conquest and Settlement of the Sixteenth-Century New World.* Berkeley: University of California Press.

Lewis, Laura A. 2003. *Hall of Mirrors: Power, Witchcraft, and Caste in Colonial Mexico.* Durham: Duke University Press.

Lima, Cabildo de. 1935 [1535]. *Libros de cabildo de Lima.* Bertram T. Lee, ed. Lima.

Lima, Concilio de 1584. *Tercero cathecismo y exposicion de la doctrina christiana, por sermones. Para qve los cvras y otros ministros prediquen y enseñen a los Yndios y a las demas personas. Conforme a lo qve en el sancto Concilio prouincial de Lima se proueyo.* Lima: Impresso con Licencia de la Real Audiencia, en la Ciudad de los Reyes, por Antonio Ricardo, primero Impressor en estos Reynos del Piru.

———. 1990 [1585]. "Tercero catecismo." In Juan Guillermo Durán, ed., *Monumenta catechetica hispanoamericana (siglos XVI–XVIII),* vol. 2, 599–740. Buenos Aires: Pontificia Universidad Católica Argentina.

Llano Zapata, José Eusebio. 1904 [1761]. *Memorias históricas-physicas, crítico-apologéticas de la América meridional.* Lima: Imprenta y Librería de San Pedro.

Lockhart, James. 1992. *The Nahuas after the Conquest.* Stanford: Stanford University Press.

Lomazzo, Giovanni Paolo. 1584. *Trattato dell'arte de la pintura: Diviso I sette libre, ne' quail si contiene tutta la theorica & la prattica d'essa pittura.* Milan: Appresso Paolo Gottardo Pontio.

López de Solis, Fray Luis. 1995 [1594]. "Constituciones sinodales." In Hugo Burgos Guevara, ed., *Primeras doctrinas en la Real Audiencia de Quito, 1570–1640: Estu-*

dio preliminar y transcripción de las relaciones eclesiales y misionales de los siglos XVI y XVII, 473–84. Quito: Ediciones Abya-Yala.

López Medel, Tomás. 1989 [1558–59]. *Visita de la Gobernación de Popayán: Libro de tributos (1558–1559)*. Berta Ares Queija, ed. Madrid: Consejo Superior de Investigaciones Científicas, Centro de Estudios Históricos, Departamento de Historia de América.

López Pérez, Pilar. 2006. "Portable Writing Desk." In Joseph J. Rischel, ed., *The Arts in Latin America, 1492–1820*, 131. New Haven: Yale University Press.

López Rodríguez, Mercedes. 2001. *Tiempos para rezar y tiempos para trabajar: La cristianización de las comunidades indígenas muiscas durante el siglo XVI*. Bogotá: Instituto Colombiano de Antropología e Historia.

———. 2002. "La memoria de las imágenes: Donantes indígenas en el Lienzo de Animas de San Nicolás de Tolentino." In José Antonio Carbonell B., ed., *Historia e imágenes: Los agustinos en Colombia 400 años, 29–39*, Bogotá: Museo Nacional de Colombia.

Low, Setha M. 2000. *On the Plaza: The Politics of Public Space and Culture*. Austin: University of Texas Press.

Luján Muñoz, Jorge. 1977. *Los escribanos en las Indias Occidentales y en particular en el Reino de Guatemala*. Guatemala: Instituto Guatemalteco de Derecho Notarial.

MacCormack, Sabine. 1991. *Religion in the Andes: Vision and Imagination in Early Colonial Peru*. Princeton: Princeton University Press.

Majluf, Natalia, ed. 2000. *Los cuadros de mestizaje del Virrey Amat*. Lima: Museo de Arte de Lima.

Mamani Condori, Carlos B. 1991. *Taraqu 1866–1935: Masacre, guerra y "Renovación" en la biografía de Eduardo L. Nina Qhispi*. La Paz: Ediciones Aruwiyiri.

Mamani Quispe, Alejandro. 1988. *Historia y cultura de Cohana*. La Paz: Hisbol.

Mannheim, Bruce. 1991. *The Language of the Inka since the European Invasion*. Austin: University of Texas Press.

Maravall, José Antonio. 1986 [1975]. *Culture of the Baroque: Analysis of a Historical Structure*. Trans. Terry Cochran. Minneapolis: University of Minnesota Press.

Marin, Louis. 1988. *Portrait of the King*. Trans. Martha M. Houle. Minneapolis: University of Minnesota Press.

Martínez Cereceda, José L. 1995. *Autoridades en los Andes, los atributos del Señor*. Lima: Fondo Editorial de la Pontificia Universidad Católica del Perú.

McAndrew, John. 1965. *The Open Air Churches of Sixteenth-century Mexico*. Cambridge: Harvard University Press.

Megged, Amos. 2010. *Social Memory in Ancient and Colonial Mesoamerica*. Cambridge: Cambridge University Press.

Mejía Gutiérrez, Carlos. 1994. *Ángeles de Sopó: Angelino Medoro y el arte colonial neogranadino*. Medellín: L. Vieco e Hijas Ltda.

Meléndez, Juan. 1681. *Tesoros verdaderos de las Indias: Historia de la provincia de San Baptista del Perú de la Orden de Predicadores*. Rome: Nicolas Angel Tinassio.

Merino Urrutia, José J. Bautista. 1958. "Los ángeles de la ermita de Allende, en Ezcaray." *Archivo Español de Arte* 31(123): 247–51.

———. 1983. *Ángeles de Calamarca*. La Paz: n.p.

Messick, Brinkley. 1989. "Just Writing: Paradox and Political Economy in Yemeni Legal Documents." *Cultural Anthropology* 4(1): 26–50.

———. 1993. *The Calligraphic State: Textual Domination and History in a Muslim Society*. Berkeley: University of California Press.

Mignolo, Walter. 1995. *The Darker Side of the Renaissance: Literacy, Territoriality, and Colonization*. Ann Arbor: University of Michigan Press.

———. 2000. *Local Histories / Global Designs: Coloniality, Subaltern Knowledges, and Border Thinking*. Princeton: Princeton University Press.

Miller, Arthur G. 1991. "Transformations of Time and Space: Oaxaca, Mexico, circa 1500–1700." In S. Küchler and W. Melion, eds., *Images of Memory: On Remembering and Representation*, 141–75. Washington, D.C.: Smithsonian Institution Press.

Mills, Kenneth. 1997. *Idolatry and Its Enemies: Colonial Andean Religion and Extirpation, 1640–1750*. Princeton: Princeton University Press.

Mitchell, W. J. T. 1986. *Iconology: Image, Text, Ideology*. Chicago: University of Chicago Press.

Monterroso y Alvarado, Gabriel de. 1609 [1563]. *Pratica civil, y criminal y instrvcion de escrivanos: Diuidida en nueue trutados*. Madrid: En Casa de Juan de la Cuesta.

Moreno Yáñez, Segundo E. 1976. *Sublevaciones indígenas en la Audiencia de Quito*. Bonn: Estudios Americanistas de Bonn, 5.

Mugaburu, Josephe de, and Francisco de Mugaburu. 1975 [1686]. *Chronicle of Colonial Lima: The Diary of Josephe and Francisco Mugaburu, 1640–1697*. Trans. and ed. Robert Ryal Miller. Norman: University of Oklahoma Press.

Mujica Pinilla, Ramón. 1996. *Ángeles apócrifos en la América virreinal*. 2nd ed. Mexico City: Fondo de Cultura Económica.

Mundy, Barbara. 1996. *The Mapping of New Spain: Indigenous Cartography and the Maps of the Relaciones Geográficas*. Chicago: University of Chicago Press.

Muñoz Camargo, Diego. 1981 [1585]. *Descripción de la ciudad y provincia de Tlaxcala de las Indias del mar oceano para el buen gobierno y ennoblecimiento dellas*. Mexico City: Universidad Nacional Autónoma de México.

Murra, John V. 1975. *Formaciones económicas y políticas del mundo andino*. Lima: Instituto de Estudios Peruanos.

———. 1998. "Litigation over the Rights of 'Natural Lords' in Early Colonial Courts in the Andes." In Elizabeth H. Boon and Tom Cummins, eds., *Native Traditions in the Postconquest World*, 55–62. Washington, D.C.: Dumbarton Oaks Research Library and Collection.

Murúa, Martín de. Ca. 1600. "Historia del origen y genealogía real de los reyes incas del Perú, de sus hechos, costumbres, trajes y manera de gobierno." Sean Galvin Collection, Ireland.

———. 1616. "Historia general del Pirú: Origen y descendencia de los incas, donde se trata, assi de las guerras civiles ingas, como de la entrada de los españoles, descripción de las ciudades y lugares dél, con otras cosas notables." J. Paul Getty Museum, Los Angeles (JPGM/LA), MS Ludwig XIII 16.

Nader, Helen. 1990. *Liberty in Absolutist Spain: The Habsburg Sale of Towns, 1516–1700*. Baltimore: Johns Hopkins University Press.

Neuschel, Kristen B. 1989. *Word of Honor: Interpreting Noble Culture in Sixteenth-Century France*. Ithaca: Cornell University Press.

Niebla, Lorenço de. 1565. *Svmma del estilo de escriuanos y de herencias, y particiones: Y escripturas, y auisos de iuezes*. Seville: Pedro Martínez de Bañares.

Nieto Soria, José Manuel. 1988. *Fundamentos ideológicos del poder real en Castilla (siglos XIII–XVI)*. Madrid: Universidad Complutense.

———. 1993. *Ceremonias de la realeza: Propaganda y legitimación en la Castilla trastámara*. Madrid: Nerea.

Oberem, Udo. 1993. *Sancho Hacho: Un cacique mayor del siglo XVI*. Quito: CEDECO.

Ong, Walter J. 1982. *Orality and Literacy: The Technologizing of the Word*. London: Methuen.

O'Phelan Godoy, Scarlet. 1993. "Tiempo inmemorial, tiempo colonial: Un estudio de casos." *Procesos, Revista Ecuatoriana de Historia* 4: 3–20 (Quito).

Ortega Ricaurte, Enrique. 1935. *San Salvador de Sopó*. Bogotá: Imprenta Nacional.

Ortiz, Fernando. 1995 [1947]. *Cuban Counterpoint: Tobacco and Sugar*. Durham: Duke University Press.

Osorio, Alejandra. 2004. "The King in Lima: Simulacra, Ritual, and Rule in Seventeenth-Century Peru." *Hispanic American Historical Review* 84(3): 447–74.

Osorio Romero, Ignacio. 1993. *La luz imaginaria: Epistolario de Atanasio Kircher con los novohispanos*. Mexico City: Universidad Nacional Autónoma de México.

Pachacuti Yamqui Salcamaygua, Joan de Santa Cruz. 1993 [1613]. *Relación de antigéedades deste Reyno del Pirú*. Ed. Pierre Duviols and César Itier. Lima: Institut Français D'Études Andines.

Pacheco, Francisco. 1990 [1649]. *El arte de la pintura*. Madrid: Ediciones Cátedra.

Padilla, S., M. L. López Arellano, and A. González. 1977. *La encomienda en Popayán: Tres estudios*. Seville: Escuela de Estudios Hispano-Americanos, Consejo Superior de Investigaciones Científicas.

Pagden, Anthony. 1982. *The Fall of Natural Man: The American Indian and the Origins of Comparative Ethnology*. Cambridge: Cambridge University Press.

———. 1987. "Identity Formation in Spanish America." In Nicholas Canny and Anthony Pagden, eds., *Colonial Identity in the Atlantic World, 1500–1800*, 51–93. Princeton: Princeton University Press.

Peña, Fray Pedro de la. 1995 [1570]. "Sinodo quitense: Constituciones para los curacas de indios." In Hugo Burgos, ed., *Primeras doctrinas en la Real Audiencia de Quito, 1570–1640: Estudio preliminar y transcripción de las relaciones eclesiales y misionales de los siglos XVI y XVII*, 460–72. Quito: Ediciones Abya-Yala.

Peña Montenegro, Alonso de la. 1995 [1668]. *Itinerario para parochos de indios*.

Critical edition by C. Baceiro, M. Corrales, J. M. García Añoveros, and F. Maseda. Madrid: Consejo Superior de Investigaciones Científicas.

Penry, S. Elizabeth. 2000. "The Rey Común: Indigenous Political Discourse in Eighteenth-Century Alto Perú." In Luis Roniger and Tamar Herzog, eds. *The Collective and the Public in Latin America: Cultural Identities and Political Order*, 219–37. Brighton, England: Sussex Academic Press.

Pérez de Bocanegra, Juan de. 1631. *Ritual formulario e institución de curas para administrar a los naturales de este Reyno los Santos Sacramentos . . . por el Bachiller J.P.B., presbítero, en la lengua Quechua general*. Lima: Gerónimo de Contreras.

Pérez-Rocha, Emma, and Rafael Tena. 2000. *La nobleza indígena del centro de México después de la Conquista*. Mexico City: Instituto Nacional de Antropología e Historia.

Perry, Mary Elizabeth. 1999. "From Convent to Battlefield: Cross-Dressing and Gendering the Self in the New World of Imperial Spain." In Josiah Blackmore and Gregory S. Hutcheson, eds., *Queer Iberia: Sexualities, Cultures, and Crossings from the Middle Ages to the Renaissance*, 394–419. Durham: Duke University Press.

Phipps, Elena, Johanna Hecht, and Cristina Esteras Martín. 2004. *Colonial Andes: Tapestries and Silverwork, 1530–1830*. New York: Metropolitan Museum of Art.

Pierce, C. S. 1955. "Logic as Semiotic: A Theory of Signs" In Justus Buchler, ed. *Philosophical Writings of Pierce*, 98–119. New York: Dover Publications.

Piñacué, Jesús Enrique. 1997. "Aplicación autonómica de la justicia en comunidades paeces (una aproximación)." In *"Del olvido surgimos para traer nuevas esperanzas"—la jurisdicción especial indígena*, 31–52. Bogotá: Ministerio de Justicia y del Derecho / Ministerio del Interior, Dirección General de Asuntos Indígenas.

Poloni, Jacques. 1992. "Achats et ventes de terres par les indiens de Cuenca au XVIIe. siècle: Éléments de conjoncture économique et de stratification sociale." *Bulletin de l'Institut Français des Études Andines* 21(1): 279–310.

Poole, Deborah A. 1997. *Vision, Race, and Modernity: A Visual Economy of the Andean Image World*. Princeton: Princeton University Press.

Portelli, Alessandro. 1991. *The Death of Luigi Trastulli and Other Stories*. Albany: SUNY Press.

Powers, Karen Vieira. 1995. *Andean Journeys: Migration, Ethnogenesis, and the State in Colonial Quito*. Albuquerque: University of New Mexico Press.

———. 1998. "A Battle of Wills: Inventing Chiefly Legitimacy in the Colonial North Andes." In Susan Kellogg and Matthew Restall, eds., *Dead Giveaways: Indigenous Testaments of Colonial Mesoamerica and the Andes*, 183–213. Salt Lake City: University of Utah Press.

Pratt, Mary Louise. 1992. *Imperial Eyes: Travel Writing and Transculturation*. London: Routledge.

Quiroga, Pedro de. 192 [1562]. *Coloquios de la verdad*. Ed. Daisy Rípodas Ardanaz. Valladolid: Instituto de Cooperación Iberoamericana.

Rafael, Vicente L. 1988. *Contracting Colonialism: Translation and Christian Conversion in Tagalog Society under Early Spanish Rule*. Ithaca: Cornell University Press.

Rama, Ángel. 1996 [1984]. *The Lettered City*. Trans. John Charles Chasteen. Durham: Duke University Press.

Rappaport, Joanne. 1980–81. "El mesianismo y las transformaciones de símbolos mesiánicos en Tierradentro." *Revista Colombiana de Antropología* 23: 365–413 (Bogotá).

————. 1988. "La organización socioterritorial de los pastos: Una hipótesis de trabajo." *Revista de Antropología* 4(2): 71–103 (Bogotá).

————. 1990. "Cultura material a lo largo de la frontera septentrional: Los pastos y sus testamentos." *Revista de Antropología y Arqueología* 6(2): 11–25 (Bogotá).

————. 1993. "Alfabetización y la voz indígena en la época colonial." In Carlos Alberto Uribe Tobón, ed., *La construcción de las Américas*, 112–29, Bogotá: Universidad de los Andes.

————. 1994. *Cumbe Reborn: An Andean Ethnography of History*. Chicago: University of Chicago Press.

————. 1998. *The Politics of Memory: Native Historical Interpretation in the Colombian Andes*. Durham: Duke University Press.

————. 2000. "Hacia la construcción de una historia propia." *C'ayu'ce* 4: 10–13 (Popayán, Colombia).

————. 2009. "Mischievous Lovers, Hidden Moors, and Cross-Dressers: Passing in Colonial Bogotá." *Journal of Spanish Cultural Studies* 10 (1): 7–25.

Rappaport, Joanne, and Tom Cummins. 1994. "Literacy and Power in Colonial Latin America." In Angela Gilliam and George Bond, eds., *The Social Construction of the Past: Representation as Power*, 89–109. London: Routledge.

Rasnake, Roger. 1988. *Domination and Cultural Resistance: Authority and Power among an Andean People*. Durham: Duke University Press.

Real Academia Española. 1990 [1726]. *Diccionario de autoridades: Edición facsímil*. Madrid: Editorial Gredos.

Recopilación de Leyes de los Reynos de las Indias. 1973 [1681]. 4 vols. Madrid: Ediciones Cultural Hispánica.

Remesal, Antonio de. 1620. *Historia general de las Indias Occidentales, y particular de la gouernación de Chiapa, y Guatemala: Escriuese juntamente los principios de la religión de Nuestro Glorioso Padre Santo Domingo, y de las demás religiones . . .* Madrid: Diego de Astor.

Restall, Matthew. 1995. *Life and Death in a Maya Community: The Ixil Testaments of the 1760s*. Lancaster, Calif.: Labyrinthos.

————. 1997. *The Maya World: Yucatec Culture and Society, 1550–1850*. Stanford: Stanford University Press.

————. 1998. *Maya Conquistador*. Boston: Beacon.

Restrepo, Luis Fernando. 2001. "Narrating Colonial Interventions: Don Diego de Torres, *Cacique* of Turmequé in the New Kingdom of Granada." In Alvaro Félix

Bolaños and Gustavo Verdesio, eds., *Colonialism Past and Present: Reading and Writing about Colonial Latin America Today*, 97–117. Albany: SUNY Press.

Restrepo Uribe, Fernando. 1986. *Los Figueroa: aproximación a su época y a su pintura*. Bogotá: Villegas Editores.

Rivera Cusicanqui, Silvia, ed. 1992. *Educación indígena: ¿Ciudadanía o colonización?* La Paz: Ediciones Aruwiyiri.

Rodríguez Jiménez, Pablo, ed. 2002. *Testamentos indígenas de Santafé de Bogotá, siglos XVI–XVII*. Bogotá: Alcaldía Mayor de Bogotá, Instituto Distrital de Cultura y Turismo.

Rojas, Ulíses. 1965. *El Cacique de Turmequé y su época*. Tunja, Colombia: Imprenta Departamental de Boyacá.

Rojas Curieux, Tulio Enrique. 1998. *La lengua páez: Una visión de su gramática*. Bogotá: Ministerio de Cultura.

Romero, Mario Germán. 1960. *Fray Juan de los Barrios y la evangelización del Nuevo Reino de Granada*. Bogotá: Academia Colombiana de Historia.

Romero Rey, Monsignor Mario Germán. 1988. "Introducción: Los catecismos y la catequesis desde el Descubrimiento hasta 1650." In Fray Luis Zapata de Cárdenas, OFM, *Primer catecismo en Santa Fe de Bogotá: Manual de pastoral diocesana del siglo XVI*, 13–26. Bogotá: Consejo Episcopal Latinoamericano (CELAM).

Rosaldo, Renato. 1995. "Forward." In Néstor García Canclini, *Hybrid Cultures: Strategies for Entering and Leaving Modernity*, xi–xvii. Minneapolis: University of Minnesota Press.

Ross, Marlon B. 1994. "Authority and Authenticity: Scribbling Authors and the Genius of Print in Eighteenth-Century England." In Martha Woodmansee and Peter Jaszi, eds., *The Construction of Authorship: Textual Appropriation in Law and Literature*, 231–57. Durham: Duke University Press.

Rowe, John. 1954. "El movimiento nacional inca del siglo XVIII." *Revista de la Universidad del Cusco* 197: 17–47.

Roys, Ralph L. 1967 [1933]. *The Book of Chilam Balam of Chumayel*. Norman: University of Oklahoma Press.

Ruiz, Teófilo F. 1985. "Unsacred Monarchy: The Kings of Castile in the Late Middle Ages." In Sean Wilentz, ed., *Rites of Power: Symbolism, Ritual, and Politics since the Middle Ages*, 109–44. Philadelphia: University of Pennsylvania Press.

Russo, Alessandra 2002. "Plumes of Sacrifice: Transformation in Sixteenth-Century Mexican Feather Art." *Res* 42: 226–50.

Sahagún, Bernardino de. 1956–69 [1579]. *Florentine Codex*. Trans. and ed. Charles E. Dibble, Arthur Anderson, and J. O. Anderson. 13 vols. Salt Lake City: University of Utah Press.

———. 1979 [ca. 1579]. *Historia general de las cosas de Nueva España, códice florentino*. Mexico City: Secretaría de Gobernación.

Sahas, Daniel J. 1986. *Icon and Logos: Sources in the Eighth-Century Iconoclasm*. Toronto: University of Toronto Press.

————. 1993. "Los pueblos de indios en el Nuevo Reino de Granada y Popayán." In Gutiérrez, Ramón, ed., *Pueblos de indios: Otro urbanismo en la región andina*, 179–203. Quito: Ediciones Abya-Yala.

Salinas y Córdoba, Buenaventura de. 1957 [1630]. *Memorial de las historias del Nuevo Mundo Pirú*. Vol. 1. Lima: Universidad Nacional de San Marcos.

Salomon, Frank. 1986. *Native Lords of Quito in the Age of the Incas: The Political Economy of North Andean Chiefdoms*. Cambridge: Cambridge University Press.

————. 1987–88. "Indian Women of Early Colonial Quito as Seen through Their Testaments." *Americas* 44: 325–41.

————. 1991. "Introductory Essay: The Huarochirí Manuscript." In Frank Salomon and George L. Urioste, trans., *The Huarochirí Manuscript: A Testament of Ancient and Colonial Andean Religion*, 1–38. Austin: University of Texas Press.

————. 1998. "Collquiri's Dam: The Colonial Re-Voicing of an Appeal to the Archaic." In Elizabeth Hill Boone and Tom Cummins, eds., *Native Traditions in the Postconquest World*, 265–94. Washington, D.C.: Dumbarton Oaks Research Library and Collection.

————. 2004. *The Cord Keepers: Khipus and Cultural Life in a Peruvian Village*. Durham: Duke University Press.

Salomon, Frank, and George L. Urioste, trans. 1991. *The Huarochirí Manuscript: A Testament of Ancient and Colonial Andean Religion*. Austin: University of Texas Press.

Sánchez Cantón, F. J., ed. 1958 [1599]. *Inventarios reales bienes muebles que pertenecieron a Felipe II*. Madrid: Real Academia de la Historia, Archivo Documental Español, vol. 10.

————. 1960 [1599]. *Inventarios reales bienes muebles que pertenecieron a Felipe II*. Madrid: Real Academia de la Historia, Archivo Documental Español, vol. 11.

Sandoval, Alonso de. 1627. *Naturaleza, policia sagradas i profanas, costumbres i ritos i catechismo evangelico de todos etiopes*. Seville: Francisco de Lira.

Santa Gertrudis Serra, Juan de. 1970 [ca. 1775]. *Maravillas de la naturaleza*. Bogotá: Empresa Nacional de Publicaciones.

Santo Tomás, Fray Domingo de. 1951 [1560]. *Lexicon o vocabulario de la lengua general del Peru*. Lima: Edición del Instituto de Historia.

Schroeder, H. J. 1978 [1564]. *The Canons and Decrees of the Council of Trent*. Rockford, Ill.: Tan Books and Publishers.

Schwartz, Stuart B. 1995. "Colonial Identities and the *Sociedad de Castas*." *Colonial Latin American Review* 4(1): 185–201.

Sebastián López, Santiago. 1985. "El arte iberoamericano del siglo XVI: Santiago, Méjico, Colombia, Venezuela y Ecuador." *Summa Artis: Historia General del Arte*. Vol. 27, 569–95. 2nd edition. Madrid: Espasa-Calpe.

————. 1986. "Las jerarquías angélicas de Sopó." In Ernesto Franco Rugeles, *Arcángeles de Sopó*, 3–19. Bogotá: Museo de Arte Religioso, Banco de la República.

————. 1992. *Iconografía e iconología del arte novohispano*. Mexico City: Grupo Azabeche.

————. 1995. *Emblemática e historia del arte*. Madrid: Ediciones Cátedra.

Seed, Patricia. 1991. "Colonial and Postcolonial Discourse." *Latin American Research Review* 26: 181–202.

————. 1995. *Ceremonies of Possession in Europe's Conquest of the New World, 1492–1640*. Cambridge: Cambridge University Press.

Serlio, Sebastiano. 1537. *Regole generale di architettura sopra le cinque maniere de gli edifici cioè Thoscano, Dorico, Ionico, Corinthio, et Composito*. Venice: Per Francesco Marcolini da Forli.

————. 1540. *Delle antichità: Il terzo libro nel quale si figurano e descrivono le antichità di Roma e le altre che sono in Italia e sopra Italia*. Venice: Per Francesco Marcolini da Forli.

————. 1547. *Quinto libro d'architettura nel quale se tratta di diverse forme de tempii*. Paris: Impr. de M. de Vascosan.

Seth, Vanita. 2010. *Europe's Indians: Producing Racial Difference, 1500–1900*. Durham: Duke University Press.

Sherman, Claire Richter. 2000. *Writing on Hands: Memory and Knowledge in Early Modern Europe*. Carlisle: Trout Gallery, Dickson College.

Silverblatt, Irene. 2000. "New Christians and New World Fears in Seventeenth-Century Peru." *Comparative Studies in Society and History* 42(3): 524–46.

Simón, Fray Pedro de. 1981 [1627]. *Noticias historiales de las conquistas de Tierra Firme en las Indias Occidentales*. Vol. 3. Bogotá: Biblioteca Banco Popular, vol. 105.

Smail, Daniel Lord. 1999. *Imaginary Cartographies: Possession and Identity in Late Medieval Marseille*. Ithaca: Cornell University Press.

Smith, Paul Julian. 1989. *The Body Hispanic: Gender and Sexuality in Spanish and Spanish American Literature*. Oxford: Clarendon Press.

Spalding, Karen. 1984. *Huarochirí: An Andean Society under Inca and Spanish Rule*. Stanford: Stanford University Press.

Spira, Gregory P. 1998. "'El Ingreso Secreto': Viceregal Entry Ceremonies and the Consolidation of Legitimate Government." Manuscript. Washington, D.C.

Stock, Brian. 1983. *The Implications of Literacy: Written Language and Models of Interpretation in the Eleventh and Twelfth Centuries*. Princeton: Princeton University Press.

————. 1990. *Listening for the Text: On the Uses of the Past*. Baltimore: Johns Hopkins University Press.

Stoichita, Victor. 1994. *Visionary Experience in the Golden Age of Spanish Art*. London: Reaktion Books.

Street, Brian. 1984. *Literacy in Theory and Practice*. Cambridge: Cambridge University Press.

Tavárez, David Eduardo. 1999. "La idolatría letrada: Un análisis comparativo de textos clandestinos rituales y devocionales en comunidades nahuas y zapotecas, 1613–1654." *Historia Mexicana* 49 (2): 197–252 (Mexico City).

Terraciano, Kevin. 2001. *The Mixtecs of Colonial Oaxaca: Ñudzahui History, Sixteenth through Eighteenth Centuries.* Stanford: Stanford University Press.

Thierry, Augustin. 1850–70. *Recueil des monuments inédits de l'histoire du Tiers état: 1. série: Chartes, coutumes, actes municipaux, statuts des corporations d'arts et métiers des villes et communes de France: Région du Nord.* Paris: Firmin-Didot.

Thomas, Nicolas. 1991. *Entangled Objects: Exchange, Material Culture, and Colonialism.* Cambridge: Harvard University Press.

Thurner, Mark. 1997. *From Two Republics to One Divided: Contradictions of Postcolonial Nationmaking in Andean Peru.* Durham: Duke University Press.

Todorov, Tzvetan. 1984. *The Conquest of America: The Question of the Other.* Trans. Richard Howard. New York: Harper Collins.

Tomlinson, Gary. 1996. "Unlearning the Aztec *Cantares* (Preliminaries to a Postcolonial History)." In Margreta de Grazia, Maureen Quilligan, and Peter Stallybrass, eds., *Subject and Object in Renaissance Culture,* 260–86. Cambridge: Cambridge University Press.

Torquemada, Juan de. 1616. *Monarquía indiana.* Seville: Matthias Clauso.

Triana y Antorveza, Humberto. 1987. *Las lenguas indígenas en la historia social del Nuevo Reino de Granada.* Bogotá: Instituto Caro y Cuervo, Biblioteca "Ezequiel Uricoechea" no. 2.

Trouillot, Michel-Rolph. 1995. *Silencing the Past.* Boston: Beacon.

Twinam, Ann. 1999. *Public Lives, Private Secrets: Gender, Honor, Sexuality, and Illegitimacy in Colonial Spanish America.* Stanford: Stanford University Press.

Urton, Gary. 1994. "A New Twist in an Old Yarn: Variation in Knot Directionality in the Inka Khipus." *Baessler-Archiv,* new series, vol. XLII: 271–305 (Berlin).

———. 1998. "From Knots to Narratives: Reconstructing the Art of Historical Record-Keeping in the Andes from Spanish Transcriptions of Inka Khipus." *Ethnohistory* 45(3): 409–438.

———. 2003. *Signs of the Inka Khipu: Binary Coding in the Andean Knotted-String Records.* Austin: University of Texas Press.

Urton, Gary, and Jeffrey Quilter, eds. 2002. *Narrative Threads: Accounting and Recounting in Andean Khipu.* Austin: University of Texas Press.

Uzcátegui Andrade, Byron. 1989. "Segundo testamento de Doña Beatriz Coquiliago Ango, Nuera del Inca Atahualpa." *Miscelánea Histórica Ecuatoriana* 2(2): 138–48 (Quito).

Valadés, Diego. 1579. *Rhetorica christiana.* Perugia.

Vallín, Rodolfo. 1998. *Imágenes bajo cal y pañete: La pintura mural de Colombia.* Bogotá: El Sello Editorial.

Valtion, Emelio. 1947. *El primer libro de alfabetizacón en América: Cartilla para enseñar a leer impresa por Pedro Ocharte en México, 1569.* Mexico City.

Valverde, Fernando, O.S.A. 1641. *Santuario de N. Señora de Copacabana en el Perú*. Lima.

Vargas Ugarte, R., ed. 1951–54. *Concilios limenses (1551–1772)*. 3 vols. Lima: Rávago e Hijos.

Villanueva Urteaga, Horacio. 1971 [1970]. "Documentos sobre Yucay en el Siglo XVI." *Revista del Archivo Histórico del Cuzco* 13: 1–148.

Voragine, Jacobus de. 1995 [mid thirteenth century]. *The Golden Legend: Readings on the Saints*. Trans. William Granger Ryan. Princeton: Princeton University Press.

White, Richard. 1991. *The Middle Ground: Indians, Empires, and Republics in the Great Lakes Region, 1650–1815*. Cambridge: Cambridge University Press.

Wintroub, Michael. 1998. "Civilizing the Savage and Making a King: The Royal Entry Festival of Henri II (Rouen, 1550)." *Sixteenth Century Journal* 29(2): 465–94.

Wood, Christopher S. 1993. *Albrecht Aldorfer and the Origins of Landscape*. Chicago: University of Chicago Press.

Wood, Robert D., S.M. 1986. *"Teach Them Good Customs": Colonial Indian Education and Acculturation in the Andes*. Culver City, Calif.: Labyrinthos.

Wood, Stephanie. 1998. "The Social vs. Legal Context of Nahuatl *Titulos*." In Elizabeth H. Boon and Tom Cummins, eds., *Native Traditions in the Postconquest World*, 201–31. Washington, D.C.: Dumbarton Oaks Research Library and Collection.

Yates, Frances. 1966. *The Art of Memory*. London: Routledge and Kegan Paul

Young, Robert J. C. 1995. *Colonial Desire: Hybridity in Theory, Culture and Race*. London: Routledge.

Zambrano Escovar, Marta. 2008. *Trabajadores, villanos y amantes: Encuentros entre indígenas y españoles en la ciudad letrada, Santa Fe de Bogotá (1550–1650)*. Bogotá: Editorial Instituto Colombiano de Antropología e Historia.

Zamora, Alonso de. 1701. *Historia de la Provincia de San Antonio del Nuevo Reyno de Granada*. Barcelona: Joseph Llopis.

Zapata de Cárdenas, Fray Luis, OFM. 1988 [1576]. *Primer catecismo en Santa Fe de Bogotá: Manual de pastoral diocesana del siglo XVI*. Transcription by Msgr. Fr. Alberto Lee López, OFM; introduction by Msgr. Mario Germán Romero Rey. Bogotá: Consejo Episcopal Latinoamericano (CELAM).

Zavala, Virginia. 1996. "El castellano de la sierra del Perú." In Hiroyasu Tomoeda and Luis Millones, eds., *La tradición andina en tiempos modernos*, 81–131, Osaka: National Museum of Ethnology.

Zuckerman, Michael. 1977. "The Fabrication of Identity in Early America." *William and Mary Quarterly*, 3rd ser., 34(2): 183–214.

Zuidema, R. Tom. 1977. "The Inca Kinship System: A New Theoretical View." In R. Bolton and E. Mayer, eds., *Andean Kinship and Marriage*, 240–81. Washington, D.C.: Special Publications of the American Anthropological Association, no. 7.

Index

tion as, 269 n. 12; painting, 35, 75, 77, 268 n. 10

Castile, Castilian, 30, 36, 46, 114, 116–17, 130, 145, 147, 215, 219, 270 n. 17; grammar and vocabulary of, 228

catechism, 6, 85, 97, 126–27, 188, 211–12, 217, 226, 229, 245, 255, 265 n. 15, 280 n. 49, 290 n. 22; ekphrasis in, 24; inclusion of syllabary in, 25; Third Catechism of Lima, 9, 62, 137, 208–12, 290 n. 22, 305 n. 24

Catholic church, 61, 63, 66, 131

Catholicism, 30, 62, 84–85, 147, 151, 188, 214–15, 237–38, 256; doctrinal images of, 212; ritual in, 190, 240; Spanish identity and, 36

cave, 80, 83–86, 102; manmade, 81–82; mural painting in, 280 n. 48; as sacred space, 78, 79–80

celebration, 98; in antiquity, 274 n. 18; civic, 48; of figure of king, 214–15; of mass, 93, 279 n. 45. See also ceremony; festival; ritual

ceremony, 21, 26, 114, 119; of possession, 120, 122. See also celebration; festival; ritual

Chandler, Nahum, 34, 41

chaos, 222; of New World, 221; order of plaza vs., 227

Charles II, King of Spain, 214–15; portrait of, 216, 308 n. 39

Charles V, Holy Roman Emperor, 30, 54, 74, 103, 183, 214, 264 n. 2

Chibcha, as common language of Muisca, 266 n. 16

Chibcha (ethnic group). See Muisca

chicha (corn beer), 137

China, 107–8; textiles from, 139

Chiquinquirá, 84, 253; Virgin of, 65, 102, 140, 252, 278 n. 39, 300 n. 27

Cholo, 58. See also race: racial mixing and

Christ, 61–63, 85, 88, 93, 98–101, 135, 209, 211–16, 252–53, 272 n. 13, 273 n. 16, 279 n. 45, 308 n. 39; body of, 215; El Señor de Sopó, 73; life of, 249; miraculous ap-

pearance of, 279 n. 45; Passion of, 70, 86, 91, 104, 249; sculpture of, 106, 286 n. 73. See also images: miraculous; Passion of Christ

Christians, Christianity, 24–32, 37, 39–46, 63, 64, 67–68, 74, 82–84, 93, 96, 98, 102, 111, 115, 130, 132, 135, 137, 142, 145, 146, 151, 154, 162, 165, 167, 183, 185, 197, 211, 213, 218, 229, 233, 247, 249, 256, 266 n. 19, 307 n. 31; authority of, 200, 304 n. 16; creation of order and, 221; conversion to, 9; culture of, 66; doctrine of, 103, 127, 210–11, 219, 226, 256, 266 n. 16; Holy Family, 212; Holy Land and, 136; Holy See, 65; performance of mysteries of, 242; practitioners of vs. non-practitioners of, 229, 255; pre-Columbian parallels with, 249–50; ritual of, 192; symbols of, 97

Chupas, 176, 178–79, 183; litigation over village of, 301 n. 31; region of, 31

church (building): courtyard of, 225, 242; interior space of, 229, 240; in town plans, 223–24

Church (institution), 54, 65, 85, 113, 130, 132, 135, 178, 188, 214, 224, 226, 233, 237; doctrine of, 127; knowledge of indigenous languages and, 118

city: foundation of, 114; planning of, 222–23

City of God (Saint Augustine), 222

civility: grid as expression of, 222; teleological movement toward, 233

civitas, 224, 226, 235

Clanchy, Michael T., 253, 289 n. 8

cleanliness, as sign of order, 219–20

clothing, 50, 51, 220; as social marker, 37

coats of arms, 4, 104, 106, 109–11, 174, 175, 187, 214; bestowal of, 183, 188; falsification of, 184; invention of, 184, 190; in relation to text, 185; royal, 195

Cobo, Bernabé, 224

collaboration. See documents: collective nature of

Colombia, 3, 5, 8, 70, 80, 86, 97, 118, 147,

crucifix. *See* cross

cultural hybridity (Bhabha), 31

Cumbal, 121, 132, 149, 196–97, 199, 201–2, 217, 226, 231; territorial organization of, 231

Cundinamarca, 22, 73, 78–79, 85, 137, 230, 238

Cuzco, 28, 31, 47–48, 142, 199–201, 216; cathedral in, 215

Dagenais, John, 12, 229

Dean, Carolyn, 28, 51, 142

destruction, 84. *See also* extirpation; iconoclasm

devil, 71, 82–83, 131; city of, 222; as deceiver, 67, 78, 81, 84, 305 n. 25; fear of, 102; protection against, 131, 210

devotional objects, 140

Diálogos de la pintura: Su defensa, origen, essencia, definición, modos y diferencias (Carducho), 61

dictation, 16, 118, 134, 210

dictionaries, 61, 210, 237; Andean, 290 n. 22; bilingual, 288 n. 7; of indigenous languages, 118, 200; standardization of language and, 210

difference: architectonic space and, 229; awareness of race and, 271 n. 6; genre and, 61, 69

diglossia, colonial, 115

disenchantment, 84, 112

doctrina, 30, 69, 237

document, documents, 33, 50, 115–17, 125, 134, 157, 220; acts of foundation in, 222; as artifacts, 24; assemblage of, 155, 254; authenticity of, 123, 126, 145, 162, 171–72; availability of, 9, 228; burning of, 183–84; collective nature of, 118, 128, 144; color symbolism in, 227; genres of, 126, 128; imprecision of, 18; in land disputes, 119, 124, 126, 142–43; in Mesoamerica, 116; in Quechua language, 116; legal, 32, 47, 118, 142, 166, 170, 174; nonwritten aspects of, 16, 24, 150, 169, 174, 227; notarial, 21, 122; as objects of power and value, 140, 160, 183, 254; ontological status of, 204; as palimpsests, 118, 142, 163; production of, 133, 153, 156, 171; quasi-sacred nature of, 148, 218; reception of, 10, 118, 148, 153, 156, 232, 254; reliance on, 114, 123, 218; ritual manipulation of, 113, 194, 204, 217, 229, 247; transculturation and, 116, 145, 156, 174. *See also* manuscript, manuscripts; *and under types of documents*

Dominican order, 68, 80, 252, 275 n. 26; 286 n. 73; pastoral work of, 253

double consciousness (Du Bois), 33–35, 43–44, 47

double voicing (Bakhtin), 44

drawing, 174–75, 220; of maps, 114; writing and, 14, 16, 265 n. 12

dreams, 101–3, 253–54

drinking, ritual significance of, 137. *See also* vessels

Du Bois, W. E. B., 33, 43, 44

Ecuador, 5, 8, 37, 47, 132, 135, 157, 173, 195, 199, 265 n. 9, 287 n. 1, 294 n. 44

Eire, Carlos, 131, 135–36

ejecutorio, 174, 183

ekphrasis, 24–25, 266 n. 22

Emblemas morales (Covarrubias Orozco), 55, 273 n. 17

emblems, 55, 59, 61, 74, 90, 112; allegorical nature of, 60; books of, 272 n. 10. *See also* allegory

empire, 61, 226; administration of, 113; hierarchical character of Spanish, 114

encomendero, 248, 251; legitimization of, 247

encomienda, 30, 39, 67, 145, 147, 292 n. 30

encyclopedia, 244; as pedagogical technique, 245

ephemeral arch, 216, 235, 245, 308 n. 38

ephemerality of ritual, 193, 215

escutcheon. *See* coats of arms

Esmeraldas, 37, 49

Espinosa, Carlos, 47–48, 270 n. 20, 308 n. 37

Eucharist, 215–16, 308 n. 39; as Christian ritual image, 304 n. 16
evangelization, 46, 67–68, 77, 84, 90, 113, 221, 290 n. 22. *See also* conversion
evidence, 140, 153, 156, 162, 232; forms of, 157, 167; fraudulence of, 300 n. 24; visual, 175, 190; written vs. unrecorded, 155, 169, 172
Exercise of Armes, The (De Gheyn), 74. *See also* Wapenhandelinghe
extirpation, 77, 79, 84, 122; through fire, 80, 83, 137; of idolatry, 73

falsity, falsification, 173. *See also* forgery, forgeries
fashion, 139, 180
Favián, Alexandro, 104–5, 107
featherwork, 103–4, 106–7, 109, 111, 119; paintings in, 284 n. 62; portrait in, 104–5
Fernández de Piedrahita, Lucas, 106–7, 285 n. 68
festival, 47; misinterpretation of, 48
Figueroa, Gaspar de, 92, 101, 140, 280 n. 46
fire, destruction by, 80, 83, 137, 183–84
Flanders, 103, 110–11, 205
Florentine Codex (Sahagún), 205
Fontibón, Christian ritual in, 98
forgery, forgeries, 126, 227; allegations of, 172; of coats of arms, 184; of documents, 145, 171, 173, 184; of genealogy, 184; prevention of, 205
France, rise of absolutism in, 213
Franciscan order, 42, 70, 80, 86, 88, 90–91, 97, 137, 148, 238, 244
Fraser, Valerie, 222, 309 n. 3
Frezier, Amédée, 71

Galíndez, Sebastián, 128–29, 159
Galle, Philippe, 74
Gante, Pedro de, 91
Garcilaso de la Vega, el Inca, 3–4, 30, 57–59, 116, 128, 189, 264 n. 5, 270 n. 18, 271 n. 6, 288 n. 5
genealogy, 159, 169, 183, 186; books of, 184;

casta and, 267 n. 2; inheritance and, 161; kinship factor and, 168; "of knowledge," 296 n. 2; among Mixtec, 301 n. 29; of nobility, 168, 264 n. 5, 284 n. 63; paintings of, 47–48
gesture, 50
Gheyn, Jacob de, 74
God, 61–63, 67–68, 88–93, 98–100, 104–5, 127, 130, 136–37, 148, 185, 208, 211, 214, 221, 224; anointing of earthly ruler by, 303 n. 13; City of, 222
Golden Legend (De Voragine), 93
González Echevarría, Roberto, 128, 288 n. 5
González Holguín, Diego, 200, 210, 305 n. 26
Goodman, Nelson, 16
Goody, Jack, 253, 312 n. 13
grammar: books on, 126; as element of standardization, 210; of indigenous languages, 118, 221
Gregory I, Pope, 42, 64, 70
grid, 6, 30, 85, 239, 309 n. 3; as expression of order, 221, 226, 231, 233, 256, 309 n. 3; as ideal, 222; graphic rendering of, 176, 225, 234; philosophical basis for, 222; sacral and secular roles of, 221, 226; in town planning, 190, 221–22, 225, 257, 309 n. 2
Gruzinski, Serge, 146–47, 266 n. 20, 287 n. 2
Guaca, 128, 129, 132, 159, 199, 287 n. 1, 296 n. 3
guaca. *See* huaca
Guacar Paucar, Felipe, 4, 183
Guachán, Magdalena, 128–29, 159
Guachocal Assa, Diego, 135, 163–65, 171, 188
Guachucal, 135, 157, 161–62, 166, 169, 173, 217, 232
Guadalupe, Virgin of, 65
Guamanga. *See* Huamanga
Guaman Malque, Domingo, 179–82. *See also* Ayala, Martín de
Guaman Poma de Ayala, Felipe, 3, 12, 14–16, 22, 25, 31, 39, 56, 97, 116–17, 128,

176–82, 192, 265 n. 12, 267 n. 24, 281
n. 50, 288 n. 5, 301 n. 31, 301 n. 33. *See
also under titles of individual works by*
Guanmanmira, Sebastián, 122
Guapastal, Juan Francisco, 125, 149
Guevara, Felipe de, 103
Guinea, 57

Hacho de Velasco, Sancho, 185–88
hacienda, 145
handwriting, 265 n. 14, 304 n. 20; dissimi-
larity of, 173; illegibility of, 172. *See also*
writing
Hanks, William, 117, 155–56, 193, 203, 287
n. 2
heir, 131. *See also* wills
Hell, 137
Henao, Pedro de, 189
heraldry, 157, 174, 183; indigenous, 186
hermaphrodite, 59
heterogeneity, 40; of colonial culture, 9,
49, 156, 232, 250; of colonial writing,
116–17; of cultural codes, 46, 48; of cultures, 26, 29–30; of images, 54
hierarchy, 6, 29, 48, 65, 69, 82, 99, 114, 121,
221; cultural, 5; geopolitical, 94, 178, 203,
232; social, 30, 35, 104, 115, 174, 226, 231,
256–57
hieroglyphic literacy, 22, 116, 254, 266
n. 20, 287 n. 2
*Historia del origen y genealogía real de los
reyes Incas del Perú* (Murúa), 179, 184
*Historia general del Pirú, origen y descen-
dencia de los Incas* (Murúa), 184
history, production of, 153
Holy Roman Emperor, 105, 284 n. 63
Host. *See* Eucharist
huaca, 198–99, 213; kissing and, 246
Huamanga, 25, 176, 178–79, 301 n. 31
Huancavelica, 136
Huánuco, 183
Huaráz, 46
Huayna Capac, 47–48
hybridity, 29–30; colonial, 188, 250; in
Latin America, 268 n. 5

Ibarra, 19, 47–48, 51, 122–25, 129, 150, 160,
231; district of, 123, 132, 135, 136, 154;
notarial record of, 292 n. 32, 296 n. 3
Iberia, 67; urban landscape of, 222. *See also*
Spain
Iberian Peninsula, 30, 35, 42
iconoclasm, 62, 66, 77. *See also* extirpation
identity, 35–36, 40, 43, 51; ambiguity of
religious, 42; blurring of, 44; construction of colonial, 41, 147; creation of, 35;
duality of, 39; modes of social, 240; relational, 34, 36
idol, idols, 68, 79–80, 83, 85–86, 213; destruction of, 78. *See also* iconoclasm;
extirpation
idolatry, 32, 40–41, 43, 47–48, 51, 66, 68,
79–81, 251; distinction between veneration and, 212; extirpation of, 84; among
Nasa, 276 n. 30; persistence of, 71; rejection of, by *indios ladinos*, 298 n. 13; similarity of Christian rites with, 67
Illescas, Alonso de, 195–96
illiteracy, 127, 134, 156, 202, 219, 228; bar-
barity linked to, 64; in legal disputes,
203; legibility of images and, 70, 196, 204
images, 9, 54, 235; allegorical, 97; of birds,
80; in conversion, 64; copying of, 175,
182–83; defense of, 62; description of,
175, destruction of, 64; for devotion-
als, 63, 252; doctrinal, 64; in documents,
175; in dreams, 101–3; emblematic, 187;
illiteracy and, 70, 204; as illustrations of
sermons, 71, 192; inspired by prints, 97;
intended public of, 61; in legal disputes,
175, 175; miraculous, 64, 65, 74, 102, 112,
252, 253, 286 n. 73; narrative pictorial,
126; as objects of power, 101, 142; production of, 193; referentiality of, 63; religious, 61, 66, 84, 111, 140, 226; secular,
61; seriality of, 70; substitution of, 85; as
surrogate of king, 215; text and, 140, 205,
212; touch and, 196; transportability of,
70; truthful vs. deceitful, 66, 68, 77–78,
112; veneration of, 212. *See also* iconoclasm; emblems; extirpation

imagined community (Anderson), 31
Immaculate Conception, Virgin of the, 86,
104, 284 n. 62
Inca, 3, 18, 28, 31, 33, 47–48, 51, 57, 59,
71, 106, 109, 115, 124, 128, 132, 150, 168,
179–80, 184, 186, 198–201, 214, 246, 248,
268 n. 9, 278 n. 39, 287 n. 1, 287 n. 2, 292
n. 28, 302 n. 35; control of Pasto region
by, 294 n. 44; deities of, 273 n. 18; indigenous references to, 248; royalty of,
54, 264 n. 5; symbols of authority of,
250; treatment of, as model, 139, 247;
use of Quechua and, 266 n. 16
Inca, Alonso Florencio, 47–51
Indies, 57, 68, 213
indio (racial category), 17, 28–29, 34–41,
44–47, 57–58, 68, 79–84, 92, 98, 107–8,
127, 133, 154, 158–60, 163, 165, 167, 172,
176, 185–86, 199, 212, 224, 246, 267 n. 2,
268 n. 9, 269 n. 12; identity of, 51; rationality of, 69, 274 n. 19; as term, 265
n. 13, 267 nn. 1–2. *See also* República
de Indios
indio ladino, 18, 40–42, 51, 91, 94, 96, 101,
126–27, 165, 270 n. 17, 278 n. 39; as blurring of boundaries, 56; as negative category, 41, 166; as positive category, 298
n. 13
indoctrination, 30, 64, 66, 70, 85, 97, 126,
209, 235, 245, 275 n. 26
indulgences, purchase of, 94
inheritance, 24, 119, 131; defined by genealogy, 161; of lands, 169; of religious art-
works, 140. *See also* testament; wills
interculturality, 126, 162, 166
interpreter, 118, 123, 134, 143, 153, 199, 281
n. 52; as government position, 293 n. 36;
as mediator, 173; testimony and, 169. *See
also* translation
intertextuality, 117, 120, 140, 143, 150,
155–56, 160–63, 187; of documents, 137;
in notarial practice, 123; of wills, 140; of
written and non-literate modes of inscription, 192–93, 300 n. 23
invasion, 114. *See also* conquest of Americas

inventory, 137, 148; khipus as, 117
Islam, 66; culture of, 30; political culture
of, 197
Italy, 104, 237
Itinerario para parochos de indios (Peña
Montenegro), 133

Jamieson, Ross, 233, 310 n. 8
Jauja, 4, 183–84
Jesuit order, 97–98, 104, 200–201, 221, 224,
242, 252–53, 289 n. 14; annual letters of,
221, 251; employment of interpreters by,
281 n. 52
Jews, 35–36; Sephardic, 42
Justice, Steven, 10, 14

Kantorowicz, Ernst, 213, 307 n. 33
khipu, khipus, 149, 175, 210, 288 nn. 6–7;
confession based on use of, 305 n. 25; as
form of literacy, 10; longevity of, 117–18;
as nonlinguistic system of inscribing
narrative, 248; as parallel literate system,
116; as record of statistical data, 117
king of Spain, 122, 126, 128, 184, 192, 246;
ritualized recognition of authority
of, 197. *See also* Crown (monarchy of
Spain); *and under names of individual
monarchs*
kinship, 230; models of, 168; networks of,
221
Kircher, Athanasius, 104–105, 107
kissing, 198; as act of obedience, 173, 209,
246; as act of reverence, 199–200, 307
n. 31; of crucifix, 211; of document, 24,
195–97, 254; of religious images, 62; of
royal seal, 21, 149, 213, 218; of Torah,
303 n. 9

lacquerwork, 140
Lake Titicaca, 71
lands: claims to, 174, 201; boundaries of,
121–22, 141–42, 158, 300 n. 23; cultivation of, 199; disputes over, 142, 147, 157,
176, 192, 194, 228, 231–32; grants of, 141;
ownership of, 119–20, 147, 169; rights to,

New Spain, Viceroyalty of, 70, 75, 90, 104

New World, 30, 58, 65–66, 74, 215, 222, 240, 244; antiquity and, 67

Nicaea. *See* councils, ecumenical: Second Council of Nicaea

nightmares, 79; appearance of images in, 101–3. *See also* dreams

nobility, 34, 42, 50–51, 183; *cacique* and, 302 n. 35; claims to, 27, 31, 186; hereditary, 176, 202; indigenous, 3, 40, 91, 93–94, 96, 104, 109, 114–16, 123, 132, 134–35, 137, 139, 157, 166, 168, 184–85, 188, 189–92, 199–200, 203, 213, 218, 230–31, 247, 250, 268 n. 7, 278 n. 39, 290 n. 20; marriage and, 35; Mexican, 3, 264 n. 4; of painting, 63; Pasto, 287 n. 1, 292 n. 32, 294 n. 42, 294 n. 44; recognition of, 143, 308 n. 36; Spanish, 35, 114, 123; titles of, 174, 179; Tuza, 296 n. 3; Wanka, 184, 186

Northern Andes, 5, 8, 18, 22, 26, 31, 36, 47, 106, 116, 118, 120, 122, 128, 134, 137, 142, 149–50, 153, 156, 186, 192, 198, 204, 210, 212, 220, 248, 254, 302 n. 35; dictionaries from, 290 n. 22; social disorganization of, 33

notary, 21, 114–16, 118, 122–24, 126, 129, 131, 134, 141, 147, 149–50, 154, 158, 167, 170, 173, 182–83, 197, 205, 222, 258; as assurance of uniformity in documents, 133; as author of documents, 128; as creator of legal truth, 20; formulaic inscription of memory by, 196; illegibility of handwriting of, 172, 227; instruction of, 127; testimony by, 171; as translator, 20; as uncommon profession, 254; validation of documents and testimony by, 140, 203, 292 n. 32. *See also* translation

Nueva corónica y buen gobierno (Guaman Poma de Ayala), 12, 22, 57, 128, 176, 179, 182, 301 n. 31, 302 n. 33

Oberem, Udo, 135

Old Testament, 106, 216, 255; Book of Judges, 67

orality, 16, 155; alphabetic documents as, 24; in Andes, 117, 288 n. 6; documentation of, 156, 201; literacy and, 5, 11, 119, 154, 169–70; as mediator, 6; of primordial titles, 146; Quechua, 15

order, 54, 56, 219; creation of, 221, 223–24, 233; distinctions of *género* and, 55; ideological notion of, 222; illusion of, 239. *See also* ambiguity

orders, Catholic religious, 115. *See also under names of individual orders*

Ortiz, Fernando, 45

otherness, 11, 42, 50–51, 157; European perceptions of, 139; ordering of, 245; as subject of painting, 39

Pacheco, Francisco, 54, 85

Pacific, 36, 196

Paéz (ethnic group). *See* Nasa (ethnic group)

paganism, 66–68, 70, 78, 253; Christianity vs., 167

pageantry, 48–49, 270 n. 21. *See also* celebration; ceremony; festival; ritual

painters, 254

paintings: *casta*, 75; on copper, 110–11; Corpus Christi, 215; as cultural literacy, 153; illusionary properties of, 238; imitation of, 106; as inheritable possession, 140; inspired by prints, 74, 86, 103, 104, 205; miraculous, 300 n. 27; murals, 22, 70, 86, 91–98, 103, 111, 137, 227, 238–39, 249, 274 n. 23, 280 n. 48; noble status of, 63; as ordering of chaos, 221; as ritual, 227; seriality of, 71, 73, 273 n. 15; theoretical writings on, 54, 62, 85, 103; used in conversion, 99–100; value of, 140, 254; writing vs., 209, 212

Palermo, Church of Sant'Angelo in, 74

palimpsest, 118, 142, 145; colonial culture as, 227; of different spaces, 241; of documentary records, 163, 169; of word, image, and space, 245

Paniquitá, 145

104–5, 284 n. 63; of Inca kings, 184; of
indigenous nobility, 94, 314 n. 25; political and social role of, 308 n. 37; royal,
54, 105; seriality of official, 77; signature
vs., 208; of Spanish royalty, 204, 215;
as surrogate of king, 214–16, 308 n. 36;
veracity of, 60, 267 n. 24; visual task
performed by, 180, 182

possession: of land, 120–21, 169, 217; physical marking of, 158, 305 n. 28; validated
by documentation, 141; ways of signaling, 174, 289 n. 12; worldly, 130

power, 154, 245

Pratica civil, y criminal y instrvcion de escrivanos (Monterroso y Alvarado), 127

Pratt, Mary Louise, 45

prayer, 131, 245

pregonero. See town crier

priest, priests, 94, 132–34, 154, 188, 195,
205, 220, 226, 228, 233, 245, 255, 286
n. 73, 294 n. 37; as abusive figure, 203; as
extirpator, 77, 79, 83–84; house of, 224;
as instructor in Christian doctrine, 97,
126–27, 170, 226; Muisca, 249

primordial title, 145, 148, 150; as appropriation of Christian discourse, 147; falsification of, 146

prints, 101; in architectural books, 235;
conversion and, 100; limited access to,
12; as model for paintings, 74, 86, 97,
103–4, 205, 238; signatures on, 205

privatization of lands, 147

Probanza de méritos y servicios, 31, 183–84,
186; as reflection of upstanding citizenship, 189; as vehicle for generating new
heraldry, 174

processions, 112, 131. *See also* celebration;
ceremony; festivals; rituals

Protector de naturales, 118, 143

Protestantism, 62, 131, 256

Puenambás, Diego, 166–67, 171, 173, 299
n. 17

Puntal, 128–30, 136, 157–61, 172, 265 n. 9;
commercial activity and lands of, 296
n. 3; region of, 10

Purgatory, 92–94, 132, 135–36

Putumayo River, 107

qompi, 136–37, 139. *See also* textile

Quechua, 14–15, 18, 116, 136, 143, 198, 201,
203, 209–13, 230–31, 246, 265 n. 11, 265
n. 12, 265 n. 15, 266 n. 16; colonial creation of literary, 287 n. 2; as cultural and
ethnic model, 8; dictionary of, 200; as
imperial language, 115; lingua franca,
287 n. 1; sermons in, 69, 71; theater in,
288 n. 5

Queen of Angels, Virgin Mary as, 282 n. 58

quellcaycamayoc, 203. *See also* notary

quero, 109, 137, 139–40, 149, 278 n. 39, 285
n. 67. *See also* vessels

quilcamayo, 12. *See also* notary

Quillacinga (ethnic group), 119

quillca, 191, 209, 210, 212–14, 217, 305 n. 16,
307 n. 33; as a colonial neologism, 265
n. 12

Quiroga, Pedro de, 41, 56

Quirós, Cristóbal Bernardo de, Bishop of
Popayán, 109, 110

Quito, 9, 36–38, 50, 124, 136, 139, 141–44,
161, 185, 203, 205, 235, 266 n. 16, 287
n. 73, 293 n. 36, 305 n. 24; Audiencia of,
158; Church of San Francisco in, 103,
241, 273 n. 15; Church of Santo Domingo
in, 38; Convent of Santo Domingo in,
313 n. 22; Museo de la Casa de la Cultura
in, 110; Museo de San Francisco in, 111;
painting in, 273 n. 15; Royal Court in,
143–44, 147–48, 150; school of painting,
208; Synod of, 212, 267 n. 23

race, 61, 98, 114, 271 n. 6; racial mixing and,
35–36, 40, 58, 115

Rafael, Vicente, 45, 203

Rama, Ángel, 3, 113, 115, 122, 171, 198, 257

Ramiriquí, and Church of Our Lady of the
Snows (*Nuestra Señora de las Nieves*),
94

readers and reading, 153, 157, 169, 188; indigenous, 201; public, 170 *real provisión*, 194–95, 197–203, 209, 212, 217

rebellion, 47

Reconquista, 30, 35, 42, 66–67, 309 nn. 2–3

recordkeeping by oral transmission, 22

reducción, 79, 84–85, 221, 224–25, 227, 230, 233, 235, 237–38, 240, 310 n. 7, 311 n. 10; bodies within space of, 234; ordered experience of, 239. See also *resguardo*

relación, 128

Relaciones Geográficas, 1. *See also* maps

relic, 273 n. 16

Renaissance, 30, 65–68, 90

repartimiento de indios, 185

representation, 45, 63

República de Españoles, 28, 36, 46, 56, 115, 174

República de Indios, 28, 36, 46, 56, 115, 126, 150, 174

republicano, 46

requerimiento, 30, 114

resguardo, 84–86, 97–98, 143–44, 147–49, 226, 295 n. 50

resistance by means of ethnic classification, 28

retrospective significance, 154, 161, 296 n. 1

Rhetorica christiana (Valadés), 6, 43, 70, 244, 265 n. 7

Río, Brígida del, 59, 272 n. 8

ritual, rituals, 29, 68, 80–81, 86, 94, 109, 114, 122, 140, 149, 196–97, 230; absence of, 303 n. 13; of chiefly investiture, 226, 232, 246, 247; Christian, 98, 103, 192; of city founding, 224, 310 n. 8; in colonial administration, 168; discourse of colonization in, 225; documents and, 113, 199, 218, 228; drinking vessels in Andean, 137; at interstices of cultures, 150, 201, 245, 247; European origin of, 21; funerary, 131; kissing in, 196; marking boundaries through, 121; medieval, 213; memory of, 201; non-literate observers of, 218; of obedience to monarch, 170, 193, 215, 217, 258; political or religious,

233; practice, 77, 230; processions of religious images, 226; Roman or Byzantine origin of, 197; social hierarchy and, 231; space of, 148, 221, 233; speech of, 115; textiles in, 249; treatment of property and, 289 n. 14; writing and literacy and, 119–20, 173, 190, 192, 219; among Zapotecs, 287 n. 2

rivers, 178, 179

Robe, Domingo de la, 37

Robe, Francisco de la, 37–39, 50

Robe, Pedro de la, 37

Rodrigo, King, 42

Roman alphabet, 130

Rome, 42, 67–68, 74, 104–5, 253, 257, 274 n. 18, 304 n. 14; culture of, 30; people of, 34

rosary, 91–92, 226, 250, 252

Royal Court, 3–4, 51, 171, 183, 213, 272 n. 8; of Quito, 36; of Santafé de Bogotá, 40, 49, 134

royal decree, 114, 142–43, 147, 158, 162–63, 165, 170, 185, 189, 194, 196, 213, 227; acquiescence to, 202, 204; ceremonial reception of, 149, 193; kissing of, 197, 199; ultimate authority and, 201

Rubens, Peter Paul, 110–11

rúbrica, 227. *See also* emblem

Sabana de Bogotá, 132, 240, 247, 288 n. 7

sacrament, sacraments, 99, 214; Mass, 229; confession, 304 n. 16; explanation of need for, 97; ordination, 233; participation of *indios ladinos* in, 298 n. 13; rituals and, 228

sacred geography as a form of literacy, 10

sacred spaces, 77, 78, 80, 84, 221

Sahagún, Bernardino de, 205, 244, 274 n. 18

saints, 61–63, 208, 209; Andrew, 136, 253; Catherine, 94, 136; Catherine of Siena, 100; Christopher, 278 n. 39; Francis, 101, 278 n. 39; Francis Xavier, 100; Gregory the Great, 42, 64, 70, 93, 212, 279 n. 45; James the Indian Killer, 66; James the

Moor Killer, 66, 85; John, 101, 136; Mary
Magdalene, 104; as mediators, 208;
Nicolás de Tolentino, 92–93, 280 n. 46;
Peter, 136; Ursula, 94
Salinas y Córdoba, Buenaventura, 239
Sánchez Cotán, Juan, 59, 272 n. 8
Sánchez Gallque, Andrés, 36–37, 39, 49,
50–51, 204, 205, 208, 254
San Juan de Pasto, 106
San Miguel de Ibarra, 129
Santacruz Pachacuti Yamqui, Joan de,
116–17, 288 n. 5
Santafé de Bogotá, 1, 3, 9, 17, 19, 22, 25,
33–34, 39, 41, 48–51, 73, 79, 91, 97–98,
111, 133–35, 139–40, 167, 191, 211, 221, 225
26, 229, 231, 235, 238, 241, 264 n. 3, 266
n. 16, 269 n. 12, 288 n. 3, 290 n. 22, 293
n. 36, 294 n. 43, 305 n. 24, 306 n. 29, 314
n. 28; archbishop of, 219; cathedral of,
17; churches in, 17, 92, 101, 110, 280 n. 46,
284 n. 62; corruption of colonial apparatus in, 266 n. 17; Monastery of Santo
Domingo in, 275 n. 26; notarial practice
in, 293 nn. 35–36; Parish of Santa Lucía
de Jesús Nazareno, 101; Royal Court in,
134; Synod of, 132, 293 n. 37, 294 n. 42,
311 n. 11
Santafé Province, 33
Santa Gertrudis Serra, Juan de, 82, 107–
109, 276 n. 30, 286 n. 73
Santander, 224, 310 n. 7; department of, 224
Santa Rosa, 82
Santuario de N. Señora de Copacabana en
el Perú (Valverde), 71
scribe, scribes, 12, 17, 115–16, 118–19, 128,
143, 162, 165, 169, 173, 201–2, 205, 227,
232; as authority, 17; as mediator, 18–19;
lesser nobility employed as, 290 n. 20;
native, 117, 126; physical and intellectual
task of, 14; transcription of indigenous
names by, 298 n. 11. See also notary
sculpture, 140, 153
seal, 214; as focus of ritual, 195, 204; as
image and surrogate of king, 193, 195–

96, 202, 213, 216–17, 227; as integral element within space of document, 227;
kissing of royal, 218; quillca and, 209
Seed, Patricia, 113
self-mortification, 100
Serafino, Ángelo, 102
seriality, 70, 74–75, 77
series, 275 n. 25; of casta paintings, 35, 75, 77,
268 n. 10; of Corpus Christi paintings,
28, 215; of documents, 50, 160–61, 163;
intertextuality of documents in, 10, 140,
143, 162; of murals and paintings, 238,
273 n. 15; open-ended, 77; of paintings of
angels, 71, 73–74; of paintings used for
indoctrination, 70; of Passion paintings,
86, 96, 314 n. 25; of portraits, 77
Serlio, Sebastiano, 205, 240, 242, 313 n. 19
sermons, 8, 24, 70, 85, 88, 126, 128, 137, 140,
170, 193, 208–10, 212–13, 226, 266 n. 22,
275 n. 23, 305 n. 24, 306 n. 29, 306 n. 29;
on Christian ritual practice, 192; collection of, 290 n. 22; as exegesis of Catholic doctrine, 214; as source of demonic
visions, 103; translation of, 40; use of
images during, 25, 69, 71, 192, 255; written in native languages, 71
Seville, 30, 98, 189, 291 n. 25
shaman, 148, 251
Shroud of Turin, 196
Sibundoy, 108
Siete Partidas (Alonso X), 127, 291 n. 25
signature, 192–93; absence of, 300 n. 24;
ambiguity of, 203–4; equivalency of
visual forms and, 208–9; forgery and,
205; inability to produce, 202; as relic,
208, 217; ritual act of, 204, 219; within
space of document, 227; as surrogate of
king, 202, 217; uniqueness of, 203
Simón, Pedro de, 247, 249, 288 n. 7
skin color as marker of identity, 36
slaves, 35, 57, 65, 97, 99, 114, 185, 235; body
of, 100–101; branding of, 305 n. 28; free-
ing of, 293 n. 35; as inventoried property,
134; patron saint of, 98

on, 221; inscribed into documents, 130; in maps, 178, 199; relation of writing to, 140; ritual space and, 241; as social creation, 220

Torres, Diego de, 1, 4, 20, 25, 27, 30, 32–34, 39–51, 57, 59, 86, 91, 154, 158, 176, 189, 263 n. 1, 264 n. 2, 264 n. 3, 269 n. 12, 270 n. 18; as author of petitions, 254; first maps of Colombia by, 257; travels of, 3

town crier, 119, 226, 247, 289 n. 9

transculturation, 26–27, 43–46, 49–50, 117, 123, 139, 146; awareness of, 116; in documents, 174; roots of, 30

transgression, 19, 48, 60

translation, 74, 119, 130, 143, 162; of announcements by town crier, 226; into codified legal discourse, 20; from Italian into Spanish, 272 n. 10, 313 n. 19; office of interpreter and, 18; of royal decree into indigenous vernaculars, 170; of sermons, 71, 305 n. 24; from utterance into text, 15

transubstantiation, 93, 237, 308 n. 39; altar as place of, 215; Mass of Saint Gregory as evidence of, 279 n. 45

Trent. See councils, ecumenical: Council of Trent

Trouillot, Michel-Rolph, 153–54, 161

truthfulness, 162. See also veracity

Tulcán, 120, 124–25, 132, 287 n. 1, 296 n. 3

Tunja, 96–98, 134, 224, 264 n. 3, 310 n. 7; Church of Santa Bárbara in, 275 n. 26; city of, 19, 25, 33; province of, 1, 81, 92, 94, 252

Tupac Amaru, rebellion of, 184

Túquerres, 132, 169

Turin, shroud of, 196

Turmequé, 1, 3–4, 20, 27, 33, 39, 40–44, 57, 59, 84, 86, 91, 96–97, 154, 176, 189, 191, 257, 266 n. 17, 292 n. 28

Tustud, 159

Tuza, 10, 121, 124, 128, 129, 132, 136–37, 139, 141, 157–59, 170, 265 n. 9, 287 n. 1, 290 n. 20, 294 n. 45

Tuza, Catalina, 136–37

Tuza (ethnic group), 158, 160

unku (Inca tunic), 106. See also textiles

Urabá, 137, 278 n. 39

urbanism, 254; centered on church, 85; gridded, 6, 30, 85, 176, 190; of indigenous Pasto and Nasa towns, 310 n. 7; layout of sacral compound and, 74; as ordering of space, 247; phenomenology of colonial visuality and, 239

urban space, 220, 226

urbs, 224

Valadés, Diego, 6, 42, 59, 70, 86, 88, 90, 244, 265 n. 7, 270 n. 18

veneration, 82–83, 101, 277 n. 32, 287 n. 73; proper vs. improper, 10, 68, 212; of relics, 108, 173 n. 16

ventriloquism, 80–82, 84

veracity: of documents, 162, 172; of memory, 167; modern standards of, 12; of testimony, 171, 200, 202; of witness statements, 266 n. 19

Veronica, Saint, veil of, 196

vessels, 137, 142; aquilla, 150; limbiquiro, 140; quero, 109, 139, 140, 149, 150, 278 n. 39, 285 n. 67; as symbol of drunkenness, 278 n. 39, 279 n. 39; totuma, 91, 139

viceroy: entrance of, 245; Francisco de Toledo as, 183–84; Núñez y Velasco as, 186; office of, 9, 48, 185, 214, 235

Vienna, 284 n. 63

Virgin Mary, 62, 63, 85, 93, 94, 101–2, 111, 136, 140, 244, 253, 279 n. 39; images of, 212; Nativity of, 195. See also under names of Marian advocations and cults

visions, 112, 251; appearance of images in, 101, 103; seen by indigenes, 252–53

visita, 227, 288 n. 7, 312 n. 15; documentation of, 229, 231; inspection of abuses of indigenous populations during, 264 n. 3; as performative act, 229, 232; recogniz-

Joanne Rappaport is a professor with joint appointments in the Department of Anthropology and the Department of Spanish and Portuguese at Georgetown University. She is the author of *Cumbe Reborn: An Andean Ethnography of History* (1994); *The Politics of Memory: Native Historical Interpretation in the Colombian Andes* (paperback edition, Duke, 1998); and *Intercultural Utopias: Public Intellectuals, Cultural Experimentation, and Ethnic Pluralism in Colombia* (2005).

Tom Cummins is Dumbarton Oaks Professor of the history of Pre-Columbian and Colonial Latin American Art, in the Department of the History of Art and Architecture, Harvard University. He is the author of *Toasts with the Inca: Andean Abstraction and Colonial Images on Quero Vessels* (2002); and, with Julio Burgos Cabrera and Carlos Mora Hoyos, of *Huellas del pasado: Los sellos de jama-coaque* (1996). He is also the editor, with Barbara Anderson, of *The Getty Murúa: Essays on the Making of Martín De Murúa's "Historia General Del Piru"* (2008); and, with Elizabeth Hill Boone, of *Native Traditions in the Postconquest World* (1998).

Library of Congress Cataloging-in-Publication Data
Rappaport, Joanne.
Beyond the lettered city : indigenous literacies in the Andes / Joanne Rappaport and Tom Cummins.
p. cm. — (Narrating native histories)
Includes bibliographical references and index.
ISBN 978-0-8223-5116-0 (cloth : alk. paper)
ISBN 978-0-8223-5128-3 (pbk. : alk. paper)
1. Literacy—Social aspects—Andes Region—History. 2. Communication and culture—Andes Region—History. 3. Indians of South America—Andes Region—History. 4. Spain—Colonies—America—Administration—History. I. Cummins, Thomas B. F. (Thomas Bitting Foster), 1949– II. Title. III. Series: Narrating native histories.
P94.65.A45R37 2012
302.2'244098—dc23   2011027539